Y0-FKX-071

UNIVERSITY OF WINNIPEG
LIBRARY
515 Portage Avenue
Winnipeg, Manitoba R3B 2E9

PERGAMON INTERNATIONAL LIBRARY
of Science, Technology, Engineering and Social Studies
The 1000-volume original paperback library in aid of education, industrial training and the enjoyment of leisure.
Publisher: Robert Maxwell, M.C.

Urban Planning Practice in Developing Countries

THE PERGAMON TEXTBOOK INSPECTION COPY SERVICE

An inspection copy of any book published in the Pergamon International Library will gladly be sent to academic staff without obligation for their consideration for course adoption or recommendation. Copies may be retained for a period of 60 days from receipt and returned if not suitable. When a particular title is adopted or recommended for adoption for class use and the recommendation results in a sale of 12 or more copies the inspection copy may be retained with our compliments. The Publishers will be pleased to receive suggestions for revised editions and new titles to be published in this important international Library.

Pergamon Urban and Regional Planning Advisory Committee

D.R. DIAMOND, M.A., M.Sc. (Chairman),
Reader in Regional Planning,
London School of Economics and Political Science

GWEN BELL, Ph.D.,
Lincoln, Massachusetts, U.S.A.

G. BROADBENT, B.Arch.,
Head of School of Architecture,
Portsmouth Polytechnic

G.F. CHADWICK, Ph.D., M.A., B.Sc.Tech., F.R.T.P.I., F.I.L.A.,
Planning Consultant,
Sometime Professor of Town and Country Planning,
University of Newcastle upon Tyne

A.K.F. FALUDI, Dipl.-Ing., Dr.Techn.,
Professor of Planning Theory
University of Amsterdam

J.K. FRIEND, M.A.,
Centre for Organisational and Operational Research,
Tavistock Institute of Human Relations, London

D.C. GILL, B.A., M.R.T.P.I.,
Director of Planning,
Humberside County Council

FRANK A. HAIGHT, Ph.D.,
Professor of Statistics and Transportation,
The Pennsylvania State University

J.B. McLOUGHLIN, B.A., M.R.T.P.I.,
University of Salford

K.C. ROSSER, M.A., Ph.D.,
Director, Development Planning Unit,
Bartlett School of Architecture and Planning,
University College London

D.N.M. STARKIE, B.Sc.(Econ.), M.Sc.(Econ.),
Professional Research Fellow,
Department of Economics,
University of Adelaide

B. STYLES, B.A., M.C.D., M.R.T.P.I.,
Formerly Divisional Planning Officer
City of Birmingham Planning Department

HT
169
.5
.U73
1982

Urban Planning Practice in Developing Countries

Editors

John L. Taylor
Consultant on Urban Planning, UNICEF, Jakarta

and

David G. Williams
Urban Projects Department, The World Bank

PERGAMON PRESS
Oxford • New York • Toronto • Sydney • Paris • Frankfurt

U.K.	Pergamon Press Ltd., Headington Hill Hall, Oxford OX3 0BW, England
U.S.A.	Pergamon Press Inc., Maxwell House, Fairview Park Elmsford, New York 10523, U.S.A.
CANADA	Pergamon of Canada, Suite 104, 150 Consumers Road, Willowdale, Ontario M2J 1P9, Canada
AUSTRALIA	Pergamon Press (Aust.) Pty. Ltd., P.O. Box 544 Potts Point, N.S.W. 2011, Australia
FRANCE	Pergamon Press SARL, 24 rue des Ecoles, 75240 Paris, Cedex 05, France
FEDERAL REPUBLIC OF GERMANY	Pergamon Press GmbH, 6242 Kronberg-Taunus, Hammerweg 6, Federal Republic of Germany

Copyright © 1982 John L. Taylor and David G. Williams

All Rights Reserved. No part of this publication may be reproduced, stored in a retrieval system or transmitted in any form or by any means: electronic, electrostatic, magnetic tape, mechanical, photocopying, recording or otherwise, without permission in writing from the publishers.

First edition 1982

British Library Cataloguing in Publication Data

Urban planning practice in developing countries.
(Urban and regional planning series; v.25)
1. Underdeveloped areas - City planning
I. Taylor, John L.
II. Williams, David G.
307.7'6'091724 HT169.5

ISBN 0-08-022225-0

Library of Congress Catalog Card. No. 81-81224

Printed in the United States of America

Foreword

The first seeds of thought for this book were sown over 4 years ago while the editors were working together in Malaysia. Both felt that, while there was a wealth of literature available on urban-planning theory, very few documented case studies existed on efforts to implement urban planning and development programmes, to evaluate the experiences or to relate them to major themes and concerns of development planning. This was particularly true of Less Developed Countries (LDCs) where many new and innovative planning and project activities were underway but little knowledge of experience derived from them was available to other planners, administrators and students in similar countries.

The book was therefore conceived as a reader in urban planning practice which would offer other practitioners and students a range of case studies, grouped into a limited number of categories which covered much of the current activities in urban planning and development in LDCs. The authors of the case studies have all been intimately involved in the subject of their study, and several of them are nationals of the country whose planning and development issues they describe. In virtually all cases the material has been written specially for this book, with the intention of providing fresh information, not available elsewhere.

The editors have limited the selection of the cases to those in Asian LDCs in an effort to limit the vast potential range of material, and to focus on a continent which they know well. Although Asian countries are extremely varied in culture, climate and income levels, they all possess strong cultural histories and administrative traditions which, the reader will observe, have coloured and moulded the style of urban planning and development and illustrate the wide range of approaches and solutions which are possible for similar problems.

In Part One, the editors have proposed a number of fundamental themes and issues common to urban development in most LDCs and suggested some planning paradigms which have been used to address them. They go on to suggest several basic criteria which are inherent in the social, economic and management issues of urban development and which are relevant to evaluating specific experiences. In Part Two, the authors describe their cases and evaluate the experiences both with respect to the case study's objectives and the editors' criteria. Part Three attempts to compare the experiences of the case studies and draw some conclusions.

Acknowledgements

The Editors' thanks are due to numerous people who have helped to make this book a reality. We greatly appreciate the time and effort put into producing original case studies by the authors, their efforts to review the experiences in the light of the editors' evaluation criteria and their helpful comments on the editors' chapters. We are particularly grateful for the critical but constructive comments on the structure and context of the book from the staff of the Development Planning Unit, London, especially to Dr. Colin Rosser, the Director, and Mr. Michael Safier. We also valued the observations and help from Mrs. Peggy Ducker and Mr. David Kellogg of Pergamon Press on the content and presentation of the book.

We appreciate the tolerance shown by the contributors and the publisher during the logistical nightmare of trying to produce a book with the editors located in different continents, the publisher in a third, and the contributing authors spread through several countries. Our heartfelt thanks to the forbearance of our wives, and to the help with typing from Harumi Williams and Gwen Ritchie, and especially to Joan Taylor for the graphics.

Finally, the opinions expressed by the editors and the authors of the case studies are entirely their own and do not necessarily reflect the views of the organisations for whom they work.

The Editors

Acknowledgements

[illegible]

[illegible]

[illegible]

Contents

CHAPTER

I

AN OVERVIEW

1

Problems and Issues in Asian Urban Areas — and the Response of Planning Practice

John L. Taylor
David G. Williams

INTRODUCTION

The essential purpose of this chapter is to provide an overview of the dynamics of the urban situation in the developing countries. It is designed to set the context for the book's main focus: an appraisal of urban planning practice by means of an empirical analysis of selected case studies of specific projects. Given this focus on practice, it is not our intention here to furnish a lengthy theoretical discussion of urbanisation, but rather to provide an analysis of the major problems and issues facing decision-makers and practitioners in the urban areas of Asian LDCs, and of the manner in which planning practice responds to these concerns.

Following these introductory comments, the chapter will first deal with what are termed "generating factors" and "consequences" of the urban condition. In combination these elements provide an effective checklist of key urban problems, but an effort is made to distinguish between fundamental or underlying causes of the urban condition (generating factors) and other factors which are simply manifestations (consequences) of the underlying causes. In actuality the urban situation can be visualised as a chain of linked generating factors and consequences or symptoms. Depending upon the viewpoint of a given individual, any particular factor or symptom may or may not be technically described as a "problem", but in general the gamut of urban problems comes from this chain, and any attack on these problems by policy-makers and practitioners must deal both with generating factors and consequences.

The chapter will then turn to a discussion of basic themes and issues for public policy underlying the urban situation in

Asian LDCs. It is our conclusion that a limited number of basic themes and issues provide the fundamental set of concerns to which urban planning practice needs somehow to respond.

Finally the chapter will attempt to analyse the response of planning practice to these problems, themes and issues. Present trends regarding the scope and methodology of planning practice in developing countries will be summarised, with the intention of drawing out some of the major lessons of experience. A tentative model of planning practice will then be presented and criticised, with some of the major questions facing the profession posed. The case studies presented in Part Two of this volume will refer to this model and to the related questions for planning practice, since the model and these questions provide one important basis for locating the empirical material which makes up the bulk of this volume.

GENERATING FACTORS AND CONSEQUENCES OF THE URBAN CONDITION

The intention in this section is to provide an analytical summary of key urban problems within Asian LDCs. As already mentioned a distinction is made between fundamental or underlying causes (generating factors) and manifestations (consequences) which together form a chain of interlinked factors characterising the urban condition. For purposes of this analysis, generating factors and consequences are divided into six basic categories - demographic, economic, political, social, environmental and technological - although there are of course important relationships between these categories. Whilst much of this information may be familar to the seasoned international expert, it is included here to introduce the student and young professional to the main problems of urbanisation - and to the literature which discusses these problems in greater detail - which set the stage for the subsequent analysis of urban planning practice.

Demographic Factors

The urbanisation problem begins with the overall scale and pace of urban growth. Underlying the widely publicised growth in total population within LDCs is the basic generating factor of public health and the related calculus of vital statistics. Improved public health measures throughout the world have led to a rapid decline in mortality which has changed the course of demographic history in LDCs.(1) Whilst mortality has declined and life expectancy has increased, however, there has been no parallel decline in fertility levels.(2) The resultant widening gap between mortality and fertility in most LDCs provides the basic explanation for their dramatic growth in total population within recent decades. By 1970, 70 percent of the world's population was concentrated in the LDCs and it is estimated that this proportion may increase to nearly 80 percent by the year 2000, in view of their high growth rates.(3)

These factors influencing overall population growth are occurring both in rural and urban areas within LDCs. In the urban areas, approximately half of the population growth is accounted for simply by natural increase. Higher natural rates of total population growth than were ever reached by present developed countries are putting increasing pressure on rural areas which are becoming more overcrowded and less capable of supporting large additional increases in population. Intensive agricultural development programmes, experience has shown, may actually reduce the absorptive capacity of rural areas. Consequently, people are "pushed" into urban areas regardless of whether economic opportunities await them there or not. This "push factor" has been particularly acute in many Asian countries where rural densities frequently exceed 500 persons per square kilometre.

Several recent studies tend to indicate, however, that the "pull factors" provide a far more powerful explanation for migration from rural to urban areas than "push factors". The rural poor migrate to cities primarily because they offer a wider variety of employment opportunities and higher incomes.(4) Associated factors include better education and health facilities, and a degree of freedom and social emancipation which the cities offer. These all add up to what is perceived by large numbers of migrants as a greater variety of opportunities in urban areas to break out of the cycle of poverty which shows no hope of release in most rural areas. A closely related generating factor is the fact that higher levels of investment in cities, incurred by both the private and particularly the public sector, increases expectations in rural as well as urban areas and further contributes to rural-urban migration. Attempts to restrain this migration flow, either by accelerated rural development or by deliberate restriction of urban services, have generally been unsuccessful.

As a symptom of these generating factors, the LDCs are experiencing very high rates of growth in urban population - currently averaging about 5 percent per year or generally twice the rate of growth in total population - and unprecedented increases in absolute numbers of urban dwellers.(5) Although most developing countries in Asia still have relatively low proportions of their populations in urban areas, these high rates of increase in urbanisation will alter these proportions in the near future.(6) In all Asian LDCs, it is estimated that the urban proportion will probably increase from about 22 percent of the total population in 1970 to about 42 percent in the year 2000. But it is the increase in absolute numbers implied by this change in proportion that is most unprecedented: the urban population will triple from 419 million to 1.42 billion between 1970 and 2000. This increment of about 1 billion persons in the urban areas of Asia represents nearly two thirds of the projected increase in total population for these countries.(7)

It is these demographic factors that create the context for the myriad of urban problems which follows; moreover, the population increases appear to be inevitable. Short of a series of major catastrophes, there is no indication that total population in developing countries will increase by much less than projected. There are clear limits as to how much more population already crowded rural areas can absorb and thus increases in the urban population of these staggering magnitudes seem likely.(8)

Economic Factors

The level of genuine economic development within these urban areas has been inadequate in relation to the scale and pace of demographic growth. This was not the case historically as the developed countries of Europe and North America urbanised. In those countries the persons who left agriculture, as its productivity rose and the need for farm labour declined, moved into more productive industrial jobs in the city. They were also able to move to the "new" lands of America and Oceania to relieve the pressure on European urban areas. The situation in many developing countries today is contrary, with the unparalleled population pressures producing a kind of "subsistance urbanisation" in which the ordinary person has only the bare essentials for survival.(9)

A second underlying economic factor consists of a basic "dualism" between the modern industrial sector and the traditional informal sector of the economy.(10) These two sectors of the urban economy, one capital-intensive and the other labour-intensive, exist side by side and in fact are closely interlinked, but are frequently in conflict with each other primarily because of questionable governmental policies. Although it is much smaller in terms of employment generated and real income created, the so-called modern sector receives most of the attention and support from governments in developing countries whilst the informal sector is either ignored or in many instances harassed. Traditional informal sector activities, while not generally as productive per head as the modern sector, can be more productive per dollar invested and are extremely important not only as the chief source of employment but also in the economic functioning of the cities and the utilisation of limited resources. The informal activities, which fall more into the "service sector" than into the industrial category, enable large numbers of people to cope in the city and survive with limited, shared resources. Thousands of small family firms engaging in trade, personal services and small-scale manufacturing create livelihoods for millions living in slums and squatter areas which, though meagre, are preferable to unemployment and probably preferable to their rural counterparts who are marginally employed. It is unfortunate, however, that the informal sector has until recently been little studied, is misunderstood and not recognised as important by most policymakers; instead authentic development is weakened by undue support from governments for impressive-looking, capital-intensive industries which benefit only a small percentage of urban dwellers.(11)

These two economic generating factors - the inadequate overall urban economy, and the dualism between the modern and informal sectors - have as their consequence several important symptoms. The first of these is that urban unemployment and "underemployment" levels are very high and growing. Despite the informal sector, there simply are not enough economic activities to provide jobs for everybody in the burgeoning labour force which will continue to grow along with the total population. Data on urban unemployment are grossly inadequate, in part because those in the modern sector who receive reported wages form such a small proportion of the labour force and the conceptual difficulties in defining "unemployment" for the others are considerable. There is evidence to suggest, however, that unemployment in urban areas generally runs between 10 and 20 percent and in extreme cases as high as 30 percent, particularly if the data include those with only occasional or marginal jobs who are so "underemployed" as to be better defined as "unemployed". And many of those who are employed must take on low-paying, unskilled jobs, which provide them and their dependants with only the barest of essentials for survival. In both modern and informal sectors, rates of pay for most jobs are very low, working conditions are poor, and opportunities for advancement are limited.(12)

Increasing levels of poverty have therefore become a tragic consequence of slow-growing urban economies. As a basis for reorienting its lending priorities, the World Bank has compiled statistics on the urban poor, in two categories. Those living in "relative poverty" are defined as persons having less than one third the average per capita personal income of the country. Those in "absolute poverty" cannot afford a minimal nutritionally adequate diet plus essential non-food items. In much of South Asia these two groups are identical. World Bank estimates indicate that, out of a worldwide total of 150 million urban dwellers in LDCs with market economies who are in absolute poverty, 46 percent are in South Asia and a further 24 percent in Southeast Asia. In most of these populous countries, over 50 percent of the urban population are in absolute poverty. Moreover, in several countries real incomes have been dropping, especially over the past few years of high inflation, and in some cases the poor are worse off now than they were at the time of independence from colonial rule.(13) Thus, despite development efforts, poverty has been increasing, mainly due to demographic expansion outpacing growth in incomes and to the characteristics of development which have worsened income distribution.

As a consequence of high unemployment and low levels of income even among those who are working, the urban economy frequently remains stagnant. It is unable to generate a large middle class and to begin to create markets for more consumer goods and improved living environments. On the contrary, urban living conditions have often been deteriorating because cities lack the financial resources required to cope adequately with their many problems. As a symptom of low personal incomes, cities are not able to generate as much economic wealth as they otherwise would, which in turn means that fewer local resources are available for urban services and facilities. This lack of resources accounts in large measure for the many settlement problems, such as inadequate housing conditions, water supply, sanitation, education and health facilities, which will be discussed below.

Another economic symptom, largely a consequence of the dualism factor, is what appears to be a widening gap in urban income distribution between a small, wealthy few engaged in the modern sector and the large, poorer mass of the urban population who are generally part of the informal sector. Although data on urban income distribution are generally poor, a recent estimate by I.L.O. for the Philippines showed that the top 10 percent of households in that country's cities receive approximately one-third of the total urban income.(14) Similar situations are undoubtedly found in most urban areas of the developing world. This imbalance in income distribution is not only a matter of equity and a possible cause of social unrest, but it also implies that the basis for an expanding middle class which a more even income distribution would create is not present. In this context of a vicious downward spiral where low incomes lead to low consumption and investment which in turn reduces public resources for basic services, it is vital that effective market demand for essential goods and services increase sufficiently to meet the needs; and this increased demand must come from the large masses of the poor. A basic needs strategy should not merely include the provision of public services at public expense, but should influence demand and supply simultaneously by government and community interventions which help to create local productive capacity and employment in small industry. This will raise incomes and allow the dormant demand of the poor to be registered in the market, leading in turn to a market response which would allocate resources to them. In this way, poverty reduction and economic growth are mutually reinforcing.

One additional fundamental economic factor should be mentioned, and that is the relation between the urban and rural economies in many LDCs. In most instances, the urban economy is not adequately integrated with that of its rural hinterland, and to the extent that there are links, they are often exploitative "core-periphery" relationships. This reflects a tendency for the primate cities in many countries to link up with the international economy and to exploit their own countryside by absorbing disproportionate shares of investment, natural resources and skilled manpower.(15)

This generating factor has at least two consequences, both of which are believed by most urban authorities to have negative implications. First, it creates a wide disparity between incomes in the urban areas, particularly within the primate cities, and those in the countryside - a disparity which often makes the worst urban jobs in the informal sector more attractive to the migrant than his alternative means of livelihood in the rural village. This disparity in wealth between city and country occurs simultaneously with the disparity which exists between rich and poor within the city, and the total effect is a kind of a four-layer pyramidal structure with a small, wealthy urban elite at the apex, government servants and workers in modern industries below them, the balance of the urban population forming the third layer, and the large mass of poor rural peasants at the base.

A second consequence of the perverted relationship between urban and rural economies is that the larger cities are receiving a disproportionate share of urban growth. This is essentially a demographic factor, but it is mentioned here because of its close connection to these economic realities. In South and East Asia combined, cities of 500,000 or more persons grew from 20 percent to comprise 36 percent of total urban population between 1920 and 1960; and in South Asia alone the percentage of million-city population in the urban population rose from 15.3 to 29.7 between 1950 and 1975.(16) In Thailand, for example, nearly half of the country's 7 million urban dwellers are concentrated in Bangkok, which is growing at nearly 6 percent per year, a rate more rapid than that of other cities in that country. And this pattern is repeated in many other Asian countries.

Political Factors

In discussing the relationship between urban and rural economies, one critical factor was not mentioned: the reality of political control. Perhaps the key generating factor which accounts for the weak integration of national economies and the excessive differences in income, wealth and opportunity is essentially political: namely, that political power is largely concentrated in the hands of the same wealthy elites who control the economy and who live chiefly in the larger urban centres, particularly in the primate cities. It is probably this convergence of political power and economic wealth which, more than any other factor, accounts for the bias of governments towards supporting the modern sector and reinforcing economic dualism, the higher levels of investment, and other policies - public and private - which favour the cities over the rural areas. This concentration of political power is, however, the source of considerable conflict in many countries, as other groups clamour for a greater voice in national affairs.

Besides having economic consequences, this important generating factor has some political symptoms as well. One symptom is that decision-making tends to be highly centralised, reflecting the concentration of political power in the hands of a small group. This centralisation has led to a trend in which democratically elected governments are replaced by dictatorships ruled by one person or a small clique. These dictatorships have tended to become increasingly uncomfortable with political opposition and dissent. Another aspect of this symptom is that decision-making has come increasingly to be of a "top-down" nature, in which governments are run through a centralised chain of command where virtually all decisions are made at the top and then passed down in military fashion. In fact, many elitist governments are fearful of encouraging participation and power-sharing in even a minor way lest the populace perceive weakness and organise to seize power. As a result, the best administrative talent is concentrated in the central government, and the quality of provincial and local government administration is frequently very poor.

A final political consequence of the concentration of power is that in many countries there is a dangerous polarisation between the interests of the ruling elite and those of the rural and urban peasantry. The policies and programmes of the central government risk becoming out of touch with the aspirations and attitudes of the peasantry. Examples include attempts to do away with the squatter settlements, small-scale public transport and other informal economic activities so vital to the urban poor. This divergence of interest between the elites who control governments and the masses of lower income groups accounts in part for the political instability so characteristic of many LDCs. Despite efforts to "keep the lid on" by resorting to totalitarian methods, countries are bound to be heading for an explosion unless their governments take steps to bridge this gap and become more responsive to the aspirations of the masses.(17)

Social Factors

In urban areas of developed countries, perhaps particularly in the United States, social factors seem to be major contributors to the urban malaise. Problems such as crime and juvenile delinquency, drug addiction and alcoholism, the breakdown of the family and alienation of the urban dweller from a sense of community all appear to be important generating factors underlying the urban condition in Chicago, Baltimore or other cities in industrial nations. But in Calcutta, Bangkok and other cities in the developing world, these problems of social pathology are less dominant in describing the urban situation. In societies where most people are poor, the urban peasant does not have the stigma of being labelled an outcast, as does his counterpart in the developed city. In making the difficult transition from what for most had been a rural origin, he/she seeks to create a friendly, supportive and informal social atmosphere in the urban bustee or kampung.(18) And, although the traditional extended family is gradually replaced by the nuclear family under the impact of urbanisation, the family as an institution and the controls which it exerts on individual behaviour appear to be a far more powerful influence in developing societies, and this perhaps accounts for the lower indices of social pathology more than any other factor.

However, it should be cautioned that these social problems are by no means completely absent and that they may be on the increase in many cities. Although reliable data are scarce (a major problem in itself), it has been reported, for example, that there are 100,000 drug adicts in Hong Kong and that crime rates are on the increase in many cities.(19)

Perhaps the most critical set of social factors is the low level of education, health and related social services in most LDCs. This is explained in large part by the economic and political factors already noted, such as the lack of financial resources and the concentration of political power. Hence, the inadequacy and irrelevancy of social services should be viewed more as consequences than generating factors. Education is clearly the most crucially needed service, and studies have shown that the education of household heads is strongly correlated with higher income.(20) In most LDC cities, educational services are not only inadequate but they are often irrelevant to the practical needs of the society and economy. Emphasis is often placed on academic rather than vocational programmes which would train people in vitally needed skills, and this emphasis frequently retards genuine economic and social development because people lack the appropriate skills.

Health and related social welfare services are similarly inadequate and often irrelevant in most LDC cities. Health problems are particularly acute in the areas inhabited by lower income groups, but health facilities serving these areas are the most inadequate and frequently unsuited to the needs of these groups. Basta shows that average urban health statistics conceal a greater variance than those of rural communities, and that health and nutrition is often worse in low-income urban areas than in the rural settlements from which the migrants came. Tuberculosis is up to ten times higher and infant mortality three times higher in lower-income areas than in the city as a whole. At the same time coverage of health facilities is usually four to six times worse in slum areas than the average published city-wide statistics indicate.(21) Specialised doctors and university teaching hospitals serve only the better off, whilst the type of paramedical personnel who could meet the needs of the masses do not exist in most countries. (The People's Republic of China is an exception in this case.)

However, it is also true that on the average a much better level of education, health and related services are offered in urban than in rural areas, and that the quality of these services tends to improve with increased city size. This is one of the factors which contributes to the demographic pull and consequent rural-urban migration.

Environmental Factors

A number of economic and political factors, including low family incomes, inadequate financial resources and disparities in wealth and political power, account in large measure for the problems of the physical environment in urban areas. Consequently, problems of urban land, infrastructure, shelter and transport which plague cities in the LDCs should be viewed largely as symptoms rather than generating factors. Nevertheless, these problems are real and critical, and in turn lead to other problems.

The use and ownership of urban land is particularly critical. In most LDCs with market economies, urban land is dealt with as a basic commodity and is largely owned by the wealthy elites, reflecting the concentration of political and economic power in the hands of the few. Speculation on urban land, which is very profitable for these few, drives land prices out of reach of most families who discover that establishing a legal foothold within the city is very difficult. This poses a major conflict between private interests who benefit from this *laissez faire* situation and the "public interest" of the vast majority of the urban population. Efforts to control land values or land uses by governments, when they are attempted at all, are inevitably met by strong resistance from influential groups, and as a consequence there is a general lack of adequate land use planning and controls, as well as public land acquisition and taxation capabilities, on the part of most governments. A further consequence of high land prices is that illegal, high-density squatments are formed by urban peasants as their way of "fighting back" and establishing a place to live in the city.

The supply of land is a closely related problem. Most cities are not preparing serviced land for development at a pace commensurate with their rates of population growth. Hence, although raw land is usually available, land which is provided with adequate urban services and properly graded is in short supply. Secondary road systems, additional water supplies and other facilities need to be planned and built at the urban perimeter to open up more land. Although these shortages of serviced urban land may be viewed as symptomatic of more pervasive factors, they are nevertheless critical.(22)

The problems of urban transport represent another set of crucial environmental symptoms which are closely related to the problems of urban land. Again they reflect the disparities of interest between the wealthy elites and the poor masses. Particularly in the cities of LDCs with comparatively high average incomes, there have been dramatic increases in the number of private motor vehicles in recent years without a corresponding increase in road capacity. In Malaysian cities, for example, motor-cycle and automobile registration has been growing at the rate of 25 percent per year. These private vehicles are affordable by a minority of the population, yet on a per-capita basis, occupy a disproportionately high amount of road space, which of course has led to marked increases in traffic congestion. The presence of both fast vehicles and also of such slow moving conveyances as bicycles, rickshaws, animal-drawn carts, etc., creates considerable congestion, particularly in the absence of facilities for segregation of these vehicles. This mixed traffic not only causes confusion but reduces available road capacity and results in traffic delays, besides being a source of accidents. These problems are further aggravated by the frequent inadequacy of mass transport systems. The spectre of grossly over-crowded buses, trams and trains is a common situation in the urban areas of LDCs. Although urban governments have generally wanted to provide cheap public transport, most resulting systems have been inefficiently operated, overly subsidised, under-capitalised, and over-regulated.(23)

These inadequacies of urban transport, combined with the lack of land use planning and control, are some of the factors which create urban patterns in cities of LDCs which are quite different from those in industrialised cities. In general, people tend to live closer to their work so as to alleviate the cost and inconvenience of lengthy trips. This in turn creates a more mixed land use pattern, with residential and non-residential activities operating on the same or adjacent parcels. Large precincts of homogenous land use found in industrialised cities, such as the central business district or suburban shopping centre, are replaced by areas which contain a fine-grain mixture of manufacturing, commercial and residential activities. Although there may be some environmental hazards in these areas, they do have some advantages: less commuting to work is necessary, secondary work opportunities are greater and there is a vitality reflecting their constant use.

In cities of the more developed countries, public service systems associated with provision of water supply and disposal of wastes have been widely installed, although there are problems of maintenance and environmental impact. However, in urban areas of the LDCs, there are tremendous deficits in the initial provision of these basic infrastructures which are very costly to install. Many governments simply have neither adequate financial resources nor sufficient organisational capability to develop these facilities. With regard to water supply/distribution systems, for example, many cities find it very difficult to keep pace with urban growth by developing adequate supply or intake sources as well as building and maintaining the pipe distribution systems. To take an extreme case, per capita supply of filtered water declined from 52.3 to 28.0 gallons per day in Calcutta between 1931 and 1965. In other cases there may be sufficient water supplied at the headworks but pipe distribution leakage and illegal tappings use up to 50 percent of water put into the system. The networks often serve only industrial and upper income areas and do not extend into lower income areas. Thus many poor families pay up to 15 percent of their incomes buying water from vendors, which would cost them only from 2 to 5 percent of income if piped water were available.

Similar problems pertain with regard to the capability of many LDC cities to collect and dispose of both water-borne and solid wastes. Again using Calcutta as an example, only 54 percent of the city area was sewered as of 1966. And, on more than one occasion, the military had to be called out to help clear away mounting piles of solid waste that clogged the city's streets and alleys.(24) This lack of basic infrastructure systems, particularly within areas where lower income groups are concentrated, leads directly to major environmental pollution problems which affect water, land and air. These hazards in turn pose not only aesthetic but public health problems which grip many urban dwellers in an endless cycle of disease and degradation. The cycle is continued as disease and inadequate diets in turn affect labour productivity and further contribute to economic depression.(25)

Shelter in Asian cities is a closely related and equally distressing problem. The quality of the existing housing stock is generally poor, and internal crowding within dwelling units alarming. One of the most striking features is that the majority of urban dwellers cannot afford even the cheapest new completed permanent housing unit built either by government or private enterprise (which usually costs at least US$ 4,000). Slums and squatments generally represent the predominant living environments for the urban poor, although conditions vary widely in these areas. Squatments portray the inability of most governments to cope with the urban services and housing problem. Recent data on Kuala Lumpur, Manila and Jakarta showed that the estimated population living in slums and squatter areas represented 37, 35 and 25 percent of the total population in these cities respectively.(26) Despite the "substandard" quality of many of these dwellings, however, it is noteworthy that the slums and squatments represent a massive unaided self-help effort on the part of lower income households, and that many of these areas have considerable socio-economic viability.

Although physical conditions with respect to both housing and infrastructure in squatments and other living environments of the urban poor are often viewed as "substandard" by the higher income official, it should be emphasised that these areas represent a major share of residential construction and of national investment in many LDCs, a fact that is generally ignored. They stand as the physical environment's counterpart to those informal sector jobs in the economy, and in fact many of the informal economic activities are situated within these very areas. Within many of these living environments, lower income people show a remarkable ability for improvisation and coping as they improve the quality of their facilities, services and shelter. In areas where such self-help activities appear to be most successful, relative security of tenure and active community organisations appear to be important factors. However, many governments have found it difficult to accept the notion of improving rather than tearing down existing slum and squatter areas, so that the question of priorities for improving these areas, of offering security of tenure and of appropriate standards of infrastructure and shelter remains one of the key issues of public policy.(27)

Technological Factors

One very basic set of generating factors which underlie the demographic, economic and social factors, and to some extent the political ones, is the impact of Western technology in civil engineering, transport, health, and management. Two broad types of technology appear to be involved. First, there is the contribution of the engineer and physical scientist to building and infrastructure development, agricultural and industrial machinery, modern medicine and health, and many other physical artifacts. Secondly, there is the technology of business and governmental management, as symbolised by the assembly line approach to industrial processing and, more recently, by systems analysis and the technocratic approach to development management. These processes were generated by the need to put together many parts of a system in an organised way.(28)

These technologies had developed in the West, and then began to be transferred to the LDCs during the late colonial period of the nineteenth and early twentieth centuries. However, their diffusion has spread much more rapidly over the past 30 years via large-scale industries, multinational corporations, technical assistance projects and other carriers. Under the general rubric of "modernisation", these technologies have severely dislocated earlier social structures, but at the same time offered an opportunity for choice and social change which did not exist before. They also promise a greater abundance of material goods, and pursuit of their acquisition is rapidly replacing traditional cultural activities among many groups in developing countries. The extent to which this aspect of development should be encouraged or controlled by LDC governments, and the degree to which new consumer demands can or should be satisfied, are major issues in the broader considerations of development, but also relate closely to governments' priorities and strategies for urban development.

This concludes our summary of generating factors and consequences, and we shall turn our attention to a discussion of basic policy themes and issues underlying the urban situation in Asian developing countries.

BASIC THEMES AND ISSUES

We can conveniently consider the following themes and issues as falling into a two-dimensional matrix, with the compenents of planning (demographic, economic, political, social, environmental and technological) forming one dimension and the scale of planning (from national and regional concerns down to project level planning) forming the other dimension. Any given theme-issue cluster falls somewhere within this matrix, and each one discussed here will be so identified. For example, the issue regarding the optimum spatial pattern of urbanisation embraces demographic, economic and political components at the national and regional planning scale, whilst the issue of how to build extensions to urban areas utilising appropriate standards falls onto the environmental category at the project planning scale. Broadly speaking three scales of planning are applied in this analysis : national/regional planning, metro/urban area planning, and project level planning. As shown in this discussion, it has been concluded that seven major themes provide the fundamental structure around which urban-related issues can be organised.

Optimum Pattern of Urbanisation

The first major theme associated with urbanisation in the LDCs is that there is no rural-urban dichotomy on the national-regional scale. Although rural development is needed, this does not mitigate the simultaneous need for accelerated urban development as well. Growth and development of both rural and urban areas should not be seen as being in competition with each other. The basic demographic reality in many LDCs is that rural areas simply cannot absorb all of the projected population and labour force, that urbanisation roughly on the scale predicted by the United Nations is inevitable, and that rural populations need products and services which urban areas are best able to supply.

The policy issue for planning practice then becomes: what should be the optimum spatial pattern of urbanisation on a national basis? How much emphasis, for example, should countries place on development of their primate city versus expansion of small and medium sized towns or the creation of new towns?

Some degree of urban concentration is undoubtedly essential to achieve a certain "critical mass" for external and internal economies of scale to foster economic growth. And, in any case, prevention of such concentration is difficult because capital investment in port and transport facilities, power, industrial plant capacity and other facilities is already considerable, and it is probably more economical to expand facilities where they exist than to establish them in new locations. On the other hand, many urban problems seem to be compounded by large agglomerations of settlement, and careful study is needed to determine at what point external diseconomies of city growth overwhelm the economic benefits which may be provided by concentration and affect adversely the prospects for new investment and growth.

This general issue regarding the optimum pattern of urbanisation is currently undergoing intensive debate among policy-makers and practitioners, and research on per capita costs and associated questions has not yielded definitive answers. It seems to us that the issue can be broken down into at least the following three sub-issues:

1. Supply of services

How do per capita costs for land, infrastructure and other services vary with city size? Who gains from and pays for these services at various levels in the urban hierachy?

2. Demand for urban activities

What kinds of population thresholds are needed to support various urban activities? How do these thresholds vary with national income and other characteristics?

3. Basic nature of economy

What kinds of demands is a nation's economy going to supply: basic needs for the poor masses or consumer services for urban elites and middle classes? Should these demands be met by letting the people come to the city, or the city come to the people? How a nation responds to this question may partially determine its urban pattern.

The need for carefully conceived national urbanisation strategies which are based on answers to these sub-issues is of critical importance in LDCs. These strategies must somehow spread urban benefits, reduce regional imbalances, minimise costs and meet other national objectives. Spatial development must be seen on a continuum from the national level down to small areas, involving both rural development and urbanisation.(29)

Integrated Spatial Development

A second and closely related theme is that, to achieve "balanced" development, urban areas need to be integrated with their rural hinterlands in a mutually supportive fashion. Broad social, economic and political disparities between the primate city, smaller towns and rural areas do not serve the long range development interests of a country. Undue concentrations of population and urban development within primate cities produce serious regional imbalances in many LDCs, sapping rural areas and smaller towns of their most skilled human resources, investment capital and vitality. To integrate urban with rural development, therefore, national and regional spatial organisation should attempt to break primate city dominance and place greater emphasis on medium-sized city and small town hierarchies which are well linked to rural hinterlands. These lattices of development are likely to yield more balanced and equitable patterns in the long run.(30) Research by Berry, El Shaks and others has shown that countries pass through trajectories of economic growth in which primacy (dominance by one centre) is often a natural intermediate stage. However, with further development, most countries move toward a "better" rank-size distribution of urban areas. Malaysia, Korea and the Indian state of Punjab are examples of this more advanced situation.(31) Factors which influence this change include the type of economic activity and income levels in rural areas, the ability of the rural population to afford public and private motorised transport, levels of services and facilities in medium size and smaller towns, telephone communications and the attractiveness of medium size towns for industrial enterprises including the cost of services and the proximity to markets.

The key issues, which are both economic and political in scope, revolve around how more balanced and integrated patterns can be achieved. Given the economic disparities and concentration of political power in the hands of a few, can more balanced and integrated patterns be achieved without major political change? If changes are necessary, can they occur without violent revolution?

It may be that the spatial reorganisation which seems to be required can occur without radical political change and that integrated rural and urban development can be achieved in a manner that will benefit all groups. The goal is to bring about more equitable participation in the development process. Each society will have to determine those means which can best ensure the desired pattern of integrated spatial development, and the degree of control which a government has over the economy and location of activities will be a major determinant in the success of a national decentralisation policy.

Dualism Between Modern and Informal Sectors

A third theme which emerges, is that there is a basic dualism and conflict within the economy between the formal and informal sectors stimulated by the generating factor of technology. Not only is this dualism reflected in the contrasting types of economic activity and employment, but also in such aspects of the physical environment as transport and residential development. Private automobiles compete for limited road space with buses and trishaws, and expensive suburbs compete for a limited supply of serviced land with low-cost squatter settlements. All of these contrasting features within urban areas are manifestations of the disparities and conflicts of interests which exist between those who are better off and the masses of urban poor. Somehow economic development must be so structured as to reduce these disparities and at the same time improve overall economic performance.

One of the key issues related to this theme becomes whether, how and when the creation of urban jobs can catch up with the expansion of the labour force in cities of the LDCs. Where are these potential urban jobs, both sectorally and geographically, and how can their creation be accelerated? How much emphasis should be placed on the informal versus the formal sector? A related issue is how can economic development be fostered so as to reduce current disparities in income and socio-economic status?

These are difficult questions, the answers to which are not immediately forthcoming. It does appear, however, that there is an urgent need to emphasise labour-intensive approaches and to spread employment around as widely as possible. Jobs in the informal sector should be given greater recognition in public planning and efforts should be made to increase their productivity and respectability. Governments should work with indigenous efforts at grass roots economic development and environmental improvement within low and moderate income areas, and realise that it is perhaps through such efforts that the greatest potential for job creation lies.

Nature of Power and Decision-making

As pointed out in the previous discussion of political factors, centralised control and decision - making from the top down, while supporting the interests of the wealthy elites, are frequently in conflict with the interests of the rural and urban poor. There is an urgent need to reduce this conflict of interests and to involve all segments of society in the decision-making process as much as possible, not merely out of altruism or democratic principle, but because it will lay the foundations for greater stability within the society.

Important issues then become: how can political power and decision-making be decentralised? Will the ruling elites be willing to voluntarily share power with broader based groups or will it have to be taken away from them involuntarily? How can the present polarisation between government decision-makers and the poor be reduced, if not eliminated? Will governments be able to resolve the politically sensitive land issue so that speculation can be brought under control and security of tenure established for lower income groups within urban areas?

Issues related to this theme are crucial because of the central importance of the political generating factor. Many of the other problems, such as economic dualism and gross disparities in the environment, can be partially traced to the concentration of power. Hence it is essential that some effort be made to bring about a decentralisation of decision-making and power.

Resources and Standards for Urban Development

With demographic growth outpacing economic growth in the cities of LDCs, these cities lack adequate resources to cope with their many problems. There is consequently an urgent need to establish priorities within cities and to determine what is adequate and appropriate within the general constraint of limited financial resources. The basic point of this theme is that appropriate technology and standards should be applied to all urban services and facilities. High standard and costly services and facilities, as frequently proposed in Western-style "comprehensive" plans, will rapidly consume limited financial resources and thus can only be made available to a small proportion of the urban population, leaving the balance of urban dwellers without anything. There is a clear need to economise on financial resources, and to make more use of available human and selected physical resources.

The issue essentially comes down to one of standards of urban settlement which are most feasible within the general constraint of limited financial resources. What are appropriate standards for social and physical services and facilities within urban areas? How should extensions to urban areas be built which provide basic facilities (such as accessways, transport and utility systems, and recreation areas) and services (such as education and health) at minimum cost and maximum amenity?

It should be emphasised that this issue involves not only minimum standards for specific facilities, but entire urban layouts and land use patterns which meet this criterion. These extensions to urban areas will be far larger than existing areas by the year 2000 and they offer tremendous opportunities for development of economical patterns of settlement. Given the limited resources available, there is no prospect for provision of high standard and subsidised housing and infrastructure for the new additions to population. Under these circumstances, governments in most LDCs should emphasise a package of programmes which encourage self-help, local self-sufficiency and maximum leverage for a given level of public expenditure. These programmes might include:

1. slum and squatter area upgrading, plus infilling with new serviced sites;
2. expansion of secondary road networks to release more land for guided development;
3. use of the techniques of such as land readjustment and relaxation of subdivision standards to encourage private development of land; and
4. selection of appropriate revenue-producing mechanisms such as the property tax, land value tax, betterment or user charges, etc. - to generate funds for an expanded programme of urban development.(32)

The Role of Government

Another theme involves the role of government vis-a-vis that of the private sector or self-help efforts in the whole field of urban development. While strong governmental initiative to establish policies and implement programmes is clearly needed, it is equally clear that governments should harness and direct the energies of the private sector into playing a useful role in urban development. They should also work with the indigenous self-help efforts at environmental improvement already taking place within many lower income communities, rather than against these efforts. Perhaps the key element of this theme, in fact, is that the best use of government may be as a catalyst to release the energies of individuals and groups and not to substitute or duplicate their efforts, but seek out those activities which are being left undone and which it can do best. This view contrasts with one which would envisage government's role as central with self-help or private sector activities playing a subordinate role.(33)

Although the precise roles here will vary from country to country, the central issue is already apparent: what should be the role of government versus that of the private sector or self-help efforts? For example, should government own urban land in toto or in part? What should be the relative public-private roles in development of infrastructure and housing settlements? How can governmental programmes support self-help activities in economic development and environmental improvement? Can housing associations and other similar community and interest-based groups be stimulated, and develop their own housing? Can the banking system be expanded to address the housing needs of lower-income groups? Is there a place for entrepreneurship in urban development, and if so where? A related issue is fundamental to improved urban development: does the political will exist to bring about needed administrative and fiscal reforms in the governance of urban areas?

Because of their magnitude, urgency, complexity and scope, problems and issues associated with urbanisation require considerable governmental action. Although Asian countries have varying policies regarding the relationship between and use of public and private sectors, it can generally be demonstrated that initiative for solving urban problems must come directly or indirectly from public policies and programmes. Massive kampung upgrading in Jakarta or housing development in Hong Kong and Singapore, cases which are presented in Part Two of this volume, could not have been mounted by the private sector. Government must be ultimately responsible for evaluation of needs and allocation of resources, for formulation of policies and programmes, and establishing a context for their effective implementation. However, government must at the same time work with self-help and private sector efforts which may be the actual implementors of most activities. Government itself should move away from being remote and centralised, towards devolving decision-making to lower levels and becoming more responsive to local needs and demands.

The Specific Role of Planning Institutions

Our final theme, and allied set of issues, relates to the specific role that planning agencies can play within government to bring about positive change in urban areas of developing countries. In a book which is dealing chiefly with an analysis and appraisal of urban planning as practiced in a number of specific cases, we are concerned with the planning function and its relationship to implementation as carried out within an institutional framework. In addition to its redistributional and protective functions, planning is also a mechanism to provide an environment for living which all may desire but which would not be attained through the fragmented decisions of individuals. It is a means to organise the public goods of society. Planning as a general activity involves assembling actions into an orderly sequence which will lead to the achievement of stated objectives, and by this definition many individual entities (including persons, households, private firms and public agencies) engage in planning to some extent. The a priori assumption is that the quantity and quality of actions will be more effective with planning than without. Our major focus here is with the nature and role of the planning function as carried out by those public institutions which are concerned with basic problems of urban development in LDCs.

Several issues are related to this theme, the most general one being: what role can public policy and planning practice play in bringing about an urban transformation within LDCs? What sorts of institutions should be fostered to engage in planning and in implementation of needed programmes? More specifically, should the planning function be consolidated within a separate agency at the metropolitan, city-wide or local levels or should it be decentralised amongst several agencies that have implementation functions as well? Should planning be closely linked to or independent from the political decision-making process? Is the quality of management and staffing of a planning institution not as important to its success as the position of the institution within government? How can planning be made effective within the cultural and institutional history of particular countries? And finally, by what criteria should we evaluate the relative success or failure of the planning function within a particular context?

This last set of issues are especially crucial to this book with its focus on urban planning practice. Throughout the case studies which have been selected for Part Two, there will be a considerable emphasis on the institutions which were responsible for planning and execution of policies, programmes and projects. It is believed that an examination of these institutions will be key to the appraisal of the success or effectiveness of urban planning.

The final section of this chapter will now focus on what has been - and what perhaps should be - the response of planning practice itself to the problems, themes and issues already discussed.

THE RESPONSE OF PLANNING PRACTICE

Scope and Methodology of Practice: Shifting Paradigms

How has planning practice responded to the above problems and issues in the urban areas of Asian LDCs? Two closely interrelated aspects characterise our definition of planing practice as applied in this volume.

1. Scope of planning:

that is, what is planning about? In terms of its substance, does it attempt to address comprehensively all concerns - social, economic, political and physical/spatial - of the type discussed above, or is its focus narrower in scope? If it is narrower, how can one describe the range of substantive concerns that a given paradigm of planning practice encompasses? There is also a geographic dimension to the scope component; that is, does planning attempt to deal with all parts of its area of concern, or does it concentrate only on specific strategic areas?

2. Methodology of planning:

in other words, what do planners do and what methods do they use to accomplish their work? An essential aspect here is the nature of the planning process and the associated sequence of steps and techniques used in planning practice. One key aspect of the planning process is the time frame for which proposals are formulated; that is, is it long range or short term?

These two components dealing with the scope and methodology of planning form a kind of two-dimensional "map" or framework within which specific planning models or paradigms can be located. Over the past three decades, a number of models of planning practice have actually been applied in LDC urban areas. Although we are generalising somewhat, it is in fact possible to characterise "traditional paradigms" and then to consider the shifts away from these paradigms which have occurred in recent years. It should be stressed that the emphasis in this discussion of recent experience is on metropolitan planning and project planning within urban areas. The national/regional scales of planning have tended to be addressed by different paradigms involving different groups of professionals.

Traditional Paradigms

The earliest paradigm of planning practice which emerged from colonial administration and which is still the most widely used is an extension of the "house-keeping" function of city administration. Sectoral agencies often linked to national line agencies are established at the city level and perform the regular functions of maintenance of city infrastructure, social and community services. Planning the expansion needs of the city and addressing the backlog is initiated by each agency through its yearly development budget, usually quite independently of other agencies. There is usually no system for assigning priorities and the city does whatever it can, partly through its own revenues, which it normally controls itself, and partly through central government subsidies which it can obtain through national allocation procedures, persuasive argument or political influence. Few cities in Asian LDCs float their own municipal bonds to obtain development finance.

In some ways, this model has much to recommend it since planning is tied into execution and to available budgets. However, it suffers from lack of inter-sectoral coordination, weak definition of objectives and priorities, lack of an area or community focus and often a lack of longer range planning. Budgets are usually very inadequate for planning the services required to keep up with urban growth, and the lack of coordinated objectives and policies and usually a low incidence of cost recovery, inhibits persuasive arguments for increasing budgetary allocations.

What can be described as the first effort to integrate sectoral activities concentrated on formulation of a long-range, "master plan" of a given urban area's physical development. The output from this approach is a kind of a photograph of how a city's basic land use and circulation pattern may look at some future point in time. This paradigm, which stems from architectural and engineering traditions going back nearly a century, has the following characteristics:

1. Long-range emphasis

The basic time frame to which the planning process is geared and for which planning proposals are formulated spans a 20- to 30-year period, usually with no phasing shown.

2. Product vs. process

This traditional approach draws up a static blueprint or map which places more emphasis on the plan-as-product than on setting in motion a dynamic planning process. As with an architect's floorplan of a building, the concept entails the strictly linear methodology of producing a city plan and then building the city as if it were a giant piece of architecture. This approach is vague as to how the city is supposed to reach the planned objective; that is, what type of phasing, short-term programming and budgeting is necessary to lay the groundwork for implementation of development? The traditional master-plan paradigm does not address this question.

3. Strong physical emphasis

The approach usually limits the scope of its proposals to land use, circulation and other physical infrastructures (water supply, sanitation, drainage, etc.); all elements which can be mapped. Analysis and projection of economic, demographic and other social elements are frequently superficial and linked to generating data that can input into future land use. (For example, demographic projections can yield estimates of needed dwelling units which, at given density assumptions, can be converted into future space requirements; and employment projections can similarly be converted into space requirements for various types of economic activity.) Very little is included in these plans on socio-economic programmes that are also required in their own right to solve urban problems and issues.

4. Non-strategic quality

Attempts are made to formulate a land use zoning plan for every square meter of the urban area, although this is irrevelant in terms of addressing many of the critical issues mentioned above, such as creation of employment opportunities, provision of low-income residential settlements, or generation of a higher level of local resources for development.

5. Lack of interaction with the users

Little attention is given to the priorities, needs and constraints of the city's population, especially to low income groups. Involvement of any users, other than government officials, in the planning decisions which affect them has been minimal or non-existent.

Although the physical "master plan" approach has found increasing disfavour in most developed countries, it was exported into many LDCs during the 1950s and early 1960s where it is still being used. In the Ankara case study presented in this volume, the approach is described and its limitations very clearly addressed. Some of these basic limitations are already apparent from the above characteristics. Because most master plans are not converted into specific short-term programmes and budgets, experience has shown that they are inadequate guides for implementation by sectoral agencies. The town planner has remained too aloof from the critical action decisions that must be made in setting priorities for the next 5 years or annually across a number of sectors. Consequently most actual action decisions are either made by decision-makers on a political basis or by sectoral agencies for a specific component. Even within the area of physical development, traditional master plans have often failed to produce usable guidelines for channeling urban growth, with the result that much growth took place in "unauthorised areas". Development pressures within strategic areas are neither understood nor managed; rather a zoning map is produced for all areas. It is usually hoped that this map can provide the land use framework for controlling private development, but this negative approach has generally not proved successful. Because of its lack of a strategic quality, the master plan approach has been ineffectual in developing policies and solutions to many key problems and issues.

Although the primary traditional paradigm described here is the "physical master plan" approach applied by urban planners to individual cities, there have also been situations in which regional planners have formulated "economic master plans" which display some of the same characteristics. In the Regional Plan initially prepared for Pahang Tenggara (Chapter 6), for example, the economists have produced documents with the same long-range emphasis, the same orientation toward the plan-as-product, and the same lack of interaction with the users. Although these regional plans are more sophisticated, there is the same tendency to neglect phasing, detailed financing, organisational and management concerns, continual adjustments from feed-back, and other aspects which are crucial for implementation.

Current Predominant Paradigm:

Since the late 1960s there has been some shift or movement away from the traditional paradigm in many LDC cities. Although this shift has taken various forms, the predominant trend has been towards a planning paradigm which is diametrically opposed to the traditional master plan model. Some of the characteristics of this emerging paradigm have been the following:

1. Short- term emphasis

The new emphasis is on formulating short-term programmes/ projects which may or may not relate to a broader development strategy. Long-term master plans which encompass entire urban areas are tending to be replaced by 5-year and annual project proposals which lead directly to action.

2. Use of budget

Included with such proposals is a budget which attempts to examine their financial feasibility. This effort to relate all proposals, including those involving physical development, to financial costs and benefits represents a relatively recent development for most urban planning practice in developing countries.

3. De-emphasis of physical (land use) planning

Another trend has been a shift away from the near-exclusive emphasis on physical, in particular land use, planning. Planning practice has taken on more of a policy orientation with greater efforts being made to formulate socio-economic programmes in addition to, or in conjuncton with, physical development projects. However, most urban development proposals still tend to remain "physical" in nature, dealing with such aspects as transport, residential settlement schemes and public utilities. But projects now being formulated are no longer limited to a physical master plan dimension; rather, efforts are made to include other policy elements within a given sector. For example, a residential settlement scheme would include elements of management and finance, and careful staging, as well as a detailed mapped plan.

This current predominant paradigm for urban planning practice has been strongly influenced by the departments of the World Bank dealing with projects in urban areas, as well as other external assistance agencies, whose economists and planners have pressed for realistic action. Local decision-makers have also shared this strong desire for more immediate results than were forthcoming from traditional master plans, although they have not always agreed with international technocrats over the specific types of projects which should be implemented. This international influence derives from an economic tradition in which individual projects are appraised for their "feasibility" and an effort made to relate a "shopping list" of projects to available fiscal resources. Several of the case studies presented under the headings "low- to moderate-income residential programmes" and "sectoral programmes" are important examples of this newer, action-oriented and project-oriented approach to planning practice. But even some recent "comprehensive plans", such as the Karachi Development Programme, described in Chapter 3, and Calcutta's Basic Development Plan (1967), have tended to emphasise a set of specific programmes/projects which are tied together by overall objectives and policies - and by a budget. The Calcutta Plan and others of this type do not include an explicit land use plan which was the main feature of the traditional master plan paradigm. This new approach has undoubtedly led to an acceleration of programme/project implementation in many LDC cities, in that the short-term action recommendations have been much more usable preludes to implementation than the traditional paradigms.

However, embedded within the orientation of this current predominant paradigm to "get things done" lies what is perhaps its most significant limitation. Frequently overall city-wide or metro-wide strategies which endeavour to tie specific projects together into an integrated whole, or to link local systems with those required at the larger scale, have been thrown out the window. In the rush to programme and execute feasible projects, the danger is that both the longer-range and metro/urban-scale perspectives may be lost sight of. In carrying out an upgrading programme in Jakarta's individual kampungs, for instance, the need to simultaneously formulate city-wide strategies for drainage, sanitation, water supply, etc. has until recently been glossed over.

A second limitation is that the current predominant paradigm still has not found adequate means for integrating formulation of socio-economic programmes with physical development projects. Whilst the latter may be appraised on economic grounds, this is not the same as broadening the scope of planning practice to enable it to encompass social and economic programmes as well as those related to the physical environment. Using the same example of Jakarta's KIP, it is a fact that no real attempt to formulate policies/programmes for support to small-scale businesses, non-formal education and other crucial socio-economic activities, and to integrate these with the KIP physical infrastructure programme, has been made. The software programmes in health in both Jakarka and Manila, and described in Chapter 12, have not received the attention and priority they deserve. In this regard, the traditional and current predominant paradigms described here are both deficient: neither have adequately built in a capacity to address such socio-economc issues as those raised under the dualism heading above.

A third limitation has been the lack of focus on institutional linkages and design. This has ranged from the mundane level of neglecting maintenance or not integrating the projects into the city administration, to a lack of focus on inter-sectoral priorities in overall planning and budgeting, and weak linkages between sectors. However, within the last year or two, some international funding agencies are making efforts to overcome these weaknesses, which are also reflected in their own organisations. In the future we are likely to see increased emphasis from institutions such as the World Bank on strengthening the forward planning, budgeting, revenue-raising and staffing of urban administrations, and a shift away from lending for isolated projects.

In fact, neither of these models of intra-urban planning practice have addressed most of the problems/themes/issues discussed earlier in this chapter. Themes/issues related to the "optimum pattern of urbanisation" and "integrated spatial development" have not generally been dealt with by urban planning practitioners, but rather by more academically oriented regional planners drawing especially on the disciplines of geography and regional economics. And the political and institutional themes/issues related to the "nature of power and decision-making", the "role of government" and the "specific role of planning institutions" have been largely ignored as well.

Some Critical Ingredients for an Appropriate Model

The above discussion has attempted to briefly summarise some of the present trends regarding the scope and methodology of urban planning practice. A recent shift in approach away from traditional physical master planning toward short-term project planning has been noted, with some of the characteristics and limitations of both "paradigms" indicated. The questions now become: where should urban planning practice in the developing countries go from here? Have some lessons been learned regarding scope, methodology and perhaps other aspects of planning which can be usefully applied in the future? The following summary outlines the essential features of a planning style which would respond to the particular conditions and needs of LDCs.

In rich countries where urban growth is slow and most agencies are relatively well staffed technically and have adequate budgets, and regulation on development is effective, the problems for planning practice are different compared to those of most LDCs where opposite conditions obtain. In the rich countries the major issues are often to prevent and slow down unnecessary physical development and to provide special assistance for small, under-privileged minorities. The planning style in these conditions often emphasises an administrative framework and regulations which provide a forum within which interested groups can advocate their position. The process is frequently very time-consuming and involves extended studies by the various parties to argue their points of view.

In LDCs, on the other hand, the need is to rapidly expand essential services and land to those who are without them, who usually form the greater majority of the population, at a price they can afford, while at the same time removing restrictions and regulations which hamper their efforts to help themselves and which depress their productivity. With the extremely limited resources at the disposal of most LDC governments, this implies careful attention to the priorities and linkages of public works and related programmes and to the design of projects which will reach the poor at standards which will not require heavy subsidies. Speed and energy are also essential qualities if the increasing deficit of services is to be overcome. Entrepreneurship and imagination have to be fostered at all levels and combined with efforts to synchronise the work of the various agencies. Key actions must be identified which will guide city growth in the most desirable directions and at lowest financial, social and environmental costs. Programmes should be selected which concentrate on services which the government is best fitted to provide and avoid duplication of those activities which can be more effectively supplied by the popular or private sectors.

The style of planning practice suggested by these needs is dynamic and iterative. It would discard long studies preliminary to action, and rely on a rapid identification and ranking of problems, a search for low-cost solutions followed by balancing the scale and timing of the programmes against resources which are presently available or which could be raised in the near future. It would then move quickly into a series of action programmes targeted at groups, sectors and locations of greatest need and in a manner which would show an early success in order to overcome the sense of inertia and defeatism which the scale of the problems in the LDC cities sometimes engenders in their administrations.

While allowing for the need for speed, efficiency and optional use of resources we must realise that planners rarely have the opportunity to act as practical Platonists, assisting society as a whole. They are usually influenced and directed by their political masters and the structure of the planning and budgeting process will also confer more power and influence on the groups which can control it, and enable them to decide who will benefit from the projects resulting from the planning. The value and power relationships in planning is discussed further in Chapter 2 and in Part Three. It is sufficient to note here that in the allocation of resources, and development of specific projects, the planning process should be open to influence by organisations representing the poorer and weaker segments of the population who are often excluded from decisions which directly affect them.

One of the most effective ways for politicians to gain popular support has proved to be broad-spread programmes which provide a small improvement for many people in services which are a high priority for them. These priorities are almost universally found to be in secure tenure of their land, and improvements in water supply, drainage and sanitation, access and transport, and health and education services. The action programmes will also be more acceptable and successful if they involve the recipients in their design, offer choices which respond to varying needs of different families and, to the extent possible and appropriate, decentralise the implementation and management of the programmes to the lowest levels of government, community groups and individual families.

Implementation should be monitored both for its effectiveness and negative impacts, with emphasis on obtaining information rapidly which can be fed back to improve the next phase or cycle of projects and also as an input to longer term strategy planning. Longer-term planning should proceed as well, with the action plans and programmes being continually modified and updated by it. There would be two main objectives. First, to develop the goals, strategies and policies for the city in more detail and precision so that each action programme and sectoral agency can harmonise its activities within this overall framework. This aspect of planning would be expressed in policy documents, performance criteria and standards, and a spatial strategy. It would be a working handbook with which to examine the consistency of specific proposals with the social, economic and environmental objectives for the city, and not an end-state master plan. Secondly and concurrently, the planning would focus on the management system of planning and implementation and look at the mechanism to coordinate the implementing agencies with the planning and budgeting agencies, allocate resources, relate expenditures to resources, expand the fiscal base of the city and review and update laws, regulations and standards.

A Tentative Model of Planning Practice

The intention here is to present a more comprehensive and dynamic model of planning practice which will attempt to overcome some of the limitations of the models described earlier yet respond to the objectives outlined in the above discussion. As shown in Fig. 1.1, our model can generally be depicted as a systems diagram of the planning/programming/implementation

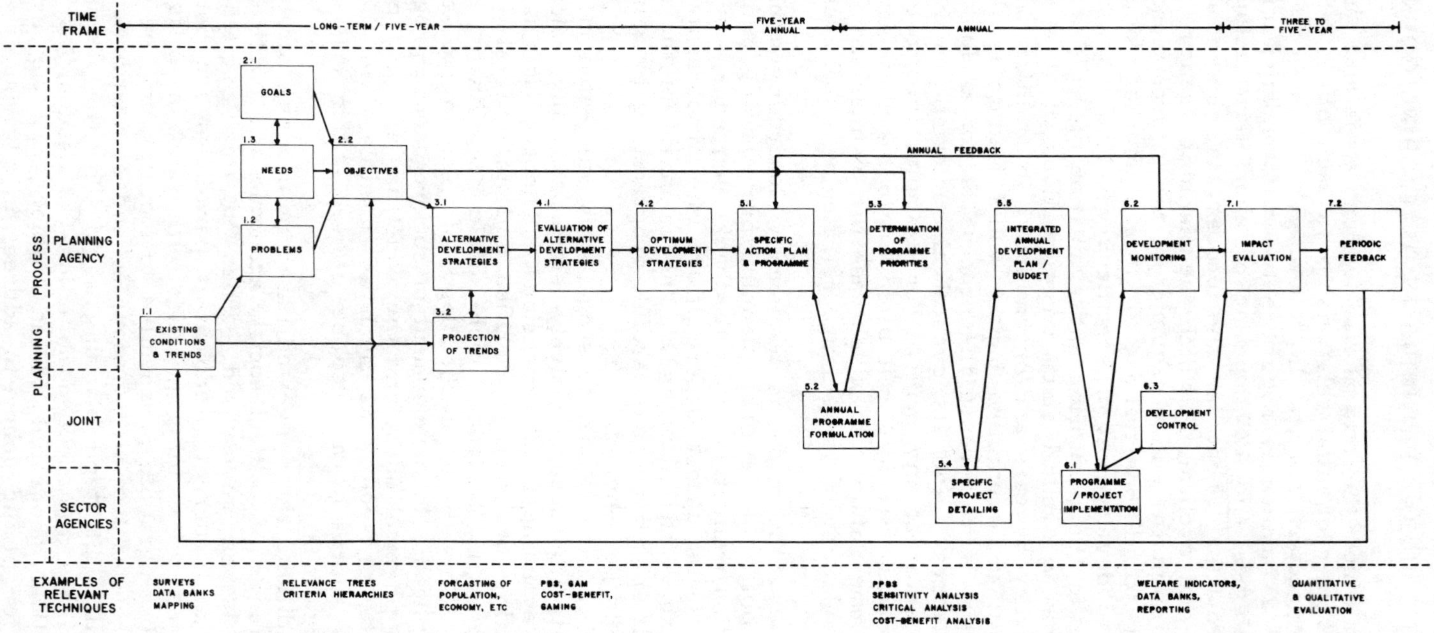

Fig. 1.1. Systems Diagram of Planning/Programming/Implementation Process.

process, in which the critical development steps and tasks are shown in their sequential relationship to each other. Some of its major characteristics are the following:

First, a balance is sought between formulation of long-range strategies and development of short-term action programmes/projects. That is, the process is viewed as both continuous and cyclical, in which the planning agency attempts to move through the entire sequence of tasks, from description of existing conditions/trends to formulation of long-range strategies to development of specific 5-year and annual action programmes to the monitoring and evaluation of implementation. This process is cyclical since large portions of it should be repeated every 5 years and/or annually; in addition, periodic evaluation of implementation impact would lead to feedback to initial tasks. In this sense the process is not as linear as it may first appear, and its cyclical characteristic enables the planner to enter at any point. For example, the most urgent desire of decision-makers will often be to formulate immediate action recommendations, in which case the planner may have to defer formulation of long-range strategies until resources permit.

Secondly, the model is not simply describing a planning process, but the entire planning/programming/budgeting/implementation/evaluation and feedback sequence, in which "planning" leads almost imperceptibly into "implementation" - and back again to "planning". The emphasis in the current predominant paradigm on careful programming/budgeting of actions would be retained.

Thirdly, with regard to scope, this suggested model has the capacity to comprehensively encompass physical/spatial, social and economic/fiscal dimensions. The emphasis is placed on formulating programme priorities and an integrated annual development plan/budget which could coordinate sectoral activities. This basic methodology of planning practice is equally applicable to development of socio-economic programmes as it is to physical ones, and the model has a robust potential to integrate all sectors as much as possible. On the other hand, this approach can also be utilised within less comprehensive situations.

In addition, the suggested paradigm can deal strategically with the range of critical social, economic and political problems and issues summarised earlier in this chapter. The traditional and current predominant paradigms are both generally limited to planning practice within urban areas - and within that geographic perspective to focusing only on some of the issues associated with "resources and standards for urban development". Strategic planning would allow the planners and decision-makers to select combinations of issues, as well as small, critical geographic areas, which may be extremely important for public policy to address in a given urban context. In this way planning practice should become more flexible and relevant in grappling with the diverse sets of key issues across a much wider spectrum. Indeed, this spectrum could also include the above-mentioned national/regional scale issues. Three other general points should be made about this model, as shown in Fig. 1.1:

1. The systems diagram makes a distinction on the vertical axis as to what type of agency is responsible for given tasks. In the upper part of the diagram are those tasks for which the intersectoral planning agency would have responsibility, whereas tasks involving line or sectoral agencies - or joint responsibility - are shown across the lower part of the diagram.

2. Also shown on the diagram are examples of relevant techniques which are required to support specific tasks in the planning process.

3. Within this process each project and sectoral programme will have its own planning sequence (5.4 and 6.1) not elaborated in the diagram. One important lesson emerging from recent experience (34) is that the nature of the project indicates the style of planning. Heavy infrastructure projects can often be planned centrally through one agency with a high degree of control by technocrats and little account taken of the political and social environment. By contrast integrated rural development projects and community-oriented urban projects which deal with individual assets such as land, and whose success is usually measured from social and economic, rather than purely physical, indicators are more dependent on the external environment for their success, deal with many different agencies and have less area of total control than the conventional sectoral projects. Not only implementation, but often goals and objectives, must emanate from lower levels of project management and sensitivity to the external social environment must be greater. Upper level management has then to provide a framework and forum for the evolution of these goals rather than imposing them on lower levels. In the context of most LDCs, where sectoral agencies are powerful and tend to define and control their own budgets, the whole planning framework described here will depend for its success more on seeking common ground and developing rationality through dialogue, than on direct control.

Some of the most important steps in the process are the following:

Task 1.1. Here existing conditions and trends are described and analysed, based on an information system which integrates data on basic resources, population, employment activities, land uses, communications and flows systems, etc.

Task 3.1. In this task alternative development "strategies" which set out "broad choice packages" for an urban area in policy terms are formulated. The time frame emphasises long-term (20-year) and 5-year periods. Alternative strategies are evaluated and an optimum one selected in Tasks 4.1 to 4.2.

Tasks 5.1 to 5.5. Having selected the "optimum development strategy", the next task is to translate this into a specific development plan and set of programmes which together can be implemented. Here a financial ceiling and other key resource constraints (institutional, human and material) must be taken into account in formulating such an integrated plan and set of programmes. A 5-year action plan should be a framework within which specific programmes can be further detailed on an annual basis. The remainder of step 5 would then be carried out annually, culminating in an integrated annual development plan/budget to be prepared by the planning agency. This document would place major emphasis on the mutually reinforcing linkages of individual programmes and projects. Responsibility for this general step is shared by both line or sectoral departments and the planning or intersectoral coordination agency.

Issues Arising from, and Relationship of Case Studies, to this Model

The suggested model sounds rather utopian; yet in fact a number of questions which face planning practitioners still remain as we consider how the model is applied:

1. What is the appropriate balance between long-range strategies and short-term action programmes/projects?

Our ideal model sounds good in theory, but how frequently has formulation of long-range strategies been used as the primary input for deriving short-term programmes/projects? In short, how consistently has this paradigm been rigorously applied in practice? Particularly in LDCs where urban conditions are changing rapidly and staffs remain sorely inadequate, formulation of sophisticated long-range alternatives does not yield the same benefits as short-term proposals which result in immediate action. And there may not be available technical resources in many cities to activate the model along all temporal dimensions. However, there are dangers in adopting a solely short-term view, and the two emphases should be seen as being mutually reinforcing. There is an international debate among planners over this issue, which takes on particular importance in LDCs.

The cases presented in this volume provide examples of planning practice which have approached the time dimension in a variety of ways. All of the metro/urban-scale planning exercises (Karachi, Ankara and Durgapur) have attempted to achieve some balance between long-range planning and short-term action programming, although only in the Karachi case is an effort made to do this thoroughly. The cases which are narrower in scope (Jakarta-Manila upgrading, Hong Kong-Singapore housing, Malaysia's UDA and Singapore's area licensing scheme), on the other hand, have largely ignored long-range planning and stressed short-term programming and implementation. An interesting exception to this generalisation is in the efforts now underway in Manila to use three sectoral programmes for community upgrading as a means to introduce a wider planning and budgeting mechanism in the metropolis. This empirical material will shed considerable light on this issue.

2. Regarding the scope of planning, how "comprehensive" should a given planning undertaking really be?

Although the suggested model has the theoretical capacity to deal comprehensively with all dimensions, the question remains: what has experience actually shown as to the success of intersectoral planning vs. efforts which have been narrower in scope? If the primary objective of planning is to expedite effective implementation, it may be that there are limits to comprehensiveness and that the system may break down if too many components (physical, economic and social) are juggled simultaneously. It becomes very difficult for any one agency or individual to integrate all of these components. On the other hand, failure to attempt an integration is also dangerous because it can lead to imbalances between sectoral programmes/projects and missed opportunities which highly synchronised development could bring about. For example, a residential upgrading programme which concentrates only on physical infrastructure may neglect the possibilities of linking such improvements with crucial job creation, community development and health programmes needed by the same target groups and neighbourhoods. As with the time dimension issue, this question of appropriate scope of planning practice is being debated internationally, and the debate takes on particular poignancy in the LDCs.

Again the cases presented in this volume address the question of scope in differing ways, thus giving us the opportunity to examine empirically which approach seems to be most effective in specific circumstances. At one extreme, the Karachi planning programme attempts to be very comprehensive in linking physical, economic and social proposals with financial and institutional/political realities. The Ankara and Durgapur exercises, although also metro-scale in geographic scope, were more narrowly focused on physical planning. At the other extreme are cases dealing only with residential development or, in the case of Singapore's ALS, traffic regulation.

3. Are there potential problems with "stragetic" planning?

The suggested model would have planning practice deal strategically with selected critical problems/issues and geographic areas within a larger jurisdiction. But there may be a number of potential pitfalls with this approach: First, who decides what problems/issues and what areas are strategic: the politician, the planner, who? What if various actors disagree on priorities in this connection? Secondly, how can the planner arrive at strategic geographic areas for more careful scrutiny? What if his projections of the extent and direction of development turn out to be wrong? Given the dynamic nature of urban growth and change in LDCs, combined with our inadequate understanding of the factors involved, this possibility is conceivable. Thirdly, what does planning practice have to say about "unauthorised" or uncontrolled development occurring outside of strategic geographic areas? Does the planner turn his back on such development or, perhaps equally problematic, does he advocate a heavy-handed programme of negative controls and sanctions to discourage or eliminate it? The model tends to implicitly advocate positive planning and programming of public development which would form the basis for subsequent actions on the part of the people, but is not there also a role for negative controls? If so, what kind of controls?

Some of the cases deal with this last question, although not as rigorously as with the time and scope questions. But the matter of who sets priorities is explicitly raised in the studies of Ankara, Karachi and Kuala Lumpur. And the Singapore-Hong Kong housing and Ankara cases both contain some assessment of the problems of negatively controlling squatter areas.

4. How should the budget be used and controlled?

It is clear that the budgeting and allocation of funds is the key link between the rhetoric of policies and priorities, and the reality of what does, or does not, happen. Furthermore, power usually resides with those who have the ability to raise and dispose of funds. In this context the proportion of funds which the city can raise and control itself is often a key element over the degree to which its officials have control over its own planning and development. In many LDCs, smaller cities are heavily dependent on central government funds for development and in the primate capitals the central government sometimes wishes to dilute its economic attraction and political power. To be realistic, any "objective" and technocratic model of planning must take these factors into account. It is not by chance that the most admired examples of efficient and rational planning are the city states of Singapore and Hong Kong where

UNIVERSITY OF WINNIPEG
LIBRARY
515 Portage Avenue
Winnipeg, Manitoba R3B 2E9

the central/provincial/local dichotomies do not exist. The more difficult situations occur in states with multiple levels of government where the issues as to which level will control the planning and budgeting function, and whether implementation will be initiated by the area government, or by national, sectoral agencies, becomes crucial.

Thus in proposing any changes in the planning and administration of a city, the historical context and the levels and powers of its institutions must be assessed. The challenge often resides in defining planning, budgeting and control mechanisms which guarantee dialogue and develop rational priorities while defining clear areas of control by implementing agencies over their specific programmes.

The case studies vary considerably both in space and time. Figure 1.2 provides a framework or "map" which shows the time dimension along one axis and the scope of planning along the other and the cases are then located on this "map". One criterion for their selection is that they offer a variety of experiences to draw upon regarding these two important dimensions of planning practice.

In the light of our own critique, the planning model we have outlined above may have to be simpler in its initial stages and evolve later towards a more precise and integrated style. There are probably four key areas which need to be addressed initially. First is the definition of priorities. Given the lack of communication between most government agencies and their separate and often unrelated sources of funds, it is important at least to have a forum where planners, the implementing agencies, and politicians can discuss the priorities for development of the city. The most unreasonable and expensive programmes can often be eliminated by exposure in such a forum. Second, budgets for implementing agencies should be formulated on the basis of the agreed priorities. Thirdly, the funds should usually be allocated to the lowest practical level of government to achieve effective implementation. Finally, agencies should be designed to reward performance, be able to pay adequate salaries to attract suitable people and, wherever possible, promote or dismiss based on performance.

In concluding this introductory chapter, we stress that the emphasis in this volume is on an <u>empirical analysis of planning practice</u>. It is our belief that too much of the international literature in this field has been deductive and theoretical. Academically based planning theorists have formulated their normative notions of planning and then attempted to fit "the real world" of planning practice to these notions. But the literature contains very few examples of case studies by practitioners which begin with empirical situations as the basis for developing more realistic theories as to what constitutes effective planning. After providing the basic framework in these first two chapters, this volume represents one modest effort to redress this imbalance.

UNIVERSITY OF WINNIPEG
LIBRARY
515 Portage Avenue
Winnipeg, Manitoba R3B 2E9

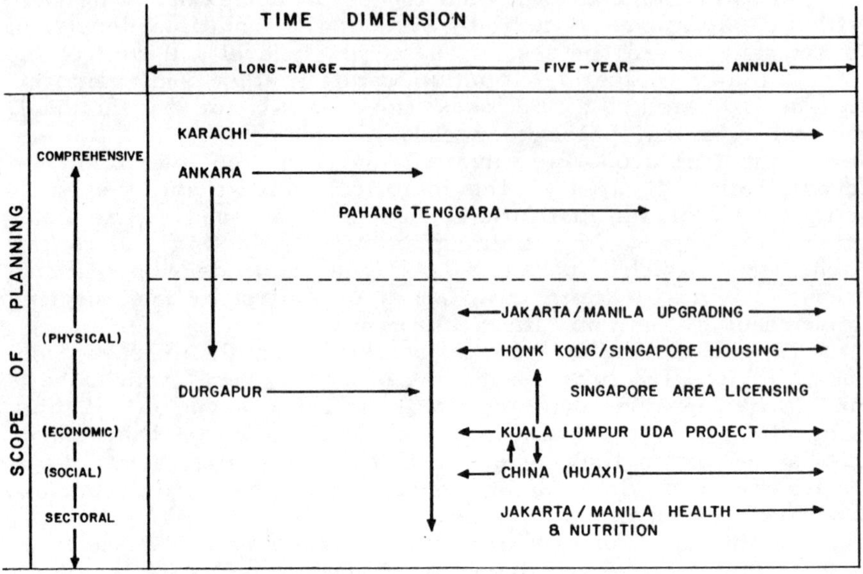

Fig. 1.2. Framework Locating Cases on Basis of Time Dimension and Scope.

In Chapter 2, we shall turn our attention to one of the key issues mentioned previously: what criteria should employed in evaluating the relative success or failure of a planning activity carried out by a given institution?

NOTES

(1) See, for example, United Nations (1971), Table 5.

(2) Ibid., Table 6.

(3) United Nations ECAFE, Bangkok, 1972.

(4) For recent reviews of relevant migration literature see Yap (1974).

(5) See United Nations (1969) and subsequent population documents.

(6) It should be stressed, however, that there are wide variations in the process of urban growth among LDCs which depend on several factors, including the present level of urbanisation, population growth and the availability of natural resources. For a useful typology which attempts to classify

the projected urban growth paths likely to be followed by most LDCs into four groups, see World Bank, Working Paper No. 209 (1975).

(7) ECAFE (1972) op. cit, p. 28.

(8) For a brief discussion in support of more recent United Nations projections made for all LDCs, see World Bank, Working Paper No. 209 (1975), pp. 12-18.

(9) For a discussion of this factor, see articles by Bose and McGee in Jakobson and Prakash (1971), World Bank Urbanisation Sector Working Paper (1972) and Berry (1973).

(10) McGee (1967 and 1971) was one of the first writers to deal with the concept of economic dualism.

(11) Examples of recent literature on the urban informal sector include Friedmann and Sullivan (1974), McGee (1974), Mazumdar (1975) and McGee and Yeung (1977).

(12) Perhaps the most useful data on urban employment and unemployment is being generated by the World Bank's Urban Poverty Task Force and the International Labour Office.

(13) Muncie (1976): Sakornpan, Tantisuk and French (1971).

(14) International Labour Office (1974).

(15) For examples of this exploitative relationship between city and country, see McGee (1974) and Freidmann (1973).

(16) These data from United Nations Conference on Human Settlements, "Global Review of Human Settlements" (1976).

(17) There is a substantial literature in political science to support these generalizations; for a recent example, see Machado (1977).

(18) Writers who have stressed this positive social role of urban low-income living environments include Clinard (1966), Laquian (1969) and Turner (1972).

(19) This figure on drug addicts appeared in an article on Indonesia's tough drug laws in the Los Angeles Times, 14 December 1976.

(20) See, for example, World Bank, "Education Sector Paper" (1974).

(21) Basta (1977).

(22) Both the United Nations and World Bank have recently sponsored studies focused on urban land problems and policies, including United Nations (1973, 1976), Grimes (1974), Doebele (1976) and Rivkin (1977).

(23) Perhaps the best summary of urban transport problems in LDCs is the World Bank Sector Policy Paper (1975).

(24) These and related data on Calcutta were published in C.M.P.O. (1966).

(25) World Bank Sector Working Papers on urbanisation, water supply and sewerage, and electric power (1971, 1972) provide one useful source of information on infrastructure in LDC cities.

(26) The statistic on Kuala Lumpur was published in Laquian (1971) and comparable figures for Manila and Jakarta in United Nations (1971).

(27) There is a growing literature on urban shelter - including Laquian (1969), Turner (1972, 1976), World Bank (1974, 1975), Dwyer (1975), Grimes (1976), and Burns and Grebler (1977) - which amplifies the points summarized here.

(28) For an excellent and profound critique of the impact of technology on society, see Berger (1977).

(29) For an excellent discussion of this issue, see Richardson (1976).

(30) A particularly strong plea for the integration of urban and rural development is made by Johnson (1970).

(31) Berry, in Jakobson and Prakash (1971).

(32) Techniques mentioned here are thoroughly discussed in several of the references, including United Nations (1971), World Bank (1974), Grimes (1974) and Doebele (1976).

(33) This point is made particularly cogently by Turner (1976).

(34) World Bank (1980)

REFERENCES

Basta, S. (1977) "Nutrition and Health in Low Income Urban Areas of the Third World", Ecology of Food and Nutrition, Vol. 6.

Berger, P. L. (1977) Pyramids of Sacrifice: Political Ethics and Social Change. London: Penguin Books.

Berry, Brian J. L. (1973) The Human Consequences of Urbanisation. London: Macmillan Press Ltd.

Burns, L.S. and Grebler, L. (1977) The Housing of Nations. London: MacMillon Press Ltd.

Clinard, M. (1966) Slums and Community Development: Experiments in Self-Help. New York: Collier-MacMillon.

Calcutta Metropolitan Planning Organisation (1966) Basic Development Plan for the Calcutta Metropolitan District. Calcutta: C.M.P.O.

Davis, Kingsley (1969, 1972) World Urbanization 1950-1970 Vol. 1, Basic Data for Cities, Countries and Regions; Vol. II, Analysis of Trends, Relationships and Development. Berkeley; Institute of International Studies, University of California.

Doebele, W. A. (1976) Land Readjustment as an Alternative to Taxation for Recovery of Betterment: The Case of South Korea. Washington, D.C.: World Bank.

Dwyer, D. J. (1975) People and Housing in Third World Cities. London: Longman Group Ltd.

Friedmann, J. (1973) Urbanisation, Planning and National Development. Beverley Hills: Sage Publications.

Friedmann, J. and Sullivan, F. (1974) Labour Absorption in the Urban Economy: The Case of the Developing Countries. Economic Development and Cultural Change.

Grimes, O.F. (1974) Urban Land and Public Policy: Social Appropriation of Betterment. Washington, D.C.: World Bank.

Grimes, O.F. (1970) Housing for Low-Income Urban Families. Washington, D.C.: World Bank.

I.L.O. (1974) Sharing in Development: A Programme of Employment, Equity and Growth for the Philippines. Geneva.

I.L.O. (1976) Employment, Growth and Basic Needs. Geneva.

Jakobson, L. and Prakash, V. (eds.) (1971) Urbanization and National Development. Beverley Hills: Sage Publications.

Johnson, E.A.J. (1970) The Organisation of Space in Developing Countries. Cambridge, Mass: Harvard University Press.

Laquian, Aprodicio (1969) Slums are for People. Manila: Univ. of the Philippines.

Laquian, Aprodicio (1971) Rural-Urban Migrants and Metropolitan Development. Ottawa: Intermet.

Machado, K.G. (1977) Depoliticization in Southeast Asia: Authoritarian Approaches to Problems of Conflict and Power. Unpublished paper.

Mazumdar, D. (1975) The Urban Informal Sector. Working Paper No. 211, Washington, D.C.

McGee, T.G. (1967) The South East Asian City. London: G. Bell & Sons.

McGee, T.G. (1971) Urbanisation Process in the Third World. London: G. Bell & Sons.

McGee, T.G. (1974) The Persistance of the Protoproletariat: Occupational Structures and Planning for the Future of Third World Cities. Los Angeles: U.C.L.A.

McGee, T.C. and Yeung, Y.M. (1977) Hawkers in Southeast Asian Cities. Ottawa: International Development Research Centre.

Muncie, P. (1976) Task Force Defines Strategy to Allieviate Urban Poverty. Finance and Development, no. 13.

Richardson, H.W. (1973) The Economics of Urban Size. Lexington, Saxon Books.

Sakornpan, C., Tantisuk, D. and French, A. (1971) Klong Toey, A Social Survey of a Squatter Slum Bangkok: Thammasat University.

Turner, J.F.C. and Fichter, R. (1972) Freedom to Build. New York, Macmillan Co.

Turner, J.F.C. (1976) Housing by People. London: Marion Boyars.

United Nations (1969) Growth of the World's Urban and Rural Population, 1972-2000, UN publication, Sales No. E. 69. XIII.3; New York.

United Nations (1971) Improvement of Slums and Uncontrolled Settlements. New York: United Nations.

United Nations ECAFE (1972) Demographic Situation in Relation to Factors Effecting Population Change. Prepared for Second Asian Population Conference.

United Nations (1973-76) Urban Land Policies and Land Use Control Measures. Vols. 1-VII. New York.

United Nations (1974) Concise Report on the World Population Situation in 1970-1975 and its Long-Range Implications. UN publication, Sales No. 74, XIII.4. New York.

United Nations (1974) Urban-Rural Projections from 1950-2000. New York: United Nations.

United Nations (1976) Habitat Conference on Human Settlements, "Global Review of Human Settlements". Unpublished conference document A/Conf.70/A/1, Vancouver.

World Bank (1971) Water Supply and Sewerage Sector Working Paper. Washington, D.C.

World Bank (1971) Electric Power Sector Working Paper. Washington, D.C.

World Bank (1972) Urbanisation Sector Working Paper. Washington, D.C.

World Bank (1974) Sites and Services Projects. Washington, D.C.

World Bank (1975) The Task Ahead for the Cities of the Developing Countries. Working Paper No. 209, Washington, D.C.

World Bank (1975) Housing Sector Policy Paper. Washington, D.C.

World Bank (1977) "Urban Poverty", unpublished materials, Washington, D.C.

World Bank (1975) Urban Transport Sector Policy Paper. Washington, D.C.

World Bank (1980) "The Design of Organisations for Rural Development Projects", unpublished working paper, Washington, D.C.

Yap, Lorence (1974) Internal Migration in Less Developed Countries: A Survey of the Literature. Urban Poverty Task Force, World Bank.

2

Criteria for Evaluating Urban Planning and Programmes

John L. Taylor
David G. Williams

"Perhaps the most startling feature of 20th century culture is the fact that we have developed such elaborate ways of doing things and at the same time have developed no way of justifying any of the things we do."(1)

INTRODUCTION

The last chapter outlined some of the principal issues and problems faced in Asian countries and discussed the response of planning practice, and the case studies in Part Two will illustrate specific efforts which have been made to try to solve some of these intractable problems through urban planning and sectoral programmes. This chapter is intended to provide a more detailed framework which the reader can use to review and compare the case studies. In later chapters the authors will evaluate their experiences with reference to the objectives stated in their respective studies and to relevant criteria outlined here.

Criteria constitute a set of tests which can be used to determine the relative success or failure of proposals and completed actions compared to original goals and expectations. They can be introduced at three major points in the planning process. First, during the initial generation of plans, to provide guidelines for translating general objectives into specific plans and programmes. Later, as an instrument to distinguish between plans and to select from alternative proposals. Finally, in evaluation of the performance of a plan or programme. In each of these phases certain objectives and their associated criteria may be more important than others, and may be ranked according to importance assigned by different interest groups. The focus of this chapter is not on the techniques and methodology of planning and evaluation as such.(2) Rather, we propose here a set of qualities and their associated criteria which we consider to be relevant to the planning of urban development and to a wide range of urban programmes and projects in the LDCs.

Since the objectives of an institution or programme constitute some of the criteria by which to evaluate its performance, it could be argued that no further external reference points are needed. Are not its own criteria sufficient? It is, of course, important to first measure the performance of a project by its own standards. But the assumptions and priorities on which proposals are based are often contested. It is useful, therefore, to have some other points of reference to help determine the strengths and weaknesses of proposals.

Criteria emerge from particular goals and from the values which lie behind them and they form the link between values and action. The structure of the planning process should thus respond both to these values and to the external conditions planning is designed to ameliorate. The criteria are social and economic values and can, in principle, be applied to evaluate any paradigm of planning practice.

Since our discussion attempts to link values to actions, but at the same time aims at a level of generality to include most cases, we examine a series of general criteria, subdivided into dimensions which are relevant to a broad spectrum, from comprehensive planning to sectoral projects, supplemented with a set of issues in the form of questions for each dimension. In a few cases we also discuss the measurement of the criterion, but this is usually dependent on local conditions. In considering the case studies, the reader can review whether the criterion is relevant to the context of the study and, if so, how well the results were able to satisfy it.

Before defining specific criteria, we will step back to look at the actors in the planning process and the principal attitudes to development which we can distinguish in operation today. We then proceed in the two subsequent sections to define the criteria which emerge from planning for the basic needs and activities of the residents in LDC cities. In "Planning for critical needs", we focus on the functions and style of planning which can respond effectively to objective needs and conditions, and to the associated essential qualities of growth and distribution. In "Planning with the users", we review the qualities and relationships needed between the planners and the eventual beneficiaries of planning. In the third section, "Matching actions with resources", criteria related to the context and constraints in supplying public services are discussed. Finally, "Managing the planning process" reviews the administrative qualities which are needed to produce action.

OVERVIEW

The Actors

A plan's objectives are necessarily based on a set of values, whether implicit or explicit. These values are derived, in turn, from one or more of the three main actors in the planning process - the technicians, the decison-makers and the users. The model of the planning process which is still extant in many planning agencies views all planning as an objective, conflict-free, technical activity contributing to the public good. The technician designs and manages, the decision-maker chooses between alternatives put to him by the technician, and the user contentedly consumes the output. These assumptions were usually intrinsic to the Master Plan approach to Planning outlined in Chapter 1, and are sometimes present in the current paradigm of action planning. The planner must, necessarily, balance the needs of the present users with those of the future ones and must also consider constraints on resources. He is, therefore, unavoidably cast in the role of arbiter. Nevertheless, the concept of planning as a detached activity has major flaws inherent in the isolation of the actors and the locus of power. While the technicians may sincerely wish to contribute to the "public good", their lack of contact with the user, their professional and class perceptions, and pressures coming from the decision-makers may prevent them from fully understanding and responding to the priorities and concerns of the people for whom they plan and may lead them to designing solutions inappropriate to felt needs. The decision-maker may also be isolated from the people if his power is not derived from a popular base, and he may be tempted to favour policies and provide resources which particularly benefit rich and more influential minorities. The users, in the absence both of consultation with the other actors, or influence over the plans made for them, often view government programmes passively or as free hand-outs, are reluctant to repay loans or cooperate in the implementation of projects, and may flare into violent action over particular injustices.

In many countries conditions do not yet exist for a closer and more equal partnership between the users, technicians and decision-makers. Barriers of culture and education, highly centralised planning and the concentration of power in the hands of a few maintain deep gulfs between the politicians and the planners, and the recipients of their efforts. In most developing countries, resources are scarce and technical expertise in short supply. The planner therefore has a further responsibility to allocate resources efficiently and to manage numerous projects rapidly. There is thus less time to devote to the intricate play of power between various groups than in societies where the speed of change is slower and pressure for basic services less acute. It is therefore doubly important for planners and administrators in developing countries to develop a clear perception of the needs of different classes of users, of solutions which are responsive, practical and efficient, and of methods in project planning which devolve as much decision making and implementation to the users as is practical.

Value Basis for the Criteria

We can distinguish a spectrum of attitudes on the part of governments which permeate the development process and which cut across conventional ideological lines. They have an important bearing on a government's attitude to urban development and give rise to many of the policies, priorities and planning styles which we find. They range at the extremes from the repressive, through paternalistic and manipulative approaches to those which are more responsive both to the needs and priorities of the majority of the people and to conserving and improving the resources of the country.

These modes are often mixed in any policy or project and can also change in a given country over time and are closely associated with the balance of power and interests of major groups in society and throw some light on the ambiguous term "development".

We have termed "responsive" an approach to planning whereby the user shares in discussions and influences decisions on the type, design and development of programmes which affect him. This attitude views development ". . . not as a cluster of benefits given to people in need, but rather a process by which a populace acquires greater mastery over its own destiny".(3) In this sense 'development' is a common struggle of all societies, and the means of development are also its ends. Although such an approach appears difficult and time-consuming, experience of cases where the users have shouldered major responsibilities for project development have shown that a responsive approach can be effective.(4) Nevertheless, its chief justification rests not in its efficiency, but in the virtue of accepting each person as having intrinsically equal worth. This attitude is the logical partner for concern with equity in material matters.

What, then, are the fundamental requirements for responsive planning? We suggest that the needs related to basic survival are essential, and programmes to supply them should have the highest priority. Moreover, apart from wasting scarce resources, projects and products which benefit the few will tend to polarise society and lead to a breakdown in reciprocity between social groups. Beyond these needs of first order, there is a further category which we can call 'life enhancing' needs, defined as those goods and services which enhance man's potential without straining resources or placing an intolerable burden on the environment. Complementing the physical necessities, are there other common values which are shared among social and national groups? Hagen(5) suggests that ". . . there is something which is valued universally, and which is the source of happiness or its lack, the source of unhappiness, of people everywhere. This, to put it in its simplest form, is the sense that one is respected." Spiritual qualities such as respect are as important as the physical necessities and they should be incorporated into the process whereby these physical goods are acquired. We have grouped them here under the rubrics of "esteem" and "freedom". The first includes qualities such as security, equity, respect, identity and self-sufficiency. The second, those of choice, participation, power and responsibility (see Fig. 2.1). Different societies, from hierarchical to more open, will express them in different ways, and they will have a variety of applications at varying scales of development from national planning down to the neighbourhood project. The planner, administrator and politician should take into account the populace's differing intensities of concern for these qualities and the speed of change in a given society's value structure. Values are often inconsistent and in conflict with each other, since they reflect the complexity of human society. The planner must find means of gauging the rank and relevance of these values, of determining their relationship with the values and resources of society as a whole,(6) and of bringing representatives of different interests into the planning process.

In our subsequent discussion, the criteria which we will consider form the value-basis of responsive planning and development.

Basic Survival Needs

The conditions of life in LDC cities, the deficits in services and employment, and the evolution of the planning which was intended to grapple with them were discussed in Chapter 1.

In summary, it is the poorest 20 to 60 percent of the urban population which lack basic essentials. Studies and practice show that the poor can afford to pay for these minimum essentials providing government policies are genuinely oriented to assisting them. Blanket criteria for hard and fast standards for these essentials are not appropriate since there will be great variation depending on income, local climate, habits and population densities. However, for each country

Basic human needs	Physical essentials		Spiritual essentials	
	Primary	Secondary	Esteem	Freedom
Component qualities	Food and water Health Shelter Tools Education Communication	Life-enhancing Goods and services	Security Identity Equity Respect	Choice Participation Power Responsibility

Interaction human natural environment human human human human human

Fig. 2.1. An outline of basic human needs.

Fig. 2.1. An outline of basic human needs.

the following basic needs can be satisfied providing standards of provision are sufficiently low and flexible:

Quality	Elements
	Adequate, nutritious food
	Clean water
	Sanitary environment
Basic needs	Minimal shelter
	Essential tools and skills
	Basic education
	Basic health care and family planning
	Easy communication

The general criterion which should cover these is: Does the planning provide solutions to these needs at a price which the poor can afford?

PLANNING FOR CRITICAL NEEDS

Consistency

The criteria we discuss in this section are fundamental to satisfying basic needs. However, in order to achieve them, consistent policies and actions are needed from national to regional and local levels and across sectoral planning. Especially in the areas of trade and industry, well-meaning efforts at the scale of urban planning can often be negated by inappropriate or conflicting national policies.

Growth and Distribution of Assets and Services

The traditional economic hypothesis which states that redistribution in favour of the poor will automatically reduce savings, weaken incentives and impair the rate of growth, and that conversely, maximizing overall economic growth will automatically raise incomes and employment more rapidly at all levels, is no longer self-evident.(7) With some exceptions,(8) the numbers in absolute and relative poverty in Asia have increased over the past two decades, with economic growth mainly accruing to the top 5-20 percent of the population.(9) In the future, pressures on urban areas will increase as the overall labour force grows from 1.7 percent/year during the

1960s to 2.4 percent/year during the following two decades. Agriculture will be able to absorb a decreasing proportion of this growth, and industry, while growing faster, is too small a sector to absorb more than a fraction. Massive expansion will occur in the services sector and, under present policies, the large pool of manpower surplus is likely to result in a decline in productivity which will also exert downward pressure in other sectors.(10) These effects will be magnified in urban areas which will receive additional rural migrants on top of natural increases which together now match or surpass total growth in rural areas.(11)

To respond effectively to the challenge of improving the productivity of the poor sufficiently for them to meet their basic needs, a twin strategy of growth and distribution is required.(12) Given the world-wide slow-down in economic growth, it is unlikely that most LDCs will show more than a 6 percent growth rate: 2 percent less than the World Bank estimates is needed even to maintain the balance in sectoral growth rates of the 1960-decade. Thus a major change is needed in the concepts of distribution and growth.

Growth in the accumulation of assets including human skills, finance, physical equipment and infrastructure is required as a precondition for increases in future consumption. But distribution of assets, especially rural and urban land, to the poor is often a precondition for stimulating productivity. If redistribution of existing assets is not possible politically, then distribution of the ownership of newly created assets should be pursued, including both fixed assets and promotion of small-scale businesses which can be managed by existing and new entrepreneurs, cooperatives and partnerships.

New public service projects should be designed to serve the poor. For example, water supply should concentrate on tertiary distribution to slum areas and should be designed as a public sanitation system integrating supply of water and disposal of wastes. Transport policies should favour public transport over road-space built primarily for the private car. Housing should focus on provision of services and land for the poor rather than more costly completed units. Health care should eschew complex techniques and hospitals and concentrate on delivering basic medical services, nutrition, family planning and environmental education to slum households. In analysing the extent to which a programme and its components serve the poor, attention should be focused on (i) its price, to see whether it can be afforded by the poor; (ii) its location, to ensure that the service is placed where the poor live; (iii) its scale and speed, to observe how many people will be served both in terms of the backlog and of the growth in demand; and (iv) its costs and standards, to ensure that large subsidies are not required which would reduce the size of the programme and encourage sale to higher income groups.

Issues:

1. What percentage of the city's population is reached by the programme, and does it assist the poorest 30 percent of the population?
2. Does the programme expand the supply of services needed by the poor (a) in sufficient volume?, (b) at a price they can afford?, (c) in the locations where they live?
3. Is the total number of unserved households less after the programme than before, or has the rate of growth overtaken the ability to supply?
4. Does the programme redistribute ownership of existing or newly created assets to the poor?
5. Do tax and administrative practices support, or conflict with, the objectives of these programmes?

Employment and Productivity

The bias against traditional sectors and small-scale businesses, and actions needed to redress the balance, have been noted in Chapter 1. In the belief that "modern" industry is the only growth vehicle of development(13) and economic independence, many governments have developed a battery of reinforcing trade preferences, monetary and fiscal shelters and incentives, licensing controls and restrictive labour practices which favour large capital-intensive "modern" industry at the expense of agriculture and small-scale traditional industries and technologies. In conjunction with food price controls, the effect has been to depress agricultural incomes, put small-scale enterprises at a disadvantage, give implicit subsidies to middle and upper-income consumers and absorb national savings in unproductive enterprises. Merely discontinuing those policies would provide a great expansion in employment per dollar invested. One indicator to determine whether a production enterprise or public service is utilising capital efficiently is to see whether the capital/labour ratio of the project, expressed as investment cost per man-year of employment, is lower than the average per capita investment for all sectors in the country as a whole. A recent research project of the World Bank(14) has reviewed the technologies used in nine important products used by the general population. Its findings are that the use of the most 'appropriate' technologies (those yielding the highest present discounted value relative to capital investment), compared with the use of more capital-intensive conventional plants, would provide up to 20 times as many jobs per unit of capital invested. Other advantages of small firms using simple technologies are that (a) they fit more easily within LDCs' social and cultural environments and easily develop links with the vast informal services sector; (b) they are often technically innovative compared to large firms using complex 'unimprovable' modern technologies and are less dependent on foreign companies and expertise; (c) they serve the limited fragmented markets of LDCs better than larger units and are more suited for dispersion, thus helping to reduce regional imbalance and urban concentration; and (d) they frequently have less negative environmental impact than more sophisticated processes.

At the same time, "employment at any price" is to be avoided. Expansion of jobs must be accompanied by improvement in productivity per job. Direct assistance with marketing, management and technology will offer some help, but the most important influence will be the competition of the market in weeding out inefficient industries and stimulating productive ones.

Issues:

1. Does the planning include policy measures to eliminate bias favouring overly capital-intensive enterprises and, instead, promote those enterprises which absorb under-utilised labour?
2. Are labour-intensive technologies encouraged both in project construction and maintenance and in new productive enterprises?
3. Is the cost per job created at or below the national average?
4. Do policies seek to improve the productivity of labour at low capital cost?
5. Is training encouraged which will help to upgrade the skills of the poor?

PLANNING WITH THE USERS

Who are the users of planning? We can discern two basic categories: the intermediate users and the end product users. The intermediate users are those who use the outputs of comprehensive and multi-sectoral planning for designing and implementing specific programmes and projects. They are often government administrators and planners themselves. We will discuss their relationship to the planning process at the end of this chapter. We will focus here on the second category which comprise the vast majority of users - those who are directly affected by the policies and projects which emanate from planning, by its process and by the distribution of benefits and costs which its results entail.

These benefits and costs exhibit several dimensions which can be roughly classified into the physical, the financial, the psychological and the legal. Planning also operates at several geographic scales, each of which has a varying impact on the users, from national and regional levels, which have more diffuse but broader effects, down to project planning which is more limited in area but affects specific neighbourhoods and each citizen more intensely. Each scale of planning should have appropriate mechanisms to allow those affected by it to be heard and to control key options.(15) At the national scale these mechanisms can include political representation along geographic area and interest group lines, referenda and the law courts. At the city scale, municipal councils, town meetings and lobbies of interest groups are often encountered, and at the neighbourhood scale, community groups and individual families will have a stronger voice. In addition to geographic scale, planning will also have an impact on various interest groups. Since urban planning generally affects the costs, price and distribution of services and land, the principal interest groups affected will be landowners, house owners, renters and producers (businessmen and traders).

Space precludes individual treatment of all these aspects, but we can discern the following over-arching qualities (illustrated in Fig. 2.1) which can be used as a test for the degree of responsiveness of the planning process.

Security

Turning to qualities under the general heading of "esteem" (Fig.2.1), the most fundamental is probably security. There is no incentive for households to accumulate assets or improve their environment if these assets are repeatedly threatened or liquidated by natural catastrophes such as floods, landslides, earthquakes, and man-made threats such as polluted air, water and noise. Economic security is needed with opportunities for employment to ensure a regular income. Finally, legal security is needed to protect people against the worst effects of private exploitation and administrative caprice. The latter is especially relevant to settlement projects where insecurity of tenure and persecution of squatters inhibit families from improving their dwellings and surroundings.

Criterion	Dimension	Urban issues
Security	Physical	Is the environment safe for human use?
	Economic	Are opportunities for employment available and predictable?

Criterion	Dimension	Urban issues
Security	Legal	Do fair legal means operate to prevent and redress oppression by private and public bodies? Can businesses operate without capricious and unexpected intervention?
	Social	Are living environments designed so as to foster a maximum sense of community?

Respect

One of the key features of responsive planning is the relationship between the planners and those "planned for". Concurrence with a traditional hierarchy of authority by both the elite and the populace in many Asian countries, compounded by the lack of skilled technical resources, may require a period of growth and adjustment before full participation in the planning process can take place. It thus becomes doubly important for policy-makers and planners in LDCs to respect the individuality and interests of the groups for whom they plan, and to sensitize themselves to their needs, means and limitations.

Criterion	Dimension	Urban issues
Respect	Psychological	Is there an attitude of empathy and willingness on the part of the planner to understand the user's problems?
	Managerial	Is the institution and its planning process organised to induce mutual respect and understanding between planners and users?

Identity

For many indigenous low income urban residents, as well as most rural migrants, the ability to form and maintain identity with their ethnic, regional or religious groups is an essential ingredient for well-being, and makes poverty more bearable.

Criterion	Dimension	Urban issues
Identity	Social	Does the planning preserve the beneficiaries' identification with their traditional or adopted group and minimize fragmentation while offering the option for integration into the wider society?
	Psychological	Is the approach consistent with the core values of the beneficiaries?

Equity

We have noted earlier that wide differences between rich and poor tend to polarise society and lead to repressive and manipulative modes of development. It is therefore important to examine whether a programme or project reduces or intensifies inequality. This can be checked by finding who it intends to assist, who actually benefits from its component parts, and how the decision process is conducted.

Criterion	Dimension	Urban issues
Equity	Economic	Do income groups obtain shares of resources and benefits equal to their number?
	Social	Do different regional, social, religious or racial groups at similar income levels have equal access to resources?
	Legal	Do all groups have equal access to legal means of redress? Is the law applied equitably and consistently?
	Managerial	Do all groups have channels for communicating their views to policy and project administrators, and vice-versa.

Choice

Apart from the intrinsic value of freedom which it confers, choice should be an integral quality in the planning process on two other counts. It is impossible for planners to predict every person's need, and a strategy which provides for a network of opportunities is likely to be far more efficient in satisfying individual needs. Moreover, an approach which offers only one option is less likely to elicit the populace's cooperation than one which emphasises variety and choice. Some of the many relevant aspects of choice are outlined below.

Criterion	Dimension	Urban issues
Choice	Economic	Are the beneficiaries' choice of occupation and employment expanded?
	Physical	Can the beneficiaries refuse, accept, or take an alternative location or product?
	Social	Are a variety of associations and interactions encouraged?
	Political	Is there a choice to acccept or reject participation in the programme itself and in decisions and management of the programme?

Participation, Power and Responsibility

The degree to which urban plans, programmes and projects include participation of the populace is closely related to the balance of power and interests at the national level. While we should not deceive ourselves that activities at the project level will lead to a rapid change of national attitudes, the value of encouraging participation and responsibility in decision making in urban projects is that, in a small but regular way, ordinary people will gain experience in controlling the forces which influence their daily lives, and thereby equip themselves to exert influence over their leaders. All nations are ruled by elites and what is important to observe is less the fact that elites exist, but rather whether they are making a genuine effort to bring people into the experience of decision-making, or whether the word "participation" is merely a palliative of national propaganda. The urban project can frequently be a litmus test for this motivation.

If the idea of power sharing is accepted, its practice can generate several qualities which are particularly appropriate to the needs of low income countries. It can lead to feelings of self-respect which are especially important where poverty and income differences are extreme. It can prepare people for responsible action at other levels in society and it can act to integrate the elites with the populace. Finally, it can even be efficient. Where government agencies are ill-prepared and unable to undertake the enormous task of supplying urban services, community groups and small businesses are often extremely effective in supplying such basic needs as transport, housing and health.(16)

Criteria	Dimension	Urban issues
	Economic	Can the beneficiaries develop their own enterprises or influence those in which they are employed?
	Social	Does the planning process encourage leadership and organisations to influence plans and make proposals?
Particiation, Power and Responsibility	Managerial	Does the planning process encourage the beneficiaries to shoulder responsibility for the design, execution and maintenance of the programme?
	Legal	Can planning proposals be challenged? What institutional arrangements are there for the users to select planning options and control decisions?

MATCHING ACTIONS WITH RESOURCES

Well-intentioned policies directed towards basic needs and a willingness by government to involve the populace in its planning will all remain empty rhetoric unless resources can be mobilised and used effectively to implement the planning. The following key issues focus on the identification, allocation and mobilisation of resources and consider means for their most efficient use.

Factor Endowment

Many plans and programmes with fine objectives have been undone through lack of attention to selection of available and appropriate resources. In some cases local materials and technologies which were available or could be easily developed were neglected in favour of distant or imported ones which were both costly and ill suited to local conditions of climate and capacities in construction and maintenance. Availability of financial resources is often over-estimated and the use of labour and local skills under-utilised.

Issues:

1. Has the best use been made of available and appropriate resources?
2. For a given performance, has the least cost solution been used?

Resource Allocation

The allocation of resources determines the importance of the project among national priorities. All public projects absorb resources in manpower, skills and finance for their preparation and implementation and some involve continuing subsidies without immediate financial return. It is therefore necessary to evaluate the importance of a programme, its beneficiaries and their needs and to determine what proportion of the total physical, financial and human resources available in the country should be devoted to it, and whether, indeed, it should be undertaken at all. The economic cost-benefit analysis orignally developed for evaluation of water resource projects can be a useful technique to answer some of these questions. It reduces the project's monetized costs and benefits to a single rate of return which can be measured against other project alternatives and to the cost of capital available in the market place. Its strength lies in evaluating the efficient use of capital among alternative single-sector projects or programmes, and it can be used to provide an incentive to minimize costs and maximize benefits. However, it is ill-suited to measure distribution and externalities, or to evaluate multi-sector and indeterminate plans such as regional or urban structure plans. For these, techniques such as the planning balance sheet analysis(17) or goal achievement matrix(18) are attempts to evaluate a wide variety of qualities and opinions which are difficult to quantify and involve issues of equity and political influence. C/B analysis can often provide an input to these wider evaluations by quantifying costs and benefits of the plans' alternative investment strategies. Allocative issues may also include spatial as well as income considerations, especially where whole regions are lagging in economic development and considerable "uneconomic" investment may be required over many years to provide an adequate productive base.

<u>Issues</u>:

1. What claim should the planned investments receive among national priorities?
2. Can the proposed projects justify the funds they require related to the impact they will have?
3. Are the resources required only for a start-up, or on a continuing basis?
4. Will the projects produce valuable multiplier effects in other sectors?

Replication, Affordability and Cost Recovery

These are useful concepts which link the demand and supply aspects of a programme together. The deficit of urban services and the increase in demand stemming from rapid population growth make it essential to determine whether the programme under consideration can satisfy both the backlog in services and the future demand. Is the programme large enough to be effective and how replicable are its projects in terms of cost and speed of implementation?

For any service or product, the population which it intends to supply must be defined, their habits and priorities with respect to the service understood, and an estimate made of their willingness to pay for the service over a specified period of time. Service levels, construction costs and quality must then be varied to match the price the population is willing to pay. Affordability also extends beyond the individual or household. The city and national governments must estimate, in the light of their current and projected financial resources, whether the plan or programme is affordable in terms of the capital costs it requires and the revenues it will generate.

While rich in labour, most LDCs have scarce capital resources, and small revenues from income and corporation taxes, and thus cannot afford heavy and continuing subsidies. Projects and programmes must therefore attempt to recover most of their costs directly from the users. Where costs cannot be recovered directly, attempts should be made to increase general revenues through indirect taxation. Real estate taxes are frequently under-exploited in LDC cities and more efforts could be made to capture increases in property values resulting from the improvement in service, through progressive property taxes which should accrue to the local government which is responsible for the maintenance and expansion of urban services. In some cases project agencies can also engage in profit-making developments and their surpluses can be used to reduce prices below cost so that poorer groups can be reached than would otherwise be possible.

Making services pay for themselves helps to ensure that they are replicable and can be maintained and expanded. The authority providing the service can then be structured on a profit making basis which usually makes for a more efficient and responsive service than can be provided by government bureaux.

Issues:

1. Is the programme of sufficient scale and can its projects be repeated rapidly enough to supply both the backlog and the future increase in demand within a satisfactory time?
2. Is the project or service affordable by (a) the beneficiaries?, (b) the local governments? and (c) the national governments?
3. Do the prices charged equal capital costs less any cross-subsidy? Can the service delivered be self-financing, or repeatable without heavy subsidies?
4. Are measures included to strengthen local government finances through indirect taxes, fees and charges?

Thresholds and Economics of Scale

One characteristic of urban public infrastructure is its "lumpiness." A road or sewer must provide a complete link before it is useful and, in cases such as sewerage and piped water supply, whole areas may have to remain unserviced until they reach a sufficient size and density to justify and economic investment in major network extensions and headworks. A whole city must reach a certain size before certain classes of service such as banking, specialized professional services and higher education can be justified. This "lumpiness" conflicts with the human growth in the city which is continuous and incremental.

Two implications arise here for urban planning, which were also touched on in Chapter 1. First, it highlights the need to examine areas for city expansions on a "least-cost" basis(19) and to guide expansion in the desired direction by means of coordinated investment in infrastructure. Second, it is desirable to design and plan urban technologies which are smaller in scale and more flexible and responsive to the incremental nature of urban growth. To gain a clear advantage over large-scale technologies, they should be at the same or lower cost per person served and be easily maintained by locally available managers and engineers. Informal transport modes such as jeepneys and pedal rickshaws are typical examples of this, as are individual household or neighbourhood tube wells for water supply and pit privy sanitation systems instead of costly piped sewerage. Further possibilities to reduce initial investment costs include techniques for upgrading levels of service of infrastructure in stages. A residential road, for example, can be built initially as a levelled dirt track, and gradually improved and surfaced as surrounding population densities and usage of the road increase and higher levels of service can be afforded. Care is needed here, however, that maintenance and repair costs are not excessive and place an unreasonable burden on the beneficiaries or the local government. Costs should thus be viewed on a "life-cycle" basis and not purely on initial capital expenditures.

Issues:

1. Does the spatial plan analyse areas with development potential on a least-cost basis and define the most economic scale for expansion?
2. Have alternative technologies and levels of service been investigated which could offer a more flexible and responsive answer to the incremental nature of urban growth?

Multipliers and Leverage

A central feature of urban development is its interlinked nature and the way in which one component of the urban system affects another. The most dramatic example is probably the impact which a new road or transport interchange has on the suroundíng pattern of land uses and prices. New growth rapidly springs up at the points of higher accessibility. Most LDC cities suffer from a chronic undersupply of services which pushes up the price of the service and therefore excludes the poor. This is especially true for serviced land for housing. Often by rapid expansion of the secondary and tertiary road network combined with taxation on idle land, more land can be brought on to the market with consequent stabilization or even reduction in price.(20)

Issues:

1. Are opportunities taken to use the pressures for urban expansion to generate better patterns of development and funds for public services through legal and other incentives?

2. Does the programme for new infrastructure use the leverage of the new investment to guide and mould city growth?

Externalities

One facet of urban development which is often disregarded are the impacts which a project or programme will generate beyond its immediate objectives. Frequently referred to as "externalities", this loose term comprises both the "inevitable side-effects of development" and the use of the so-called "free goods of the economy", usually meaning air and water. It is rapidly becoming clear that there is no such thing as a "free good" and that many human activities can inflict detrimental impacts on the physical environment and on other social groups. The poor are normally the ones who suffer the most impacts of a deteriorating environment. Urban development(21) absorbs prime agricultural land, liquid wastes pollute rich fishing grounds and directly cause human diseases, bad construction techniques and poorly sited development cause massive erosion and siltation problems, and vehicular exhausts cause air pollution which is often worse than in cities of developed countries. Until recently, few urban infrastructure projects made arrangements for the housing and employment needs of squatters who had to relocate from the right of way. More research is needed to demonstrate the financial values of natural ecosystems in terms of the work they do for man cost-free, and the costs to society of over-loading them beyond their sustainable limits.

Solutions to environmental impacts may have to be curative and often involve high costs of treatment, disposal and restorations. However, problems can often be avoided by fore-thought and planning together with the requisite controls, incentives and monitoring to make them effective.(22)

<u>Issues</u>:

1. Does the planning set standards of air and water quality and land development which avoid continuing deterioration of the long-term balance of the ecosystem and climate and degeneration in the health and safety of the present and future populations?
2. Will the project stimulate the extraction of irreplaceable natural resources before adequate substitutes are developed?
3. Are adverse social and economic impacts to households and businesses minimized and, if they are unavoidable, are those affected adequately compensated?
4. Is the planning oriented towards preventing environmental problems in the future and integrating environmental concerns into the planning process?

Adaptability, Uncertainty and Risk

LDC cities are growing so rapidly that their problems change in orders of magnitude, requiring adaptable and flexible solutions. Changes occur in available resources, in the level of services needed, and in the character and direction of city growth. Rapid social shifts occur through the expectations, perceptions and composition of their populations. Yet policies and implementation programmes have often remained relatively static and frequently begin to address a given problem when it is too late and sometimes after it has changed. Flexibility and open-mindedness is thus a key quality for institutions, policy-makers and managers. In physical design, solutions which have a "loose fit" and are robust and adaptable should be explored.

Projects should also be examined with respect to the risk of failure of the project itself and the risks it may imply for the wider economy and the physical environment in which it is set. Projects which are more modest but are likely to succeed may be more desirable than those with high potential benefits but with equally high levels of risk. Thus, risk anaylsis would examine the scale, complexity and type of programmes chosen. Particular care should be paid to avoid systems which, if they break down, would most adversely affect the poor. Those technologies which are simple and decentralised are frequently the most robust, since breakdown of one part of the system does not affect the whole.

Issues:

1. Is the planning flexible enough to incorporate necessary changes in emphasis and direction and does it include a monitoring system to signal needed changes at an early stage?
2. Are the institutions and managers chosen for programme implementation responsive and open-minded?
3. Are the physical designs and standards adaptable to a range of possible future needs?
4. Are the technical, financial, economic, environmental and managerial risks adequately estimated in the analysis of project feasability?

MANAGING THE PLANNING PROCESS

Thus far we have focused on criteria which evaluate the products of planning and the relationships between the planners and the society which planning is expected to serve. In this final section we will conclude with some brief observations of the criteria for operation of the planning process itself, emphasising the managerial features of the proposed model of planning practice outlined in Chapter 1.

Many of the qualities needed for effective urban planning are similar to those required in good management of a private business, including the proper identification of the outputs and inputs, clear definition of functions and responsibilities of staff, ability to delegate decision-making as far down the hierarchy as possible and a responsiveness to the changes in external conditions. Especially in LDCs, planning should have a dominant concern to effectively deliver essential public services. Planning is more complex than business management to the extent that it deals with multiple objectives and usually involves more interests and actors than the private corporation. It is also concerned with regulating access to assets and resources and ensuring that they are not unduly absorbed by more powerful groups. It must also be responsible for protecting the quality and the common use of the natural environment and other public goods. While it is concerned with harmonising numerous social objectives, it also operates among and through multiple institutions and agencies whose interests must also be considered to ensure that the aims of planning are realised. There are a number of key concerns which arise from the context described above.

We mentioned earlier in this chapter the need for consistency in policy and actions between the national, regional and local levels of planning. Emerging from this is our first concern: the need to match the level of planning to the nature of the problem. A strategic framework is required which defines the goals and priorities for development in an urban area and the rules and guidelines within which sectoral programmes and projects should operate. From the evaluation of existing problems and sectoral programmes, this level of planning should define a spatial strategy, a fiscal and investment strategy with time horizons, and define requirements and methods to analyse the impacts of sectoral projects on different social groups and on the natural environment. It would also define the incentives and penalties which will guide private investments towards socially acceptable ends. Within this framework sectoral planning should define the scope of the programmes to match the needs, lay down affordable standards and unit cost, define means of recovering costs and identify critical links and contacts within other sectors. Project planning, involving the smallest scale of operation and being closest to its physical products and the human beings who will use it, must concern itself not only with efficient production, but also with sensitivity to the users' needs and where appropriate the direct involvement of the users in planning and implementation.

The second concern is the need for an effective mechanism to coordinate the levels of planning both vertically and across the various sectors. The most effective means to do this is usually through budgets and financial allocations without which sectoral plans and projects cannot operate. The procedures and timing for budget allocation and review, and the definitions of powers and responsibilities in this process are key elements.

Budget allocation is rarely decided by a single omnipotent planner but usually depends on the political power and influence of top sectoral administrators and political figures. An important element in planning is therefore to develop shared objectives and concerns and to mould a commitment and concensus among the various actors. This requires continual discussion and exchange of information and often a slow process of gradual persuasion.

Finally, an essential quality of good planning is its responsiveness and flexibility to new conditions. It should seek to manage change as it occurs and this requires a system to define and update key information and to feed it back to those who can act on it. This cyclical quality of planning, where regular review leads to changes in policies and programmes, is essential to match the rapid changes occurring in Asian cities today.

NOTES

(1) C.W. Churchman (1961).

(2) These matters are covered exhaustively in other works including Chadwick (1971), Lichfield, Kettle and Whitbread (1975), Dasgupta, Sen and Marglin (1972), Hill (1968), among others.

(3) Goulet (1971), Chap. 7

(4) Examples where bottom-up development has produced satisfactory results include the urban squatter movements in Peru, the slum improvement project in Tondo, Manila, village communes in China, and earlier, organisation of farmers' cooperatives in Japan. These achievements have sometimes been made in the face of opposition by the government.

(5) Hagen (1968).

(6) Lindblom (1959) and Davidoff and Reiner (1962) consider the intensity, timing, adjustment and authorship of values in greater detail.

(7) Chenery (1974), in a review of sixty-six fast and slow-growth countries, found no evidence of correlation between rate of growth and improvement in equity.

(8) Singapore, Korea, Taiwan and possibly China.

(9) The ILO (1976) notes that in most LDCs the richest 10 percent of households receive 40 percent of personal income whereas the poorest 20 percent receive about 5 percent. (p. 22).

(10) World Bank estimates (1976).

(11) Even in predominantly rural India, urban population increase is expected to be 223 million over the next 25 years, compared to 260 million in rural areas (Beier et al., 1975).

(12) A model developed by the ILO (1976) indicates that, in order to supply basic needs by the year 2000, medium- and low-income countries in Asia would require a 9.7 percent/year growth rate under rapid growth oriented policies and 7.2 percent/year under income redistribution policies (p. 41).

(13) In fact, they are often both costly and inefficient. In Pakistan, for example, Little, Scitovsky and Scott (1970) found that the actual contribution of large scale manufacturing to the economy was only 0.4 percent of domestic value added, but amounted to 6.6 percent of total domestic investments.

(14) Quoted by David L. Gordon (1979).

(15) Fagence (1977) reviews the attitudes and mechanisms concerning citizen participation in planning in more detail.

(16) In transport, examples include Manila's jeepney system where over 17,000 licensed vehicles provide an excellent low cost transport service for almost 70 percent of Manila's public transport travellers. In housing, examples abound in every city of the poor building their own houses themselves or with the help of small craftsmen at a fraction of the cost of housing produced by agencies. China has been able to provide an adequate medical service by wide use of para-medicals and the skills of traditional healers.

(17) Lichfield et al., (1975).

(18) Hill (1968).

(19) Techniques developed by Maliscz and others in threshold analysis of urban development are useful here. (In Fisher, 1966.)

(20) This guideline approach to planning is being taken by governments of smaller cities in Brazil. Other examples of city governments who have been able to use this kind of leverage include the rationalization of suburban development by means of land readjustment procedures in Korea, Taiwan and Japan, the use of infrastructure and coordinated neighbourhood development to guide growth in Singapore, and advantage taken to guide land use by the stimulus to development generated by the new underground railway terminals in Toronto.

(21) The most serious impacts, however, are in rural and forested areas of tropical countries, where the scale of destruction and change in the ecosystems amount to an environmental Armageddon of global proportions within the next 20 years. SCEP (1970), The Ecologist, January 1972, Washington Post, 23 April 1979, among many other sources.

(22) Some suggestions on integrating environmental concerns into the planning process in LDC cities are outlined by the World Bank's Environmental Handbook (1980).

REFERENCES

Beier, Churchill, Cohen and Renaud (1975) The Task Ahead for the Cities of the Developing Countries. World Bank Staff Working Paper No. 209, July.

Chenery, H. et al. (1976) Redistribution with Growth. Oxford University Press.

Chadwick, G. (1971) A Systems View of Planning. Pergamon Press.

Churchman, C. W. (1961) Prediction and Optimal Decision. Philosophical Issues of a Science of Values. Prentice Hall Inc. Quoted from Chadwick (1971)

Dasgupta, P., Sen, A. and Marglin, S. (1972) Guidelines for Project Evaluation. U.N. Publications.

Davidoff, P. and Reiner, T. (1962) A Choice Theory of Planning, Journal of the American Institute of Planners, Vol. 28.

Fagence, M. (1977) Citizen Participation in Planning. Pergamon Press.

Gordon, David L. (1979) The Bank and the Development of Small Enterprises Finance and Development, Vol. 16, No. 1, March.

Goulet, D. (1971) The Cruel Choice. Atheneum Press.

Hagen, E. (1968) Are Some Things Valued by All Men? Cross-Currents, Vol. XVIII, No. 1.

Hill, M. (1968) A Goals-achievement Matrix for Evaluating Alternate Plans. Journal of the American Institute of Planners, No. 34.

International Labour Organisation (ILO) (1976) Employment, Growth and Basic Needs: a one-world problem.

Lindblom, C. (1959) The Science of Muddling Through. Public Administration Review, Spring 1959.

Litchfield, N., Kettle, P. and Whitbread, M. (1975) Evaluation in the Planning Process. Pergamon Press.

Little, Scitovsky and Scott (1970) Industry and Trade in Some Developing Countries. Oxford University Press, for OECD.

Maliscz, B. (1966) "Urban Planning Theory: Methods & Results" in J.C. Fisher (ed.) , City & Regional Planning in Poland. Cornell University Press.

S.C.E.P., Man's Impact on the Global Environment. (1970 and 1971). M.I.T. Press Cambridge, Mass., U.S.A.

Warwick, D. (1968) "Human Freedom and National Development" Cross-Currents, Vol. XVIII, No. 1.

World Bank, unpublished papers, December 1974, July 1976.

World Bank (1980) Environmental, Health and Human Ecologic Considerations in Economic Development Projects.

II
SELECTED CASE STUDIES

Comprehensive Planning of Major Cities

The first group of case studies to be presented in this volume deal with initiatives which have involved comprehensive planning in major urban areas. Three quite different situations are taken up in turn: (1) Karachi, a large and established metropolis; (2) Ankara, the rapidly growing 50-year old capital of Turkey; and (3) Durgapur, one of India's steel cities which has been developed since World War II. Although these cities are all quite large, they are representative of the widely varying conditions found in major cities throughout the LDCs. With respect to age, they range from an old city to a new town. With respect to economic base, they range from a highly diversified commercial, industrial and institutional centre (Karachi); an administrative capital which has recently been diversifying its employment (Ankara); to a city which depends largely on capital intensive industry (Durgapur). But, despite these contrasts, the major problems and issues are strikingly similar in all three cities. They include such matters as how channelize urban growth, how to plan and programme the timing and standards of infrastructure development, how to build decent living environments for low- to moderate-income families, and what kinds of institutions to develop to undertake these and many other tasks.

In the initial contribution, John Herbert describes and evaluates the recent experience in plannning and programming development of metropolitan Karachi. Within the past two decades, several major Asian cities have been the focus of metropolitan planning studies supported by international technical assistance. The Karachi planning project, supported by the UNDP, was one of the largest such studies to take place during the early 1970s. This case study reviews both the many problems of Pakistan's largest metropolis as well as some of the solutions which emerged from this important planning study. In stressing practical, realistic approaches to such problems as low-cost housing, public transport and development control, Herbert's chapter anticipates some of the major themes of this book.

Ilhan Tekeli and Tarik Okyay follow with their "Case Study of a Relocated Capital", tracing and evaluating the growth of Ankara over the past 50 years. One of the particularly interesting aspects of this study is the way in which it links physical development of the city to socio-political factors, most importantly that of who benefits from urbanisation. In Ankara's case, it was clearly the "emerging national bourgeoisie" who controlled and chiefly benefited from urban development. Although the growth of Ankara has become self-sustaining and has had considerable impact on the national urbanisation pattern, its intra-urban development has been fraught with many problems. Several of these problems are discussed.

K.C. Sivaramakrishnan then presents his case study of the largest Indian new town to emerge since World War II. The steel city of Durgapur is traced from its beginnings a generation ago, and the study reviews the problems of economic, physical and institutional development which the authorities have had. Several difficulties are stressed, including the economic problems in achieving self-sustained growth in a city whose chief base is capital-intensive industry; the physical problems associated with creating an integrated city out of a disparate collection of factories and their associated townships; and also the institutional problems which are involved in planning, building and managing a major new city.

3

The Karachi Development Programme: 1976-1985: An Interim Appraisal

John Herbert

THE SETTING

The overall geographic unit selected for the Karachi planning work was the Karachi Metropolitan Region.(1) At the southern end of Pakistan, surrounding the port of Karachi, it lies predominantly in the Province of Sind but its western end extends into the Province of Baluchistan. Its southern border is the Arabian Sea. With an area of 19,675 square kilometres the Region had an estimated population of approximately 4.5 million in 1974 of which 93 percent were in urban occupations. The Metropolitan Area had approximately 94 percent of the Region's total population.

With the exception of the Metropolitan Area and an agricultural area in its south-eastern portion, the Region is semi-desert. Its physiography imposes very few limits on urban expansion. But its desert character is misleading since there are large areas of excellent soils which could be brought into use in intensive agriculture if they could be watered adequately.

Water is the physical resource that threatens to impose the most severe constraint on growth. The only significant source in the mid-1970s was the Indus River; a dam designed to utilise the Hab River on the west was under construction, but even under the programme proposed through 1985 the Metropolitan Area will continue to receive three-quarters of its water from the Indus.

The potential and the problems of Pakistan's urbanisation are highlighted in Karachi. The city has a pre-eminent advantage in its capacity to accelerate economic and social development nationally, as well as locally. In the mid-1970s the Metropolitan Area supported 6 percent of Pakistan's total population and 22 percent of its urban population; it contributed approximately 15 percent of gross domestic product; generated approximately 42 percent of value added and 35 percent of employment in large-scale manufacturing; it accounted for approximately 50 percent of bank deposits and, according to one estimate, it generated approximately 25 percent of all Federal revenues. Karachi is Pakistan's only significant seaport. From 1947 to 1961 it was the nation's capital.

The population loads to which the Metropolitan Area has been subjected are awesome. One hundred and thirty years ago Karachi was a walled township of 14,000 on a site of 14 hectares. As recently as 1941 the population of the Karachi District was less than half a million. Between 1947 and 1951 approximately 600,000 displaced persons migrated into the area from India as a result of the creation of Pakistan in 1947, bringing the total population to 1.13 million. By 1961 it had almost doubled again to reach 2.14 million. By 1974 the metropolitan population had reached the 4.2 million referred to earlier and continued in-migration was accounting for almost 50 percent of growth. The average annual compound growth rate for 1961-1974 was estimated at approximately 5.3 percent.

Like that of many major urban areas in the developing world, household income distribution was highly skewed. The metropolitan estimates for 1973/1974, with an exchange rate of PRs9.9 - US$1, were as follows:

Household monthly income	percent of households
Less than $30	44.52
$30-50	35.35
$50-100	14.42
$100-200	3.43
$200 and over	2.28

Although located in the Province of Sind, Karachi has become so cosmopolitan through its functions as a port, a haven for refugees and a major center for rural-urban migration, that it stands in complete constrast with the more purely Sindi city of Hyderabad, 160 km to the east, and many Sindis regard it almost as a foreign city.

The power structure is far too complex to describe in this brief discussion but even a drastic over-simplification would have to include: the land-owning, industrial and commercial elites; the military establishment which has controlled the country from time to time (and is in power at present); the senior civil service -- often linked closely with the elites through familial ties or long-standing "working relationships";

an emerging middle class of smaller industrialists and businessmen, many of whom have established themselves after emigrating to Karachi at Partition in 1947; and the elected political leadership and senior party members which are active in the interludes between military regimes. On another dimension are the middle-level bureaucrats who are able to influence many negotiations, including land deals; the housing societies -- loose, often fictitious, associations of households and investors established to benefit from large-scale purchases of land (at less-than-market prices if they have the right connections); and some communal groups who are able to protect their territorial holdings in the Metropolitan Area, even though they are operating outside the formal legal system.

These groups, severally, control most of the decisions governing industrial and commercial development, the availability of urban services in the Metropolitan Area, access to credit, land ownership and housing. Over 50 percent of the Metropolitan Area's households, the poorest, have little or no influence in the formal decision making through which key metropolitan resources are allocated. They do have their own mini-power structures, to be sure, but these influence principally the allocation of the "leftover" resources in which the major wielders of power are not interested. Those leftovers are vital to the survival of a majority of the Metropolitan population and the processes through which the informal system allocates them deserve a separate study, beyond the scope of the present chapter.

Massive and erratic population loads, major fluctuations in economic growth at the national level, a chronic shortage of resources at the local level, a lack of coordination among public agencies and persistent deficiencies in administration have had very predictable results on the level and distribution of employment opportunities and urban services. Somewhere between 15 and 30 percent of the labour force is unemployed or under-employed. A majority of metropolitan households are unable to afford adequate food, yet approximately 191,000 hectares of potentially good agricultural soils in the Region lie unutilised for want of water. In 1971 average domestic water availability to households was only about 112 litres per capita per day, with ample supplies for the affluent (450 litres per capita per day or more at less than half a rupee per thousand litres) but only a trickle, intermittently (as little as 45 litres per capita per day) for the poor, who frequently are forced to pay 20 to 30 rupees per thousand gallons to have water carried to their hutments; in 1971 only about 30 percent of the Metropolitan Area's households had individual connections. Installed sewage treatment capacity was only 180 million litres per day, relative to a water intake of 450-540 million gallons per day; only half of that capacity was operative, for want of proper management, and the entire sewerage system was capable of handling only 4 percent of the biological oxygen demand generated daily; only about 20 percent of the Metropolitan Area's households had individual sewer connections but sewer pipes are often installed in outlying areas in advance of the need for settlement. Several hundred thousand of the Metropolitan Area's inhabitants had (and still are) settled in areas subject to flooding in heavy monsoon rains -- flooding that costs lives, brings sewage into huts and results in considerable property damage. Somewhere between 1500 and 2000 tons of refuse were being generated daily in 1971 but less than half of this was being collected and disposed. There were only 1.5 hospital beds per 1000 population and 1.1 health centres per 100,000 population; 38 percent of the metropolitan population 10 years of age or older was illiterate. There were perhaps as many as 800,000 persons living in extreme squalor with only rudimentary infrastructure or none at all. There were severe deficiencies in metropolitan transport -- with long and costly commutes for many low-income households (absorbing 10 percent of their monthly incomes in northern and eastern Karachi). However, the arterial road system was lavish. Approximately 90 percent of it was under-utilized and approximately 57 percent of it was utilised up to only 50 percent or less of its capacity. There were only 1400 buses for a population of approximately 4.2 million with only 950 buses operative on an average day because of poor management and maintenance.

The physical form of the Metroplitan Area reflects very clearly its typography, its economic institutions (informal as well as formal), its laws and the laxity of their application. Most of the land (perhaps 80 percent of the developable land in the Metropolitan Area) is publicly owned -- a rare and potentially great advantage in a metropolis of Karachi's size. This provides a remarkable opportunity to guide metropolitan growth. Unfortunately, it also makes land development decisions very vulnerable to political pressures. The local economy and, specifically, the distribution of income, is such that an elite minority is able to manoeuvre freely in the land market while a majority of the urban population -- the poor majority -- is crowded into the least desirable areas at densities of up to 1300 persons per acre (3250 per hectare) in structures of only one to four stories. The principal agencies responsible for physical infrastructure have a considerable capacity for construction. Unhappily, this is not coupled with a corresponding capacity for management and maintenance. The private sector is not equipped to compensate for this. The public agencies have been seduced rather readily into extending major infrastructure at high standards into the outer reaches of the Metropolitan Area in advance of the real need for development, supporting speculation. Even in areas ready for settlement only the peripheral infrastructure is installed by the public agencies, leaving the "inner" development to housing societies and other private entities, many of which are not equipped (or never intended) to install the necessary improvements.

Military areas have played a major role in physical growth. Karachi Cantonment, the first of a series of extensive holdings, was established after the British occupation in 1839. Even then it occupied 650 ha; it has since been expanded to 1,200 ha. This and the other cantonments that have been added since total approximately 11,600 ha. They are massive islands of under-development in the inner area of the city and in the path of its growth.

All of these factors together, plus a willingness to lease or sell public lands at below-market prices, have resulted in a very extravagant use of metropolitan land. The gross urban density of 168 persons per ha in 1970, excluding vacant developed land and defence lands, was extremely low relative to actual space needs and results in very high transportation costs. If vacant developed land and defence lands are included in the calculations, the gross density was only 98 persons per hectare.

The nature of the administrative system through which the planning and development of the Karachi Region occur is determined largely by the national Constitution of 1973. Pakistan is a Federation. Certain powers are granted exclusively to the Federal Government, others may be exercised concurrently by the Federal and Provincial Governements, and residual powers are vested in the Provinces. National planning and national economic coordination are the exclusive prerogatives of the Federal Government. In the absence of express mention of "physical planning" in either the Federal or Concurrent Legislative List, this subject is left to the Provinces. However, since physical planning is an integral part of the development functions with which it is associated, much physical planning has been deemed to be beyond the control of provincial planning authorities. Problems of Federal-Provincial conflict in physical planning are minimized, in principle, through an integrated Federal-Provincial system for economic development planning. A National Economic Council stipulates that each proposed public sector development scheme be scrutinised by, and subject to the approval of, a Provincial Development Working Party and, above specified cost levels, subject to review by a Central Development Working Party.

Although there was in the early 1970s a Physical Planning and Housing Section in the Provincial Planning and Development Department in Sind, primary responsibility for planning in the Karachi Metropolitan Area rested with the Master Plan Department of the Karachi Development Authority (KDA). The KDA was also responsible for water supply and sewerage, a large part of all road construction, land development and land-use controls related to the development areas under its jurisdiction, and building regulations covering much of the Karachi District.

Development functions in the Region, as distinguished from planning and regulatory functions, are shared by Federal Government agencies, the Provincial Government, local governments and special bodies. Public development and the regulation of private development are characterised by the arbitrariness, fragmentation, inefficiencies and inequities that characterise metropolitan development in many parts of the world. The major land developers in the Region are public agencies. Their activities are not governed by a common set of policies. Some share their plans with the KDA, the main control authority; others do not. Many of the regulations supposedly in force are unrealistic in relation to households' economic capabilities and are simply ignored. The KDA does not have the resources for effective enforcement and the rewards for arranging exceptions can be considerable. There are various means to avoid regulations. In some cases, for example, a "no objection certificate" is signed by the landowner, indicating that if he is allowed to depart from the regulations (by building on a public right-of-way, for example), he will make no objection and seek no compensation if the government later exercises its rights and, if necessary, demolishes his structures; the chances of the government enforcing the provisions of such a certificate are slim. Under another provision in which land is allocated to private individuals subject to the land being used for residential purposes within a specified number of years, a standard device for retaining property rights without having to make the investment needed for normal housing is to build a small (2x2 metres) hut for a _chowkidhar_ (watchman) in one corner of the lot and then claim that the land is being used as a place of residence. The property tax has similar loopholes. There is a tax on the income from building space, but not the income from furnishings. For those who are conscientious enough to go through the formalities of reporting income, a simple device is to attribute most of the rent to furnishings and as little as possible to the building. The author once received a bill from a relatively respectable hotel which read "daily tariff Rs.270 for furnishings (the bed, the air conditioner and a meagre miscellany), Room Rs.30".

The financing of Karachi's development in the early 1970s was meagre relative to the area's needs. For the fiscal year 1972/73 the total public resources assigned to development in the Region by all levels of government amounted to about US$32 million(2) - a little less than $8 _per capita_, compared to the average of $85.49 _per capita_ for development expenditures in municipalities of one million or more in the United States in 1970/1971, excluding direct federal and state expenditures.(3)

Karachi depends heavily on the central government for its development financing; of the total $32 million in 1972/73, $10.5 million was from the central government, $5.5 million was from the Province of Sind and only $16.4 (51 percent) was local. The shortfalls in funding were aggravated by programme imbalances relative to the area's social needs, a shortage of programming and project preparation skills and a shortage of management skills.

THE PLANNING AND DEVELOPMENT REPORT OF 1971-1976

Antecedents

The previous overall planning exercise for Karachi prior to the planning and development effort that is the subject of the present chapter was published almost 20 years earlier. It was preoccupoied with physical development. The metropolitan physical form recommended has never developed but some of the major infrastructure proposed as a prelude to that form -- in particular, a series of major arterial roads -- have been built at very high standards. Still under-utilized because of a lack of "fit" between actual settlement patterns and economic conditions and the preconceived forms and standards of the earlier plan, these investments represent a very inefficient allocation of public resources.

Between the earlier plan and the work of 1971-1976, the other planned development that occurred included the creation of two new townships designed to help absorb a part of the sudden growth in population which followed Partition. Within 7 years, 44,000 households were provided with housing and basic infrastructure. This was a considerable achievement but does not represent a relevant solution to the growth and poverty problems facing the Metropolitan Area. The locations of the new townships were poor in relation to job opportunities and the physical standards of development were far too high to be affordable by a majority of the metropolitan population. Their internal layout does not reflect local behaviour patterns and many spaces and facilities (including space constructed for commercial use) have been converted to other uses or are underutilized. Coupled with poor project administration, these factors have made it impossible for the townships to be viable socially or economically.

There has been considerable experimentation with a variety of types of settlements and housing on a smaller scale. Almost everything has been tried -- open plot development (an early version of sites and services, but the planned services were never fully installed), core housing, "low-cost" housing (that was not nearly low enough in cost to be relevant for a majority of the population), workers' flats, publicly constructed apartments, housing cooperatives (middle and upper-middle income), and the ubiquitous (sometimes infamous) housing society schemes (also limited almost exclusively to middle and upper income groups).

The work of 1971-1976 thus benefited from considerable evidence as to what would work and what would not.

The Master Plan Project

The planning and development work to be discussed here extended from 1971 through early 1976 as part of the Master Plan Project for the Karachi Metropolitan Area which was undertaken with the assistance of the United Nations Development Programme. The Karachi Development Authority (KDA) was the Cooperating Government Agency and established a new Master Plan Department for the project and for the permanent planning and regulation of metropolitan development. The United Nations established a staff group with a Project Manager, U.N. individual experts and the principal U.N. Contractor, PADCO Inc., an international consulting firm with its head office in Washington D.C., in association with POLYTECHNA/TERPLAN of Prague. For the transportation planning aspects of the project, PADCO utlized the services of an affiliated firm, Alan M. Voorhees (AMV) Ltd. of London.

The project was misnamed. It was not intended to produce a "Master Plan" in the traditional sense. Indeed, a conscious effort was made to avoid the pitfalls of such planning, and focus instead on the identification of opportunities for immediate action to deal with the crises facing the Metropolitan Area, the formulation of a medium-range development programme as a framework for project decisions - rather than a detailed long-range master plan of the type described in Chapter 1 - and on building up local institutional capacities so that the planning and development effort could continue later without outside consultant support.

THE MAJOR FEATURES OF THE 1974-1985 DEVELOPMENT PROGRAMME

The Cyclical Structure of the Planning Process

Policies and programmes were formulated in three major "cycles". The first cycle, extending from February 1971 through September 1972, produced two major outputs - recommendations defining two alternative long-term development strategies that appeared to deserve serious consideration by government and a series of recommendations for immediate action that could be initiated even before overall planning was completed.

The second cycle, extending from October 1972 through July 1973, was concerned with the development of more specific policies within the general orientation established by the first cycle, an examination of alternative physical development options for the Region (with attention focused on the Metropolitan Area) and continued work on immediate action projects.

The third cycle, extending from August 1973 through June 1974, was required to complete the proposals for the preferred development programme, including recommendations for the legal, administrative and fiscal instruments necessary for its implementation, and further recommendations for immediate action.

Following these three cycles of basic programming, attention was focused on the detailed preparation and implementation of one of the major immediate action projects - the first "Metroville" project in the low-income settlement programme that was identified as a major component of future growth.

This cyclical structure was designed to force at least preliminary decisions to the surface quickly enough to identify the major issues which should be confronted in more detailed planning, to enable the government to establish policy guidelines at an early stage in the work, and to generate proposals for specific projects that could be implemented without waiting for the full formulation of a medium-range or long-range programme.

The Policy Alternatives

The two alternative strategies considered were labelled the Distributive Investment Plan (DIP) and the Concentrated Investment Plan (CIP). They were presented as extremes of a spectrum of viable policy choices in order to clarify the issues to be faced. The DIP strategy was designed to reduce the major inequities among income groups as quickly as possible, sacrificing productivity and the growth of aggregate output in the short run, if necessary. The CIP was designed to increase net output as quickly as possible, even if this would necessitate continued inequities in the distribution of basic urban services and the other benefits of growth in the short run.

A Policy Advisory and Steering Committee was appointed at the beginning of the project to establish objectives for the development of the Region and to review and recommend on the programme and its components during their preparation. This Committee included representatives of the central, provincial and local governments, the military authorities, the KDA and the United Nations. An international panel of experts in metropolitan planning was provided by the United Nations to review the output of each cycle of the planning work. Working groups were also established in each of the areas of major concern, including Agriculture, Industry and Commerce, Water Resources, Transportation, Ports, Tourism, Housing, Utilities, Health, Education and Land Policy. The membership of these working groups included policy-level representatives of government, agency administrators and representatives of private groups. The working groups helped to establish objectives for each sector and to evaluate sectoral policies and plans.

The DIP strategy was selected as a guideline for subsequent planning work. Within this overall strategy there was a desire to utilize Karachi's productive potential as fully as possible (i.e. to incorporate some features of the CIP alternative).

Development Objectives

The basic objectives established for 1974-1985, in the DIP strategy, were as follows:

<u>Priority I</u>:

Short-run Survival, through measures including:

- adequate short-run levels of employment and income, with highest priority for the unemployed or underemployed;
- the provision of basic infrastructure, services and financing for enterprises generating employment;
- adequate public transport for journeys to work;
- minimal adequate food supplies at price levels that would permit at least subsistence consumption;
- the provision of minimal adequate supplies of safe potable water;
- the provision of basic environmental sanitation and flood protection;
- the fiscal and organisational changes necessary for these actions;

<u>Priority II:</u>

Sustained Improvement and Growth, including:

- sustained production, employment/and incomes at the levels necessary to provide surpluses for investment in continued growth in Karachi, the Region and priority areas elsewhere in the nation;

- expansion of essential suport programmes including financing, technical assistance and training for small enterprises;
- provision of key health services, with an emphasis on preventive services designed to reinforce improvements in water supply and sanitation and reinforce other measures intended to increase productivity;
- improvements in education services, with priority for an increase in basic literacy, primary education, technical training and community development programmes;
- provision of basic shelter, with emphasis on support for households to help them to improve their own housing, rather than the provision of public housing;
- improvements in public transport beyond the basic journey-to-work emphasised under priority I;
- organisational and fiscal changes necessary for sustained development, including the establishment of metropolitan planning as a permanent part of the machinery of government and the establishment of a permanent metropolitan development policy group.

Priority III:

Additional Improvements Needed to Upgrade the Quality of Urban Life, including:

- expansion of recreation facilities;
- development or improvement of facilities for domestic and foreign tourism;
- preservation and enhancement of areas of high environmental quality;
- establishment of higher standards for the design of public facilities.

The Programme for Regional Development

The urban population of the Region is projected to reach somewhere between 6.4 to 7.3 million by 1985 and between 11 and 15 million by the year 2000. In addition to this, Hyderabad, defined prior to the project to be outside the Region, is expected to grow to somewhere in the vicinity of 2 million by 1985 and 3 million by 2000. An additional rural population of the order of 417,000 was projected for 1985 and about 1.6 million by the year 2000.

The development proposed for the regional economy up to 1985 would take the fullest advantage of the economic potential of Karachi within the constraints imposed by federal concerns to reduce disparities in levels of development throughout the nation and to achieve a more equitable distribution of household incomes in the Karachi Region itself. Changes in the composition of non-agricultural output are expected to be relatively minor, although the addition of a new steel mill will be an important change within the manufacturing sector. Agricultural output is expected to increase by approximately 40 percent by 1985, based on an assumption that it will become possible to use urban waste water and improved groundwater management to bring a large additional acreage into intensive agricultural production.

It was recommended that urban growth in the Region up to 1985 should be concentrated in and around the Karachi Metropolitan Area, although Hyderabad is also likely to grow substantially. Apart from this, urban or semi-urban growth should be limited to small service centres supporting the substantial growth in agriculture that is proposed. The physical development recommended is sketched in Fig. 3.1.

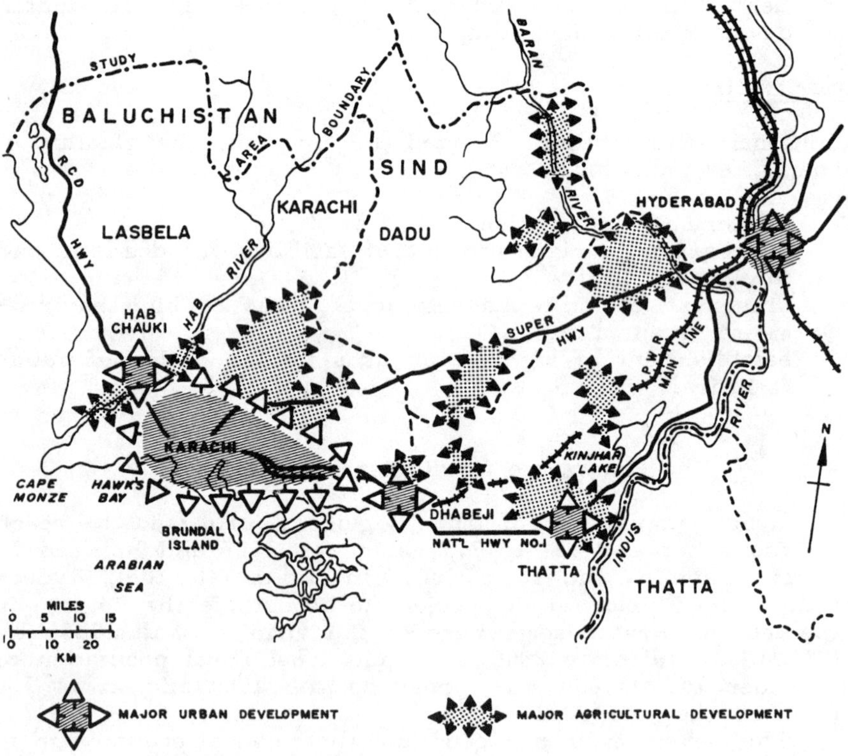

Fig. 3.1. Regional Growth Strategy, 1974-1985.

Alternatives for the distribution of urban development were considered. A somewhat different strategy may become feasible after 1985, but the advantages of consolidated growth up to 1985 in and around Karachi appear, in the words of the Development Programme report, to be "overwhelming". The strategy proposed emphasises the fullest possible use of existing infrastructure as a prerequisite for new investment, achievement of the highest possible productivity within the constraints imposed by distributional concerns, and the maintenance of acceptably low levels of risk in the early stages of development.

A series of critical additions to regional infrastructure are required to implement this strategy. These include the completion of the Hab Dam to the north-west of the city and the bulk water supply canal connecting it with Karachi, several new water treatment plants, a protective drainage canal and other flood control works to the north of the Metropolitan Area, the expansion of the existing Karachi Port and the creation of a new port to the east of the existing built-up area, improvements to the existing civil airport, a new railway marshalling yard near the new port and rail and road links to a new steel mill close to the new port complex, several new power stations and two high-tension transmission lines from the Kotri-Hyderabad area into Karachi, a second gas transmission line into Karachi from the Sui gas field and a series of groundwater management projects to support agricultural development.

Two alternative regional strategies are identified for the period 1985-2000, one with relatively dispersed urban development in between Karachi and Hyderabad and the other with a continuation of the concentrated development recommended for the period up to 1985. The Development Programme also examines very briefly the prospects for longer-term development, envisaging the possibility of a vast coastal conurbation stretching from an area west of Karachi to Hyderabad with a total urban population of the order of 25 million by the year 2050.

Metropolitan Growth

The regional strategy recommended for the period 1974-1985 envisages that the population of the Karachi Metropolitan Area will increase to approximately 6.8 million. By the year 2000 it may have reached 12 million. Between 1974 and 1985 the Development Programme foresees some improvement in the distribution of household income: the percentage of households with monthly incomes of less than US$30 is expected to decrease from about 45 percent to about 26 percent; however, the percentage of households with monthly incomes between $30 and $100 is expected to increase from about 50 percent to about 65 percent (constant 1974 dollars).

The overall strategy for the metropolitan economy is focused on the improvement of conditions for households with monthly incomes of $50 and less, contributing as fully as possible to the public and private capital formation necessary to sustain economic growth, reducing foreign trade deficits and external debt and the achievement of acceptably low levels of risk in development.

The physical growth recommended is shown in Fig. 3.2. It has three major components: (a) provision for new growth; (b) the intensification of existing development; and (c) restraint and upgrading.

The new growth areas are ones where it is relatively easy to achieve a reasonable balance between residential development and existing or new job opportunities; they are areas which can be provided with infrastructure and essential urban services relatively inexpensively; and they are areas in which the risks associated with new development will be relatively low. The major areas for intensification are those having substantial under-utilised infrastructure capacity and a large amount of serviced land which was not occupied at the time of the preparation of the programme. Restraint on growth and major renovation (upgrading) was recommended for the heart of the Metropolitan Area which contains a large proportion of the metropolitan population, much of it occupied by desperately poor households living at high densities in localities with only rudimentary urban services.

Water-resources Development and Agriculture – A Major Innovation

The present water resource technology is costly, wasteful of water, makes Karachi vulnerable to system failures and does not support agricultural development or environmental enhancement effectively. Water demand is increasing rapidly. The waste water generated by the urban area is simply discharged into local rivers (rivulets for much of the year) or the sea. Inland, most of the meagre rainfall is lost through surface runoff or evaporation; there are very few surface impoundments to reduce runoff, to encourage percolation and build up groundwater reserves, yet seasonal concentrations of rainfall make many parts of the urban area subject to serious flooding.

The objectives established for water resources development and water management in the Region were:

(a) To provide water for both urban and rural use at reasonable standards (180-270 litres per capita per day for all

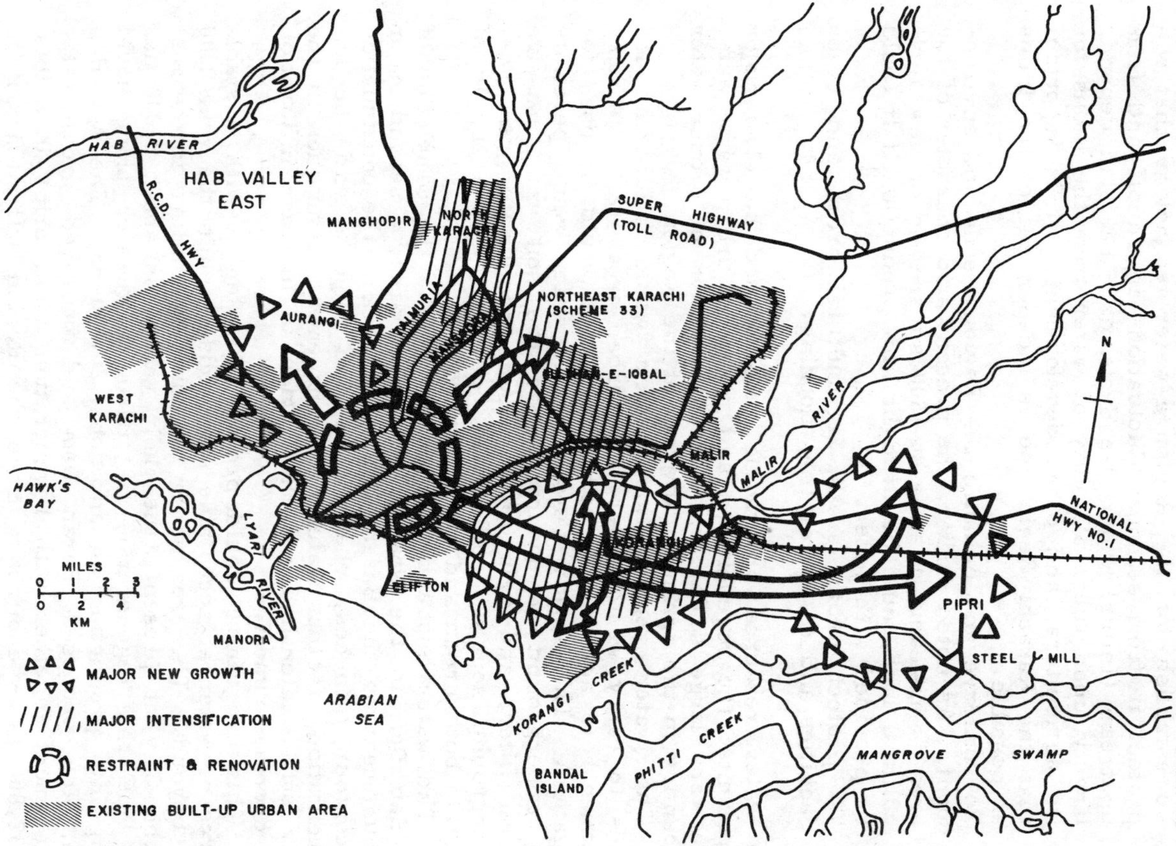

Fig. 3.2. Karachi Metropolitan area basic physical growth strategy 1974-1985.

uses by 1985, 90-180 litres *per capita* per day for household consumption in urban areas and 70-90 litres *per capita* per day for household consumption in rural areas.

(b) To establish for the Region a water technology that will protect it from seasonal fluctuations in runoff and from upstream (Indus) water use decisions. Pakistan depends largely upon the availability of water from the Indus for its agricultural and other development. It is important that the Karachi Region be as independent of the Indus as possible.

(c) To conserve and enhance the Region's soils and environment. As noted earlier, the present arid character of the area is misleading; at least 1800 square km of new agricultural land could be brought into production if it could be provided with water.

(d) To protect urban areas, agricultural areas and other facilities and resources from flooding.

The water resource programme recommended has two major components: the regeneration and re-use of urban waste water on a very large scale; and the introduction of proper water husbandry in the agricultural areas of the Region.

The water regeneration system would utilize unlined canals to carry waste water from urban areas (after primary treatment) to agricultural areas, where it would be used for irrigation. The steady flow of waste water would percolate into underground reservoirs, using the soil as a massive natural filter, and help to build up groundwater reserves. Underground sources would then be used for the supply of water to both urban and agricultural areas.

The water husbandry proposals include the completion of the Hab Dam to the west of the urban area, a second major impoundment on the Baran River to the east, the construction of contour trenches, check dams and dugouts and the implementation of other watershed management techniques in the many small watersheds of the Region to increase infiltration and decrease runoff.

This programme would provide the Region with a stable source of water at acceptable standards through the year 2000 and beyond. The area under intensive agriculture to the east of the City at present (the Malir valley) is about 8,000 ha. By 1985 the regeneration of urban wastewater alone could bring into production an additional 20,400 ha. The new Hab Dam, the proposed Baran Dam and improved groundwater management together with regeneration could bring in a total of 32,800 ha - enough to make the Region self-sufficient in milk, meat, vegetables and fruit and generate direct employment in agriculture for approximately 63,000 workers; an additional 20,000 jobs might be created in related activities and irrigation. At present roughly 70 percent of the vegetables, fruit, milk and meat consumed in the Region originate outside it.

A continuation of this strategy might make it possible to bring into production a total agricultural area of approximately 191,000 ha in that part of the Region designated as the water husbandry area.

Industrial and Commercial Development

Economic growth in Karachi has been fairly rapid, but it has benefited only a part of the population. Unemployment and under-employment are severe and incomes are very low for most households. In part this is due to the overall low level of development of Pakistan's economy, shortages of domestic capital and the large flows of in-migrants that have inundated Karachi. It is due also to an inability to develop markets for the goods and services produced and an inability to use capital and labour efficiently in the Region.

The objectives established for industrial and commercial development included (a) improvement in the growth and distribution of incomes and consumption; (b) improvements to private and public capital formation and efficient use of existing physical resources; (c) reduction in foreign trade imbalances and external debt and support for export-based industries; and (d) reduction in economic risks, involving diversification of the metropolitan economy, reduced dependence on external economic activities, and encouragement of the productivity of "marginal" corporations.

The recommended programme involved (a) financial assistance to small-scale businesses; (b) technical assistance in marketing and business management; (c) development of strategically located land for industry, and (d) encouragment of commercial areas with a four-level hierarchy of centres which include small-scale manufacturing and respond to existing and emerging trends in sub-district growth. However, emphasis would be placed on strengthening and consolidating the exisiting metropolitan centre through 1985.

The Basic Strategy for Housing and Related Services

According to a survey in 1967/1968, approximately 54 percent of the privately owned dwelling units in the Karachi Urban Area had only one habitable room and an additional 31 percent had only two habitable rooms.(4) Approximately 18 percent of the housing stock was <u>kutcha</u> (made of temporary and/or substandard materials such as cardboard, old packing cases or adobe), 37 percent was <u>semi-kutcha</u> and only 45 percent was pucca (built of permanent materials at officially acceptable standards). Only 30 percent of all dwelling units had piped water; only 20 percent had sewer connections; only 16 percent had water, sewerage and electricity.

It has been estimated that 489,000 new households will require shelter and services in the Karachi Metropolitan Area between 1974 and 1985. Most of these households will be poor. Although the public sector has experimented with a variety of types of shelter, the government has never been able to achieve financially viable public housing or construct at a pace which, together with private sector construction, is anywhere near sufficient to provide an adequate supply of even minimal pucca housing for all of the Metropolitan Area's urban population. In Korangi and North Karachi, the two "new township" schemes launched in the 1960s with foreign financial and technical assistance, only US$17 million has been collected out of the payments due, leaving $11.7 million in arrears, in spite of the fact that both of these schemes were heavily subsidised.

In the face of this situation, a number of the following objectives were proposed for shelter which were consistent with those established by the Central Government and included (a) an adequate plot or rental accommodation for every household by 1985; (b) expansion of water sanitation and electricity supply to individual households from 16 to 60 percent by 1988; (c) regularisation of existing unplanned settlements and expansion of the open plot programme to allow for growth; (d) encouragement of private developers to expand the housing stock with assistance of improved insitutional finance and land development, thus minimizing government-managed housing; and (e) minimization of the demolition of substandard housing.

The basic strategy recommended would provide low-income groups better access to the pool of capital and management allocated to housing in order to help to achieve the fastest possible improvement in their standard of living. It does not propose any massive subsidy to low-income groups because a meaningful level of subsidy simply is not possible with the resources estimated to be available. The programme gives highest priority to low-income groups but recognizes the importance of addressing the needs of all income levels. It also includes a land policy component designed to reverse the practices of the past through which the advantages of public land ownership have been squandered. The three specific components of the programme are:

(a) Regularisation and improvement of existing unauthorized areas with an appropriate form of land tenure, improvements in water supply, sanitation and drainage, paving of central paths, street lighting and improvements in social services; costs would be recovered through a quarterly fee designed to recoup capital investments, and water, electricity, conservancy and sanitary charges.

(b) Open plot development for newly forming low-income households and a utility wall core unit for low to moderate income groups. Land and construction costs would be recovered from beneficiaries. The principal advantage of this component of the programme is that it provides secure land tenure at low capital cost in planned areas. The plots thus provided can be improved gradually by increasing the levels of service and through housing construction undertaken by the households themselves. Satisfactory settlement is achieved, eventually, at much lower cost and with much greater flexibility than if an attempt were made to create a pucca neighbourhood initially.

(c) High standard development - pucca dwelling units with full utility services. The threshold income for affording a high-standard unit without subsidy was estimated to be \$50 per month.

Within this overall programme it was recommended that immediate action be taken to reduce land speculation, achieve secure land tenure for low-income households, and implement three specific types of shelter: (i) an initial new low-income settlement project incorporating shelter of types (b) and, (c) identified above, with a majority of the settlement devoted to (b) and (c); (ii) an initial regularisation and improvement project; and (iii) the construction of a small demonstration project designed to test the utility-wall concept.

Education and Health

The education programme proposed incorporates the following elements:

(a) An expansion of general education with enrolment targets of 100 percent in primary education, 60 percent in secondary education and 8 percent in college education by 1985. To reduce costs and make optimal use of buildings and facilities, it is proposed to continue the practice of two shifts per day.

(b) Specialized education programmes, including training skilled craftsmen and technicians through work in the private sector, as well as formal schooling, training teachers to support the ambitious primary and lower secondary programme and training doctors and nurses for the proposed health programme.

(c) A series of adult and informal education programmes, including one in adult literacy to be conducted in work places and, in the evenings, in school buildings and other facilities not then in use; a mass media programme which includes the installation of public television sets in community centres and parks; and a series of community development activities which incorporate important learning-through-doing components.

Considerable importance was given to a better geographic distribution of schools in order to increase access to education, for lower income groups in particular. In all of the primary, lower-secondary and informal education components of the programme priority was given to improvements in staffing, curriculum content and teaching materials, rather than expending the funds for high standard school buildings.

In health, the major emphasis was on a preventive programme which incorporates health education, improvements in water supply, sewarage and refuse collection, improved food quality control at all stages of production and distribution, population planning, inoculation services and a series of malaria eradiction measures.

The curative health programme placed major emphasis on the expansion and improvement of the system of local health centres which can deal with relatively common health and injury problems, rather than fully equipped and large-scale hospitals. A somewhat higher level of curative services is to be provided through several new 300-bed hospitals. Intensive care and special therapy will be provided through improvements in existing major hospitals.

Transport

At both the regional and metropolitan levels the objectives established for transport were: (a) to provide for efficient movement of goods and persons with minimal dislocation of actual and potential urban activities and (b) to locate facilities so that desirable long-range urban growth patterns would be supported.

The project was undertaken in the middle of a controversy concerning port development - the issue being whether further capacity should be created through an addition to the existing port or through the construction of a new port to the east of the city. The project team supported the eastern location, whose development could be coordinated with the location recommended for the new steel mill, the construction of a major railway marshalling yard and the expansion of the Metropolitan Area to the east, towards Hyderabad. Some expansion of the existing port is to take place, but the new location of the port to the east was eventually adopted.

For air transport it was recommended that the existing international airport be developed to handle traffic up to the year 2000; two alternative sites further from the city were identified as possible locations for a new airport to be developed later.

It was recommended that the regional rail system be improved by increasing line capacity between the city and the new port to the east. The new marshalling yard was already under consideration and the project became a proponent for a change in its location that would have been better from both a transport and an urbanisation point of view; however, that battle appears to have been lost - for reasons that will be discussed later.

As regional water management and agriculture are improved it will be necessary to improve and develop the regional network of rural roads -- all-weather, but at minimal standards consistent with the relatively modest traffic loads they will bear.

Major improvements are needed in the metropolitan transport system. The recommendations included:

(a) Restraints on the use of private passenger cars to reduce the need for capital investment in the road system and encourage the use of public transport, in conjunction with minimal key road links.
(b) Susbstantial immediate improvements in bus services through an increase in the number of buses available and improvements in operations and maintenance.
(c) The efficient use of existing tramways in the first stage and later in improvements to and expansions of an existing ring railway for passenger movements.
(d) Support for the continued operation of autorickshaws, _tongas_, victorias, camel carts and donkey carts to provide low cost, short-haul services for low-income groups within high-density areas, and to support continued employment through these modes.
(e) Improvements to the administrative and regulatory framework necessary to secure coordinated development and operation of transport within the metropolis.

A striking reflection of the present inefficiency of land use and the improvements potentially achievable through the development recommended for 1985 is the transport system analysis which shows that in 1985, for all modes except walking, where the differences are very slight, low-income people could make shorter trips, on the average, than they did in 1975; in spite of the expanded size of the metropolitan population, the average length of all work trips could be less in 1985 than it was in 1971.

The Financing of Development

The total resources likely to be available for the development of the Region in the period 1974-1985 (the Total Resource Pool, or TRP) were defined as the development resources of the public sector (the central and provincial governments and six local bodies), the semi-public sector (utility agencies and port authorities) and the semi-private sector (the House Building Finance Corporation and public sector transport financing agencies). A development Resources Pool (DRP) comprising public-sector and semi-public sector resources was estimated within the TRP; the DRP was assumed to be available for financing the programme; it was judged that the use of semi-private resources could be influenced by the use of the DRP but would not be determined directly by the programme. The expenditures of the private sector, similarly, cannot be determined by the programme, but it is hoped that they will be influenced by it; the ratio of private to public expenditures is expected to be high and private expenditures are likely to be channeled into industrial, commercial and high-income residential development, in particular.

Even with the programme pared down to minimal acceptable levels there was found to be a "gap" between the DRP and the expenditures needed. Although the TRP and DRP were found to be very sensitive to variations in the rate of growth of national output, it was decided that specific recommendations should be made for closing the resource gap, rather than relying on optimistic projections for national growth.

Five principles helped to shape the recommendations for financing: (a) the revenue system should be designed with the real limitations of the existing administrative system in mind; (b) there should be a concern for the income-distribution effects of taxes; (c) the revenue system should have beneficial, or at least neutral, effects on urban land use; (d) economic distortions caused by taxes should be minimized; and (e) the revenue instruments used should each produce significant amounts of revenue.

There has been for some years a significant "net fiscal drain" on Karachi - that is, Karachi has generated for the central and provincial governments much more each year than it has received back in the form of development expenditures. One possibility for closing the resource gap for financing the programme would be to reduce this drain. However, it is reasonable for the Metropolitan Area, which represents the nation's largest single concentration of urban resources and wealth, to be generating capital for investment elsewhere in the country. It was therefore judged unrealistic to expect a significant increase in Karachi's share of central and provincial outlays -- although the absolute level of those outlays can be expected to increase as development proceeds even if Karachi's share stays the same.

Two principal measures were proposed for raising the necessary revenues. The first was to increase central government revenues (and, therefore, increase the total size of the pie to be divided between Karachi and other areas) through improvements in income and corporate taxation and through selective increases in indirect taxation on goods and services consumed primarily by upper-income households. The second measure consisted of three improvements in the local fiscal system: the introduction and proper administration of a site value tax (it was estimated conservatively that approximately $30 million could be raised annually in the Karachi area, compared to the $5 million being raised through local and provincial property taxes in the early 1970s); improvements in the leasing and selling of public lands, with prices being raised to market levels; and levying financially sound user charges for urban services.

As a part of the overall financing strategy, it was recommended also that metropolitan budgeting should be integrated fully with provincial and national budgeting - to achieve more rational patterns of expenditures by the several levels of government and to make it easier to analyse the contributions to expenditures at each level.

The Institutional Framework Recommended

Four key judgements were made in shaping the institutional recommendations for the planning and development of the Region:

(a) The administrative mechanisms used must be intergovernmental, with the active participation of the central, provincial and local levels of government, in order to reflect the reality of the sources of funds and political power and, at the same time, provide for a more effective local voice in local development.

(b) Public leadership and incentives, rather than restrictive controls, must provide the basis for guiding growth.

(c) The development regulations that are necessary, including land use regulations and the standards embodied in them, should be realistic in relation to the economic capacities of the households and businesses expected to conform to them and they should be flexible -- allowing for the exercise of sound judgement in the face of the rapid changes confronting the Region and providing for a gradual upgrading of standards and procedures as improvements in real income makes this possible.

(d) The actions recommended should be within the capacities of existing institutions. It would be futile to propose changes requiring an administrative revolution for their implementation. Such a revolution is unlikely to occur; even with considerable political upheaval there is a substantial inertia in the bureaucratic machinery of Pakistan, as in most countries. Change can be expected, but it is likely to be incremental.

With these principles in mind, it was recommended that there should be a series of specific improvements in the administration of individual sectors and that the overall structure for integrated planning and development in the Region should be based on four mechanisms: a high level federal body concerned with aspects of regional planning and development having federal implications; an Interprovincial Karachi Region Planning and Development Committee dealing with matters having interprovincial implications; a mechanism for dealing with planning and development outside the Metropolitan Area in that part of the Region that is in Sind; and an intergovernmental Metropolitan Planning and Development Committee which will be responsible for planning and development in the Karachi Metropolitan Area.

A number of changes were recommended in the functions of the Karachi Development Authority, the single most influential local development agency in the Region. These were designed to focus its resources on detailed planning for land development (compared to the overall planning and budgeting that would be the responsibility of the Metropolitan Planning and Development Committee) and the construction of appropriate infrastructure, and discourage its past practice of disposing of large amounts of public land at bargain prices through its *ad hoc* schemes.

The change in land pricing recommended was combined with the introduction of an annual tax on site value, improvements in practices for leasing public land and a series of other measures to constitute an integrated package of instruments to reduce land speculation.

PRIORITIES FOR IMMEDIATE ACTION

The urgency of the problems confronting the Region and, in particular, the Metropolitan Area, demanded that the project identify the immediate actions that could be taken to improve conditions in the area, even in advance of the basic development programming just described. The following were the most important immediate actions recommended:

Optimisation and Upgrading of Existing Service Systems

Attention was focused, in particular, on: (a) reducing losses in the bulk water supply system through improvements in metering, repair of service reservoirs and the repair of valves; (b) reducing wastage in the water distribution system; (c) economic pricing of water; (d) optimising the existing sewerage system through connecting sewered but unserviced areas to the main collector system, clearing blocked trunk sewers, recommissioning and proper maintenance of under-utilised sewage treatment plants and terminating the practice of dumping street sweepings into sewers; (e) clearing and proper maintenance of the main drainage system, the installation of key additions to that system and the construction of flood protection works; (f) improvements in refuse collection and disposal; (g) the introduction of unified management for metropolitan water supply and sanitation; and (h) upgrading the metropolitan bus system through an increase in the number of buses available, improvements in bus operations and maintenance, and increases in bus fares to economic levels to allow sustained improvements in the system.

Upgrading Existing Low-income Settlements

It was recommended that an improvement and regularisation programme should be undertaken immediately for upgrading those unauthorised low-income settlements which have the potential for becoming viable long-term settlements. The actions recommended were: (a) final selection of the areas to be upgraded (more than 70 <u>jhuggi</u> (shanty) settlements had already been identified by the Government but the question of whether they should be demolished or upgraded was still an open one when the project work started); (b) a series of surveys in the selected areas to determine the facilities to be provided and the other actions to be taken; (c) preparation of an administrative and financial plan for upgrading; (d) establishment of appropriate forms of land tenure in each area; (e) installation of appropriate facilities and services with as much community and self-help participation as possible.

The first upgrading project was subsequently initiated with World Bank support in the single largest concentration of low-income households in the Metropolitan Area -- Lyari, with a population of approximately 500,000.

The Integrated Development of New Low-income Settlements

It was estimated that approximately 160,000 members of new low-income households would be added to the metropolitan population in 1974; a larger number would require settlement support each year thereafter. The "Metroville" programme was conceived to address this need. This is an integrated programme for provision of land, physical infrastructure, employment opportunities, transport services, social services, credit, support for community mobilisation and an administrative and legal framework to expand similar low income settlements throughout the Metropolitan Area. The programme is to be scheduled to reflect the rate of growth of the metropolitan population. Each Metroville project is to include a variety of households, with a corresponding variety of levels of urban service and types of shelter -- in each case, within the means of the households involved or with minimal and very selective subsidies to support those who cannot possibly launch improvement of their own condition.

The first project, designed to support a population of approximately 35,000 people, was constructed during the planning effort described in the present chapter, with assistance from the planning team. The form in which it was implemented was the result of an extended dialogue between the foreign consultants in the team and their local colleagues and the government officials involved. The original layout proposed is shown in Fig. 3.3. The actual project incorporated higher standards for development and a more "orthodox" layout than the one shown but it was built, rather than just talked about, and that was considered to be more important than the preservation of an unimplemented "purist" concept. More will be said about the successes and shortcomings of the first Metroville project later.

Immediate Improvements in Urban Management and Finance

A series of actions were proposed for improving the management of individual urban functions. In addition, it was recommended that an interim Metropolitan Planning and Development Committee be formed by the existing Policy Advisory and Steering Committee to coordinate ongoing planning and plan implementation.

The immediate fiscal improvements recommended were an investigation of the potential for introducing the proposed site value tax to help to finance regional development and the establishment of an improved system of user charges for water supply and other essential urban services to make them financially viable.

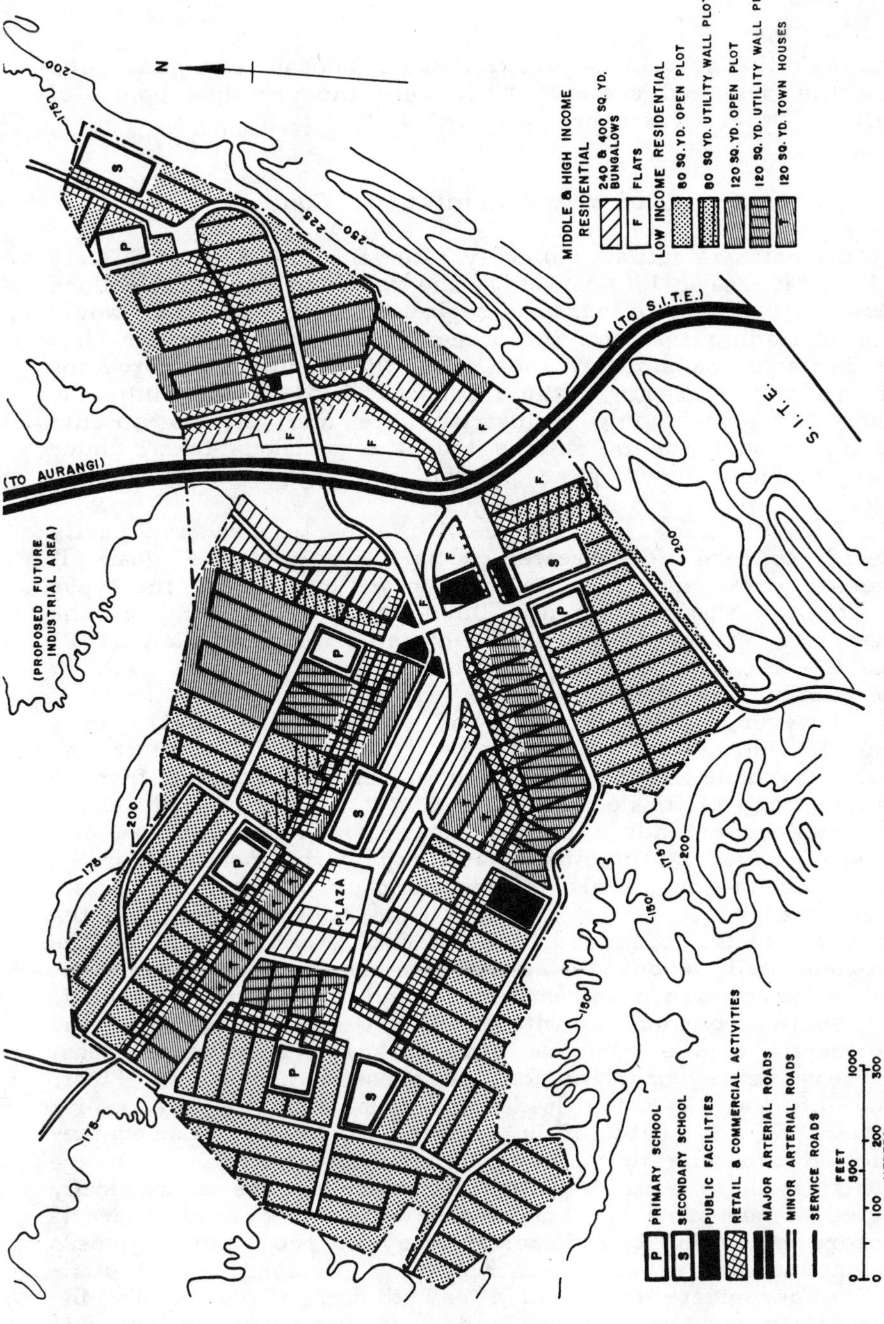

Fig. 3.3. The First Metroville Project - Major Land Use.

THE PROCESS

What was the context in which these proposals emerged? Who were the principal actors? What were the principal points of conflict? Where was concensus achieved?

The Political and Institutional Context

The project was initiated shortly after the PPP (People's Party of Pakistan) came into power as the result of popular elections following a series of military regimes. "Dictatorships" would be a misleading term for those regimes; they were severe, but the decisions made under them were the result of compromises between the interests of the traditional land-owning elite, the newer but overlapping industrial elite and the not-so-elite military. What can be said is that the decisions taken under those regimes never gave particularly high priority to the poor.

The PPP came into power with a partly real and partly avowed concern for greater social equity. The goals it espoused provided a formally satisfactory context for the types of action recommended in the Development Programme and the Government adopted the Distributive Investment Plan (DIP) from the two alternatives presented to it in the first cycle of the planning exercise.

However, the membership of the PPP was itself partly from the old elites, or the sons of the elites, and it was clearly burdened with a tradition of self-interest and favouritism in much of its decision-making. It could not easily shake off practices extending back at least to the Moghul era and reinforced by the protectionist and exploitative practices of the British occupancy. This influenced many of the political and administrative practices shaping the development of the Region. These practices were particularly virulent in the decisions made about the groups to be served through the installation of urban infrastructure and the allotment of land.

Another burden inherited from the more recent past was the inertia of the technical bureaucracy. This had at least two components important for the present discussion. First, many of the decisions made are dominated by the senior members of an elite of a Lahore, Oxford or Cambridge-educated bureaucratic club. The principals of this club are concentrated in Islamabad but its members are strategically located at the provincial and local level also. Second, there is a cadre of senior technicians - many of them the engineers responsible for urban infrastructure - steeped in the standards appropriate for London or Edinburgh but totally inappropriate for the economic and social conditions of Karachi.

Peppered through this structure are a number of younger, and often very capable, potential party leaders who perceived the reality of the crisis facing the nation and the Metropolitan Area and who were willing to fight for productive and fairly radical breaks with tradition.

The capacities and the degrees of commitment to realistic programmes varied greatly among the principal executing agencies and factions within those agencies. Some were almost hopelessly inefficient and corrupt, requiring major renovation. Some were relatively efficient but not at all socially oriented. Some were established specifically to serve social ends but were without significant political power. One or two were socially oriented and potentially powerful but still without much experience at the time at which the Development Programme was beng prepared. At least one major entity was struggling to reorient itself under dedicated leadership but was encumbered by a massive staff, most of whom were ill-equipped for the responsibilities they held. There was not a single major agency that combined a sound social orientation with efficient management and the political power and financial independence to launch and sustain programmes to benefit the Metropolitan Area's low-income population. In other words, there was no ready-made institutional base for the Development Programme - not that this makes Karachi unique among the metropolises of the Third World, but it goes a long way to explaining the partial successes and false starts experienced in the initial attempts to implement important programme components.

The institutional situation was not only fragile but also volatile. During the first 2 years of the planning effort four different Directors General were responsible for the Karachi Development Authority within which the Master Plan Department was located, and there was so much dissatisfaction with the track record of the KDA that at least one abortive attempt was made to dismantle it.

The planning project's genesis was not much more promising than its context. Although there was a recognition of the massive problems facing Karachi in the higher levels of government and a general sense that something should be done about it, the real thrust for launching an integrated planning and development effort came from United Nations technicians who had been viewing the situation with alarm for some time and a small group of Pakistani professionals -- some of whom were in the central government and some of whom were on the staff of the KDA. In other words, much of the initiative came from outside the real power structure.

Coupled with this, the composition of the project's technical team at the beginning of the work was, on the surface at least, unpromising. The group consisted of local professionals with widely varying capacities, some of whom bitterly resented the fact that foreign consultants had been called in at all and felt that the job should be done entirely by Pakistani technicians; a small group of individually recruited United Nations technicians from several different countries; and a consulting consortium made up of a U.S.-based private firm and an Eastern European government-sponsored technical institute. On top of this, the U.N. Project Manager had both a technical and an administrative role and this post itself changed hands twice during the 5-year planning and development effort. In spite of this awkward set-up the team, through a series of ups and downs, became a quite close-knit and effective group -- partly, perhaps, because of the personalities involved, partly because of shared professional concerns on the part of a majority of the team, partly because of strong support at various crucial times from various levels of the government and from the United Nations and partly because there were enough successes or semi-successes to make it all seem worth while.

The international community was spearheaded by the United Nations, which was the sponsoring agency. The other "interested" members of that community who participated to varying degrees and at varying times during the work included the World Bank, the Asian Development Bank and the Karachi consulates of several countries. Although motivated by a variety of political concerns, there was a shared concern with the plight of the city, and support from the United Nations and several other members of the international community at critical times was important to the continuation of the planning effort and to its impact on actual development.

Local community groups at the "grass roots" level played a minor role in the formulation of the development programme - in retrospect, a much too minor role. Their involvement was limited principally to that of contributors of information and opinions in the course of the many field studies undertaken as a part of the basic analysis. Their almost total absence from decision-making was due partly to the Government's reluctance to allow the project team to encourage more active participation, partly to the time pressures on the team and its reluctance to make the additional effort needed to awaken and deal with community involvement, and partly to the fact that many of the potentially relevant community groups were not particularly well prepared to participate.

Another important feature of the political context was the long-standing distrust with which the rest of Sind regards its overgrown orphan city. Much of the leadership of the Province of Sind is aligned with traditional land-owning interests in its rural areas and with the elites of its truly Sindi towns, rather than with the cosmopolitan port city whose population is largely non-Sindi. The allegiances and investment interests of much of Karachi's leadership, on the other hand, are internal, national, or even international, at least as much as they are provincial.

Given this context, it is not surprising that a wide variety of orientations were involved in the formulation of the overall development programme and its individual projects - the Party political leadership with promises to keep and newly won positions to defend, the entrenched bureaucracy concerned with the protection of old positions and practices at least as much as progress, younger technicians impatient for change, private-sector elites perceiving change as a threat, local community groups interested by the necessity of survival before all else, Provincial interests with a fundamental antagonism towards Karachi and certainly not anxious to see it grow further, the sponsoring international agency preoccupied with a reputable end-product and a visible impact on development, other international agencies with specific investment interests, factions in the project team polarised from time to time around government intervention on the one hand, and free-market development on the other, and a majority of the project team pressing for an exploitation of Karachi's locational advantages, and promoting realistically low standards for development against opposition from some government factions which wanted to slow the growth of the city substantially and/or abhorred any strategy which they perceived as a "perpetuation of the slums".

The Varieties of Concensus and Conflict that Emerged

Some issues were resolved by what might be called safe consensus. These were generally postponable issues or issues revolving around more or less unavoidable trends. In the former case, the groups conceding could feel confident that there was no real concession since the issue could be taken up again later - for example, the question of whether there is or is not likely to be a more or less continuous belt of urban development between Karachi and Hyderabad by the year 2050. In dealing with unavoidable trends, the opponents to the position adopted were eventually persuaded of the reasonableness of the decision and could rationalise their concession as inevitable - for example, in the judgement that the urban population of the Metropolitan Area is likely to be between 6.5 and 7 million by 1985, a prospect that was protested vigorously by some groups at the beginning of the analysis.

In some cases significant consensus was achieved with minimal compromise on the part of the project team. This usually occurred only after extended dialogue and the technical information generated by the planning process was often crucial to achieve consensus. An important example was the final decision to locate the new steel mill on the eastern side of the city, rather than the west. The project team was faced with the obstacle of a site already purchased, but went to considerable trouble to prepare a series of technical papers to reveal the negative pollution, transportation and urbanisation consequences of using the western site.

In other cases a significant consensus did entail substantial compromise. The most important example was the decision to go ahead with the construction of the first Metroville project. The whole concept of the Metroville was resisted strenuously at first by groups close to the highest levels of government, largely on the grounds that the standards being proposed were too low and that each Metroville project would be nothing more than a grand jhuggi (slum). The project team, or at least a large part of it (there were initial differences in the team itself on this issue), judged correctly that construction at higher standards would waste capital and make it impossible to serve the lower income groups that were an important part of the target population. However, key members of the PPP had promised every Pakistani worker a roof over his family's head and decent basic housing; a large part of the original Metroville programme consisted of utility wall units, which have no roofs, and an even larger part consisted of open plot development. It became clear that the programme would never be launched if the project team insisted on what it judged to be appropriate (low) standards. It was decided that it was much more important to get something built - and begin to build up badly needed confidence in the concept of organised low income settlement, even with the lowest-income groups omitted or subsidised - than to have the technical satisfaction of seeing a sound scheme published in the official international documents but never implemented. One important benefit of this compromise, in addition to the fact that the first project was built, is that several key government administrators and senior technicians who saw the reality of the situation and had confidence in the project team, fought the political battles necessary to keep the utility wall units and the open plots as important, though reduced, components of the programme. A second benefit was that in the course of the construction of the first project, confronted by the physical reality of the higher standards (including unneccessarily wide roads and unnecessarily large plots), some of the original opponents of lower standards finally became convinced of their reasonableness. Hopefully, this will make it possible to reduce standards in future projects.

Some technically sound recommendations were frustrated because they simply posed too great a threat to vested interests. A major example of this involved proposals to modify a very large land development scheme on the north-west of the city to incorporate more low-income households, with higher densities than those envisioned originally and with a more efficient use of land. The recommendations of the project team in this case violated too many traditions and posed a threat to too many upper-middle class housing societies and key individuals anticipating enormous speculative profits. Although those recommendations remain in the Development Programme document, the project staff eventually abandoned the daily campaign it had been waging for a reorientation of the scheme because a continuation of that campaign might have built up so much resistance that the whole planning effort would have been jeopardised.

The implementation of other technically sound recommendations was frustrated or delayed because they threatened established or bureaucratic positions. The immediate optimisation of the existing water supply system was delayed, even though such delay poses a threat to the very survival of the city, partly because the identification of leaking valves, inadequate metering, system imbalances and other deficiencies was embarrassing to the senior technicians responsible. The recommendations for an alternative location for the new railway marshalling yard were frustrated because of the entrenched position on the part of the administrators and technicians responsible for the already-completed preliminary design work for the original site and because technicians in the international agency financing the project were so frustrated by previous delays that they discouraged any reconsideration of the project.

A number of sound recommendations were undermined by bureaucratic indifference or inertia. Perhaps the most striking example was the failure to upgrade the metropolitan bus system aggressively even though its deficiencies are extreme and well recognized.

Some of the proposals for major innovations remain unimplemented because of conservatism, administrative overloads and higher priorities. The in-depth analysis needed to evaluate the feasibility of the proposed regeneration of urban waste water still has not been undertaken, even though the Government of the Netherlands expressed interest in supporting the necessary studies.

Some recommendations, of course, remain unimplemented because they were weak or incomplete. In retrospect, there probably was not enough operational detail in some of the administrative changes recommended. This was partly intentional, because of the sensitivity of some administrative issues, but when the total number of dynamic and competent policy-makers and administrators is small and the daily demands on their time are extreme, even inherently sound changes may not be made unless the actions required are specified and scheduled unambiguously and in detail.

There were also some false starts that reflected underlying conflicts and, perhaps, over-optimism about administrative capacities. Two of the most dramatic cases, both of which are important for all future development, are the first project for the upgrading of an existing low-income settlement and the first Metroville project.

In the case of upgrading, an ambitious scheme backed with international support to upgrade Lyari - the largest single concentration of low-income households in Karachi - was stalled for a combination of reasons. Despite dedicated leadership by the Administrator of the Karachi Municipal Corporation, the Corporation was too over-loaded with daily tasks, could not recruit sufficient technical staff and employed rather inexperienced consultant assistance to undertake the task, especially in view of the onerous and excessive technical requirements from the international funding agency, and the need to move quickly to respond to the community pressures. But the most important factors were that entrenched interests in property ownership were threatened, the Government was reluctant to recover costs from the low-income beneficiaries which supported it and, when the Bhutto regime which had been supporting the project was overthrown, the political backing was removed, and the scheme fell into limbo.

The first Metroville project was launched after great difficulty, with considerable fanfare. It had the support, at least temporarily, of the highest levels of government - and it has been constructed. Virtually all of the infrastructure is in place, and row after row of utility wall units have been built. Moreover, the site was ripe for development and well located. However, only a few hundred people have actually occupied plots on the site, which has been designed to provide for a total population of approximately 35,000. As in the case of the upgrading project, there has not yet been a systematic analysis of the problems encountered and the following comments involve a lot of second guessing. As always, part of the problem is political. The project has not been able to sustain the high-level interest that was convenient when it was launched. There is also a legal difficulty; the site was owned originally by the Sind Industrial Trading Estate, which was opposed to the scheme, and title never has been transferred to the KDA as executing agency, so that it has not been possible to offer households lots with titles which could be used as security for the financing of housing. The physical standards used for development, higher than those recommended by the project team initially, are beyond the affordability of many of the types of households that would find the location attractive; many higher-income households probably are reluctant to settle there. The Government is not in a position to be able to subsidise the programme on a continuing basis and for this reason, among others, presumably is reluctant to subsidise what might become a precedent-setting project. (Part of the whole concept of the Metroville programme was that it would not require significant subsidies.) The author has been told also that the main water supply has not yet been connected to the project's system; this should be a minor technical problem, since the main distribution network is nearby and the on-site infrastructure is in place, but it may reflect a much more intractable political or administrative unwillingness to encourage the settlement of the area. Another factor may have been that international support was focused on the upgrading project in Lyari rather than the Metroville. This was reasonable in principle, since the Metroville programme was designed to be handled internally; but perhaps the initial project needed the additional momentum that international support might have provided. Indeed the upgrading of Lyari might have been implemented if the International Agency had also backed Metroville, thereby diversifying its base of support. It certainly is to be hoped that the first site will be settled fully and that the programme will continue, for at least four projects of approximately the size of the first one are needed each year to keep pace with the Metropolitan Area's growth. There appears to be some chance of this, since designs for three more sites have been prepared and work is said to be going ahead for their development.

THE STATE OF PLAY 2½ YEARS LATER - AN APPRAISAL

The period since the foreign technical assistance to the Master Plan Department terminated in 1976 is short in relation to the dimensions of the problems of the Region, the ambitiousness of the project, the overall planning horizon and the political uncertainties that Pakistan still faces. It is too soon to pass any overall judgement on the effectives of the Development Programme, but it is not too soon to point out some of its strengths and weaknesses and to suggest what might be learned from them.

Technical Soundness

The major recommendations of the Development Programme still appear technically sound and a number of them are particularly innovative and sensitive to local conditions. The sins are those of omission, rather than commission. Some of the recommendations - for example, several of the administrative proposals - were presented in a form too general to be immediately implementable; as noted earlier, the immediate action and entire 10-year activity should have been more precisely scheduled. Over-scheduling is a waste of time in a situation fraught with the uncertainties common to most developing countries, but at least annual priorities should have been specified for the first 5 years of the programme to enable the agencies responsible for implementation to mobilise more effectively. Priorities for the recommended actions should also have been made so that the government could decide more easily which items to postpone (or abandon altogether) if resources turn out to be less than anticipated or if the administrative system becomes overloaded in an attempt to implement the entire programme.

Political Responsiveness

Considering the complex political and social context and the multiple composition and origin of the planning team, the team's performance can be considered fair - not spectacularly astute but generally sensitive to the policy concerns of the government and reflecting central, local and community priorities. The specific objectives and strategies proposed are consistent with established national and local objectives. Members of the project team took the initiative during visits to Islamabad to promote ideas and responded to government requests for participation in policy meetings and for their inputs to annual and 5-year planning, and also made efforts to obtain international support and funding for specific projects in the Region.

At the same time, the team did not simply go along with every policy guideline and project suggestion received from the national, provincial or local level. It has attempted, thus far unsuccessfully, to reorient the major land development scheme referred to earlier. It prepared a negative technical evaluation of an extravagant road-widening scheme proposed (and later carried out) by the central government. It fought for an alternative and better site for the new marshalling yard, with the very active support of several autonomous and local entities, but was overpowered by the central agency involved. It fought, successfully, for the launching of the major low-income settlement programme, against substantial opposition to the whole concept and specific opposition to the low, but realistic, standards proposed. Other successes included the relocation of the proposed steel mill and the partial implementation of the Metroville development.

Beneficiaries

Who has benefited from the planning and development effort apart from the experience gained by the master plan team? Thus far, the answer must be: some of the property owners in the vicinity of the proposed second metropolitan centre; landowners in the vicinity of the new steel mill, now under construction; the handful of low-income households who have settled in the first Metroville project; the low-income households benefited by the limited implementation of the major upgrading programme recommended; and the low-income households whose removal from existing settlements has been avoided, or at least slowed down, by a broader acceptance of the reality of low-income settlement as a major component of metropolitan growth. But clearly, the planning and development effort to date has been of only minimal benefit to the urban poor who constitute a majority of the metropolitan population and whose needs are the most desperate.

However, the "thus far" in the initial question is important. The development initiated through the 1974-1985 Programme promises to be of major benefit to low-income groups as well as to the metropolitan and regional communities and the nation as a whole. The first Metroville project is virtually ready for occupancy as soon as the tenure problem has been resolved; three more Metroville projects are on the drawing boards. The steel mill and the new port which the project team supported together will form the nucleus of a new urban subcenter offering a wide variety of types of employment.

Looking beyond what is actually being implemented to what has been proposed, it is clear that a major thrust of the entire Development Programme is the improvement of conditions for the urban rural poor of the Region; it is simply too soon to judge how much of the programme will be implemented and how much of the expected impact will be achieved.

Participation

Government agencies actively, and at times hotly, participated in discussions on policy proposals, and efforts made to integrate their existing schemes and projects. News on plan ideas were fed regularly to the local press by the KDA and was frequently published. Interest from multilateral and international financing agencies was actively solicited. But the greatest weakness was the almost total absence of representatives from community groups in the major discussions. Their only input came through the project team's field surveys and informal soliciting of opinions in the course of the work. However, the formulation of the Programme and its implementation would have been greatly improved if community groups had had an opportunity to be heard. The low-income settlement programmes, in particular, would probably have had a better chance of sustained implementation through the political and administrative upheavals which have occurred (and undoubtedly will continue) if low-income groups had had a voice directly in their formulation.

Efficiency

An underlying theme of the Development Programme is efficiency in the use of land, capital, water and the other resources of the Region and the nation. As in the case of comments on the beneficiaries of the Programme, it is too soon to judge its real efficiency. The specific projects that have been built are few but they probably are reasonably cost-effective. The existence of the Programme and the discussions and arguments which contributed to its preparation probably have helped to avoid major extravagances in regional development that might very well have occurred without it. No new towns have been begun outside the Metropolitan Area, although they were being promoted actively when the planning work began. The steel mill and the new port have been located efficiently. The extravagances of past patterns of land development have been exposed; although the wastage involved has by no means stopped, it may at least have been slowed down. With the exception of one major street widening which was dictated from Islamabad, no large-scale additions to the road system have been undertaken. On the other hand, the optimisation of the existing road and public transportation systems has not made any significant progress. In other words, results are mixed and the impact of the planning effort is still uncertain.

Risk and Flexibility

In the opinion of the project team, a low-risk strategy was adopted. It is hard to say what would have happened if resources had been more abundant, but the combined effects of the policies proposed and economic constraints have certainly discouraged high-risk expenditures such as those associated with an attempt to shift a significant proportion of future urban growth from Karachi to Hyderabad or to new major centres elsewhere in the Region. Major additions to infrastructure in outlying areas prior to a fuller use of the existing road, water supply, sewerage and drainage systems have been avoided, but again it is difficult to determine whether this has much to do with the planning proposals or simply reflects a general shortage of capital. The risks associated with a continuing reliance on the Indus as the principal source of water have not been reduced significantly; the water regeneration option which could greatly reduce those risks has not been pursued aggressively. Once again, a mixed record.

The low-risk nature of the Programme is coupled with considerable flexibility. The long-range regional strategy leaves open the option of substantial later development between

Karachi and Hyderabad. The intensive and extensive agricultural development that could result from proper water management would provide for a variety of lifestyles, including seasonal agriculture close to urban job opportunities. The development of a second metropolitan centre would open up options in the inner structure of the urban area and reduce the risk of overloads on the existing core. The use of a light-rail system as the next major technological change in transportation would help to preserve rights-of-way for the later introduction of rail rapid transit if that proves to be desirable. However, these are still only proposals and it remains to be seen whether a strategy focused on flexibility and low risk will be implemented when the political situation becomes calmer and more resources are available.

Institution Building

Draft federal legislation of the type needed to ensure participation of federal bodies in the planning and development of the Region and to provide for the interprovincial coordination needed was prepared by the project team, submitted to the federal government and subsequently circulated, with modifications, as the National Physical Planning Act, 1973. A draft Model Provincial Urban and Regional Planning Act was prepared also, as an instrument for helping to achieve the coordinated participation of provincial and local entities in regional development; this draft was modified and circulated by the Ministry of Production and Presidential Affairs to the provinces for their consideration. Shortly thereafter, sections of the Model Provincial Act were incorporated in legislation for the North-west Frontier Province, the northernmost Province in Pakistan. The author was not able to obtain information on the current status of the draft legislation elsewhere at the time of writing. The changes recommended in local land use regulations have not yet been adopted and applied systematically.

The principal organisational improvements recommended, including the creation of an intergovernmental Metropolitan Planning and Development Committee, have not yet happened. Nor has the recommended reorientation of the responsibilities of the KDA, but this may be achieved in the fairly near future through the added impetus of international support for the financing of major improvements in water supply and sanitation of the kinds recommended in the Programme.

At the provincial level, a regional planning body whose creation was supported actively by the project team (outside the original scope of work) has been functioning for several years and is building up its staff capacities through both local and overseas training. At the metropolitan level, the Master Plan Department created for the initial execution of the project has been preserved under the new name Master Plan and Environmental Control Department. The original technical cell created for launching the first Metroville project has been preserved and is continuing work on the overall Metroville Programme.

The impact on institutional change has thus been very modest, but at least positive rather than negative.

LESSONS TO BE LEARNED

Technical Soundness

There is no substitute for technical competence. A simple, well-presented but technically unsound plan may receive enough support to have some of its components implemented - particularly if it is filling a void in a situation where there is a strong desire to do something (including almost anything to get foreign funding) rather than nothing. But such planning can be very costly. The earlier (1952) plan for Karachi was partly implemented in the absence of anything better and is largely responsible for the very wasteful investment in metropolitan highways that has taken place. Technically shallow planning for the two new townships built in the 1960s has similarly resulted in considerable waste. Because the Development Programme for 1974-1985 is basically sound it can at least provide a sensible framework for project identification and preparation as resources become available for its individual components; and has influenced some key development decisions.

Sufficient Operational Detail

Planning at a general level is likely to be of little value unless there is the capacity to follow it through with detailed and operational project preparation. The Metroville Programme was translated by the project team into a specific first project which was subsequently built.

The Use of Scarce Technical Resources

In most developing areas, even in the larger cities, there is, at least in relation to the scale of the problems to be faced, an extreme shortage of technical skills for planning and programme implementation. That skill clearly should not be wasted on projects of minor importance. Nor should it be wasted on elaborate long-range planning of the kind traditionally associated with "master plans" - work that will be out of date long before the proposals associated with it can be implemented. Instead, the skills which are available should be focused on implementable projects designed to deal with urgent and major issues, with the effort spent on long-range programming being just sufficient to provide a sensible framework for project identification. In retrospect, although the Karachi work was very much concerned with responsiveness to urgent issues and with immediately implementable projects, an excessive amount of time was spent in the preparation of the overall programme; a shorter framework would have been sufficient.

Involving all of the Relevant Levels of Government

A plan must be addressed to each of the real sources of political power and executive action upon which its implementation will depend. This obviously includes the individuals and entities which control basic financing and the budgets for individual sectors. Just as importantly, it includes the executing agencies whose administrators and technicians will be responsible for supporting the negotiations for individual projects and for their successful execution. In the development of a metropolitan area as complex as Karachi this means that the central, provincial (or state) and local levels of government should be given the opportunity to participate as fully as possible in all of the relevant stages of programme development - including identifying issues, establishing objectives and priorities and programme formulation, as well as detailed project preparation and project implementation. Only if such participation has been achieved will the programme be likely to benefit fully from their specialised insights in their own subject areas, their understanding of the programme and their roles in it, and their energetic implementation of the specific projects for which they are responsible.

ENGAGING THE COMMUNITY

A genuine involvement of the ultimate "user" in the planning and development process is important for at least two reasons. First, it is likely to result in programme and project design which is sensitive to the real priorities of users and realistic in relation to their capacities to pay for, or contribute in other ways to, project implementation. Second, the longevity of specific implementing agencies, the availability of government funding and even the stability of government almost always are very uncertain. If user groups have participated in programme formulation and project preparation and projects have their full understanding and support, there is a fair chance of sustained implementation (and subsequent project maintenance) being possible through all but the most severe financial, administrative and political crises. Without such grass roots support even relatively minor upheavals in the public sector can result in the stalling or abandonment of a program.

Administrative Capacity

Although some administrative upgrading is likely to be necessary, in most situations it is extremely important that at least the initial phases of programme implementation be designed as fully as possible to be within the capabilities of existing public and/or private entities. Endless numbers of potentially promising programmes have been aborted or failed to even get off the ground because they were beyond the current capacities of any existing entity or feasible combination of entities. It is often better to accept a highly simplified version of a project which is capable of being improved upon later than to hold out for comprehensiveness.

Economic Realism

In most situations, if there is a real desire to achieve sustained programme implementation, a good general rule is to avoid both internal and external (foreign) subsidies as fully as possible. Most LDC governments cannot afford large-scale and sustained subsidies, even if they manage them during times of relative prosperity, with the help of temporarily high agricultural export prices or by other means. But when times are tougher many development activities are likely to be abandoned, and some of the first to go are likely to be socially oriented programmes benefiting low-income groups with little political power. External funding is always uncertain, often painfully slow in coming and, in the long run, is unlikely to be very significant in scale in relation to the scale of many urban and rural development problems. These factors together mean that, wherever possible, the physical standards or other features incorporated in programmes should be low enough that the programmes are affordable by their beneficiaries; they are the ones with the strongest motivation to keep a programme going, in bad times as well as good.

Treatment of "Hot" Issues

Particularly in the early years of a planning or implementing agency's existence (but also later, as some over-confident agencies have discovered to their cost), insistence on "technically correct" but politically unacceptable positions concerning major projects can undermine or destroy both the project and the agency.

This does not mean that "hot" issues have to be avoided altogether. Some can be tackled if the agency is simultaneously working on, and gaining support for, a larger set of programmes and projects in which there is a substantial consensus. Provided there is this kind of security in its other activities, an agency may take the risk of supporting a sound but temporarily unpopular position in the hope of achieving a gradual reorientaton of policy. In Karachi, the large land development scheme favouring predominately middle- and upper-income groups is a case in point. The Master Plan Department did, and could afford to, protest the scheme fairly vigorously, in the hope of affecting later land policy, even if not much could be done about the scheme itself.

Strategic Compromise

It is often difficult to get anything substantial implemented - especially if it involves a new policy direction or innovative project design - but the social and economic costs of delays can be very great, particularly in a developing area. It may well be better to compromise and support a less-than-perfect project than to insist on technical purity and get nothing done at all - particularly if the project is the beginning of a sustained programme which can be improved later. This was the case with the first Metroville project.

Local Initiative

It is frequently tempting and easy for an outside funding agency or foreign consultant group to take the real initiative in programme formulation. Except in a crisis in which there is no alternative, it is also a mistake. At least some of the local policy-makers, administrators and technicians have a fair chance of remaining in place after the outsiders have gone. It is they who will have to achieve sustained implementation. Moreover, they are likely to have much better insights into many local problems than any outsider can and their solutions, though perhaps less facile, may be more effective in the long run. It is up to the foreigners to listen and learn, as well as give leads. And it is important for the local policy makers, administrators and technicians to take the real initiative in final decision-making - not only because this is likely to mean that they will be fully behind proposals and that the proposals are likely to be sensitive to local realities, but also because it is likely to increase greatly the chances of sustained follow-through.

Sufficient Time for Effective Dialogue

In addition to being technically sound and sensitive to local conditions, programmes must be implemented energetically and, if they are to have a chance of reasonable longevity, they should be embedded in a policy framework which is supported at the highest levels of government. Even with all of these things in their favour, the odds against sustained success are considerable. One of the factors most vital to sustained success is the time and opportunity for the extensive dialogue needed for sound programme formulation and project preparation. There should be time to gain adequate insight into local problems and idiosyncracies. There should be time for executing agencies and ultimate user groups to have contributed to, and internalised, programmes sufficiently to be willing to give them the fullest possible support. They must believe in the programmes and the programmes must deserve their belief. There should be time for policy-makers to have adopted programmes wholeheartedly enough to create the policy framework necessary for sustained support.

All of this takes time and the staff of a planning agency has a special role to play in achieving the necessary dialogue. There is little hope that executing agencies on the daily firing line of implementation will be able to take the initiative in opening up appropriate dialogues, but the best of them, at least, are likely to respond to initiatives if they are encouraged to see how their own interests can be served.

The dialogues likely to be necessary include: those internal to the planning agency itself; exchanges between local professionals and their foreign consultants; dialogues with the agencies responsible for international assistance; dialogues between the planning agency and executing agencies; dialogues with the various publics involved; and the ultimately crucial dialogues with policy-makers at all of the relevant levels of government.

A part of the planning agency staff should be made explicitly responsible for ensuring that the necessary dialogues occur and they should have sufficient status and time to do so. The Karachi planning effort, even prior to project preparation, took longer than expected. This was due partly to avoidable delays and an over-concern with comprehensiveness, but it was due principally to the fact that time was taken to respond to urgent issues outside the original scope of work and to dialogue until there was a reasonable consensus over the many issues which arose in the formulation of the 10-year programme itself and the first immediate-action projects.

Tenacity and Follow-through

Even the most well-conceived programme will depend partly on good luck for its success. The key officials whose support has been gained after months of dialogue may be shifted to other posts just when the vital policy decisions are to be made. The best local professionals are likely to be recognised eventually and rewarded with a training fellowship abroad or seduced into the international professional market. There is likely to be strong and persistent opposition from specific groups to even the best-substantiated proposals. Revolutions and wars are becoming the rule, rather than the exception. Among all their other qualities, policy-makers, administrators and planning technicians must have the tenacity to survive the disappointments and upheavals that are likely to be simply a fact of their professional lives.

Initial successes in the form of laws passed, policies adopted or projects implemented can be very misleading. Institution building to provide a permanent foundation for programme continuity is likely to be vital, as noted earlier. In addition, all of the protagonists of a programme - local, national, bilateral or multilateral - should be prepared to provide the sustained support likely to be needed until such time as it has achieved a stable momentum and they should be prepared to rally around with additional support if a worthy programme starts to falter. It is easy and tempting to become frustrated by repeated setbacks or get cold feet when unexpected and major problems arise. In the Karachi case, for example, it was decided that the programming effort had had enough external support after 5 years and should be capable of continuing on its own. The Metroville programme was expected to be sustained with internal resources and outside aid was focused on upgrading. Both have faltered but not totally collapsed, yet no back-up support has been forthcoming in spite of the fact that all three activities could have an enormously positive impact on the future of the Metropolitan Area and the Region. Five years is really a very short gestation period in relation to the size and complexity of the problem.

In addition to these specific clues as to what might be done in future, the Karachi experience raises a potentially important question. Perhaps, if the various clients involved at both the programming and project levels are willing to de-emphasise the importance of a relatively complete programme as a basis for other decisions, a minimal 10-year framework for development could be defined with just sufficient information to guide decisions on the most urgently needed and implementable projects. The scarce technical and other resources available could then be focused on the preparation and implementation of such projects and on the strengthening of the institutional machinery needed for continued planning and, in particular, implementation. But that is a subject for another chapter of another book. More importantly, and before that chapter can be written, it is a subject that deserves experimentation with alternative approaches in the field.

NOTES

(1) The author lived in Karachi for 2 of the 5 years in which consultant support was provided for the development planning effort, directing the consultant team during that time and maintaining supervisory liaison with the project thereafter. The reader should be aware that while the present appraisal is based on an intimate knowledge of the project it may also be subject to the biases which are likely to be associated with such a close involvement in the work. Parts of the descriptive material are adapted from the Karachi Development Plan 1974-1985, in the preparation of which the author participated. The views expressed are entirely those of the author.

(2) Karachi Development Plan 1974-1985. National Pilot Project 3 for the Government of Pakistan. Master Plan for Karachi Metropolitan Region, assisted by the United Nations Development Program. Karachi: Master Plan Department, KDA August 1974, p. 355.

(3) The Municipal Yearbook 1973 (ICMA).

(4) Karachi Development Plan 1974-1985, p. 177.

REFERENCES

Government of Pakistan. "Karachi Development Plan 1974-1985."

International City Management Association "The Municipal Yearbook 1973." ICMA. Washington, D.C.

4

Case Study of a Relocated Capital: Ankara

Ilhan Tekeli
Tarik Okyay

INTRODUCTION

The case study of Ankara is an important illustration of the national spatial planning issues met in the former colonial or semi-colonial regions of the world. It also serves as an informative example of the kinds of urban planning problems faced in LDCs. In such countries national political independence is often followed by a decision to relocate the capital, seen as the foreign-linked control centre of the country.(1) This is viewed as a strategic decision in the transformation from a foreign-linked economy to a national one. The Ankara experiment provides the first example of this type of approach to spatial planning. Now, half a century later, we can look back on a unique planning experience.

The idea of selecting an inland location on the Mid-Anatolian plateau owes its origin to a reaction against the semi-colonial status of the Ottoman Empire. The Empire suffered from a disintegrated economy long before the First World War that gave her the final deadly blow. One could speak of the integration of individual regions with various foreign economies but not of interregional linkages within the Empire. One immediate problem caused by this fragmented internal structure posed itself at the end of the First World War, in the organisation of the armed resistance movements against the occupying victorious foreign powers. Almost all of these armed resistance movements were in the form of regional uprisings with little or no coordination.

In the poorly integrated Ottoman Empire all communication lines branched off from Istanbul, the established capital. This city was the nest of countless political groups and social movements, the most powerful group being the bourgeoisie consolidated with foreign commercial and political interests. The leaders of the nationalistic independence movement renounced imperialistic relationships and the associated native bourgeoisie. Moreover, the greatest disadvantage of the old capital was its geographic vulnerability to likely military occupations. Istanbul was, in many respects, an unsuitable location for the organisation and guidance of an independence war.

The decision a few years later to locate the new headquarters of the resistance movement and to found the capital of the new republic at Ankara was not the result of a random selection process among many mid-Anatolian towns. Ankara was historically situated at the crossing of the caravan routes going east, west and south. It was also the unique production centre of Angora wool until the second half of the nineteenth century.(2) The railroad reached Ankara in 1892, even prior to the construction of the Baghdad Railway. This infrastructural superiority was no doubt of prime importance in considering the town as a supply base for the western battle fronts as well as the new communications centre for coordinating disparate regional liberation movements (Fig. 4.1).

Fig. 4.1. Ankara Within Turkey's Urban Settlement System.

The relocation of the capital could also be interpreted in terms of the "growth pole" theory.(3) According to this theory, a group from the small bourgeoisie falls into conflict with the colonial bourgeoisie and the concurring political administration. They form a "social pole" at the periphery and utilise this new centre to take over power. Around this social pole a new style of life, that of the national bourgeoisie, emerges. Indeed, the relocation of the capital in Turkey carried a significant cultural dimension; it represented a wilful effort to create a new national bourgeois culture. The leaders of the new republic were against imperialism but they never denied the capitalist line of development.

The basic reasons for the selection of Ankara as the location of the new capital can be summarised as follows. It was the best alternative for the headquarters of the Independence War. With a relatively good set of transportation and communication links, it could unite disparate regional resistance movements and control the battle fronts. In the early days of the Republic it became the symbol of reaction against Istanbul, the former colonial decision centre, and was visualised as the seedbed of a nationalist bourgeois culture.

DESCRIPTION OF PLANNING AND DEVELOPMENT OF ANKARA

Overview

In this case study we shall describe the major stages of planning in Ankara from 1923 to the late 1970s. For each stage we shall try to summarise the key policy themes and related administrative efforts. In evaluating the early planning experience of Ankara, however, planners of today face a difficulty. Both urban planning education and practice of the last two decades have placed great emphasis on the complementarity between physical planning and socio-administrative policies set down for implementation. At times partial or project planning, as opposed to comprehensive planning, has gained the upper hand among planners, but a close harmony between physical plans and administrative policies has been the common recommended theme.

The early planning efforts in Ankara, however, did not follow this norm. To develop the city as the new capital appears as a clear and deliberate objective, but the path followed in implementation has been quite different. Looking back on the early days of the Republic, one detects a series of disjointed administrative and legal policies with little or no physical planning. Later on physical plans were introduced as a formula for a comprehensive approach to urban planning. But it is difficult to commend them as an effective tool for planning the city. On the contrary, physical plans have somehow remained as addendi to existing administrative policies and they have contributed only marginally to the actual development of Ankara. Therefore, in presenting the successive stages of the city's planning history, we shall not be able to separate the discussion of the chief problems and conflicts from the explanation of key policy themes, nor be able to give priority to the description of physical plans. The historical sketch of the early planning efforts in Ankara will perhaps leave us with the following question: Do physical plans have a major influence on the ensuing development of the city? Is urban planning at all possible independent from the solution of national planning problems?

Initial Piecemeal Planning Efforts (1923-1928)

When the Republic was declared in 1923, Ankara was a small town with a population barely reaching 20,000. A major fire during the First World War had destroyed a sizeable part of the housing stock.(4) This town was to compete with Istanbul, a lively, cosmopolitan metropolis of 1.2 million people. In addition to the planning and construction problems of the new city, there were significant social and political objections against displacing the ancient capital. Some foreign countries were opposed to such a relocation long before the decision was officially declared. The native elite groups, on the other hand, were so used to the pleasant life of the large coastal city that they hoped for only a temporary stay in Ankara; no longer than the end of the Independence War.

For the founders of the new capital, there were equally important constraints at the intra-urban level. Following the Independence War a dual social structure could be observed in Ankara. One component consisted of existing property owners, mostly the former townsmen. The other component emerged with the immigration of the new residents, mostly bureaucrats. As the town grew, the interests of these two groups inevitably fell into conflict. Even the simple proclamation that Ankara would henceforth be the capital boosted all land and property values. This was a godsend for the old Ankara folk while the newcomers had to pay the price for it.

One could say that such constraints helped increase the perseverance of the founders. The success of a new city was closely identified with the triumph of the republican regime. Ankara had first priority in the political agenda. The constraints had to be overcome.

The first organisational undertaking was the founding of the Ankara Municipality (<u>şehremaneti</u>), a heritage from the Ottoman municipal experience.(5) But in consideration of the conflicting groups in Ankara, the composition of the traditional council was altered. In its traditional form a person had to be a taxpayer on property exceeding a given value in order to elect or become a council member. The condition of property ownership was abolished in the Ankara council, decreasing the power of the old landowners and placing the newly arriving bureaucrats on an equal footing.

By far the largest undertaking of this period was the expropriation of 400 hectares of land on which the modern section of Ankara called the Newtown (<u>Yenişehir</u>) was to be built. This was a deliberate policy discouraging higher densities within the old town. If the city was allowed to grow in and around the old town, land speculation would counteract all efforts to construct a "modern" town. Indeed local property owners strongly supported the idea of developing the existing urban area against the alternative of planning on a completely unattached, unbuilt area.(6) Since the balance of power no longer favoured the previous property holders, it was possible to proceed with the desired plan; land was purchased for Newtown.

Among the vital needs of the rapidly growing town were construction materials and basic infrastructure. There was no other organisation than the Municipality itself which could undertake their production. Soon brick, tile, lumber and lime factories were built and a power plant was started. Workmen's dwellings were provided next to these production units. A power mill, a modern bakery, a fumigation house and gasworks were also set up by the Municipality. Foreign capital did not remain indifferent towards such modernisation projects in Ankara.(7) But the leaders of the new regime were to remain reluctant to accept any type of foreign cooperation for a few more years of the early Republican era.

During the early years the expenditure by the Municipality was so high that money spent per capita in Ankara was 28 times the average municipal expenditure per person in Turkey.(8) It was impossible to cover these costs from the municipal incomes of Ankara. The central government had to make income transfers or find means of crediting the Municipality. The parliamentary debates of 1925 can be of interest to students of planning law. The main argument at the time was, should the state purchase land by paying an amount based on the landowner's declared tax value or the current market price of the land? It was also claimed that the increase of urban land values was a surplus that should be accrued by the public rather than by the individual. But the Republic did not intend to leave the capitalist line of development.(9) Therefore such parliamentary debates did not result in the adoption of planning measures to constrict private gain on urban land and to allow the Municipality a fund from the land value increments. The government's political attitude on state intervention also marked the strategy of tenant subsidisation. Bureaucrats had to endure high rents charged by the local property owners in the city. The State, instead of taking over the production of new housing, preferred to pay a tenancy indemnity to bureaucrats. This strategy was fully consistent with the policy of remaining respectful to the claims of property holders while helping out the bureaucrats.

By 1927 it became clear that a series of such disjointed decisions and such a piecemeal approach would bring no solution to the city's rapidly expanding problems. So far the development process of Ankara was being revised by the method of trial and error. The errors indicated the necessity for at least two basic changes. In the first place, the organisational and financial power of the local authority was insufficient to tackle the problems; a more powerful, centralised organ was needed to take over this task. Secondly, a more comprehensive approach to planning would pave the way to success. The first type of change was realised by handing over various responsibilities of the Municipality to new authorities mostly attached to the central government.(10) For example, the planning task was taken over by the Directorate of Development for Ankara (Ankara Şehri İmar Müdürlüğü) attached to the Ministry of Internal Affairs. The plans and the annual budgets of the Directorate were to be approved by the Council of Ministers. The Directorate would be responsible for the 5-year plan of the city. It would take over the possession of public land,(11) and it would contract debts and issue bonds.

It was thought and recommended that comprehensive planning would bring further remedy to the problems; this approach emerged in the form of physical plans.

The Jansen Plan and Difficulties in Implementation (1928-1954)

The Jansen Plan, completed in 1932 is generally known as the first comprehensive physical plan of the city. There were two previous partial plans drawn up by Heussler, known as the Löhler Plans.(12) The plan for the old town was considered impractical and turned down, while the plan for the new town was rapidly implemented due to an acute shortage of housing.

The new comprehensive plan of the greater city was prepared by three competent architects of the period: H. Jansen, the winner of the competition for Berlin's city plan, Professor M. Brix, his colleague from Berlin Technische Hochschule, and L. Jausseley, chief state architect from France. The year 1927 was hence the beginning of a new period in which the Turkish leaders began turning to the Western world for technical expertise. The jury, however, consisted of Turkish technocrats closely associated with Mustafa Kemal, and they were to decide on the best plan. Following a meeting with the President, the jury gave the first prize to H. Jansen. He signed an agreement to complete the details at the Directorate of Development and remained as consultant until 1938. The plan was approved by the Council of Ministers in 1932 and a programme for the first 5-year period was put into action 2 years later.

In the first section of this chapter, it was stressed that the physical plans of Ankara were more or less doomed to make but marginal contributions to the city's overall development.

The Jansen Plan could not escape the same fate though it left some important visible imprints on the city. In the beginning it was drawn as a comprehensive plan. In the end it was only a partial plan. Some of the reasons are stated in the following paragraphs.

When the three competitors formulated their proposals in 1927, basic decisions on the growth direction and pattern of the city had already been given. The decisions of the preceding years, such as the construction of Newtown, the President's choice of residential location and the existing main road that connected this location to the parliament in the old city, were some of the crucial constraints limiting the planners' range of choice. Furthermore, the competitors were advised on the orientation of other main roads, the locations of a few prestige buildings and the preservation of the old town. All competing plans assumed that the population of the city was to reach 300,000 in 50 years; it barely exceeded 74,000 in 1927. Despite this four-fold increase, it was assumed that the growth rate would decline with increasing size. The actual growth rates in the following two decades were to show the shortsightedness of this projection.

The three plans judged by the jury, however, were dissimilar in their conception of the town as a human environment. Jausseley's plan displayed the grandeur of what the French conceived as the capital city. The plan by Brix emphasised sanitary engineering aspects. Jansen's plan was concerned more with social issues, housing and workers' dwellings. The human scale was valued above all. Favouring a design that dwelled on social issues rather than on grandeur was a clue to the regime's attitude towards power and society. Jansen proposed an extensive system of green areas. The settlement structure was composed of low-rise buildings with gardens. The road pattern started from culs-de-sac and pedestrian alleys in residential areas. A workers' community and a university community were to be built. The national government centre consisted of moderate size buildings and small squares. But the reasons for the plan's subsequent inadequacy can be attributed to the structure of social and political power prevailing during its implementation.

Ankara experienced an annual population growth rate of 6 percent as soon as it gained the status of capital city (Fig. 4.2). At the time, it was the single town in Turkey with such a high rate of growth. Two-thirds to three-quarters of the rate of growth was due to immigration. There were mainly two types of migrants: The first type was the unskilled worker arriving from the rural region of Ankara. These constituted the main body of the low income inhabitants. The second type of migrant was skilled and could have an origin anywhere in the country. Indeed, more than 50 percent of the migrants came from other urban centres. These formed the middle and upper-middle class groups in the city.

Fig. 4.2. Stages of Growth in Metropolitan Ankara.

It was the acute housing shortage of the low income groups that gave rise to the phenomenon of gecekondus.(13) Due to spontaneously spreading gecekondu areas, neither the university district in Jansen's plan nor the workers' dwellings could be built. Some of the proposed green areas around the town were already covered by these low income dwellings. The gecekondu districts were called "The Third Ankara", the first two being the upper- and the middle-income areas. The planners did not attribute this phenomenon to a structural condition in society, and assumed that a few assertive measures could wipe out such areas forever. Such measures, however, never achieved success.

As for the middle income groups in Ankara, the housing question was far from being resolved, in spite of the existence of a plan. As one remedy, housing cooperatives were formed to build dwellings for bureaucrats and middle class families. The largest of these cooperatives could not build more than a hundred dwelling units. These were located within the general scheme of the plan, like Bahçelievler (the gardenhouses district). The Real Estate Bank played a decisive role as the credit providing institution, but it was ineffective for the lower income groups who lacked a sufficient and continuous income.

In addition to the difficulties in the organisation of finance, the largest handicap to the rapid production of a sufficient number of dwellings for all income groups was the dominant production type in construction. This could be called petty-production. The growth of Ankara provided numerous opportunities to an increasing number of private building contractors. This was in perfect harmony with the regime's policy of creating a new national bourgeoisie class. The rising bourgeoisie was conjunct with the upper echelons of the bureaucracy. But as businessmen they had very little capital; therefore their production capacity was severely limited.

The difficulties in the implementation of the plan were closely related to the political pressure coming from such groups. For example, the previously expropriated land in Newtown was reopened to private use. This policy induced land speculation leading to departures from the plan. The conflicts on the use of urban land soon caused serious disagreements between the governor-major of Ankara and H. Jansen. Jansen's further dissidence with the new cadres after Mustafa Kemal's death in 1938 made it impossible for him to renew his contract.

The contradictions noted above are a reflection of the tension at the national level between the sense of national pride resulting in 'etatism'(14) and consequent state control on the one hand and, on the other, the influence of the nationalist bourgeoisie who were committed to capitalist development.

By 1945 sizeable gecekondu areas could be observed in almost all large Turkish cities. It was only then that the problem was viewed from a larger perspective. The uneven distribution of income, the dominance of small contractors in the building sector, the rapid rate of population growth and other structural problems were seen as the cause of the gecekondu phenomenon. A specific law was passed in 1948 to "ameliorate" the conditions in the gecekondu areas of Ankara. "Amelioration" meant that the act of building a gecekondu could, under certain conditions, gain a legal status. The areas to be legalised were clearly mapped.

Public land within these boundaries would be divided into building lots and handed over to the gecekondu people. All gecekondus remaining outside the legalised areas would be demolished a year after their inhabitants were granted a building lot within the legalised areas. The legalised areas were beyond the already planned areas, since there was still a concern to keep the Jansen Plan as intact as possible. The result was a distinct separation between different social strata. In other words, what was introduced as a partial plan to cover the inadequacies of the existing comprehensive plan was soon to create other problems.

Ironically enough the gecekondu act gave the Municipality a chance to plan a low- to middle-income district, Yenimahalle. An area of 105 hectares was divided into lots of sizes 175-300 square metres and was offered to low income employees at cost price and a 10-year payment basis. The holders of land were to have a house built in 2 years, using a range of type plans. Under these conditions, a new district emerged in 3 years with a population of 20,000. This amounted to 10 percent of the city population.(15)

Why was it that the Yenimahalle example could not be further developed to solve the gecekondu problem? First of all, the building cooperatives and credit mechanisms were relevant for low- and middle income employees with fixed and continous wages. They were of no use to the lower strata, largely consisting of marginal sector members with no fixed wage and working place. Secondly, the large masses migrating from the rural areas into the cities had introduced a new solution for the housing problem that minimised the cost of labour. The solution was the gecekondu. In the eyes of the leaders who looked forward to a flourishing bourgeois life in the city the gecekondu was a problem. It disturbed the image of a modern, prosperous city. But the bourgeoisie regarded the gecekondu as a solution. Therefore, there was little reason left to reapply the Yenimahalle experience to the lower urban strata. Thus a dual structure emerged in Ankara, easily discerned by planned areas on the one hand and gecekondu areas on the other.

The Need for Further Rearrangements: The Yücel-Uybadun Plan (1954-1965)

By the early fifties the population of Ankara had risen to 228,000, the target for the Jansen Plan. But it had been reached in 20 years instead of the expected period of a half a century. The urbanised area touched the boundaries of the existing plan while the growth of the city continued at an undiminished rate. Therefore a new physical plan was required. Specifications for a second international planning competition were prepared in 1954. The 30-year population projection was 750,000 and it was indicated that new developments be confined within municipal boundaries.(16) Among the competition judges were well-known post-war city planners like Patrick Abercrombie and Luigi Piccinato. The winners were two Turkish planners, Rasit Uybadun and Nihat Yücel. The project was designed as a comprehensive plan and approved in 1957. The decisions brought by the new plan and the new institutional rearrangements more or less meant nullifying the Jansen Plan.

In the year that the Yücel-Uybadun Plan was ready for implementation there were some serious bottlenecks in the economic development of Turkey. International economic relations of the fifties had resulted in a deterioration of the balance of payments and in rapid inflation. Menderes, the Prime Minister of the period, chose the urban planning activities as a political showpiece to cover up more substantial unsolved issues. Ankara took a small share of these investments. The strengthening of foreign ties in the fifties had pulled back the attention to the port cities of Istanbul and Izmir. Therefore the previous ideal of building an exemplary Turkish capital city, symbolising the achievements of a national bourgeoisie, was no longer relevant. Ankara was to have no priority over other large towns.

High rates of urbanisation had encouraged land speculation and values had shot upwards. It was no longer possible for a middle income family to own a new garden house in the city. Given this structure of the land market, middle income groups could only settle in fringe areas where land prices were within their payment range. The result of this locational choice was an urban pattern with numerous empty lots near the city centre. This pattern increased municipal infrastructure costs. Pressure from various groups soon led to a new real estate ownership pattern. In 1954 the concept of "flat ownership" was introduced to the modern Turkish civil law. This enabled a number of families to get together, build a multi-storey apartment and thus meet the high land prices.

In actual fact most middle class families would not readily get together without entrepreneurial initiative. Thus a new species of contractor emerged who organised the building process by combining the capital of a number of individuals, constructing a multi-flat building, and selling some of the finished extra flats to other individuals. Similar to the term gecekondu, a new word was made up for these petty entrepreneurs: builder-and-seller (yapsatç). Their functions were different from the contractors of the previous periods who were responsible for construction only.(17) The yapsatçs soon became the most prominent interest group in the development process of Turkish cities as well as the chief dynamic force of the housing market.

In the period after 1955, the market conditions produced a big stress on planners and planning administrators. Garden houses were rapidly pulled down and replaced by multi-storey buildings on small parcels of land originally designed by Jansen. The increase of densities well above the intended levels resulted in a lack of sufficient infrastructure; and social services also became substandard. The consequence of all these residential developments was a city with a dual social and physical structure, the pseudo-planned middle and high income areas at the centre and the unplanned low income gecekondu areas at the periphery, both lacking in basic infrastructure and the required social services. The gecekondu was by then an acknowledged and unsolvable problem, but the development trend of other (so-called planned) areas was also unpromising.(18) The inadequacy of road, electricity and gas networks, the lack of playgrounds, school spaces and, above all, the newly fragmented ownership pattern would soon pose grave planning problems.

Issues of urgent concern were by no means confined to housing areas. There was scarcity of public transport facilities in the city even when the car ownership level was extremely low. Combining the electricity, gas and transportation boards into a single organisation (EGO) did not provide sufficient capital to purchase buses. A new type of petty entrepreneurship now emerged in the transport market. As a variation of the jitneybus prototype in early twentieth century San Francisco, or the jeepneys in Manilla, the dolmuş (pooled car) emerged as an alternative mode of transport and started to carry a larger percentage of the daily urban passengers.

Ankara's emerging pattern of residential development and associated transport system requires some background explanation. A consistent feature of Turkish city development is the high density of residential areas together with a low percentage of land use devoted to roads and public space. To some extent this is a reflection of the urban traditions of the Middle East. The development of a lower density 'garden city' envisaged by Jansen would have required much greater expenditures on secondary and tertiary road networks. This would have allowed greater accessibility to the perimeter of the city, and a more extensive public transport. This in turn would have the effect of opening up more land on to the market, hence reducing the price of land and thereby the density of residential development. Thus, while the development authorities of Ankara spent money on acquiring land for the city and investing in industries to produce building materials, very little proportion of investment went into building road and transport systems in advance or in step with development. This approach resulted in the high density residential developments we see today.

The 1965 population of Ankara was 805,000. The 30-year population projection cast in 1955 had been well exceeded in 10 years. Ankara was now ready for a third stage in planning.

The Third Stage of Planning in Ankara: The Metropolitan Planning Bureau (1965 to present)

The phenomenon of rapid urbanisation was now conceived as a nationwide issue and it was found necessary to have a central organisation specifically dealing with the problems of towns and cities. The founding of the Ministry of Urbanisation and Resettlement dates back to 1958. Therefore, the third stage of planning in Ankara is a direct undertaking of the central government. Furthermore, the experience of the past half a century had shown the inadequacy of competitions as a method of selecting the best town plans. It was believed that scientific research and continuous evaluation were inevitable requirements for planning metropolitan cities and this could be better achieved by standing bureaus directly attached to the Ministry. The Istanbul Metropolitan Planning Bureau and the Ankara Metropolitan Area Planning Bureau (AMAPB) started collecting preliminary data in 1967 and 1969 respectively. The mission of AMAPB was to design a comprehensive plan for the year 1990. The maximum target population was 3.6 million.

With the AMAPB there emerged three separate and more or less independent authorities dealing with the plan. The Municipality was responsible for building infrastructure, issuing construction and dwelling permits or making amendments to the master plan. The Urbanisation Directorate of Ankara supervised the implementation of the plan while the Metropolitan Planning Bureau proposed long term goals and the general direction of urban development. This organisation, resembling a three-headed monster pulling its body to pieces in different directions, often caused conflicts in decision-making. But this was a desirable situation from the point of view of different interest groups in the city. If the demands of one group were turned down by one authority, chances were that it would be accepted by another. For example, at a time when the AMAPB decided to freeze densities within the city due to aggravating pollution and health hazards, the mayor was promising his electors, during an election campaign, that each apartment house would be allowed to add on another storey. Such a permit would naturally increase the rent gained by property owners.

The AMAPB has managed to produce a metropolitan plan at a scale of 1:50,000 after a period of almost 10 years.(19) More detailed plans at 1:5000 scale are presently being prepared in the Bureau. Since these plans are not yet officially approved, the former plan keeps its validity with numerous amendments and addendi. There are local master plans for areas lying beyond the boundaries of the old plan.

In fact, the Ankara experience tends to call into question the relevance of the physical master planning approach. Planning personnel were insufficient to prepare detailed plans at a pace commensurate with development, and in any case the approach was too rigid, cumbersome and static to cope with the dynamic growth and change taking place. Master plans, at whatever scale, present a static land use map of the city at some future point in time, but fail to address the "strategic" nature of development in space as well as the critical dimension of time. In the case of Ankara, the physical planning approach used failed to address the problems of low income residential development and also failed to keep pace with the overall rate of city growth. In addition, the programming and budgeting procedures for specific sectoral projects were pursued separately from the preparation of physical plans.

Two significant issues which have posed urgent planning problems in the seventies need mention here. One is increasing private car ownership, the other air pollution.

Before the seventies car ownership was not a widespread phenomenon. At most, traffic congestion was observed at peak hours in the city centre and there was a negligible amount of air pollution originating from exhaust fumes. The number of cars rising exponentially within the present decade(20) not only caused greater congestion and pollution, but introduced a new settlement pattern directly related to metropolitan planning: suburbanisation.

Before the seventies spatial proximity to the city centre was still the principle criterion in choice of residential location. The result was a highly dense and compact urban form. With increasing spatial mobility there has been a great demand for land outside the urban area. Most of the demand has come from housing cooperatives formed by middle class groups. The upper middle class has shown a desire to own one or two-storey garden homes. These trends have posed completely new planning issues. First of all, almost all suburban development has started to take place beyond the areas covered by the approved plan, and the new plan has already fallen behind the suburbanisation movement.

The AMAPB has suggested a minimum development area requirement (15 hectares) with the hope that in planning these new residential neighbourhoods the necessary public areas will be reserved and the social services will be fully provided. Thus the lack of a comprehensive plan has been temporarily covered by a control on such private, neighbourhood development plans.

The suburbanisation trend is not expected to aggravate the second urgent urban problem, air pollution. But the present pollution level is so high and the expectation of decreasing city densities is so low that even Leibnitz would not have left the solution to the course of events. Indeed in the seventies Ankara took its place among the five most polluted cities in the world. This pollution was different from its prototypes in the industrialised countries, where the principle pollutant was industry. It originated from domestic heating, and thus became an acute problem in winter months only. Jansen's plan had placed the town in a bowl-shaped topographic formation surrounded by hills on the east. The lack of wind and the existence of an inversion-effect were the factors which gave the town a high pollution potential. When the population was only 300,000, smoke could disperse readily. As the density was increased to accommodate one million people in the same area, this potential turned into a serious hazard. No plan was earnestly undertaken to counteract a danger that was so certain to arise; instead of heating the city from a few central terminals, about 300,000 individual chimneys were allowed to emit smoke simultaneously. This increased the difficulties of control. The political pressure to raise densities and thus to increase individual benefit at one time resulted in an exponential rise in social costs for which the whole town had to pay and payment was in years of human life.

EVALUATION

The case study of Anakara covers a period of over 50 years. This introduces obvious evaluation difficulties; in fact, it becomes largely irrelevant to evaluate an historic experiment with criteria carrying value judgements pertaining to recent planning practice. In a period of over half a century, planning and decision-making styles have changed. Therefore, it would be more meaningful to measure the success of each planning experiment under the particular conditions and criteria of each given period. We have no evidence that recent criteria had sufficient relevancy for historic periods. On the other hand, recent criteria - whether those mentioned by the editors or others - do take on increasing relevancy when they are applied to the more current phases of planning and development in Ankara, that is to the periods since 1954.

In Turkish planning practice today the most prestigious institution is the State Planning Organisation. The basic criterion used by this organisation in distributing the national resources is short-run economic efficiency. There are no models or criteria for evaluating long term efficiencies due to structural changes in the economy. In such a planning environment it would be impossible to make a decision such as the relocation of the capital or the creation of a new city. In retrospect it can be said that the Ankara decision has had a facilitating role in the solution of spatial population distribution problems in Turkey. In truth, the success of the Ankara experiment lies more in the solution of spatial planning issues at the national rather than the intra-urban scale. Therefore separate evaluations are required for these different levels of planning.

The leaders of the Republic have no doubt been effective in changing the semi-colonial type of settlement pattern. This pattern, distinguished by the concentration of foreign affiliated urban activities in and around a few port towns, was transformed into a more evenly distributed urban population pattern, reflecting a more integrated national market. The urban population distribution in Turkey today closely approximates the rank-size rule, a rare circumstance among under-developed countries (see Fig. 4.1). This argument can be supported by a comparison with the population distribution in Egypt. During the past 50 years the total population of Turkey and Egypt have been more or less equal. At the turn of the century Istanbul and Cairo were at equal population levels. But in the following years the two cities have experienced completely different growth trends; Cairo has reached a population of 10 million while Istanbul has not even reached the 4 million mark. In the dissolution of the primate distribution pattern in Turkey, Ankara has undoubtedly played a decisive role. The median point of the national population distribution has moved 200 km to locate itself at Ankara. In other words, Ankara has become the minimum-transport-cost point of industry satisfying the total national market. Augmentation of the previous primate distribution pattern would have no doubt aggravated the urban-planning problems in Turkey.

Ankara can also be evaluated as a growth pole. Has it been sufficiently effective in developing its immediate region as the growth pole theory suggests? Today there are two new towns, surviving on military and industrial activities within a distance of 90 km of Ankara. Other settlements around Ankara, mostly former Ottoman cities, have experienced population decline due to the dominant effect of the new capital. Therefore Ankara cannot be considered as a classical example of a growth pole stimulating development in its immediate hinterland.

It is also possible to evaluate the degree to which Ankara's economy has acquired the desired internal dynamics(24) of self-sustaining growth. Most new towns in the world suffer from imbalances in social structure such as in the distributions of age, sex and employment. Employment opportunities implanted through exogeneous decisions may not create the desired multiplier effect. Therefore the new town often lacks the impetus to grow into a self-sustaining natural settlement. In terms of this criterion the Ankara experiment can be considered a success. Having originally started as the centre of national governmental functions with a high percentage of civil servants, it has also become an important business centre. Apart from these organised sectors there are widespread marginal sector activities in the city. In terms of the concentration ratios of different employment sectors, Ankara follows Istanbul. With an urban population of 2 million, a balanced sex ratio and varied activities, Ankara has fulfilled the threshold requirements for a settlement possessing internal dynamics of growth. In that sense it can no longer be distinguished as a new town different from older cities in Turkey.

As to the evaluation of intra-urban planning efforts, this can be best be done by considering changing styles of planning in time. Following a period of early trial and error, the planning style in the thirties can be identified as paternalistic. This style had emerged as a necessity under the particular conditions of the period. The leaders of the Republic were aspiring to create a new style of life, that of the national bourgeoisie, and urban planning was conceived as a tool for its materialisation. A plan brought forward by an administration that asserted to lead a nation was bound to be paternalistic. Such an attitude did not contradict the German urban planning practice of the era. In Jansen's view the guide to building a successful city lay in the planner's supreme authority.

Since 1950 this paternalistic view has changed and taken on a completely different character. Today's style of planning has reduced the authority of the planners to a minimum. Planning has more or less been reduced to an activity whereby all fait accomplis are given a legal status. The decision makers under such circumstances are land speculators, gecekondu builders and other pressure groups in society, rather than planners or administrators. Of course, such a transformation is not exclusive to urban planning; it has a direct relationship with the changing political structure of the country. The development of the democratic, parliamentary political structure since 1950 has exposed the governmental system to the influence of pressure groups; urban planning has been no exception to this trend. In a sense, the paternalistic planning of the thirties has turned into a total denial of planning in the seventies.

It is astounding that, in spite of the changes in the planning environment, the attitude of the planners has remained unaltered: They are still paternalistic. The participation of different users in the decision making process is not considered. The Ankara experience does not score well in terms of the editors' criteria of participation, power and responsibility. This brings to mind the following question: How is the paternalistic attitude of the planners to be reconciled with the actual state of affairs in the urban arena? There are numerous complex institutional mechanisms that have undertaken the reconciliary role. As a result of such mechanisms the gap between planning and implementation process is continuously growing. While metropolitan planning bureaus are encouraged to make general decisions on large scale maps, the actual development of new urban areas within the metropolitan region takes place through small-scale local plans. Often the approval of the local plans precedes legalization of the metropolitan plans. With such mechanisms planning itself becomes the denial of planning.

With the emerging new style of planning in Ankara, the investment priorities in the country have also changed. In the early years of the Republic, top priority was given to the creation of a national bourgeoisie life style; hence the success of Ankara as a new town was identified with the triumph of the new regime. Ankara thus continued to utilise a large share of the national resources until 1950. Under one-party rule Ankara became a unique settlement somewhat alienated from the rest of the country. By the seventies the new balance of political power within the country began to deny this privilege to Ankara. It was not the capital city alone that was undergoing a rapid rate of growth. There were other large cities that required urban investment. Furthermore, a new national objective had appeared on the political agenda: industrialisation. According to some economists increasing urban social investment meant decreasing economic efficiency. The resources of the country were not sufficient to meet urban investment requirements and satisfy the industrial growth targets simultaneously.

The shortage of urban investment resulted in a dual social structure in urban areas. The modern section of the cities absorbed most of the investment while the gecekondu areas received a small share. Planning laws merely legalised this dual structure. Although equity is a criterion stressed by the editors in Part One and a favourite campaign slogan of all politicians, escape from the dilemmas of investment allocation could only be achieved through inequality, under the selected mode of development. Hence, with regard to several other criteria mentioned in Part One, such as employment and productivity and distribution of assets and services, which stress that urban development should favour the poor, the

Ankara experience is not positive. The aforementioned style of planning served certain other mechanisms in the system. The in-migrating low income groups were allowed to remain in the city as members of the weakly organised marginal sector, with little power to demand their share of the national resources and without creating notable social stress. They formed their own living environment, the gecekondus.

The Ankara experiment makes at least one fact clear with regard to urban planning in the developing capitalist countries. Concentration of all efforts and resources into one city may create an orderly urban environment, but such an achievement is often short-lived. It is not possible to bring a solution to urban problems without tackling the basic and larger development issues of the country.

NOTES

(1) Tuğrul Akcura, (1960), "Ankara: ses Fonctions Urbaines" and "Les Fonctions d'Ankara sous la Republique," <u>La Vie Urbane</u>. January-March, pp. 35-64; April-June.

(2) See Avram Galanti (1950) and Halit Ongan (1974).

(3) See, for example, John Friedmann (1973).

(4) Rusen Keleș (1971).

(5) An Ottoman local authority of the late nineteenth century responsible for keeping municipal order, taking sanitary and aesthetic measures in the capital city, the <u>șehremaneti</u> is appointed by the central government.

(6) See Fehmi Yavuz (1952).

(7) U.S.-based Ulen Company made various proposals to the leaders. (See <u>U.S. Secretary of State Dept</u>. Document Index no. 1101).

(8) See Ilhan Tekeli and Ilber Ortayli (1978), p. 285.

(9) Mustafa Kemal himself, in the years 1924-5, acted and dressed in a manner that would set the personality image of the "national bourgeoisie". As a pioneer Turkish entrepreneur, he established the largest private bank of the country (Is Bankasi). A year later, in 1925, he set up his Atatürk Forest Farm (<u>Orman Çiftliği</u>) on 2000 hectares of land. This was a multi-purpose venture. Kemal wished to demonstrate that farming <u>is</u> possible in mid-Anatolia contrary to the opinion of those who claimed that this steppe-land was good for nothing. A second purpose was to provide the city with a sizeable green area.

(10) Housing credits were to be organised by a central finance institution, the Real Estate and Orphans Bank (Emlak ve Eytam Bankası). The production and distribution of gas and electricity was transferred from the Municipality to the German Didier Company. The provision of drinking water was taken over by the Ministry of Public Works.

(11) Land belonging to the Municipality, the Treasury and the pious foundations.

(12) Fehmi Yavuz (1952), p. 25.

(13) A gecekondu is usually a single-storey, one or two-room house built overnight on public or private property without a planning permit. A similar form of the gecekondu is the Latin American barrio.

(14) Many political scientists writing on the Middle East use the word "etatism" instead of the more general term "statism".

(15) See Mehmet Uğur (1954).

(16) Bericht Der Baukomission Betrefens Des Neueu Bauplans Fur die Stadt Ankara (1954).

(17) Yapsatcı organises the capital collection process as well as marketing the finished flats. His financial power enables him to build not more than two or three buildings simultaneously.

(18) See T. Okyay, O. Altaban and V. Yazar (1975).

(19) Ankara Metropolitan Alan Nazim Plan Bürosu (1977).

(20) The opening of three car assembly plants in Turkey is no doubt responsible for this change, since in previous years customs regulations severely limited the importation of cars.

REFERENCES

Ankara Metropolitan Alan Nazım Plan Burosu (1977) Ankara Nazım Plan Şemasi Raporu, 1970-1990. Ankara.

Bericht Der Bankomission Betrefens Des Neuen Bauplans Für die Stadt Ankara (1954).

Friedmann, John (1973) Urbanization, Planning and National Development. Beverley Hills: Sage Publications.

Galanti, Avram (1950) Ankara Tarihi. Istanbul: Birinci Kısım and Ikıncr Kısım.

Keles, Rusen (1971) Eski Ankarada Bir Sehir Tipolojisi. Ankara: Siyasal Bilgiler Fakultesi.

Okyay, T., Altaban, O. and Yazar, V. (1975) "Housing and Environments Standards as a Product of the Free Market Mechanism; an Example: Ankara", M.E.T.U. Journal of the Faculty of Achitecture. 2:1.

Ongan, Halit (1974) Ankara'nin Iki Numaralı Seriye Sicili. Ankara: Türk Tarih Kurumu.

Rivkin, M.D. (1965) Area Development for National Growth: The Turkish Precedent. New York: Praeger.

Tekeli, İlhan and İlber Ortayli (1978) Türkiyede Belediyeciliğin Evrimi. Ankara: Türk Idareciler Dernegi.

Uğur, Mehmet (1954) "Yeni Mahallenin Kuruluşă ve Ucuz Mesken Politikası", Ankara Belediye Dergisi, Year 3, No. 10.

Yavuz, Fehmi (1952) Ankara'nin İmar ve Şehirciliğimiz. Ankara: Siyasal Bilgiler Fakultesi Yayınları.

5

Durgapur: Case Study of an Indian New Town

K.C. Sivaramakrishnan

THE ORIGINS OF INDIA'S NEW TOWNS

The railway towns of British India can be regarded as the beginning of India's new towns. In some cases they were only a collection of employees' quarters and station buildings, but in many parts of the country these settlements formed the nuclei of urbanisation. One may wish otherwise, but the form and substance of many post-independent new towns are much the same as the railway towns built several decades earlier.

The partition of the country, followed by the influx of refugees and their resettlement, added a few new towns in post-independent India. Faridabad near Delhi, Nilokheri in Punjab, Gandhidham in Gujerat and Asokenagar in West Bengal are some of these refugee resettlement towns. There were also a dozen or so "model towns", mainly in the Punjab area, that were built in the forties as planned extensions to existing cities. Most of these were suburbs which were eventually incorporated into the main city and in that sense cannot be regarded as new towns of significance. In addition, Chandigarh in Punjab, Bhubaneswar in Orissa and Gandhinagar in Gujerat are the capital cities built after independence.

However, new towns, as a major Indian urban phenomenon, commenced with the construction of several industrial townships from the late 1950s. It was part of the National Plan strategy to locate new industries away from large cities. The Third Five Year Plan, in particular, emphasized the preference for backward areas in the location of public sector projects. It was felt that the lack of facilities in such places could be resolved. There was also a latent hope that the effects of such large projects would trickle down to the surrounding areas. This was the general background in which over a hundred new towns were developed in the country after independence.

Several points emerge from a preliminary assessment of India's new towns. One is that the objectives for their creation have not been very clear. In most cases the building of a particular industry has been taken to be the main objective and the settlement itself has been treated as an adjunct. Where some spatial goals were indicated these appear to have emerged from the personal views of the officials in charge of building the plant or township at the time. Density, house types and location of community facilities were often determined by the same small group. Neither the physical nor the socio-economic issues of raising and nurturing a town seem to have been recognised.

The poor comprehension of the social issues in an urban community have been further complicated by the rapid growth of the new towns and the inability to cope with the heterogeneity brought in by migration from different parts of the country. The influence of the industry continues to be dominant, and the Indian new town is often described as an "employee town" rather than a "citizen town". These are some of the issues examined in this paper with reference to Durgapur, a major new town.

DURGAPUR

Located 150 km north-west of Calcutta on the Calcutta-Delhi rail and road corridor, Durgapur is one of the largest concentrations of heavy industry to be set up anew in the country. With a population over 300,000, it is also a major urban centre in Eastern India (Fig. 5.1).

Durgapur emerged when the plans for the Damodar Valley region took shape. The taming of the Damodar River and its tributaries and the creation of large capacities of thermal power gave a generous stimulus to the region. In 1955 it was chosen as the location for the third steel plant in the public sector which was to be built on a turn-key basis by a consortium of British firms. The availability of land close to coal and the proximity to Calcutta as a port and a major point of consumption for the plant's products were the reasons which prompted the decision. In October 1956 construction on the steel plant commenced.

By then, some other major investment decisions had been taken for Durgapur. One was to locate the Damodar Valley Corporation's thermal power plant at this site. Another was a coal based industrial complex comprising a thermal power plant, a coke oven plant to supply the much needed metallurgical coke for Bengal's engineering industry, a chemicals

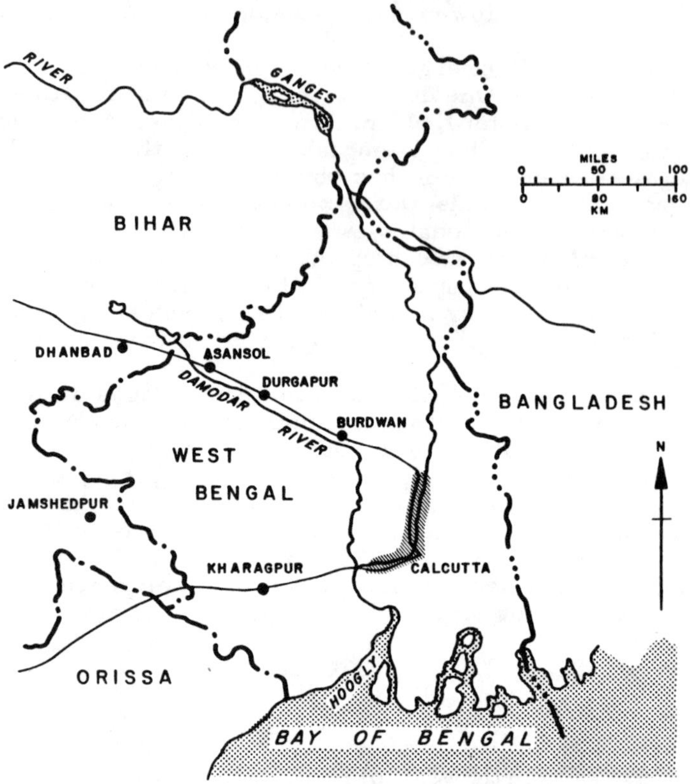

Fig. 5.1. Location of Durgapur within Eastern India.

plant to utilise the by-products from the coke oven and a gas-grid that would feed ½-million cubic metres of gas to Calcutta. By 1959 decisions had also been taken to locate three other large plants, one for special steel, the second for manufacturing coal mining machinery and the third to produce ophthalmic glass. Other engineering units to produce boilers, pressure vessels, automobile wheels, electrical wire, heavy castings, etc., followed. By 1961 nearly fifty large, medium and small industries had made Durgapur their home. The Central Mechanical Engineering Research Institute, a Regional Engineering College, and an Industrial Training Institute were added soon after as major supporting facilities for the area.

However, despite an encouraging beginning, the dream of an integrated industrial city did not materialise. An important reason for this was the decision of the larger industries to build separate townships for each. The biggest was the steel plant township covering some 30 square km but built sparsely. Other companies followed suit and set up their own townships of varying sizes and standards, all adjoining each other but not providing linkages in utilities or facilities; not even a road connecting them.

The Durgapur Development Authority, formed as a statutory body in 1958 to ensure the planned and coordinated development of the complex, did not regard these disparate developments as serious. On the contrary, it confirmed the trend by deciding to set up another township of its own to provide residential support to medium and small industries. Thus, by 1961, less than 5 years from its beginning, Durgapur became a sprawling mixture of factories and housing to the north and south of a 15 km stretch of the Grand Trunk Road. In the next 10 years the gaps between the townships began to fill; but slowly and always with shacks and slums. Employment rose until 1966 to some 34,000 factory jobs but declined thereafter. People, however, continued to come. The 1971 census indicated the area's population as 206,000. By then some attempts had been made to bring the townships together through a common plan. Work began on a major city centre to serve as the "downtown" for the area. But industry has not been expanding and the funds for city building have been scant. Durgapur has remained, as so aptly described, a collection of townships in search of a city (Fig. 5.2).

The Planning Concepts

Like Durgapur, most other industrial new towns failed to reach their potential. The reasons for this are to be sought in the premises or concepts behind their creation. Two appear to stand out: one is self-containment and the other, particularly for industrial townships, is the image of a model employer. For all its widespread use in town plans, self-containment is a concept vaguely defined and rarely understood. Since many new town locations were on greenfield sites and quite distant from existing towns, the industry's management felt self-containment was an essential prerequisite in the plans for the new town. However, commuting could not be avoided while new town residents always found a gap in facilities that could be satisfied only in some other town. Self-containment and the exclusiveness it implies can be traced back to the colonial traditions of the country. Cantonments and railway towns have had an important influence on layout planning. Townscape, in British India and even now, is viewed mainly in three segments, the Civil Lines or the Cantonment, with detached bungalows, wide roads, rows of trees with their trunks whitewashed, with law courts and some government offices nearby, is the first or the premier segment. The Bazaar, with its crooked lanes and by-lanes and the honky-tonk of assorted vehicles, is the second. The third segment

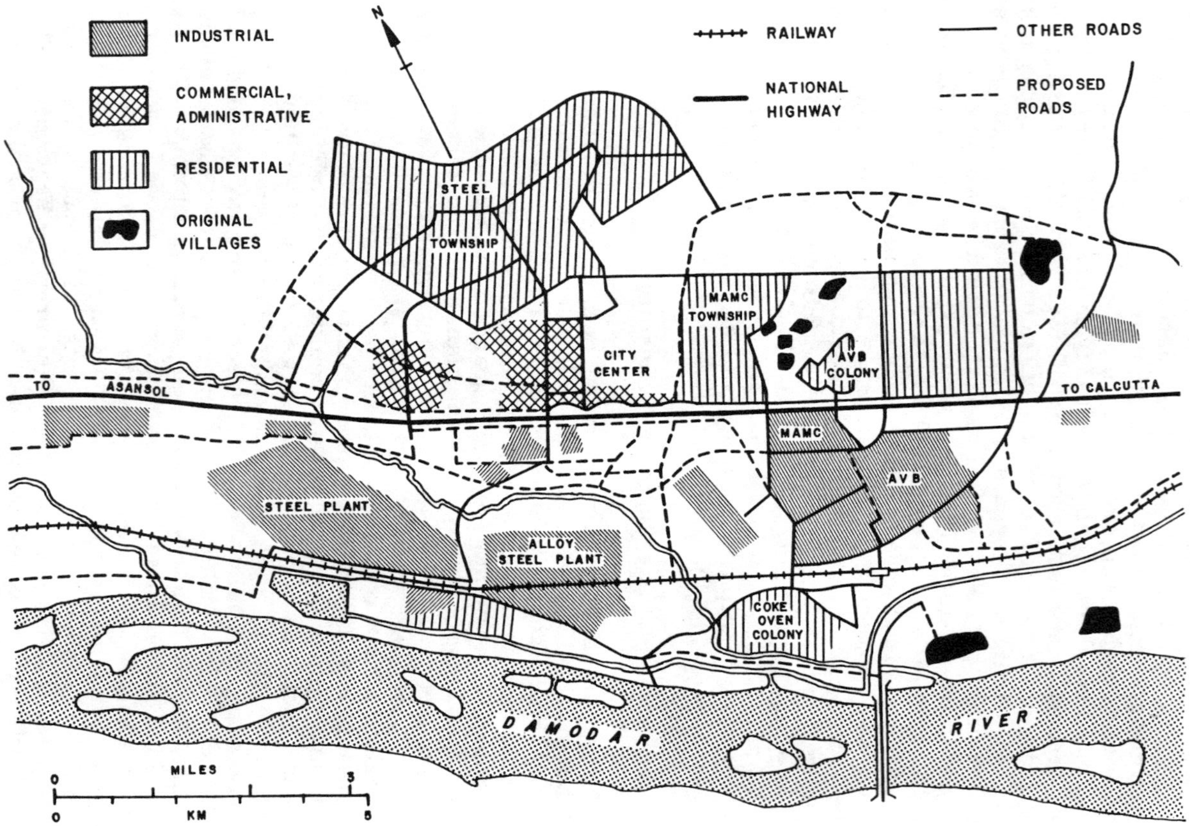

Fig. 5.2. Durgapur: General Land Uses.

is the native quarter, a congested motley of houses and hovels, narrow winding streets, street taps and open drains. The numerous railway colonies built in the country repeated this pattern. Even latter day extensions to some of the cities in the 1920s and 1930s, the so-called model towns, as in Punjab or in the south, were closer to this segregated style of planning.

There was another strong influence, a constant overtone, that characterised the planning and building of these new towns. This was the concept of a model employer, valid especially for the public sector. Given the liberal and socialistic traditions of the leadership that guided India's struggle for independence, the public sector was regarded not only as the dominant segment of industry, but also the catalyst to achieve socio-economic change. To be an ideal employer was thus a cardinal point in their creation. The colonial elitist background in physical planning, interacting with idealism in the sphere of labour welfare and amenities, tended to cause several distortions.

Planning Standards and Costs

In determining the norms and standards for the use of land, for housing, for utilities and for the provision of community facilities, the image of the model employer has been the most important determining factor. The capital costs involved have been quite high. Inevitably the running charges have risen and these are a major item of deficit for the industrial managements. In many cases, it is also seen that the technology adopted has not been appropriate.

In Durgapur about 48 percent of the land is assigned to residential use while circulation and open space take 20 percent and 14 percent respectively. Extravagant use of land, especially in the initial stage when land acquisition did not seem too difficult or expensive, has resulted in very low densities. The density has been around five to twelve dwellings or even less per hectare in Durgapur. Capital costs on services such as water supply, drainage, sewerage and roads came to about $184 *per capita* (1962 prices).

If the cost of residential and other buildings for community facilities are included, *per capita* costs came to $490 (Ved Prakash). This is more than twice as high as the *per capita* cost for suburban developments that have been built in Indian metropolitan cities. Along with these high capital costs, *per capita* running costs have also been very high. According to 1971-1972 figures, *per capita* annual expenditure on maintenance of the townships, excluding expenditure on buildings and also items like education and health, is $10 in Durgapur steel town compared to $7.50 in a reasonably well-maintained city like Bombay. It is not so much the quality or scale of service that has determined the high cost as the wage component. Since wage levels are usually very high in the steel industry, the wages of persons engaged in the township activities also tend to be higher than those engaged for identical work in other cities. Subsequent wage agreements have tended to increase these costs further.

Land and Shelter

Although the townships in all cases had the advantage of publicly owned land, policies with regard to land ownership and utilization of land for shelter have not been clear. Initially the managements had the desire to provide housing to most of their employees. In fact, this was to be an important component of the so-called self-contained township. There was also the feeling, though not openly expressed, that provision of housing within the industry's own township would lead to better industrial relations and, hopefully, better control of the work force. In effect, however, complete provision of housing by the companies has not materialised due to the increasing cost of housing and its increasing proportion to the total township costs.

Slums and Marginal Settlements

As mentioned earlier, the industry itself has been taken as the dominant force in the planning of the townships. But in terms of employment, tertiary sector activities have accounted for an increasing share of total employment in the towns. In 1961, out of 26,000 workers in Durgapur, about 17 percent were in the tertiary sector and 59 percent in manufacturing. By 1971 percentages had changed to 31 and 57 percent respectively. Nevertheless, in the context of the policies discussed earlier, persons engaged in tertiary activities were regarded as "outsiders" by the township management and they had to fend for themselves for residence and working space. Those industrial employees who were not fortunate to be housed in the company's quarters were also in a similar position. The only accommodation they could find was either in the villages, which were pockets in the township area left out of acquisition or located at the periphery, or in the huts of paper and board, tin or straw which grew on the townships' fringes.

The village pockets were the only "neutral cushion", so to say, to absorb the migrant industrial or other workers who rapidly lost their earlier identity and character. Limited facilities like the village pond or well that existed before were quickly overrun by increasing population. Demand for rented accommodation prompted new construction but usually in a haphazard way. Improvements like electricity, drainage, paved roads, etc., were not extended to these villages as they were outside the township. Still, people denied of space in the township proper continued to move into these villages which became, in the process, the poor quality components of the new town's growth. This is particularly evident in Durgapur where the villages, which accounted for 75 percent of the Notified Area's population of 41,700 in 1961, degenerated into slums 10 years later.

Other new towns like Bhilai, Rourkela and Bokharo have had similar problems with 20 to 30 percent of the people living in slums. The main reason for this phenomenon in so-called planned new towns appears to be the failure to understand the dynamics of urbanisation and the policies needed with regard to the villages in the designated town area. It was apparent that, in due course, the character of these villages would change substantially. It was also clear that, if minimum facilities such as water and drainage were not extended to these villages, their environment would rapidly deteriorate. Yet, while preparing the plans for developing the township, these villages were excluded as pockets. Lack of expertise does not seem to be the reason, since some techniques for dealing with such villages had been devised by the industrial managements themselves in other circumstances. In the case of villages acquired while setting up the plants or the townships, elaborate arrangements were made for rehabilitation of the displaced families. Fresh layout plans were made, plots were earmarked and basic facilities such as water supply, roads, lighting, etc., were also extended to the rehabilitation sites. Although the state governments participated in such rehabilitation arrangements, undeniably the initiative and much of the expertise came from the project authorities. Gopalmath, in Durgapur, is a good example where over 1200 families, shifted from several villages at the steel plant site, were brought together in one location. A system of roads, water supply and electricity was extended to the area. Primary and secondary schools and a health centre were constructed under the state government programmes with assistance from the steel projects. Today Gopalmath, with a population of 8000, is regarded as one of the more homogeneous and reasonably serviced components of Durgapur. Of course, the advantage of designing a new layout was there in Gopalmath, but the concept of providing services and amenities to villages, thereby enhancing their livability, could have been followed in the case of existing villages as well, although these were not covered under acquisition. The financial outlay would not have been much.

One reason why this has not happened in the case of existing villages appears to be the lack of a decision as to who should pay for these services and whose responsibility it would be to look after their maintenance. Another may be the idea that these villages were outsiders, messy and disorganised, and could either be safely cold-shouldered, or left for redevelopment at a later date.

Shopping

In the design for shopping at the neighbourhood and sector(1) levels, the new town plans have focused more on the architectural than the functional aspect. The rents for the built-up shops have been quite high and the locations unattractive. The number of shops built in a sector market have also been somewhat inadequate. In almost all cases, the design has been somewhat inflexible and sufficient regard was not given to the native characteristics of shopping. In most Indian cities daily supplies such as vegetables, eggs, etc., are sold by hawkers and petty stall keepers who operate on very low overheads and cannot afford built-up shops. It is an activity of low margins sustained by low overheads. Invariably, they have been "priced out" of the high quality sector market, but the need for this trading persisted; hence, instead of quality shops, the activity moved into wayside shacks and "lean-to" sheds put up in the vicinity of the quality market. Depending on the township managements' mood and disposition, these "unauthorised commercial encroachments", as they are called, have stayed on or have been pulled down, only to be re-erected from time to time.

In Durgapur the sector markets in the township have never been important at the city level. The main trading centre is Bhiringi-Benachity, a poorly built commercial strip of about 900 shops which, according to a 1966 survey, accounted for 60 percent of the total sale of groceries, cloth and apparel and 80 percent of all other retail sales. The clustering of shops and its size have been Benachity's manifest advantages. It is also a classical illustration of locational advantage being exploited within a short time span. Situated along an old village road which also marked the shortest distance between the steel plant and the township, Benachity initially resisted all attempts at land acquisition in the area. Eventually sizeable parts of the area were acquired. For no particular reason it was decided to settle in this acquired land many persons displaced by land acquisition for the steel plant. Of course leases for these rehabilitation plots were granted on the strict understanding that they would be used for residence only, but the location, enhanced by the siting of a sector market in the steel township close to its northern tip, clearly pointed up Benachity's commercial potential. Within less than 4 years, or by 1961, about 600 establishments were developed.

Most of the so-called residential rehabilitation plots were converted into non-residential use. Faced with such a massive flouting of the lease conditions, the local administration could do little. In 1970 the Durgapur Development Authority began construction of a city centre in a more central locaton for all of Durgapur. With the sub-divisional courts and other government offices, the city centre is now emerging as an important focus. But it is doubtful whether it will ever be able to wrest from Benachity the premier commercial role.

Transportation

In the preparation of the township plans, transportation was viewed mainly in terms of circulation space rather than modes of transport. It was generally assumed that the bus and the motor car would be the principal means of transport and this is reflected in the very large rights of way, the high standards of construction and several types of roads provided in the town plan. The sight of a 30-40 metre wide road brilliantly lit, going nowhere in particular and bereft of all traffic, is a familiar feature of Durgapur and other Indian new towns. But the attention given to circulation space was not matched by a comprehension of activity locations and traffic potential. In Durgapur, the main centre of activity, the steel plant, is at a distance of more than 15 km from the township. The steel plant's management maintains a large subsidised bus fleet, but it serves mainly the factory-residence movement. Facilities for transport within and between the townships are severely limited because of vast and "non-paying" distances. Poor transport has seriously affected communication between people and is considered a major cause for Durgapur not emerging as a community.

Community Services

The concept of "model employer" has been more pronounced in this regard. Like other industrial townships the managements in Durgapur provide a variety of services, such as subsidised transport, medical care, education, recreation, cultural facilities, etc., apart from the usual range of statutory welfare activities in the plant. Here at least there is not much distinction between public and private sector managements. The welfare and model employer approaches were, in fact, evolved in Jamshedpur where the range of services, even today, is much wider. But the cost of providing these services has been quite high. During 1974-1975 the expenditure incurred on these welfare services amounted to nearly $75 million for the Durgapur steel project. Since the income derived from the delivery of these services is very little (school fees, hospital fees, etc.), the expenditure is mainly a subsidy. The welfare activities comprise a wide range such as primary and secondary education, medical care, maternity child welfare and family planning, social and cultural activities, transport, dairy, etc.

In the administration of such a wide range of services, the managements have had to set up an elaborate machinery. The set up is usually divided between the factory and the township managements. Services such as transport, subsidised canteen, amenities for sports, etc., would be looked after by the factory, whereas services such as health and education are dealt with by the township. The managements have had to assemble quite a number of senior officers to provide these services. In addition, they also maintain fairly large units for administering educational facilities. Each have a full-time education officer supported by a number of deputies and assistants. The Durgapur steel plant management, for instance, has to deal with 865 teachers and more than 22,000 children.

MANAGEMENT ISSUES

Of the hundred odd new towns built in India, no more than six are municipal entities. The rest are an assortment of town communities, municipal boards, town panchayats, notified area committees and so on. Of course, management forms do not convey any inherent worth and the process of governance and its effectiveness merit more attention. Being new and therefore free from the traditional patterns of government, the new towns could have experimented with new forms and reformed existing ones. However, this has not happened. Institutions set up for management of new towns appear to be ad-hoc intrusions into the scene rather than conscious efforts towards providing a viable administrative structure.

In India the responsibility for creating and supervising local government institutions rests with the state governments. Initially they did not have a very clear idea about the issues involved in major industrial projects or their townships. Steel plants, in particular, were considered to be highly prestigious developments to have in a state and whatever was sought for such projects was given (e.g. land). Because of their size and complexity, the state governments did not become involved in the planning or development of the project townships. Their concern, if any, was limited to rehabilitation of displaced persons and later to recruitment of local people, personnel management, law and order, etc. Since a number of industries and townships were to be developed side by side, the need for an overall plan framework and coordination was obvious. The

Durgapur Development Authority was set up by a special statute in 1958 to provide for such planning and coordination. However, the Authority, which included the representatives of industries, resolved at one of its early meetings that industrial management could be depended upon to observe correct planning principles and, in so far as their townships were concerned, the planning jurisdiction of the Authority need not apply.

Much later, when proposals for establishing some machinery for levy of taxes and provision of services were mooted, the response varied from town to town. The attitude of the industrial managements, especially those of the large steel plants, was that their townships were well provided with services at much higher levels than average; that an adequate organisation existed in the town administration office of the plant for upkeep; that the services were being treated, for the most part, as amenities to labour; that establishing a Notified Area Committee or municipality would therefore be superfluous for the townships; and that, therefore, the company townships should either be kept out of the jurisdiction of any such NAC or municipal body, or the townships should be created as separate NAC's with the steel plant officials as chairmen and members. In Bhilai, Rourkela and Bokaro the plea was heeded and the townships remained as before.

In Durgapur the West Bengal government took a hard line. A Notified Area Authority was set up accordingly for all of Durgapur and the different plants and the townships were included within its limits as holdings. For instance, the steel plant was one holding and the township was another. All the company holdings were to pay the NAA the holding rate assessed on its property value. Other rates for water, conservancy, lighting, etc., were not payable as these services were already being provided in the townships. A pattern thus emerged in which the company towns were included in a municipal structure as ratepayers. Out of the DNAA's annual income of approximately $450,000, about $250,000 are derived as holding rates from the company holdings, half the amount coming from the steel plant and its township. In 1968 the chief executive of the Development Authority was made the chairman of the NAA as well, to ensure better coordination between the two. The general division of work between the two bodies envisage planning, development control and capital works in the DDA's purview, while operation and maintenance, municipal rates and other regulatory functions are performed in the DNAA.

While the two bodies have been able to sustain modest programmes for building and operating infrastructure, mainly in the areas outside the township, both continue to be restrictive in composition and cannot be regarded as participative platforms for the city's upkeep and thinking about the future.

Community involvement, whether in civic or social affairs, continues to be scant. A comparative study of voluntary organisations in two new towns, Durgapur and Jamshedpur, indicates that associations for cultural activities, such as sports, music and drama, predominate. Men are the principal participants, and employment ties tend to be the main determinant for association membership. Activities for women and children are limited. Identity with the town as opposed to the workplace does not seem strong and militancy for securing more facilities or better conditions is hardly present. One can say that the policy of a "model employer" has been successful to the extent that it has engendered a passive and satisfied labour force, but the system has not encouraged the development of indigenous institutions for improved local management.

The concept of a self-contained company town, poor appreciation of the problems of urban governments, reluctance to accept local self-government as a goal, absence of a strong motivation to levy taxes since funds for maintenance of the town are met by the industries, and the generally poor public awareness or response for participative management of the towns appear to be major reasons for the weakness of authorities in industrial townships.

EVALUATION

Despite the high investment, technology and skills which have gone into the creation of Durgapur as a major complex of heavy industries, its impact on the region has been limited. It may be pertinent to ask what kinds of impact were expected. As in the case of other industrial new towns, no regional analysis preceded Durgapur's planning, although there was the usual expectation that the benefits of the investment and industrial development would somehow trickle down to the surrounding region. In effect some of this did happen and many parts in the region have witnessed considerable change. Ranigunge, traditionally the wholesale commercial centre for the region, expanded its business to serve Durgapur 20 km away. The administrative functions were added on to Asansol, the sub-district's headquarters, 35 km away. Immediately west of Durgapur, one of Asia's largest railway marshalling yards was developed at Ondal. To the east, a group of three adjoining villages, Panagarh, Debipur and Kanksa, attracted several service industries, especially auto repairs; and doubled its population from about 7400 in 1951 to 15,000 in 1971. However, to the south across the Damodar River, the Banbura District has maintained its predominantly rural character.

It may be argued that these changes could have been anticipated, planned for and integrated with Durgapur's development. The belated start that the Durgapur Development Authority made in spatial planning did commence with an exercise for the region. In 1963 the Indian Institute of Technology, Kharagpur came up with the outline of a regional plan for an area of about 3,100 square km around Durgapur, with an existing population of 700,000. Envisaging Durgapur at the centre of a regional system, the plan identified the types of industries and economic activities to be developed and what the linkages should be. But the DDA had no mandate for the region which encompassed three revenue districts. Even within the Durgapur urban area its efforts towards spatial planning did not go far. Little, therefore, came out of the IIT exercise.

At the intra-urban scale where, in view of tighter administrative control, a critical evaluation of Durgapur is more justified, it would appear that this major new town has not been very successful in "matching actions with resources", as the editors have put it in Chapter 2. With regard to factor endowment and thresholds and economies of scale, the physical development of the city has been wasteful of space and has not allowed for infrastructure provision and expansion on a least-cost basis. Both capital and operating costs for such facilities as water supply, sanitation and circulation have been relatively high, not only within each particular township but throughout the entire urban area. Consequently, the provision of urban services for all Durgapur residents poses serious difficulties with regard to replication, affordability and cost recovery. Although the major industries appear to have subsidised high-standard facilities and services within their townships, the village pockets and other marginal areas have not been adequately served. Hence, wide disparities exist within the urban area. In addition, measures have not been taken to strengthen local government finances.

Another set of observations deals with the relationships of Durgapur's planners and managers to its users. If we refer to the editors' criteria of respect, equity and participation, some of the problems emerge from this brief evaluation. The industrial managements have concentrated paternalistically on the welfare of their own workforce and on the settlements they have built for them, thus causing this population to feel very dependent on its providers. In contrast, the needs of those forced to live in pre-existing villages and in the new squatter settlements have been neglected. Thus, from the standpoint of equity, all groups do not have anything approaching equal access to Durgapur's resources and benefits. In addition, a stiuation has been allowed to develop in which the transport, social and economic linkages between various parts of the urban area are overlooked. From the standpoint of participation, power and responsibility, it is unfortunate that the management of Durgapur and other post-independence Indian new towns has not allowed for experimentation with institutional arrangements which would have encouraged local leadership and control. If a stronger urban development and management authority which was more independent from the major industries had been established at the beginning, and had called for substantial popular participation and levied contributions for development costs, perhaps the "company town" quality of Durgapur's physical layout and social life would have been reduced.

NOTES

(1) In Indian towns, a sector is a community or major component of the urban area for which facilities such as major markets and secondary schools are developed.

REFERENCES

Bose, Ashish (1973) Studies in India's Urbanisation (1901-1971), Tata. Bombay: McGraw Hill.

Census of India, 1971 (1973) General Population Tables, West Bengal, Part II-A, Series 22. West Bengal, Calcutta.

Census of India, 1971 (1973) District Census Handbook, Burdwan District Part X(A&B), Series 22. West Bengal, Calcutta.

Census of India - 1971 (1975) General Population Tables - Series 1, India, Pt. IIA (i). New Delhi.

Chattopadhyaya, B.C. et al. (1967) Planning for a Coal Steel Complex, Mimeo, APO, Asansol.

Committee on Plan Projects (1963) Report on Industrial Townships. New Delhi.

Durgapur Development Authority (1969) Administrative Reports, Durgapur.

Govt. of West Bengal, APO (1969) Socio-Economic Survey in the Asansol-Durgapur Region.

Govt. of West Bengal, APO (1966) Interim Development Plan, Asansol. Durgapur, Calcutta.

Govt. of West Bengal, APO, CMPO, DDA (1968) A Perspective Structure Plan for Durgapur. Mimeo, Durgapur.

Govt. of West Bengal, APO and DDA (1969) City Center for Durgapur. Mimeo, Durgapur.

Hindustan Steel Limited, Annual Reports - 1957-1975. Mimeo, Calcutta.

Indian Institute of Technology, Kharagpur (1963) Durgapur Regional Master Plan, Draft Report. Mimeo, Kharagpur.

Report of Planning Commission, Third Five-Year Plan. New Delhi.

Sivaramakrishnan, K. C. Durgapur - A Decade's Growth. Mimeo, APO, Asansol.

Ved Prakash (1969) New Towns of India. Monograph and Occasional Paper Series, Monograph No. 8, Duke University, U.S.A.

The Role of Urban Settlement in Rural Development

Although this is essentially a book about urban development, two case studies have been included which deal with predominantly rural regions. The following contrasting regional studies have been included: (1) Pahang Tenggara, Malaysia, which is an extensive area of jungle being converted to plantation agriculture; and (2) the Huaxi production brigade, Huashi Commune, Jiangsu Province, China, a typical rural settlement in the world's most populous nation. One objective of presenting these projects is to point up the wide variation in socio-political orientation toward both rural and urban development which national policy-makers can take. The Malaysians are concerned with opening up new regions for agriculture, and see in a decentralised programme of small urban centres an important positive vehicle for achieving their objectives. The Chinese rulers, on the other hand, have adopted an anti-urban stance to date. The transformation of rural development, according to their model, will come about via the local production brigade in existing rural areas. These studies also demonstrate that the role which urban settlements can play in rural development is not uniform.

John Taylor and David Williams describe and evaluate Malaysia's most ambitious regional planning and development project to date. Pahang Tenggara is an organised programme to convert a large chunk of jungle into agricultural use. At the same time, it is hoped that the concentrated settlement pattern proposed will eventually offer diversified economic opportunities, particularly for the country's poor Malays. The study presented here describes the vast Pahang Tenggara region and the plan for its transformation which was drawn up by a team of foreign consultants. It then proceeds with a brief status report on efforts to implement the plan, and concludes with an overall evaluation of the programme.

Richard Kirkby presents the Chinese case study of an essentially rural district in Jiangsu Province. Given the very different socio-political orientation, and specifically the different attitude which the Chinese have adopted toward urbanisation, this contribution begins with a comparatively elaborate review of these and related matters. Developments in a single production brigade area (Huaxi) are then discussed and assessed. With its utterly anti-urban philosophy, the Chinese situation stands in marked contrast to the cases presented from democratic/capitalist societies. It throws up a challenge to all countries to carefully think through the role of urbanisation in development.

6

Towns for Plantation Agriculture: Pahang Tenggara, Malaysia

John L. Taylor
David G. Williams

INTRODUCTION

Malaysia has had considerable experience with rural development, and with relating urban areas and other settlements to this development, during the 22 years since it became independent. This experience has attracted some international attention. For example, the Federal Land Development Authority (FELDA), which has developed nearly 400,000 hectares of land and settled about 45,000 families, has been the subject of considerable scrutiny by other Asian countries. The first area to be planned and developed on a regional basis was the Jengka Triangle, and the plan for this region is well summarised by Johnson.(1)

Within the past 9 years, however, comprehensive regional plans have been drawn up in two much larger regions, Johore Tenggara and Pahang Tenggara (see Fig. 6.1). These plans have been prepared in conjunction with the Second and Third Malaysia Plans (1971-1975 and 1976-1980) and in the light of "the New Economic Policy" which is designed to provide accelerated opportunities for the Bumiputras (Malays). Both in scale and concept, they represent a considerable advance over the Jengka Triangle, and should receive more international publicity than they have to date.

The purpose of this case study will be to describe the regional planning study and plan which was prepared for the Pahang Tenggara Region, and also to review the status of efforts to implement the plan. Particular emphasis will be placed on the settlement programme for the Region, which proposed a concentration of all settlement and population into a series of urban places ranging from 4000 to 75,000 persons in size. After describing the plan recommendations and reviewing

Fig. 6.1. Regional Planning Project Areas in West Malaysia.

the status of implementation, our study will conclude with an evaluation of the entire planning and implementation effort.

THE PAHANG TENGGARA REGION

The Pahang Tenggara Region covers nearly 10,400 square km along the east coast of Peninsular Malaysia, an area 10 times the size of the Jengka Triangle (see Fig. 6.1) or about the size of Belgium. Presently it is the largest single planning region in the country. The Region is sparsely populated, the 1971 population being less than 60,000, with most of it along the Pahang River and along the coast of the South China Sea. The interior of the Region, except for scattered settlements of Orang Asli (aborigines) and recently developed plantations, consisted primarily of jungle. This dense jungle formed part of the lush tropical rain forest that still covers much of the land in Malaysia. As can be seen from Table 6.1, 54.4 percent of total land area before development commenced was under dense forest, and of this wooded area about one-third was virgin forest. Only 15.7 percent of the Region was considered non-forest, made up chiefly of agricultural plantations.

Table 6.1. General Existing Land Use Summary

	Hectares	Percent
Virgin productive forest	361,000	35.9
Logged productive forest	187,000	18.5
Peat swamp forest (potentially productive)	110,000	11.0
Non-productive lands and swamps	190,000	18.9
Non-forest (including plantations, clearings, water, etc.)	158,000	15.7
Total Area	1,006,000	100.0

Source: FENCO, vol. Forestry Development in Pahang Tenggara, 1972.

The general topography of the Region is undulating with blocks of low mountain ranges in scattered locations. A broad band of peat swamp, 22 to 30 km wide, runs along the coast. A corridor of land with high agricultural potential runs in a north-east to south-west direction, and it is along this corridor that the proposed Kuantan-Segamat highway is aligned. The Region is drained by several river systems, all flowing into the South China Sea.

Existing roads into the area consisted mainly of logging tracks, and until recently access was very poor. By the end of the Plan period, a whole network of roads are proposed to be constructed, not only to connect the various new towns and areas within the Region but also to connect the Region with other parts of the country. The major highway already mentioned, which will become part of the national route along the east coast, will figure prominently in development of the Region.

Much of the rationale for future development of the Region hinges on exploitation of the rich agricultural and forestry potential of the land. The Region is presently rich in timber and it is expected that, during the process of land clearing, this resource will be effectively used. Unfortunately, however, the smaller trees and presently unmarketable species -probably amounting to 70 percent of the total standing bio-mass - are simply being burnt and hence wasted in the land conversion process.

It is not only the jungle which is threatened by future development. The way of life of the orang asli who live inside the jungle is bound to be altered beyond recognition. Also an impressive array of wild life in the Region, including many elephants and the last remaining Sumatran rhinoceros, will be threatened by the Plan.

But Pahang Tenggara is clearly a vast area with considerable potential for economic development. Although Malaysia has a large land area (330,590 square km) relative to a comparatively small population (10.7 million in 1970), its commercial or planatation agricultural sector has been very successful and has had an insatiable appetite for consuming more land for its purposes. Situated on the relatively unexploited east coast, Pahang Tenggara now lies in the path of development.

THE REGIONAL PLANNING STUDY AND PLAN

The Pahang Tenggara Regional Planning Study, financed by a Canadian International Development Agency loan and prepared by a consortium of Canadian consulting firms, was a major 2-year effort costing US $4 million and involving fifty experts which was completed in mid-1972. The results of this study are contained in eleven volumes of written material, plus a one-volume atlas of planning maps and seven volumes of technical appendices. At least in terms of sheer volume of output, it must be considered one of the most massive regional planning studies ever undertaken.

Plan Objectives

The Plan set forth the following objectives:(2)

1. The creation of efficient, well-managed, technically advanced and large scale enterprises in agriculture and forestry, and the assurance of employment opportunities for participation of Malays in these enterprises at all levels. Potential agricultural land is being alienated to investors in blocks of 5000 acres (about 2000 ha) each. With the exception of the 25 percent of the Region which would be developed by FELDA, which promotes government-controlled cooperative schemes where settler families will eventually own 14 acres (5.7 ha) of farm land each, agriculture in Pahang Tenggara would generally be owned and managed in large units.

This decision to opt for large scale private corporate ownership and management of the land instead of cooperative or individual ownership is one of the most controversial and is bound to have implications for the overall programme. Although the decision was taken in the interests of efficiency, it is likely to lead to formation of a rather unusual social phenomenon: a town-based agricultural proletariat.

2. The promotion of substantial amounts of industrialisation and urbanisation of a kind which provides opportunities for Malays as well as for other Malaysians to find employment at all levels in the modern sector.

3. The Regional Plan should contribute towards the reduction of regional disparities. This objective requires a pattern of development which will boost present levels of income and social welfare in the Region above the national average, and should permit substantial migration from relatively low productivity sectors of the poor regions to Pahang Tenggara.

4. Providing means of acquiring higher levels of skills, particularly for Malays but also for other Malaysians.

5. Providing productive employment opportunities, in which the quality of these opportunities is as important as the quantity.

6. Building a base for attracting manufacturing and service enterprises not directly related to resource exploitation.

Plan Recommendations

In summary, the Plan recommended the following actions:

1. The clearing of forest land for agriculture should proceed at the rate of approximately 25,000 ha per year until 1980, and logging operations should proceed in sequence with the opening of land for agricultural development.

2. A total of 28,000 ha of land are to be planted with oil palm, rubber and diversified crops within the Second Malaysia Plan period (1971-1975), while another 100,000 ha are to be opened for similar agricultural development in the Third Malaysia Plan period (1976-1980).

3. Two integrated forest complexes are to be established on the basis of a potential sustained yield resource of 96,000 ha of productive forest. These two plants would have a combined capacity of 320,000 cubic metres of processed timber to produce high-value products such as plywood, particleboard, and component parts for prefabricated housing units.

4. Five areas totalling 67,000 ha are to be set aside as parks and conservation areas because of their special biological significance and tourism potential. A further 104,000 ha are retained more or less in their natural condition as protective forest to safeguard the soil and water resources of the Region. These areas consist chiefly of steeplands and floodplains. Ecological management of the Region is also emphasised in the Plan.

The above-mentioned actions involving agricultural, forest, conservation and recreation development would lead to a future land use allocation in Pahang Tenggara, as shown in Table 6.2.

5. Population in the Region is to be housed in concentrated settlements. A total of thirty-six new towns are proposed to be established and these towns will form a complete urban hierarchy within the Region. This proposed settlement pattern will be discussed in greater detail below.

6. It is strongly recommended in the Plan that services within the Region be provided at a level above standards prevailing at present in other parts of Malaysia. To achieve the necessary level of migration and investment, an attractive environment should be created. This is proposed by means of well serviced urban areas readily accessible to settlers, who can thus fully benefit from the development opportunities throughout the Region.

7. To coordinate implementation of the Plan, it was recommended that a Development Authority with wide planning powers be established. Although the Regional Planning Study suggested that the Authority play mainly a promotional, coordinating and service role, and refrain from becoming involved in specific developments, early experience has shown that the Authority must take greater initiative, particularly with regard to development of the towns.

Table 6.2. Future Land Use Allocation

	Hectares	Percent
1. Land allocated prior to commencement of Masterplanning Study (mostly under development for agriculture)	200,000	20.0
2. Land recommended for allocation, 1971-1980:		
Agricultural development	128,000	12.7
Forestry complexes	96,000	9.5
Special Mentiga Forestry Concession (net area)	8,000	0.8
Parks and conservation areas	67,000	6.6
New townsites	2,000	0.2
	301,000	29.8
3. Land available for allocation after 1980:		
Agricultural development	127,000	12.6
Peat swamp with logging potential	81,000	8.0
Steepland and protective forest	104,000	10.4
	312,000	31.0
4. Land not recommended for agriculture or forestry (mostly swamp and other lowland areas)	193,000	19.2
5. Total land area of Pahang Tenggara	1,006,000	100.0

Source: FENCO, vol. The Masterplan for the Development of Pahang Tenggara, 1972, p. 52.

8. Finally, the progress and implementation of the Plan should be monitored, so that it can be adjusted to absorb deviations and unexpected changes in policy and situations. Since the full span of the Plan period is 1971-1990, a major mid-term review is proposed for 1980.

In essence, the Pahang Tenggara Regional Plan represents a major effort to raise income levels and increase employment opportunities, hence fulfilling the objectives of the

Second Malaysia Plan and New Economic Policy. It is expected that some 180,000 jobs are to be created in the Region by 1990, half of them in the primary sector (agriculture and forestry) and half in the secondary and tertiary sectors. It is estimated that this will lead to a Regional population of about 500,000 persons. Figure 6.2 indicates the proposed structure of the urban settlements and regional development.

The Urban Programme

Perhaps the most unique set of recommendations to emerge from the Regional Planning study relates to the proposed spatial pattern of new settlements. The following discussion of the settlement programme deals with (a) the justification for a pattern of concentrated settlements, (b) the hierarchy of settlement categories, and (c) the proposals for the region's relationship with other urban centres.

A pattern of concentrated settlements:

The basic urbanisation strategy employed in the Pahang Tenggara Regional Plan is to agglomerate all hinterland population, including agricultural workers and their dependants, into about thirty-six concentrated urban settlements. This settlement pattern deviates from the normal practice of scattering labour lines or small villages within commercial agricultural undertakings. By concentrating the Region's population into a limited number of towns, it becomes financially feasible to provide the population with the physical amenities and social services associated with an urban environment. The thesis is that this process of urbanisation will create socio-economic conditions that foster the development of modern values and attitudes among the settlers, who will be primarily Malays. Although the Region's economy will be chiefly agricultural, the new towns will provide physical and social infrastructures which are esssentially urban in character and which will aid the settlers in making the transition from a rural to an urban way of life.

An important justification for this concentrated pattern is that it will further the objectives of the New Economic Policy and Second Malaysia Plan, in particular the goal "to accelerate the process of restructuring Malaysian society to correct economic imbalance, so as to reduce and eventually eliminate the identification of race with economic function".(3) The economic dichotomy between the two dominant racial groups in Malaysia, Malays and Chinese, may also be viewed as a rural-urban dichotomy, the Chinese being strongly represented in the modern urban sectors of the economy while the Malays are largely confined to traditional rural pursuits. The traditional

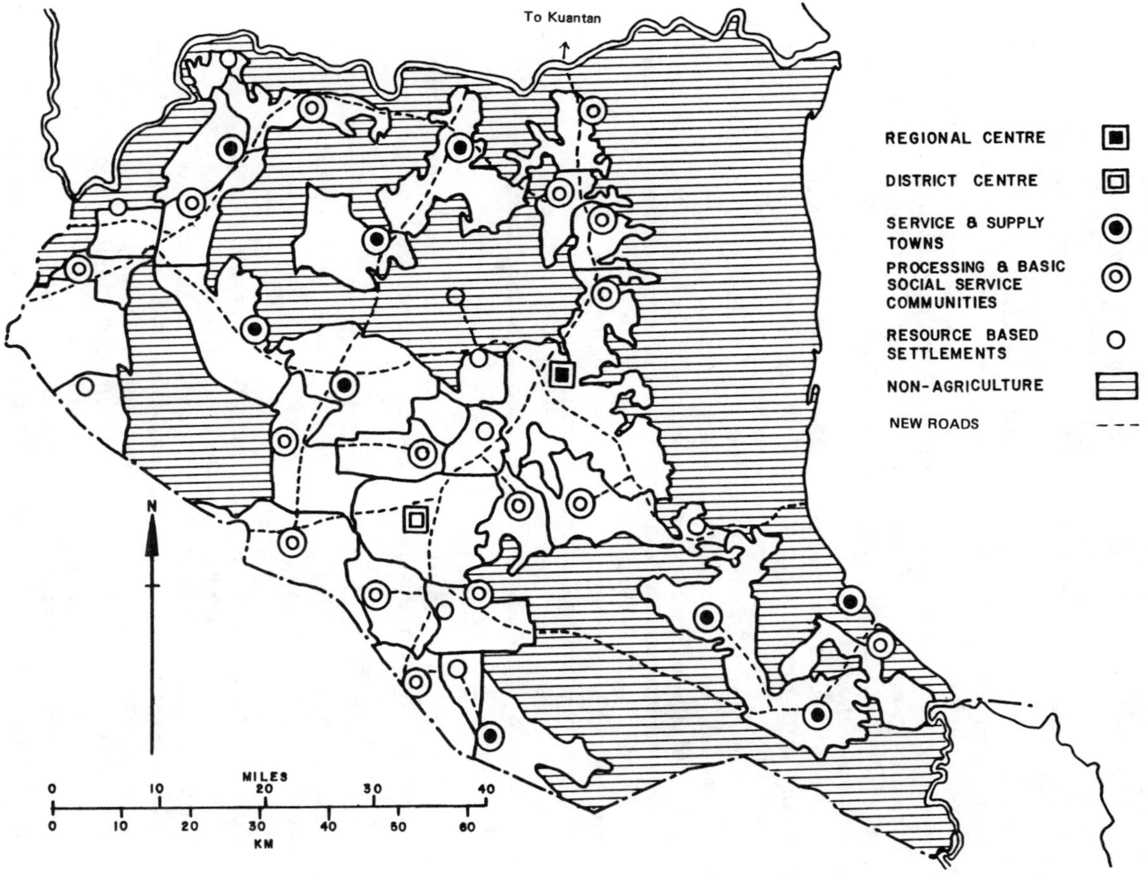

Fig. 6.2. Proposed Hierarchy of Towns and Immediate Agricultural Hinterlands.

culture and values of the Malays are believed to be an impediment to their progress and ability to capitalise on the economic opportunities available in the country.

Therefore, to ensure that the political tensions between the two races will eventually dissipate, government policy makers believe it is important that the economic participation of Malays be upgraded and their penetration into the modern sectors of the economy be accelerated. Chinese society in Malaysia has developed a solid urban-based middle class, while the Malay community of entrepreneurs and professionals is still small and weak. It is imperative that a Malay urban-based middle class be nurtured in order to break what has grown to be a racial monopoly of certain economic functions. Urbanisation of Malays is therefore a critical contribution to political planning in Malaysia.

Although it is no panacea, the strategy of concentrating population into urban centres in Pahang Tenggara is definitely promoted by this drive for urbanisation of the Malays. Through such induced urbanisation, the Malay settler will have greater social and economic mobility, increased productivity, access to better information and generally greater freedom than he has experienced in existing agricultural estates or traditional kampungs. This is, in any case, the rationale put forward by the planners of Pahang Tenggara, with support from the policy-makers in Kuala Lumpur.

Migrants into the new towns of Pahang Tenggara will also benefit from a high level of amenities and facilities, including the following:

1. electricity, water and sanitation provided for each house;
2. proximity to qualitatively better educational and health facilities;
3. proximity to good shopping facilities; and
4. proximity to greater variety of social and entertainment amenities.

Concentrating the population into relatively few settlements not only furthers social and political objectives, as discussed above, but also turns out to be financially preferable. In the study, a cost appraisal of six alternative settlement models, ranging from twelve settlements to a single one for an agricultural hinterland of about 26,000 ha, demonstrated that considerable savings in the cost of infrastructure can be effected by concentrating the population into one large settlement. This potential savings in both capital and operating costs in an agricultural development with a more concentrated settlement pattern, as compared with the more traditional approach, was a significant factor in the planning of Pahang Tenggara. In addition to costs savings, further benefits accrue to the concentrated settlement pattern, in that people will have immediate access to the higher level of services mentioned above than would be possible under the more traditional pattern. Hence, the economic justification for a concentrated settlement pattern coincides with the social and political objectives of the New Economic Policy.

The hierarchy of settlement categories:

The Plan calls for a hierarchy of settlements, ranging from resource-based settlements of under 5000 persons, to processing and basic service towns of 5000 to 15,000, service and supply towns of 15,000 to 30,000, a district centre of 40,000, and a regional centre of about 75,000 persons. The distribution of towns by settlement category is shown statistically in Table 6.3 and graphically in Fig. 6.2. The distinguishing characteristics of each of these settlement types relates chiefly to the amount and type of non-resource based economic activity; i.e. to the urban functions and role that they will play in rural development. In the towns of less than 15,000 persons, the majority of workers would be engaged in agriculture and other resource-based economic activity, but in the larger centres increasing proportions of workers would be employed in industrial, commercial and service activity. The larger urban centres would also contain more sophisticated public services in fields such as education, health and government administration. These settlement categories and the functions of each were developed after a thorough study of existing occupational structure, thresholds and town size within Malaysia.

Table 6.3. Distribution of Towns by Settlement Category, 1990

Population size	Number of towns	Population	Percent of total pop.
Under 5000	9	30,000	6.0
5000-14,999	16	165,000	33.0
15,000-29,999	9	190,000	38.0
40,000 (±)	1	40,000	8.0
75,000 (±)	1	75,000	15.0
	36	500,000	100.0

Of the thirty-six towns proposed in the Plan, half were programmed for planning within the Second Malaysia Plan period and the balance would be planned and constructed during subsequent periods. On the average, there would be about three processing/basic service communities or resource-based settlements for every one service and supply town, although factors related to topography and to the agricultural hinterlands prevent this from becoming a symmetrical pattern. However, there would be a definite central place hierarchy established, which would involve an intermeshed rather than dendritic market system. The Regional Plan stopped short of preparing detailed plans for the individual settlements.

The relationship with other urban areas:

The development of the region was intended to reduce regional disparities by creating a strong link with the economically more backward eastern half of Malaysia(4), Kuantan, the town immediately to the north of Pahang Tenggara, was expected to be the focus for new development with a new deep-water port creating an export centre for the agricultural products of Pahang Tenggara and other regional development schemes. In order to develop close links with Kuantan and avoid capture by the influence of the established southern and western urban centres, phasing of agricultural and infrastructure development was to commence from Kuantan and the north and to move southwards. Only after the region was oriented towards Kuantan and had also received a substantial number of settlers from the poor north-eastern states, was any link to be made with the thriving towns of Segamat and Johore Baru, to the south.

STATUS OF IMPLEMENTATION

Establishment and Evolution of the Regional Development Authority

The Pahang Tenggara Development Authority (DARA) was established in February 1972. It was conceived as a mixed-function public-private corporation with three principal powers: (a) approval over land use in the region, (b) power of financial evaluation and approval of expenditures by other government agencies and (c) the power to evaluate and arrange contracts. It has a Board composed mainly of high-level Federal and State government officials which appoints a General Manager who has responsibility for choosing his staff, implementing the policies of the Board and translating them into plans and action. Following the Master Plan recommendations, DARA was to have very limited implementation functions and would rely on coordinating and approving the budgets and plans of Federal and State line agencies to implement its programmes. Subsequently this approach was modified to allow DARA to plan and implement development in designated town-sites with its own funds. However, the intention was that capital expenditures by DARA on development outside the town sites would only be made as a last resort. In addition to planning and coordination, DARA was to play a leading role in manpower planning, promotion and training. It was expected that the investments in regional infrastructure by national line agencies would make the Region so attractive for industrial investment and migrant labour that spontaneous growth would spring up in these areas. This did not occur to the extent expected and DARA subsequently took an increasingly larger role in organising joint-venture industrial and business operations using its own equity as leverage.

Reflecting the functions expected of DARA, its initial organisation was a simple one. Under the General Manager were three main divisions: The Land Control Division directed a land administration section and a land use section. The Regional Performance Division comprised a regional control section and a regional development section. The Manpower Development Division administered task forces responsible for promotion and training. Since DARA was to concentrate on planning and control, a large staff was not envisaged and most of them were expected to be seconded from Federal and State government agencies. For its first 2 years the technical staff numbered from twenty to forty. There was no division for town planning since it was expected that the Federal Town and Country Planning Office in Kuala Lumpur would do this work for DARA.

In 1975 DARA's organisational structure was changed to reflect the increasing need to manage and direct regional and town infrastructure programmes, to coordinate land development with infrastructure planning, to promote new industrial investments and to manage its own joint venture companies. Two major branches were established, one for development, and the other for finance, administration and land control. These were linked by a coordination, monitoring and research section reporting to a coordination committee composed of divisional and branch directors. After some initial problems this has proved to be a more effective means for integrating the numerous facets of DARA's planning, administration and implementation responsibilities.

Progress with Regional and Detailed Planning

The planning and timing of regional and town development was driven by the expected speed of agricultural and forestry development. These inputs provided the basis for projecting the location of development and the characteristics of the population attracted into the Region, initially those to work on the agricultural estates, followed by the "induced" population who would provide the workforce for the support services and for industry. The strategic plan was to develop along the axis of the new major Kuantan to Segamat highway, commencing from the northern end. This strategy would support the development of the small agricultural-based towns along this axis and promote the major regional centre called Bukit Ridan, which would be developed at the cross roads with the other principal road running across the Region. For reasons we shall touch on later it became difficult to coordinate development along this axis, and land development started to occur both in a sporadic manner and faster than originally projected. The major road system was initiated from the south instead of from the north as planned, and Kuantan's deep port development was delayed. Consequently the region become oriented towards the south and west and not towards the poorer and migrant-sending east coast region. The development of infrastructure and town sites lagged behind the agricultural development and therefore could not provide the necessary services and exert the organising force on the land development. The lack of services and housing also made the region less attractive to migrants who were also being attracted to other developments schemes in the country, and the land developers therefore resorted to temporary contract labour and more capital-intensive techniques in order to develop their projects within the time framework they had agreed to with DARA. The developers were obliged to put up temporary "labour lines" on the traditional pattern on each of their developments in order to provide accommodation for their workforce. They agreed to move these settlements into the town sites when they were developed, although their own preferences had always been for the "labour line" approach since this gave them better control over their workforce. At the same time, it became clear through analysis of town to field commuting times and from the projections for reduced in-migration noted above, that too many small towns had been planned for the Region. Because of these factors, DARA reduced the number of towns expected to be built from thirty-six to about twenty-four, and concentrated on rapidly establishing basic services in what were called "reception areas" in a few key town sites located in the centre of the most developed areas, so that the town-based strategy could become a reality and not be completely undermined.

The lag in development of both regional and town site infrastructure has proved to be a major stumbling-block for the development of the Region as originally planned. The cooperation from national line agencies did not materialise as expected, since each agency was fully occupied with its existing commitments programmed through its own budget. DARA eventually had to call on expatriate consultants and had to set up its own planning and implementation capacity, especially for town planning and development. This took time and delayed the planning process. The town site areas were selected early and on a purely notional basis. When town planning started it was found that these sites were often on bad land, frequently the residual areas which were not wanted by the agricultural developers, and the negotiations for moving and adjusting some of these sites took time. Considerable discussion also took place on the site planning and standards appropriate for the towns which were a new venture for Malaysia. The approach eventually adopted was very suitable, and provided an environment which would be attractive to migrants yet at a reasonably low cost. This was reached following social and anthropological studies of settlements in migrant sending areas. The complexity of town development had not been appreciated during the Masterplan study and all this work took more time than expected.

Difficulties also arose in the planning of agricultural and forestry areas. These had been designated according to market analysis for crops, crop productivity related to soil type, and to a lesser extent, ecological criteria. Due to the subsequent strong demand for palm oil, the pressure to develop oil palm estates over-rode the more balanced patterns proposed in the Masterplan and the Region has tended to develop in a one-sided manner and exposed itself to the risk of an economic downturn if the international price of oil palm drops. Eventually DARA had to consider a ban on future oil palm development. Ecologically sensitive areas which, under the Masterplan, and in some cases according to State law, were required to be kept in forest, were developed into oil palm with serious effects which are now appearing on the hydrology, water quality, climate and wildlife in the region. There was inadequate attention in the Masterplan to estimating the ecological impact of the massive deforestation and land development it proposed, or to investigating alternative land-development patterns which could have reduced the destruction of forest and integrated more productive multi-cropping patterns into the existing environment. The public land development agency, FELDA, was an even worse offender on environmental matters than the private developers and, being a powerful central government agency, was more difficult for DARA to control.

Rational planning of the Region thus tended to become the victim of weak control, bureaucratic and coordination difficulties, and lack of early foresight and attention to realistic timing. The planning task for a new and inexperienced agency was truly gargantuan and was grossly under-estimated in the Masterplan study. Nevertheless DARA has learned much during its 8 years of operation and is now achieving a better output and operating more effectively than before. It has completed numerous studies (5) which have been able to define and guide policy and investment decisions and has also completed physical and financial plans and detailed engineering for about twelve towns. The physical planning and engineering sections of DARA have been greatly strengthened and are now more capable of undertaking their important role.

Implementation to Date

As of the time of writing (1979/80), the physical development of the Region is fairly advanced, especially in the agricultural sector where most of the areas scheduled for development in the Masterplan have been planted, albeit mostly with oil palm. Almost 103,000 hectares have been planted in oil palm with about six oil-palm mills processing the fruit. Only 2800 hectares have been planted in rubber, a small fraction of that projected in the Masterplan, due to the greater attractiveness of the return from palm oil. There are two centres for cattle raising, totalling 3000 hectares and supporting 8000 head of cattle. Other crops include cocoa and fruit. The FELDA areas are on schedule and the settlers are now living in the FELDA towns. The two projects for sustained yield forestry are proceeding although more slowly than expected. Although far behind the original schedule, the primary regional infrastructure of roads and water supply is nearing completion and the major Kuantan to Segamat highway now provides a complete link through the Region. The first phase of infrastructure and housing has been built for about six towns. Joint venture industrial operations in wood processing, timber housing, building materials, gem production and poultry farming have been established.

Compared to the achievements in land development, the development of the towns and the resulting settlement of the farmers and permanent workforce has lagged far behind expectations (apart from the FELDA projects). Only about 13,000 workers have immigrated into the region together with a further 22,000 dependants, a small fraction of the 500,000 settlers projected for 1990 by the Masterplan. Moreover, most of these are temporary workers on the agricultural estates and in construction. This shortfall is partly due to the difficulty of attracting migrants, and the inadequate state of preparation of the towns, points which are discussed later. But it also highlights a change in conditions not expected at the time of the Masterplan. The national economy has grown considerably in the last few years and jobs in urban areas compete with land settlement schemes. Demand for palm oil is high and the newer developers prefer to use more capital-intensive means of production, to use their labour more intensively and to accept a lower standard of estate maintenance.

The financial expenditures in the Region are difficult to estimate since they run through so many different budgets, but government expenditures on regional and urban infrastructure to date are roughly on the order of $300 million. Private, joint venture and FELDA investments presently amount to about $500 million. The Asian Development Bank has assisted in financing some of the regional roads and water supply, and the World Bank has financed the FELDA Keratong Land Development Scheme (about 8000 ha).

EVALUATION OF THE PAHANG TENGGARA EXPERIENCE

Problems with Implementation

The shortest volume of the eleven-volume Regional Plan was the one which dealt with implementation. This lack of attention to implementation was unfortunate, because there have been considerable problems in getting the ambitious regional development programme moving during the first 5 years after the Plan was published. The Masterplan tended to look at "end-state" conditions and did not sufficiently emphasise the need for continuous on-going planning. The only planning review it proposed was to be in 1980, seven years after the initial Masterplan. The Pahang Tenggara Regional Plan can therefore be seen as a prime example of the "economic master plan" described in Chapter 1 as one variant of the traditional paradigm of planning practice. More serious, however, was the failure of the Masterplan to deal realistically with issues of public organisation and management, phasing, financing of public infrastructure, incentives for migrants and several other matters which have been crucial for implementation. In migitation, it should be pointed out that the terms of reference for the study emphasized analyses for physical outputs and did not lay sufficient stress on the institutional and management issues. The consultants were therefore inhibited by time and cost to address these important issues.

This "end-state" mentality transmitted itself to DARA, inhibiting continuous monitoring and reappraisal. As we have seen, the Plan underestimated the effort required to plan and implement the infrastructure and town development programme.

The primary infrastructure and first phase of town construction should have been well underway before the hinterland areas were leased for agriculture. There were tremendous pressures on DARA to allow logging and agricultural development to proceed immediately. Logging is a very profitable activity and is also the main revenue-earner for Pahang State. Most of the land in Pahang Tenggara is State-owned, its management being taken from the Sultans at the time of independence. The Sultan as the Head of State nevertheless still retains considerable influence over the distribution and use of land. Under Malaysia's constitution, land is a State matter, and DARA being a Federal agency had, in the last analysis, little control over the speed and even location of logging and land development. The private profits from logging are enormous and can capitalise the subsequent development of a whole oil palm estate on the logged land. The fees from logging due to the State are very low relative to the private profit margin and State supervision of the actual yield is rather weak. Consequently pressures to obtain forest land for logging and development are considerable. To date 238,000 hectares have been approved for development and are logged (adding the illegal logging would inflate this figure considerably), more than half of the total area scheduled for development in the Masterplan.

Another implementation problem which weakened DARA's influence was related to its inability to control the budgets and project priorities of the major sectoral infrastructure agencies, expecially those constructing regional highways and water supply. Whereas DARA had legal control over the town sites, it could only request the major sectoral agencies to incorporate the key regional and inter-town infrastructure into their budgets.

In addition to attracting private capital, the success of a balanced regional development also rests on bringing in nearly half a million migrants from other parts of Malaysia to provide the labour. It is assumed that, by paying wages and offering urban amenities that are more attractive than elsewhere, this migration can be induced. However, it is an open question as to whether the inducements being offered will be sufficient to create a migration stream on the scale desired, especially when the settler discovers that, outside the FELDA schemes, he has no stake in the agricultural land itself. Moreover, since the Pahang Tenggara Plan was prepared, there have been plans prepared for other regions in the country which will be competing for the same limited migration pool. Consequently, we see that there is a need for spatial policy at the national as well as regional scale, so that Peninsular Malaysia can determine the optimum settlement pattern not solely for one region but for the entire country.

Impact on National Urbanisation Strategy

As the Israelis have already discovered, there are economic as well as social advantages for a more concentrated pattern within agricultural regions. As Johnson mentions, the Israeli experience has been that the larger C and D centres have undergone the most vigorous growth. The Pahang Tenggara Plan has demonstrated that economies of scale are possible through concentration of agricultural populations into larger towns. In both Israel and Malaysia, this policy serves a crucial spatial objective to encourage the growth of small and intermediate-sized urban centres in an effort to slow down metropolitan growth. In both countries, this objective is at least to some extent being achieved. The population distribution in Malaysia exhibits less concentration in large cities and a more even rank-size distribution of towns than in other countries in the region such as Thailand, the Philippines and Indonesia. This can be partly attributed to the lower population density in Malaysia and consequently more rural land available per family than in these other countries, and partly to the level of commercialisation of the agriculture where cash crops yield a reasonable income even for the smallholders. Another reason may be the traditional reluctance of many Malays to migrate to cities which they see as the preserve of Malaysians of Chinese and Indian extraction who dominate the industrial and commercial sectors of the economy. The large private and government-run agricultural estates which comprise a significant proportion of the country's land area are in effect factories in the field employing wage labour, and in that respect offer employment more akin to an urban life-style than the self-employed subsistence smallholder.

However, a question arises here as to the future of rural versus urban functions in the country and the consequences of migration in peninsular Malaysia. The available land for new agriculture is rapidly disappearing, as are the forest resources, yet the population continues to grow at 2.7 percent per year. The labour-absorption potential of large scale commercial agriculture is very low due to capital-intensive techniques and mono-culture cropping systems. If the present labour scarcity problem turns into a labour-absorption problem as trends indicate, then a strategy oriented towards increased manufacturing and service functions is appropriate. These would have to be located in medium to large size towns to be viable. In the rural areas, however, there is still considerable opportunity to expand and improve smallholder operations where a family could own 2 to 3 hectares of land and develop it intensively with multiple crops. To expand this approach, which would offer 2 to 3 times the employment level of estate agriculture and a lower cost per job, would involve a political decision to gradually expropriate the large private estates in favour of the smallholder - a policy which so far has been resisted by the Government. The reluctance of potential settlers to migrate to regional development schemes such as Pahang Tenggara would indicate that the most effective way to reduce under-employment and to raise incomes would be to develop projects in the areas where these poor smallholders live, rather than expecting them to move to the new schemes. Further, the real attraction for the poor farmer is to own more land rather than become an agricultural employee. The self-evident nature of these facts leads one to question the seriousness of the stated objectives of these type of land development schemes to addressing the problems of under-employment.

By undertaking agricultural development through large private commercial units, and by concentrating hired labour in small towns, Pahang Tenggara is likely to pay some social costs. In consciously separating the farm family from the direct physical relationship to the fields it would have if living in a scattered settlement, is not the planner creating a strange kind of alienation whose long range consequences are difficult to predict? The positive argument is of course that social integration can be achieved through a more gathered settlement pattern, as Johnson's discussion of the Israeli case points out.(6) However, the concentration of agricultural labour in small towns (bear in mind that two-thirds of Pahang Tenggara's settlements will be made up mostly of farmers) may lead to a proletariat that will eventually become a force for radical change. Although possible long range changes in ownership and control of production may not be what the planners had in mind, it would not necessarily be a bad thing.

In theory, however, the proposed concentrated pattern of settlement may have some real social advantages if Malays as well as Chinese and Indians can be attracted into the larger towns and over time into non-agricultural occupations. It may be possible to overcome the "undesired social consequences" mentioned in Johnson's description of Israeli spatial design, in which "rural communities (A and B centres), particularly those composed of immigrants from oriental countries, tended to segregate themselves from the emergent urban communities (C and D centres), thus retarding the social integration in the newly created settlements that had been visualised by the planners."(7)

In the Pahang Tenggara settlement programme, nearly all families would live in the equivalent of C and D centres, thus assuring at least some degree of social integration among the various racial communities. It is of considerable interest that the chief justification for a concentrated settlement pattern is the desire to restructure Malaysian society by urbanising the Malays and creating a new set of social and economic opportunities. The rationale, as described earlier in this chapter, provides a fascinating case study of using spatial organisation to achieve political and social goals. It will be important to monitor and evaluate the results of the experiment as it is carried out.

A related benefit from concentration will also be achieved if the high level of social and physical infrastructures and facilities advocated in the Plan are actually built and put into operation. Since it has been demonstrated that these facilities can be provided more efficiently in a concentrated settlement pattern, it will also be essential to study the impact of higher level facilities on human behaviour. For example, to what extent is social and economic mobility or productivity furthered by making better facilities available?

Fiscal Issues

While the Masterplan devoted considerable space to detailed feasability studies for private agricultural and forestry operations, economic analyses of production sectors and their impacts on the economic rate of return to the region as a whole, less emphasis was placed on reviewing alternative methods for recouping the costs of government investments in infrastructure. Costs of regional and town site infrastructure were estimated, but little attention was paid to price inflation which turned out to be much more severe than expected. The infrastructure costs were not expected to be recouped directly, but instead through quit rent, royalties and land premia resulting from forestry and agricultural operations, and from export duties on sales of oil palm and rubber grown in the region (the latter two amounting to over 49 percent of all revenues). All the regional and town site infrastructure would be paid by government grant, leaving only the housing and water supply to be paid directly by the settlers through mortgages and user charges. This left the collection of most of the revenues to State and Federal government tax-collection bureaux who were not connected with the agencies spending the monies. There was consequently no linkage between costs and revenues and no pressures on implementing agencies to reduce costs. Cost recovery was left to the mercy of the market prices obtainable for the region's main commodities. It became very difficult to know, in face of rising costs, whether the government was gaining or losing on its investments in the Region.

As soon as DARA began operations, contracts were made with agricultural developers which omitted any mention of contributions to regional or town-site infrastructure or housing costs. The town-site approach meant that the labour lines on the estates which normally represent a considerable cost to the developer were no longer needed and the developer was consequently relieved of those costs. The settlers, on the other hand, had to pay for housing which would normally be provided free by the developer. Subsequently, during studies on town-site development, housing and transport, and in view of rising costs of town-site development and housing, the agricultural developers were approached for contributions to these costs, but they were naturally reluctant to become involved since they already had possession of their land. The developer who managed to obtain a lease on land in Pahang Tenggara can thus count himself extremely fortunate.

Who Benefits from Development?

One important reason why Malaysia's rural development programme has been relatively successful is that the country has utilised foreign capital to build an efficient commercial agricultural sector. This is a tradition that began with the British development of the rubber industry, and has continued with oil palm and other crops. Although there has been an increase in local capital ownership, mostly Malaysian-Chinese with Malay partners, the majority of commercial agricultural undertakings is still foreign-controlled. Despite attempts to represent local participation through joint ventures involving the Development Authority, this pattern of heavy outside capital investment will continue in Pahang Tenggara. It is clear that a critical decision was taken in Kuala Lumpur that large private companies, and state-managed organisations such as FELDA, rather than cooperatives or other units controlled by the Malay settler more directly, were to own, manage and control the means of production. Perhaps the economic planners are right in their assessment that only these companies have the know-how and funds to make development happen, and it is significant that there is no dearth of interest on the part of such companies to place bids for participation in Pahang Tenggara. But are not we not faced with a variation on the efficiency vs. equity theme here? In opting for what may be the most efficient means of agricultural development in terms of high-volume production, is not Malaysia sacrificing a tremendous opportunity for experimentation with new socio-economic arrangements in ownership and control that would achieve the "restructuring of society" they desire? One is left with the feeling that the main beneficiaries of this type of development tend to be the large private owners more than the poor kampung Malay.

Ecological Issues

An issue with which all planners concerned with regional development in Malaysia must contend is the pace at which the virgin jungle should be torn down and replaced by agriculture. It must be stressed that Malaysia's tropical rain forest is a non-renewable resource and, although it may be acceptable for portions of it to be replaced by agriculture, there are limitations as to how far this process should go. Some would argue that it has already gone too far and that the rain forests of Southeast Asia represent a finite world resource which is crucial to the local eco-balance and to the world's climate and should not be destroyed. For a developing country such as Malaysia, however, the issue seems to come down to the expedient of short-term economic growth through exploitation of the land for agriculture versus the harbouring of their forest resource for potential long-term benefit. Although the jungle is very limited on a global scale, it is not perceived as such in a country where over two-thirds of the land area remains in forest. Tropical soils are extremely fragile and the volume of biomass in an equatorial forest acts as a giant sponge to conserve water and maintain ground water levels. With the massive destruction of forests, Malaysia is now experiencing severe flood and drought cycles and the consequent drop in aquifer levels is reducing available water both for the remaining forest and agriculture and for human needs. Erosion is increasing as more sloping land is turned into agriculture, since the plantations of rubber and oil palm do not provide the same protection for the soil as does the forest. Despite careful practices to terrace the land and plant creeping ground cover, erosion is over 3 times greater under plantations than under the natural forest. In order to counteract the reduced fertility and in order to maximise production, massive doses of artificial fertiliser are used together with heavy pesticide spraying which is required for mono-culture crops. These chemicals run off into the streams, poisoning the water for the fish and rendering it difficult to treat for human consumption.

All of these effects are occurring on a massive scale in Pahang Tenggara where virtually every last piece of forest in areas designated for agriculture is being destroyed due to the pressures for land development and the weak environmental controls mentioned earlier in this chapter. In addition, raw and semi-treated effluent from oil-palm mills is being discharged into the rivers, killing the fish and making the water untreatable except at extremely high cost. Since ground water is not available in most areas, the Region's settlements depend on these rivers for their water supply and a major problem now confronts DARA regarding its water resources. These environmental changes also have direct social effects. Some of the poorest Malays in the region, deprived of their livelihood from fishing in these rivers, are now forced out of their traditional occupations. But those worst affected are probably the orang asli, the native forest dwellers whose habitat is being entirely removed and for whom little alternative provision is being made. Two ancient lakes, the Tasek Bera and Tasek Chini, which are major cultural and economic centres for the orang asli, are now silting up due to erosion and changes in the Region's hydrology. The last in the list of victims from environmental causes which we have space to mention here are the wild life of the region. They are called "pests" by the developers and are systematically eliminated either by direct killing or through the elimination of their habitat. Elephants, tigers, monkeys, boar and the last group of the extremely rare Sumatran rhinoceros are in the final stages of extinction. Even the Rompin-Endau national park in the south of the Region, which had earlier been designated as an inviolate reserve for wild life and tourism, has recently been opened for logging by Pahang State.

The tragedy is that most of these effects could probably have been minimized if a more sensitive approach to land development had been taken, whereby plantations would be restricted to the flattest areas and interspersed with wide belts of forest linked together in a linear pattern which could have protected the stream system and given refuge to the wildlife, the riverine Malays and the orang asli. The forest could have been a productive resource if managed on a sustained yield basis. While this would have considerably reduced the areas available for plantations and the numbers of settlers, it would have secured the long-term future of the Region.

Summary Evaluation

In evaluating the Pahang Tenggara experience according to some of the criteria noted in Chapter 1, a mixed picture emerges. The <u>effectiveness of the planning process</u> is questionable given the lack of attention to the dynamics of planning and timing of development in the early stages, the weak powers conferred on DARA regarding forestry practices, land alienation, and control over regional infrastructures budgets, and the difficulties in staffing up and managing such a gigantic undertaking. Nevertheless, after a hesitant start DARA is becoming a more effective agency as it catches up with the backlog of infrastructure and town construction. The <u>efficiency</u> of development in terms of the scale and speed of plantation agriculture is impressive and the volume of palm oil exported from the Region will amount to almost one-third of Malaysia's production in a few years' time. The degree of detail on agricultural and forestry development which was contained in the FENCO plan did help DARA to start quickly on this aspect of the region's development.

However, this tremendous <u>productivity</u> is being achieved at the cost of <u>heavy externalities</u> which are falling chiefly on the natural environment and on the small communities which depend on it and secondarily on the public sector, in terms of the water resources needed by the new settlements. The growth in income and assets is also phenomenal, but their distribution is generally regressive, accruing mainly to the large private estates, with the exception of the FELDA projects where each family will own 4 to 6 hectares of land and will enjoy a higher income, providing product prices remain bouyant. The town developments will yield some positive distributional effects, since the settlers will be able to own their housing and offer a partial escape from the bondage of the "labour line". Efforts to induce service activities and processing industries into the towns will help to diversify the opportunities there, although this entails considerable risk for the entrepreneurs in the early stages before a large enough market has been established. Employment will be expanded in the Region, although the most efficient way to do this on a national scale may be through more smallholder development and through expansion of industry and services in larger urban areas. Participation by the settlers in decision-making has been non-existent, although this is likely to increase as the settlers flow into the towns. Whether the public investments in the Region are affordable by the government, and by the settlers in the case of housing, is an open question in the light of rising costs and uncertainty in market prices.

NOTES

(1) Johnson (1970).

(2) FENCO, vol. The Masterplan for the Development of Pahang Tenggara, 1972, p. 1.

(3) Government of Malaysia (1971), p. 1.

(4) Higgins (1976).

(5) These include a major study on migration potential to the region, demand studies of the attractiveness of the town to migrants and businesses, and an anthropological study of the orang asli, all undertaken for DARA by Universiti Sains, Penang. Other in-house studies and policy papers include ones on hinterland transport, environmental and ecological matters, forestry use, housing finance and programming tourism, financial analyses, manpower projects and training, and numerous feasibility studies for joint venture businesses. Over the first 5 years the numbers of working papers and policy memoranda ran into the hundreds.

(6) Johnson, *op. cit.*, p. 306.
(7) Johnson, *op. cit.*, p. 304.

REFERENCES

FENCO (1972) Pahang Tenggara Regional Master-planning Study. For the Government of Malaysia and the State of Pahang, Kuala Lumpur, 11 vols. and technical annexes.

Government of Malaysia (1971) "Second Malaysia Plan 1971 - 1975." Kuala Lumpur: The Government Press.

Higgins, B. (1976) "The Unified Approach To Development Planning at the Regional Level: the Case of Pahang Tenggara," in Kulinski, A. (ed.) Regional Development in Worldwide Perspective. The Hague: Mouton.

Johnson, E. A. J. (1970) The Organisation of Space in Developing Countries. Cambridge: Harvard University Press.

7
Settlement Prospects in China: A Rural Case Study

Richard Kirkby

The following contribution departs from the urban orientation of this collection. In order to justify the choice of a rural case study, I find it necessary to provide some preliminary background on the general state of urban China, and on the implications for human settlement of China's much vaunted 'Four Modernisations' programme. This introductory information constitutes the first of my four main sections. The following second section, the core of the study, consists of a description and tentative evaluation of the development plan for the Huaxi Production Brigade. Further evaluatory remarks are developed in the third section. Finally, the study is drawn together and related to a wide context in a brief Conclusion.

THE CHINESE URBAN SCENE, CURRENT ECONOMIC STRATEGY, AND THE IMPLICATIONS FOR SETTLEMENT

Urbanisation and City Structure

The view put forward by a number of Western students of the Peoples' Republic in recent years is that China has found a new form of urbanism, that in its essential structural features the Chinese cityscape differs qualitatively from those of both the industrialised and the industrialising worlds.(1) However, first-hand observation of many of China's large cities and discussions with planners(2) lead me to conclude that the above view is not supported by the evidence. Furthermore, in the coming period of modernisations, there will be powerful forces constraining the emergence of a novel and innovative urban practise in China.

Much is made by the optimistic school of the measures China has taken (and continues to take) in order to contain the city, to avoid unrestrained urban growth which would cause inherited urban hierarchy/primacy patterns to be even more pronounced. But focusing on these regulatory and remedial policies tends to obscure the severe problems of urban congestion which give rise to them. We are not concerned here with the precise figures for China's current urban and rural population composition - a subject fraught with problems of definition and meriting specialised study. Most observers agree that during the initial push to industrialise in the 1950s, the urban proportion of China's total population rose from around 10 percent in 1949 to 19 percent in 1960.(3) The 77¼ million registered in the 1953 Census as urban had increased by roughly two-thirds a decade later - to an estimated 130 million in 1964.(4) One careful estimate puts the annual average increase of urban population at 7.6 percent for the 1949-1960 period; for the Great Leap Forward year (1958) the figure stood at a massive 20 percent.(5) In short, the larger cities grew enormously during the 1950s. Between 1953-1958, the number of 'million-plus' cities leapt from nine to fifteen,(6) at the end of the period accounting for perhaps 30 percent of the country's total urban population.(7)

The true significance of this array of figures can, perhaps, best be judged by a cursory examination of the panic measures adopted by the Chinese authorities since the mid-1950s in order to deal with over-burgeoning city populations:

1. The imposition of strict migration controls.
2. From 1957 on, the periodical waves of 'sending down' (xia fang) of millions of cadres and assorted intellectuals.
3. The 'Up to the Mountains and down to the Rural Areas' (shang shan xia xiang) programmes for resettling young urban school-leavers in rural areas - many on a permanent basis. By mid-1975 it was claimed that 10 million young people had been decanted from the cities in this way.(8)
4. A comprehensive rationing of urban food comsumption.
5. Since the early 1970s, strict birth control programmes in the urban areas.
6. The drive to lessen the burden on the countryside by reducing the proportion of dependants to employed population in the cities. This has been done by setting up a myriad of small neighbourhood level workshops mainly employing women.

These measures have certainly met with success, and the city authorities of many major centres can report very low growth rates since the early 1960s.(9) But in the long term they have sown deep social tensions, with which the present post-Mao leadership in China is now grappling.

As for the effect on the urban fabric, gross over-population in the cities has caused a decline in the quality of the urban environment. City planners have had to run very fast in order to keep still. Certainly, in the early years, an admirable effort was made to give basic shelter to the millions who had previously been living in the most appalling conditions. But this achievement was gradually over-shadowed in the 1950s by a decline in housing standards for the majority of city dwellers. At the outset of reconstruction, 9 square metres of floorspace per head was provided in new projects, but this figure had dwindled by almost two-thirds by the early 1960s.(10) Studies have shown that urban housing and infrastructure was accorded a very low priority during the First Five Year Plan (1953-1958).(11) Regardless of the tortuous changes in national policy in China, one aim has remained constant since 1949: to transform the parasitical 'consumer cities' into 'producer cities'. The determination to minimise levels of 'non-productive' investment in the cities has created a situation in which there has been little scope for ambitious planning experiments. There are, of course, some 'grand schemes' of urban construction, but they are generally confined to the erection of monumental public buildings whose purpose is to awe - to give witness to the greatness of the era.

Today, 5 years after the Cultural Revolution was called to a close, it is no longer heretical in China to call for better housing, public transport and urban services. Indeed, Mao's successors are responding to the pent-up demand for improvement by initiating large housing projects (for the first time, of the multi-storey variety) in almost every major city. The administrative dislocation of the decade of strife (1966-1976) is a more obdurate problem; it had become customary for each enterprise to determine its own construction plans without reference to municipal planning bureaux. A serious start is being made in the area of pollution control, and for the first time since 1949 factories are being prosecuted for infringements of pollution regulations.(12) But the present wave of activity in the cities is basically corrective in nature; it is an assault on past problems rather than an attempt at any radical re-statement of socialist urbanism. Such remedial work on the existing fabric of China's cities (the new projects referred to are usually infilling on small sites) will continue to absorb the energies of city planners.

China's current political climate (basically a retrenchment, with radical social experiments being pushed into the background), combined with the requirements of the industrialisation phase now anticipated, together imply little in the way of qualitative change for the fabric of the existing cities. By examining the "Four Modernisations" programme in greater detail, the following section will elaborate on this assertion, and suggest that the latitude for innovative spatial planning will be greater in China's countryside than in the cities.

The Post-Mao Development Strategy and Prospects for the Urban Scene

Future settlement changes in China will occur in the context of economic plans. The drastic changes in the country's political orientation associated with the eclipse of the Maoist strategy have set the stage for a comprehensive modernisation programme apparently more akin to conventional strategies. The keystone of the "Four Modernisations", begun in the early 1970s and taken up in earnest in 1977 (industry, agriculture, technology and defence), is the import of high-level techniques from the West.(13) Successful implementation of the long-term plan would necessitate a gradual transformation of production methods both in the cities and on the farms. But it seems that in one vital respect China's industrialisation will differ from that of the already-developed nations: in a quarter of a century's time, around four-fifths of the population will still be rural-based.

Industrial targets and their implications:

For the 1978-1985 period, China plans that investment in capital construction will equal that of the entire preceding 28 years of the People's Republic. In his speech at the fifth convening of China's quasi-Parliament (the National People's Congress held in February 1978), Premier Hua Guofeng disclosed that the chief thrust will be in 120 large projects, among them nineteen metal complexes, eight giant coal-mines, and ten oil and gas fields. These developments, combined with existing plants, will form fourteen spatially distinct regional bases. Although the details of their distribution throughout the country are only partially known, it would appear that most of the new development will take place in or near established industrial centres. This is certainly the case with the many foreign turnkey chemical fertiliser plants constructed from 1975 onwards and now coming into operation. With oil, gas and other newly discovered mineral deposits, the location of extraction installations is of course predetermined; but the settlement patterns encouraged at these sites will almost certainly follow the dispersed "Daqing model"(14) - about which more will be said later. The exceptions may be those very large coal deposits to be exploited under the current plan which are located near to existing mines. Here the small towns may be considerably expanded, as for instance, in the case of the East Shandong coalfield where the city of Zibo and the town of Zhoucun appear to be the objects of exceptional attention of China's spatial planners. During the 1950s, when a number of important industrial bases were developed according to the Soviet model, there was massive migration from the villages to the factories. The Four Modernisations, however, will not give rise to a comparable swelling of the urban centres. Briefly, there exists in the cities an obvious (but unquantifiable) pool of surplus labour. Inattention to labour productivity during the 1966-1976 period gave rise to considerable over-manning of industry. Problems with the 'sending down' programmes have made it politically inexpedient to pursue them in the same form:(15) in the future the majority of young school-leavers will probably enter the urban labour force directly or after a few years of the rustication experience. The vast numbers of women presently employed in workshop-type enterprises operating with primitive technology will also provide a ready source of labour for the planned industrial plant as their production methods are upgraded. The Chinese are purchasing foreign plants incorporating the most advanced and thus capital intensive processes; apart from the period of construction, which may rely heavily on contracted (temporary) labour from the rural areas, the demands for an expanded labour force will be limited.(16)

A parallel component to present plans for the development of an ultra-modern basic industrial sector is the continued expansion of small and "medium-sized" plants. These will be located in the metropoli - where they already constitute a prominent feature of China's cityscapes. But it is in the smaller townships - especially the county (Xian) towns - where they will acquire an enhanced significance as catalysts in the modernisation process. By 1978, as many as half of the country's 2000-odd Xian had their own small chemical fertiliser plants. In the dual system of large and small developments, the lower tier has been told to concentrate on the mining, power, cement, fertiliser, iron and steel and even non-ferrous metals; county-owned industry is expected to provide its raw materials from local sources. The county towns will continue in their role as assembly, manufacturing and repair points for agricultural machinery. As agricultural productivity is raised - partly through mechanisation - greater quantities of agricultural raw materials will made available to a principally county-town-based processing and light manufacturing sector.

What impact will such developments at county town level have on the overall pattern of rural settlement? Up until recently, within the administrative hierarchy of Province, Prefecture, County and People's Commune it is the county town that has undergone the least change in political role and the least physical transformation. In the three decades of the People's Republic, the county towns have been divested of some of their former importance of imperial times by the establishment of the communes. But in matters of vital national policy (investments made under the State plan, education, etc.) their traditional powers, though changed in form, are undiminished.

At present, most county towns are small in relation to the populations they serve: the national mean for county population size is around one third of a million, yet the typical county town lies in the 5000 - 15,000 range. The trends of the past decade or so, reinforced by the new emphasis on industrial development in general, will accelerate the growth of the county towns. The effect on the surrounding countryside, however, will be more marked in the economic and cultural spheres than in the political and spatial. That is to say, the agricultural sector will benefit from an increased availability of county town-produced machinery, fertiliser and other inputs; peasant incomes will be boosted thereby, as well as through a greater number of farm workers being drawn into the industrial economy. But unfettered expansion of the county town is unlikely, for China cannot afford to permit its urban development to encroach on limited agricultural land.(17) The recruitment of rural labour for small town industry will continue to be strictly regulated according to the annual global figures arrived at by the State Council in Peking. Provincial allocations are further broken down; the lowest tier in the chain, the County Labour Bureau (Xian Laodong Ju), being finally informed of the precise number of workers to be recruited (jiao gong) for the current year. Most of the new recruits to county town enterprises are not in fact fully recruited - that is to say, they do not attain full 'non-agricultural' status (fei nongye hu) until they have passed through a probation period. The duration of the latter depends both on the size of the State allocations (referred to above) and on the personal qualifications and/or connections of the recruit. Until he undergoes the vital change in status ("agricultural" status but resident in an urban area, to "non-agricultural" status), the probationer is obliged to pay as much as half of his monthly salary to the Commune Production Brigade from whence he came.(18)

Almost without exception, this is considered to be a small price to pay, for one foot in the urban economy means a hand in the "iron rice bowl" of the State system. Despite advances in basic security for China's peasants, the collective rural existence (in which income is directly determined by local annual output) is essentially precarious. So much so, that a new urban recruit will go to enormous lengths in order to avoid marrying back into the villages from which he so recently escaped.

One of my purposes in outlining the tight set of controls governing migration from the village to the nearest point of urban contact - the county town - is to emphasise the continued rift between urban and rural worlds in contemporary

China. There is perhaps a need to do so, for hitherto the impression conveyed by outside observers of the Chinese scene is that the age-old attractiveness of the cities has been turned on its head in the case of China.(19) With a few notable exceptions, this appraisal is contrary to the reality I have found. Yet if the urban alternative will only be open to a minority, what prospects are in store for the great majority of China's 700 million peasants? I have opted for a rural case study precisely in order to attempt an answer to this question. By describing and evaluating the development process at Huaxi (one of the "notable exceptions" par excellence), I hope to demonstrate that most of the advantages - and few of the undesirable side-effects - universally associated with an urban existence can be brought to the Chinese rural scene.

Agricultural targets and their implications for rural settlement and organisation:

The Chinese are acutely aware that poor agricultural performance would jeopardise industrialisation plans. The modernisation of agriculture and the rural economy rests on (1) mechanisation, and (2) development of small non-farming service and production enterprises, mainly at Commune and Production Brigade (PB) levels rather than at the lowest level of rural organisation - the Production Team.

Mechanisation has been on the agenda at least since 1955. In the Chinese literature, the term is usually ill-defined; but generally it implies that the chief processes of ploughing, irrigation, harvesting, threshing and transport are taken care of by small machines. Despite the disruption of the Cultural Revolution years, the farm machinery industry has continued to expand at an impressive rate: the period from 1966 to 1976 saw a 20 percent annual rate of increase in the output of farm machines. But the enormity of rural China and unequal distribution policies have meant that efforts so far have failed to make much overall impression. In the wake of a number of national conferences on agricultural development(20) (particularly the two meetings to propagate the experience of the agricultural model brigade of Dazhai held in 1975 and 1976), certain concrete aims have been set. The Fifth National People's Congress called for a doubling of grain output by 1985, when 85 percent of all major agricultural processes should have been mechanised. Besides expanding the output of machines, the programme calls for a remodelling of small field systems at present unsuited to the introduction of heavy equipment. This work began in earnest in 1975: field levelling and amalgamation projects, undertaken usually during the slack winter season, can be observed everywhere in China's countryside. Normally, land-shaping efforts rely solely on human muscle power and the carrying pole or wheelbarrow. Around large cities such as Shanghai modern earth moving equipment is beginning to be brought into play.

Enterprises. Communes and PBs are encouraged to establish their own small workshops for the repair or manufacture of simple farm equipment, dehusking of grain and so on. Commune factories occasionally produce more sophisticated items, often under contract to an urban factory. By 1975, 90 percent of the Communes and 60 percent of the PBs were said to have their own "enterprises". Many of these are non-industrial, as the term includes such activities as fish farming, fruit-growing and personal services such as cobbling and tailoring.

In the Chinese system, increased rural production of all kinds should accrue directly to the producers. This is possible because of the regressive State Agricultural Tax. The more the peasants produce the more they can retain for augmented investment and consumption at the lower levels of Production Brigade and Team which have legal ownership of most land, tools and machinery. In the long term, the development of the productive forces will pave the way for an upward transfer of ownership - from the present collective system to State ownership. The initial stage of this "statification" process, achieved by only a small minority of China's three-quarters of a million PBs, is the upward transfer of Team(21) collective property to the PB. This step is far more than a simple juridical act. Under the present moderate leadership in China, it is supposed to be taken only when the level of development of the productive forces merits it, when there is sufficient economic parity between the villages to be organisationally merged, and so on. The significance for rural settlement patterns lies in the fact that the field system rationalisation (a concomitant of mechanisation) can provide the occasion for the network of scattered villages left over by history to be physically merged. Thus mechanisation of agriculture may create both the extra resources prequisite to structural change in the rural economy, and the stimulus for a profound transformation of China's traditional rural habitat. This is what has happened at Huaxi.(22)

THE HUAXI PRODUCTION BRIGADE PLAN - A DESCRIPTIVE ANALYSIS

Introductory Facts and Data Sources

The Huaxi Production Brigade is one of the twenty six PBs belonging to the Huashi People's Commune, situated in Jiangyin Xian not far from the large county town of the same name. Jiangyin, one of the seventy-odd counties of Jiangsu Province, is part of the traditionally prosperous belt of the Jiangnan

("South of the River") zone. Its northern border is in fact the Yangzi. The Huaxi PB is one of those relatively few Brigades that has made the transition from Team level accounting to Brigade level; this transfer has been accompanied by the merging of the original constituent hamlets of the Brigade into one large village. This Brigade has 258 households (mid-1976) and a total population of 1022. Almost half (480) of the Brigade members are economically active. Of these 480, half are women. Huaxi's total cultivable area is around 57 hectares; there is one-eighteenth of a hectare for every man, woman and child in the Brigade.

My information on Huaxi stems from a visit in August 1976. It is complemented by reports in the provincial and national press between September 1975 and December 1978.(23) The clarity of the information on Huaxi stems in great part from the fact that it is a fairly self-contained experiment. This stands in contrast to the development process of, say, an urban neighbourhood, where a large number of municipal agencies may play a part.

Huaxi Prior to the Brigade Development Plan

The setting:

In 1964, when the "Learn from Dazhai" movement had just been initiated, Huaxi was by local standards quite unremarkable. The member teams of the Brigade corresponded to twelve scattered villages. In the broad plains of the Lower Yangzi, surface water is the dominant physical feature. Viewed from the air, the countryside is a lattice-work of canals, streams, ponds and lakes. Maps of old Huaxi show that much of the area was ill-drained and marshy: even the best land was subject to periodic waterlogging. Settlements were small and isolated from one another. Often the only routes between villages were the narrow muddy ridges separating the paddies. Village layout followed the traditional rectangular pattern, the single line of dwellings around the perimeter enclosing a central threshing ground of sun-baked earth. Of shops, schools or other public buildings - except perhaps for the occasional small temple - there were none in these tiny hamlets. In place of the boundary wall of baked mud characteristic of the North China village, here the settlements were surrounded on three and sometimes four sides by a narrow moat - more for household water supply than for defence (see Fig. 7.1). Though the terrain was fairly even, multiple land ownership and the needs of irrigation meant that there was some variation in level between adjacent fields. These should more accurately be called plots - as an earlier description of a similar area shows:

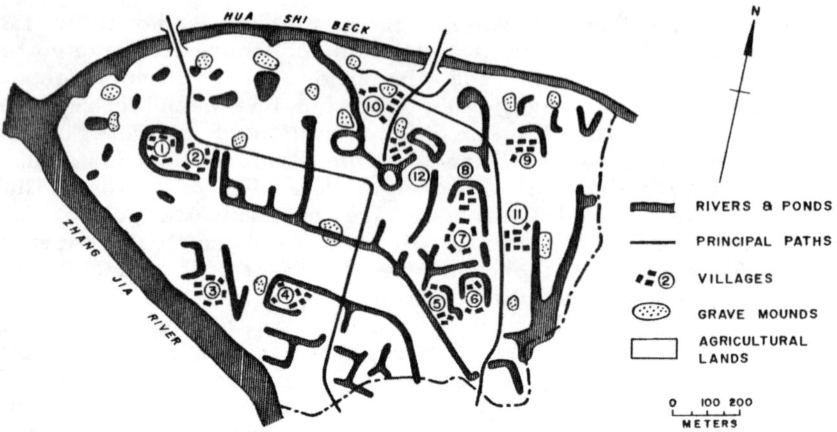

Fig. 7.1. Hauxi Brigade and its twelve scattered villages in 1963.

Source: Jianzhu Xuebao, No. 3, 1975

> "Few fields exceed 90 metres in length; many are only 30 metres long by 15 metres wide. A crop such as soybeans may be planted in two or three rows along a path, and much corn is grown in odd patches less than three metres in diameter."(24)

Individual plots at Huaxi must have been even more minute, for in 1964 there were 1300 of them.

In this part of China, considerable importance has traditionally been attached to the design of the home. But the breakdown of the rural economy over the century preceding the Communist victory meant a sharp decline in construction standards. By 1949 kiln-fired bricks and tiles had become a luxury that only the richer landlords could afford. As in other less-endowed regions, mean mud-brick huts covered by a straw thatch served as home for the ordinary peasant. The roof beams comprised the only valuable component; they would be carefully used and reused until they finally rotted. The average dwelling was low (often the roof ridge was less than 2 metres high), windowless and crampled. Average per capita space for Huaxi's twelve original hamlets was a mere 4.6 square metres. Superstition decreed unhealthy design - still prevalent in many neighbouring areas today: the traditional practice is to build the floor level rather lower than the outside ground level. The packed earth floors are transformed into a morass of sticky mud during the wet season. The local belief is that a high floor allows all the riches (literally the "gold and silver") to flow out of the home.

Farming methods were those of the countless centuries of traditional China. A buffalo or a pair of oxen (huang niu) might have been available for ploughing, and primitive wooden pedal-operated machines for threshing. Water lifting was by hand or by the traditional 'dragon's back' device. The only modern item of farm equipment in the entire Brigade was a diesel engine and pump attachment. The village lands were dotted with ancestral grave mounds which hindered cultivation and prevented any reform of the ancient irrigation networks.

Grain output (in rice and winter wheat) averaged 6.75 metric tons per hectare in 1964. In many parts of China, this would be a high figure, but for Huaxi the low level of technique allowed only a part of the potential of the fertile earth to be tapped. In the Chinese rural system, standards of living and the surplus available for expanding production are determined directly by the level of collective grain (or cash crop) production. In 1963, annual per capita grain allocation stood at 250 kilogrammes (500 jin) and cash income at 91 yuan.(25) The resources of each Production Team and of the parent Brigade were limited because of the small size of the grain surplus which could be sold to State purchasing authorities. Consequently there was little available for collective educational, health and other services. Children benefited from a few years of rudimentary primary schooling in the Brigade school, but for the mass of the peasants cultural horizons had changed little with the coming of the new society of Socialist China. Finally, the spatial configuration of the Brigade, with its poorly linked hamlets, militated against any advance in economic or social conditions of life.

Formulation of the plan:

One of the most intriguing aspects of the Huaxi experience - indeed of any emulation model - concerns the nature of the initial impetus, and of the circumstances which allowed exceptional development to be sustained. With respect to natural conditions, the skills of its labour force, etc., Huaxi in 1964 did not differ from the countless other Brigades of the Lower Yangzi region. The purposeful planning for a transformation of production and lifestyle was not triggered off by any particular material input - for instance, a State grant, the sudden availability of a number of agricultural machines, etc. There was, however, an external catalyst of a less tangible nature: propagation by the Party apparatus of the broad principles of "self-reliant" rural development associated with the then-new national model of the Dazhai Brigade. The lowest formal level of the Communist Party's organisational net in the countryside is the Brigade Party Branch, presided over by its Secretary. The decisive force in the initiation and supervision of the Huaxi development process has clearly been the Brigade's far-sighted Party leaders. It should be emphasised that the demonstrable success of this body in acting as a reliable vehicle for the implementation of Party policy is highly atypical.

According to later accounts of the early planning process, the stages were as follows: (a) study of the Dazhai example; (b) Party Branch decision to press for sweeping changes in the Brigade: on the basis of a prior expansion in agricultural productivity the old village patterns were to be transformed; (c) consultation with each family conducted by Brigade cadres, mainly on ways of improving village lands; (d) detailed survey of existing land and irrigation system; (e) detailed elaboration of a 15-year plan for farmland improvement and crop targets. For grain, the goal was to raise per hectare output from 6.75 tons (1963) to 15 tons (1979). Also spelt out were the schemes for remodelling irrigation and surface water, as well as for the merger of existing settlements; (f) publicising of the details of the plan to Brigade members; and (g) continuous evaluation of initial results and adjustment of targets.

It would appear that, at the outset, specific production targets (other than those for grain) were left unstated. Similarly, little was said initially about the many aspects of life which might be improved during the course of the plan. The reasons for this vagueness on the part of the Party Branch can be hazarded: the Party leadership itself was unable to foresee the spin-off from grain output increases; it did not wish to raise expectations which could not ultimately be met; it did not want to frighten off the peasants by holding out an image of a too highly collectivised future; the Party Branch wished to maintain the maximum leeway in the planning process, so that readjustments and additions could be made as time went on. Indeed, new aims were fed in: in 1968 Brigade leaders visited Dazhai, returning with plans to save even more land by constructing underground irrigation channels and a new pumping station. Brigade members were constantly reminded of what the future held by a large plan of the proposed layout which was erected in a prominent position in the village. Brigade cadres kept details of the amount of labour and equipment to be used, the quantity of earth to be shifted, and the perceived priorities at each stage of the plan's implementation.

The Hauxi Plan - Results and Preliminary Assessment

The following section will detail the plan's achievements and comment on the process of implementation. The reader may justifiably observe at this point that, since Huaxi is well publicised, by commonly accepted standards it is, predictably, going to turn out as a great success story. I believe that this fact in no way diminishes Huaxi's relevance, for by making available information on the Brigade's plan the Chinese authorities are conceding by default that its positive experience is encountered only rarely in China's countryside. My own evaluatory remarks are necessarily limited.

Production achievements:

By 1976 the 1300 tiny plots of 1963 had become 400 fields. Figure 7.2 shows how surface water was rationalised; irrigation was simplified and channels put underground. A modern electric pumping station was built to regulate the flows of the water system. Grain output (the basic indicator of success) rose gradually through the 1960s - from the 1964 figure of 6.75 tons per hectare to 10 tons in 1967. By 1972 the 15 year target of 15 tons per hectare was attained - some 7 years in advance. As the Brigade's annual grain surplus increased, more equipment could be purchased. Today most of the ploughing, planting (including rice transplanting), irrigation, threshing, plant protection and transport tasks are done with the aid of small machines. Of the really arduous jobs, this leaves only the back-breaking work of harvesting and carrying the rice seedlings from their beds to the paddies. Most field construction was done by hand, but in the future any large-scale earth moving will be assisted by mechanical diggers. The initial 15 ton per hectare target for grain proved to be conservative: by 1976, 19 tons had been reached, and this figure was exceeded in 1977.

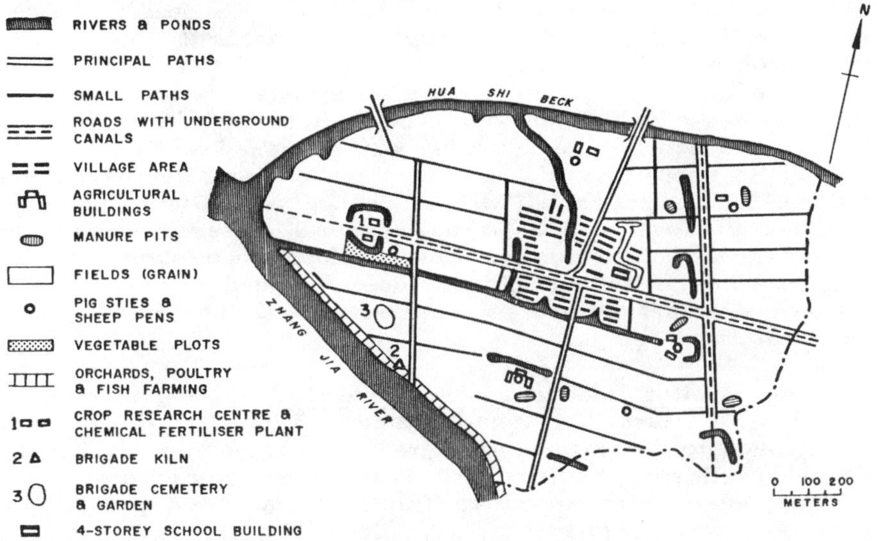

Fig. 7.2. Huaxi Brigade in 1976

Source: Jianzhu Xuebao, No. 3, 1975 and R. Kirkby, 1976)

The Brigade had managed to diversify production. By 1978, 78 percent of the total value of output came from its thirty-one non-cultivating enterprises. These include pig-breeding and poultry units, fish ponds, metal workshops, a grain processing and noodle-making mill, and so on. Of these thirty-one enterprises, some are oriented towards "export" while a number provide services consumed within the Brigade. By 1978 over seventy items of agricultural equipment had been acquired by the Brigade with its own funds.

Consumption aspects:

(a) Income, food availability and retail services. Cash income per capita (working members and dependants) has more than doubled, from 91 yuan (US $37) (1963) to 185 yuan (US $99) (1975) and 220 yuan (US $132) in 1978. These figures do not include the value of the grain and straw (used as fuel) distributed to each household periodically throughout the year. *Per capita* grain allocation rose from 250 kilos in 1963 to 310 kilos in 1978.

Numerous other foodstuffs have become available, many at prices subsidised through the Brigade's collective welfare fund.(26) Some examples: eggs are sold to Brigade members at roughly half the market price; peanuts, sunflower seeds and several varieties of bean are supplied cheaply. Vegetables (almost a kilo per person daily) are provided completely free of charge - a fact which has greater significance than meets the eye: perhaps the most sensitive aspect of rural policy concerns the question of private plots for each peasant household. With a free vegetable supply the necessity for private land is largely obviated.

The new Brigade village has its own tailors and cobblers, the services of which are 50 percent subsidised from collective funds. Household grain supplies are dehusked and polished in a Brigade shop free of charge. Noodles - preferred during festivals - are processed without charge to the individual who supplies his own flour. A new general store provides most everyday household wares, while a food shop supplies non-staples which are not locally produced. The Brigade generates its own electricity which is supplied to each new home at half the local rate.

(b) Cultural, educational and health. The upper floors of a new "Cultural Services Building" (*Wenhua Fuwu Lou*) are given over to meeting rooms, a reading room and small lending library, and study/cultural activities rooms for each section of the Brigade. With collective funds it has been possible to purchase two television sets and film projectors. Next to the Cultural Building there is a small sports ground with two basketball courts. Slightly to the east of the village centre, a recently constructed five-storey building houses a nursery, kindergarten, and primary and secondary schools. In contrast to the usual situation, all education, including senior middle schooling, is provided free to Brigade members out of Brigade funds. Each household contributes a few yuan a year to the Brigade's health insurance scheme. The Brigade clinic takes care of minor health problems free of charge, while patients referred to county or high-level medical services need pay only half of their medical bills.

(c) Shelter and village construction. From the legal point of view, all land belongs, as it does throughout China, to the peasants. The tenure is collective; that is, the individual peasant is not at liberty to buy or dispose of land; nor may he directly decide on which crops to grow, and to whom to sell. Broadly considered, the degree to which ownership can truly be considered collective is determined by current national policy (which may regulate peasant life strictly or less strictly), and the vagaries of local leadership. In the case of the Huaxi plan, no formal questions of land prices or compensation arose when the individual villages were required by the plan to put their lands into the hands of the higher collective body - the Brigade.

Since 1963 every household has been rehoused. Peasant homes in this part of China are traditionally measured in terms of jian (standard-sized room units). Most housing units are of the single-storey terrace type (670 jian), but since 1975 the Brigade has decided to rebuild in two-storeyed terraces. 190 jian of this space-economising type of construction has been completed. Housing conditions have, of course, improved immensely: per capita space is up five-fold on the 1963 figure; each home has electricity, while running water is supplied to the most recently built housing; materials are superior - kiln-fired bricks and tiles; the interiors are provided with plenty of light and walls are whitewashed, while concrete is replacing the traditional sunken packed earth floors. No part of the village, including the school building, is more than a few minutes walk from the home, and the various sections of the village are linked by dry, paved paths.

The new village layout was selected with a view to maximum utilisation of land. The present village centre - meeting-cum-sports ground, shops and the 'Cultural Services Building' - occupies an area which was formerly a marshy island in the Huaxi Beck. The laymen-planners were successful in utilising this unfavourable site, even managing to meet traditional requirements of aspect. For most of the terraces, the ancient principle of "facing the sun" (chaoyang) was adhered to (see Fig. 7.2).

Rural housing in China has never been collectivised. The Huaxi planners decided that new housing units would remain privately owned, and to this end a housing finance scheme was devised which was sufficiently flexible to allow even the poorer households to repay loans without undue hardship. In fact, all loans had been repaid by 1972. Construction costs were kept to a minimum by a variety of means: bricklayers and carpenters in the Brigade trained a team of peasants, and set up a full-time construction team which was paid by the work-point system rather than in cash; no outside expertise had to be hired by the Brigade; locally found materials were used, and a kiln was built; all salvageable materials from the demolished homes were reused.

The result of this economy was construction costs at roughly one quarter the level of those in the nearest large city - Wuxi.(27) The overall plan for demolition and rebuilding was drawn up according to the principle of the greatest need. In addition to organising the assembly (and, where necessary, the purchase) of building materials, the Brigade forwarded all the ready cash required for construction of the individual's home. The crucial point is that no external source of finance or labour was required for the entire housing scheme. This is also the case with the two multi-storey public buildings.

A BROAD EVALUATION OF THE HUAXI PLAN

From the Perspective of the User

It is clear that the development plan has brought with it a great measure of physical security - a deep-rooted obsession in this land which for centuries has known a cycle of drought, flood, famine and destitution. But what of less tangible aspects than physical security?

Legal security:

It can be argued that in China's socialist system, one of the greatest barriers to an enthusiastic acceptance by the peasants of collectivising policies is the strong measure of irrevocability of the process. If it fails to provide the promised advantages, there can be little right of redress. For instance, during the Cultural Revolution private plots were abolished; the peasants in many areas have had the greatest difficulty in getting this premature and unpopular measure reversed, even though private holdings were clearly sanctioned in the State Constitution of 1975.

At Huaxi, as elsewhere in the country, the greatest potential threat to legal/economic security lies in the State's ability to readjust the present agricultural tax system.(28)

The continued development at Huaxi would be jeopardized if taxation directly proportional to output were to replace the present system based on a fixed amount of grain per hectare. It should be noted that at Huaxi, the State Agricultural Tax has gradually dwindled as a proportion of total output - from around 7 percent in 1963 to 1.6 percent in 1976.

Thus threats to legal security emanate from national policy, over which the peasants of the Huaxi Brigade have little control.

Respect for the "planned for":

We are dealing here with a country only just emerging from its long feudal past. The tendency towards hierarchical authority, towards a monopoly of new skills by a minority, make it especially important that planners in China be aware of the dangers of isolation from the planned for. Despite the upheavals of the Cultural Revolution period in China, the belief that those with power should exercise it, and those without should obey, is an enduring one. Thus the mode of implementation of the Huaxi plan was almost certainly paternalistic - the Commuist Party's self-defined image is that of a guide for the people. Yet in the Chinese rural context, there are definite limitations on the prevailing paternalism becoming authoritarianism. The bare facts of the situation are that, unlike in the Soviet Union during its phase of collectivisation, the organised forces of mass State repression are logistically extremely limited.(29)

Since the 1930s the Party has stressed that its rural cadres should rely on techniques of education and persuasion. Huaxi cadres relate a case which illustrates the non-commandist nature of their own methods: one of the villagers was pleased at the thought of getting a new home, but he wanted it to be built on his ancestral land. He refused to move to the new village, so the Party Branch decided that his wishes be respected and gave him materials and assistance in rebuilding his home on the old site. Later this recalcitrant individual realised the advantages of living in the new village and he was rehoused there.

The methods of the Huaxi leadership are prescribed by the general policy of the Party, which considers itself to be the ultimate authority in all spheres of life. In a more important unit (danwei) than a PB, such as a university, the Party Secretary might well be a stranger sent in (often as deus ex machina) by higher quthorities. But the Huaxi Brigade leadership is made up of local people, many being from former poor peasant families.(30) Though not elected by and directly answerable to the local community (they are selected by a higher tier of the Party), Brigade officials are at least familiar with local problems and aspirations. They too are subject to the successes or failures of the plan - a necessary though clearly insufficient condition for sensitive government.(31)

In the urban setting, detailed participation in neighbourhood development issues, or in production planning in the factories, is virtually an unknown concept.(32) Information is of course a prerequisite to participation, and at Huaxi a high priority has been accorded to access to information and plans, both for production and for settlement.

The leaders of Production Teams in rural China are not necessarily Party members. Although the lowest tier of Party organisation - the Brigade Party Branch - obviously takes a close interest in the leadership of the constituent Teams, it cannot actually appoint Team Leaders. The latter are supposed to be selected by Team members by consensus; the procedures, intervals and so on for this selection process are left vague so there is in fact a great deal of room for manipulation, favouritism and family nepotism. In the case of Huaxi, with its apparent unity of effort and successes, one can assume that the leaders of the eight functional Teams have been responsive to their "constituencies".

Problems of identity:

In rural China as in other peasant societies there exists a strong sense of identity with one's kinfolk. This is despite the efforts of the authorities over the past 30 years to supplant kinship ties and feelings with an identity with the collective and the nation. My information regarding the structure of kinship at Huaxi is unfortunately inadequate. Thus it is difficult to judge whether significant group feelings have been infringed or enhanced by the Huaxi plan, and especially by the resettlement plan. This remains an area for future study; all that can be said at this stage is that it would be difficult to practise the present high level of collective expenditure (subsidies, welfare, education, etc.) if vital social ties had been ignored by Huaxi's planners.

Equity:

Economic. Considering firstly indirect income, the point of central importance to equity between households is that the Brigade's annual allocation to its Welfare Fund is very high in comparison with other rural units. Every Brigade member is equally eligible for subsidised food, services, and for free educational, cultural and health facilities. Consumption in this sphere is not related to the individual's contribution to production. Direct income in cash and kind, on the other hand, depends on the number of working members in the household and the assessed value of their contribution. Normally the tougher or more highly skilled jobs are awarded higher values. Yet in Huaxi in 1976, Brigade officials claimed they were implementing a policy by which all jobs were considered as of equal value, regardless of the amount of skill or energy required in executing them. In this system, any variation in pay between individuals stems from the degree of efficiency with which each performs an allotted task. The creation of a large number of enterprises at Huaxi, as well as the introduction of mechanised agriculture, has not led to the emergence of a skilled elite with special privileges. Brigade cadres explained that they were perfecting a system which they dubbed "The Three Gradual Equalities": firstly, Brigade officials should be rewarded in the same way as the ordinary members; second, individuals from the Brigade recruited by outside enterprises (at commune or county levels) should not be awarded a high cash wage but should be paid partially in kind; thirdly, Brigade machinery operatives should be paid the same amount as unskilled peasants.

This statement should be qualified in the light of the political changes in China since 1976. Currently, extreme egalitarianism is under fire, for it is said to inhibit peasant initiative by denying incentive.(33) Although such criticism of egalitarianism is demonstrably appropriate in the case of backward units (where income equity may imply "common poverty" rather than common prosperity), it may not be so valid in such cases as Huaxi where a strong production base has already been established. It is interesting that current publicity on this Brigade does, pointedly, refer to some income inequality; in 1977, for example, 9.5 percent of households received over 1000 yuan, while 50 percent got less than 500 yuan.

Those with no income from labour - the retired and disabled - are supported out of Brigade funds. They receive free grain, fuel and vegetables, as well as a small monthly stipend. Those with no family receive free housing.

Sexual equality. As a result of the payment policies outlined above, women receive not only equal pay for equal work but also equal pay for unequal (less skilled or easier) work. Most of the workers in the machinery shop are women. Nursery and kindergarten provision, and communal canteens during the busy agricultural seasons, release women from their burdensome roles of tradition. A number of leadership positions in the Brigade are filled by women: four out of ten numbers of the Party Branch, including the two Vice-Secretaries; and six out eleven members of the Brigade Revolutionary Committee.

Housing equality. For those peasants who could not afford to purchase their new homes outright, the flexible repayment policy for interest-free housing loans meant that household income has not determined access to the rehousing scheme. At present, one-storey terrace housing and the superior two-storey structures exist side by side, a fact which must give rise to a certain degree of inequality. But this situation is temporary as the plan is to demolish and rebuild the first-stage housing in order to save land. Generally, the advent of standard design housing units and equality per capita space allocation have meant a high degree of equity in the provision of shelter.

Huazi and the Objectives of China's Rural Development Strategy

Background - A self-contained experiment:

Moving on now to the "supply" aspects of the Huaxi plan, that the Brigade conforms to national development aims is palpably demonstrated by the intermittent attention it has been given in China since 1975. Broadly, these aims are summed up in the Chinese political slogan of "self-reliance". In the early 1960s, the CCP concluded that as the central State authorities lacked the material and administrative resources for the development of local projects the only recourse was to rely on local initiative. Mao, of course, is inextricably identified with self-reliance. But despite many changes in the Cultural Revolution policies in the 3 years since the overthrow of the "gang of four" radicals, the present leadership in China is finding that it is obliged by circumstances not to dismantle this aspect of the Maoist edifice. Indeed, it has no reason to do so.

For its production and settlement plans the Huaxi Brigade has not required any external assistance. This, despite the initial disadvantage of owing a sizeable sum to State organisations - a sum borrowed at an earlier period to meet normal operating costs. After repayment of debts it is claimed that Huaxi's transformation has been entirely self-financing.(34)

From the ideological point of view, the CCP emphasises that improvements in peasant living standards must be founded upon a significant and sustained prior increase in grain output.(35) In short, higher consumption cannot be paid for out of locally accumulated funds required for basic investments in the productive base. At Huaxi the decision to demolish the first batch of old housing came in 1965, as it could be justified on the basis of the previous year's 35 percent increase in grain production. Furthermore, to minimise interference with production, all construction was done during the slack winter season, and even then only a small proportion of the labour force (a maximum of 12 percent) was assigned to village construction.

A further ideological/proganda aspect of great import to State policy is the rooting out of harmful feudal superstition.

Family graves which previously took up much valuable land are now centralised in a Brigade burial ground. Cremation - unheard of in rural China - is successfully encouraged.

CONCLUSION

This case study focuses on a fragment - albeit not an entirely representative fragment - of China's administrative system. It is a system with a fair degree of uniformity, which means that a description of the part casts some light on the whole - the broader context of China's economic and spatial planning policies. It is this broader context which, in my concluding remarks, deserves further, if brief, mention; thereby, it is hoped that the general utility of the Huaxi experience to China will be underlined.

The Model per se is, of course, regarded as an important vehicle for change in contemporary China; the concept has its origins both in Chinese tradition and in the Stakhanovism learnt from the Soviet Union. Can Huaxi be considered as a model? With regard to its economic aspects it surely is upheld as one. But the general absence of debate on the question of the relationship between social and spatial dimensions has relegated the settlement aspects of the plan to a poor second place.

The first section of this study attempts to show that China's cities are weighed down under the burden of unplanned and incremental growth which occurred both before and after 1949. And in examining the current "Four Modernisations" proposals, it can be concluded that there will be little latitude for future large scale urban expansion or for the innovative planning solutions which such an expansion might afford. So what model are Chinese planners being exhorted to follow? Periodically that of the Daqing Oilfield is mentioned in the literature.(36) But in my own view it is quite inadequate, irrelevant even, to the needs of the rural and urban condition of China. Briefly, the "Daqing model" proposes that a radical departure from the traditional ("capitalist") concentrated urbanism can be achieved through the establishment of dispersed settlement/production points. The interstices between industrial installations and housing are used for farming purposes, with the dependants of industrial workers producing the bulk of the grain and vegetables required by the non-farming section of the population. An added virtue of Daqing is said to be its unprepossessing and cheap self-help housing, built of baked mud bricks and other local materials.

This is all very well for an oilfield in virgin territory, but the value of a model lies in its transferability: the long term industrial modernisation programme China is embarking on suggests a more concentrated, perhaps more conventional, form of urbanism. It should be pointed out at this juncture that those foreign observers who (taking their cue from the official Chinese accounts) state that China's cities have already somehow been "ruralised" and the countryside "industrialised" are far from the reality. All the evidence shows that today in China the city remains very much the city and the countryside - regardless of some advances in basic security - very much the countryside.

But if Daqing as a spatial model is as much a backwater, a diversion, as I assert, why is it fixed on by the Chinese? The reasons can be crudely divided into ideological and economic. The former have their basis in the long-standing and powerful strand of socialist utopianism and anti-urbanism in the Chinese Communist movement. In so far as the Chinese are guided by theory, these trends imply a misreading of Marx's formulation concerning the contradictory relationship between town and country. Marx was essentially speaking of a contradiction founded on the antagonistic relations (economically, politically) between city and countryside. The remedy of the socialist era is, therefore, not the obliteration of the physical differences between the two, but, rather, the removal of these exploitative relations. As for the second set of reasons (economic) - they arise from the CCP's oft-stated policy of limiting non-productive urban investment.

During the present period of pragmatic leadership we cannot perhaps expect much attention to be given to theoretical formulations of the model. The tasks confronting Chinese urban planners are obvious and practical: the rehabilitation, depolluting, revitalisation and general rationalisation of the two dozen or so "million" cities. Very basic work has yet to be done to the fabric of the cities - the provision of modern, standardised electricity and water supplies, the introduction of an underground sewerage system and so on.

As for the vast countryside - there, development-cum-spatial models which relate to the coming mechanisation of farming will have a very practical use in the next 20 years. Much work on local design and customs remains to be done by China's urbanists, in order that the best traditions of an ancient culture be preserved and enlarged. But in the meantime, the developments at Huaxi and a few other outstanding rural units hold out the broad guidelines for the future for China's hundreds of millions of farmers. A generalisation of the Huaxi-type experience would create an entirely new tier of sub-county town level settlements in the 750-1500 population range. Only then could we begin to speak of a novel Chinese agropolitan model, consisting of a network of small and manageable agriculturally oriented self-contained townships. The experience of Huaxi shows how, at a small scale of settlement, it is possible to provide enhanced standards of living and an impressive range of cultural, educational and other services not at present generally seen in China's countryside.

NOTES

(1) See, for example, Sawers (1977).

(2) Between 1973-1979. I have lived in China on and off since 1975.

(3) Sen-dou Chang (1976), Chang's figures also indicate that the urban proportion fell somewhat through the 1960s.

(4) See Onoye (1971), p. 113.

(5) Chao (1966), p. 382.

(6) Sen-dou Chang (1968), pp. 128-153. The entire article is extremely useful.

(7) Blumenfeld (1978).

(8) Guangming Daily, 17 May 1975.

(9) For instance, city planners in the Provincial capital Changsha reported an annual average growth of population of only 1 percent since 1960. A visit to Chengdu, capital of Sichuan Province, in March 1979 revealed the same situation.

(10) Chao (1966).

(11) Chao, and Li (1959).

(12) During a visit to the Province of Jiangsu in March 1979, I was told that twenty-nine enterprises were being closed down or prosecuted.

(13) All information on specific targets is taken from the Chinese press. It is published in collected form in English, in Documents of the First Session of the Fifth National People's Congress of the P.R.C., Peking, 1978.

(14) Daqing (an oilfield development in NE. China) is better known as the nation's industrial emulation model.

(15) In the spring of 1979 there was a wave of unrest amongst the sent-down youth, especially those from Shanghai sent to border areas.

(16) Evidence of over-population of the cities (and under-employment) can be seen in the Central Committee Directive of 3 March 1979, which outlined various new schemes for early retirement for urban employees.

(17) Some of the best land is situated on the peripheries of towns and cities, where plenty of night-soil has been applied over the centuries.

(18) In return, he or she is paid a certain amount by the Brigade in kind. I found this system in Linxian, Henan, in 1975.

(19) See, for example, Murphey (1976), p. 313.

(20) As far back as 1955, Mao called for mechanisation. Three national conferences on mechanisation have been held - in 1966, 1971, and January 1978.

(21) The Production Team is the lowest level of rural organisation. A number of Teams make up a Brigade. Teams often correspond to natural villages.

(22) I must stress once again that what has happened at Huaxi is quite atypical.

(23) These include "The Construction and Planning of the Huaxi Brigade's New Village" (Huaxi Dadui Xin Cun de Guihua Jianshe) in Jianzhu Xuebao (Architectural Journal) No. 3, 1975, pp. 13-17; "A New Village", China Reconstructs, October 1976, pp. 22-30; "The Peasants Like this Kind of Socialism", Renmin Ribao (People's Daily), 6 December 1978. I have found a high degree of consistency between the various reports, and between them and the information gathered at first-hand.

(24) From Cressey. Quoted by Dwyer.

(25) 1 yuan = US$0.63 approx. But the official exchange rate is almost meaningless in a discussion of Chinese prices and incomes. For a peasant country, the purchasing power of local currency with regard to the food staple may be a good indicator. Huaxi's peasants do not have to purchase their grain allocation out of their cash income. But supposing they did, 91 yuan would be sufficient for a year's supply of grain for one person. In the cities, most families spend around 15 yuan (US$9.45) per head on all food monthly. Of that figure, about one third goes on grain. On the other hand, a radio (transistor) might cost the equivalent of a monthly wage packet for the average urban worker (male), i.e. 55 yuan. If available in the countryside at all, this would account for a sizeable proportion of annual cash income.

(26) The Brigade Party Branch, in conjunction with that of the People's Commune to which it belongs, will decide on the proportion of Brigade income (from sales to the State) to be invested in new plants, accumulated, paid out in cash to Brigade members at year's end, or spent on collective welfare (goods and services).

(27) Planners in Wuxi said in August 1976 that the Municipal Housing Bureau's estimate for new housing construction was about 60 yuan per square metre (overall). The cost at Huaxi was about 15 yuan, so that the average cost for an entire house was around 1100 yuan.

(28) And the arbitrariness of local leaders, who may at times distort national policy beyond all recognition. I do not mean to imply that there are any plans at the present to rethink the tax system.

(29) The political upheavals of the past few years have shown that the Chinese State does not have the comprehensive and unified apparatus necessary for the coercion of a vast population. Local loyalties intervene even in the army and security forces.

(30) The People's Daily article (see Note 23 above) commented that mere "dragging, pushing or exhortation" is insufficient - indeed it is often counter-productive. The Huaxi Party Branch was praised for its practice of initiating projects which have immediate and visible results for peasant standards of living and lifestyle.

(31) Until 1978 Huaxi had a Revolutionary Committee as well as a Party Committee. Membership of the two committees was overlapping, but the Revolutionary Committee (its functions more executive) was rather broader based.

(32) Surprisingly, according to versions of Mao's unpublished speeches from the Cultural Revolution, Mao specifically forbade the urban population from taking part in urban planning decisions. 1971, p. 17.

(33) For an up-to-date critique of egalitarianism in rural China, the reader is referred to Beijing Review, No. 9, 2 March 1979. The article is entitled "Let Some Peasants Become Well-off First".

(34) It must be borne in mind that many so-called self-reliant models have in fact been carefully fostered by certain leaders (local or national) over a long period. I have never heard Huaxi mentioned in this connection.

(35) China's peasants are provided with an apt slogan from the national model of Dazhai: Xian zhi po, hou zhi wo (literally, "First deal with the slopes" - i.e. field construction - "and then deal with the nests" - i.e. home construction).

(36) A summary of the arguments in English can be seen in "Taching Impressions", Peking Review, No. 22, 27 May 1977. For a full description of the spatial configuration of Daqing see Buck (1975-6), pp. 24-35.

REFERENCES

Blumenfeld, Hans (1978) "Correspondence", Monthly Review, June.

Buck, David (1975-76) "Directions in Chinese Urban Planning", Urbanisation Past and Present, No. 1.

Chao, Kang (1966) "Industrialisation and Urban Housing in Communist China", Journal of Asian Studies, 15, No. 3.

Chao, Kang and Li, Choh-Ming (1959) Economic Development of Communist China. Berkeley.

Cressey, George, B. "The Fenghsieu Landscape; A Fragment of the Yangtse Delta", quoted by Dwyer (Ed). (1974) China Now, originally published in 1936, Geographical Review No. 26.

Lewis, John Wilson (Ed). (1971) The City in Communist China.

Murphy, Rhoads (1976) "Chinese Urbanisation under Mao", Urbanisation and Counter-urbanisation, Vol. 2. Sage Publications.

Onoye, Etsuzo (1971) "Regional Distribution of Urban Population in China", Developing Economies, Vol. 8, No. 1.

Sawers, Larry (March 1977) "Urban Planning in the Soviet Union and China", Monthly Review.

Sen-dou Chang (Sept. 1970) "The Changing System of Chinese Cities", Annual of the Association of American Geographics, Vol. 66, No. 3.

Sen-dou Chang (1968) "The Million Cities of Mainland China", Pacific Viewpoint, 9.

Low- to Moderate-income Residential Programmes

In the following group of cases, both the geographic focus and the scope of concern narrow considerably. In these studies, the authors are dealing with housing and related residential development programmes within specific urban areas. As was discussed in Chapter 2, many urban problems and issues revolve around how best to provide decent living environments for the masses of low and moderate income dwellers. These case studies have been chosen to demonstrate some of the major policy options available as solutions to these problems. Three very different programmes are presented: (1) the large-scale public housing programmes of Singapore and Hong Kong; (2) residential upgrading or improvement programmes being implemented in Jakarta and Manila; and (3) a prototype sites-and-services cum upgrading project conceived by the Urban Development Authority for Kuala Lumpur. Although these cases serve to emphasise the fact that the physical solutions vary widely, they also point up in a number of ways the tremendous importance of institutional, financial and social factors in residential development.

Yue-man Yeung and David Drakakis-Smith lead off with a comparative study of the massive government housing programmes in Singapore and Hong Kong. Despite some important differences, these two programmes are basically similar, and constitute Asia's prime examples of meeting residential needs by building new, finished housing units in large government estates. It should be stressed at the outset that this approach was subsidised, and would not have been possible in less wealthy nations which lacked the city states' efficient tax collection systems. Nevertheless, these cases illustrate programmes which have been well managed and provide some positive lessons for more typical LDCs, even if the particular physical solution is not always appropriate.

In the case which follows, John Taylor and David Williams contribute a second comparative study of residential development, this one dealing with upgrading programmes in Jakarta and Manila. This approach stands in marked contrast to the public housing solution, directing little or no public investment into houses per se but rather focusing on provision of physical and social infrastructures within existing low-income communities. Policy-makers in many LDC cities have been reluctant to adopt upgrading, fearing that the standards are too low; yet, as this study points out, it enables a large proportion of a given city's households to see some short-run improvement in their environments, and can provide the base for further improvements at a later date.

The third case study in this group is different, in that it does not really present a city-wide programme of residential development as in the case of the other two. Rather, this is a study of a unique LDC institution, Malaysia's Urban Development Authority, which has used real estate as the primary vehicle for achieving the socio-economic objective of improving conditions for the Malays. Peter Amato provides an overall institutional analysis of the goals, policies and programmes of UDA before concentrating on a specific residential project which represents that country's initial attempt to implement the sites-and-services (and upgrading) approach.

8

Public Housing in the City States of Hong Kong and Singapore

Yue-man Yeung
D.W. Drakakis-Smith

INTRODUCTION

Among the developing countries, the city-states of Hong Kong and Singapore are often regarded as outstanding examples of rapid transition from vulnerable entrepot-based economies to prosperous export-oriented manufacturing communities. Accompanying this development has been a remarkable improvement in the economic and social life of the inhabitants themselves so that at present their per capita gross national products (GNP) are the highest in Asia after that of Japan.(1) It is noteworthy that the high rates of growth in Hong Kong and Singapore have been sustained over a long period without significant assistance from abroad, and in many ways the rapid development must seem somewhat paradoxical given their small territorial size.

Despite these exceptionally high rates of economic growth, it could be argued that the developmental experience of Hong Kong and Singapore, particularly the manner in which industrialisation has occurred, is relevant to other developing countries. This paper examines one aspect of these developmental experiences, viz. the urban planning lessons which may be derived from their extensive public housing programmes. While Hong Kong and Singapore have achieved equal international distinction for their massive developments, their planning philosophies and approaches are sufficiently distinct to make a comparative study instructive.

THE PROBLEM OF SHELTER

In 1976 the British Crown Colony of Hong Kong had a land area of only 1045 square km, but its population was 4.4 million. This represents a seven-fold increase over the immediate post-war population of 650,000 in 1945. The contributory causes of this phenomenal increase were the return of former residents from China after liberation from the Japanese, the refugee influx caused by the civil war on the mainland, and, until 1961, a very high natural growth rate. While movement from China itself has fallen substantially since the imposition of border controls, the flow of both legal and illegal migrants is still considerable. Between 1961 and 1971 there were 101,000 legal entries to the Colony while another 132,000 were admitted in the 3 years before 1975. Illegal migrants also enter Hong Kong in a steady stream and estimates put the annual influx between 30,000 and 80,000 persons.

The problems of population density in Hong Kong are compounded by a rugged topography which has severely restricted urban growth. The resultant pattern of development is such that 88 percent of the population is crowded into the relatively level land on either side of the harbour, land which despite extensive reclamation still constitutes only 19 percent of the total area. Urban population densities are among the highest in the world and at their peak in 1961 reached 238,000 persons per square km in the old tenement district of Sheung Wan on Hong Kong Island. Such densities are indicative of the acute housing problems which affect the entire population, irrespective of status.

To a certain extent the extreme metropolitan densities have eased over the last 15 years following piecemeal urban renewal and population shifts into government housing in Kowloon and the New Territories. Nevertheless, chronic housing shortages persist and the massive public housing efforts of the government are unlikely to be relaxed in the foreseeable future, although they will be concentrated more on new town developments than before.

Like Hong Kong, Singapore had ample evidence of overcrowding and housing shortages before World War II, but the problem of shelter was enlarged to critical proportions in the post-war period by rapid population growth. The combination of an unusually high birth rate (the annual average rate was over 4 percent until the late 1950s) and sizeable immigration from Peninsular Malaysia led to a heavy demand for housing. Widespread substandard living conditions were reported in the 1950s. Even as late as 1966, densities reached 34,500 per square km in the central city area of Singapore.

PUBLIC HOUSING - HONG KONG & SINGAPORE

The island-nation of Singapore, which became an independent republic in 1965, shares with Hong Kong two common characteristics: both possess a small land area and a population predominantly Chinese in origin. With an area of 602 square km Singapore has a population of 2.3 million, or half that of Hong Kong. Although most of Singapore is low-lying land amenable to development, land is nevertheless scarce. The traditional urban pattern has been subject to waves of immigrants, mostly from China and the Indian subcontinent, converging on the old part of the city on either side of the Singapore River. Over the years housing in the central city area had become increasingly substandard and overcrowded. An avowed objective of the Master Plan approved in 1958 was to decongest this part of the city. Through successive large-scale public housing programmes, complemented by urban renewal and resettlement projects since 1960, the decentralisation objective has to a large measure been achieved. The centrifugal tendencies are further reinforced by the recent public housing developments which centre on new towns at much greater distances from the city centre than those completed in the 1960s (Fig. 8.2). In fact the whole island is now conceived as an urban complex for the purpose of development planning.

PUBLIC HOUSING PROGRAMMES

Along with their success at industrialisation, Hong Kong and Singapore have also achieved international recognition for their efforts in public housing, particularly through the steady upgrading of planning standards and the increasing proportion of the population which has benefited from such policies. In Hong Kong, by 1975 over 1.8 million people or 41 percent of the total population were living in public housing; in Singapore the proportion was even higher with 51 percent or 1.1 million of the Republic's population housed in government-built flats.

Despite the many differences which underlie the public housing programmes in the two city-states, there are certain common features. For example, land availability has been a principal determinant in shaping the pattern of development. In Hong Kong, resettlement estates, which are found predominantly in the Kowloon peninsula, were built largely on sites made available by deliberate squatter clearance programmes. This location factor particularly applies to resettlement estates in the 1950s, since later developments in resettlement housing involved more distant sites, such as Sau Mau Ping and Kwai Chung, which were relatively free of squatters. Because of the hilly terrain and the earlier development of Hong Kong Island, most of the better public housing has been built on flat land, peripheral to the Kowloon metropolitan area (see Fig. 8.1). Those projects developed on Hong Kong Island have been planned to adapt to the often more rugged topography. In like manner, large-scale construction programmes since 1960 in Singapore have been dictated by land availability in the outlying areas where large tracts of land could be assembled at considerably lower costs. The outer parts of Toa Payoh, Queenstown, and Macpherson estates are about 5 miles from the city centre; this was estimated to be an effective distance for commuting without severe economic strains. This planning policy which characterised the earlier development in the 1960s is being succeeded by the necessity to develop new estates at much greater distances from the city centre (see Fig. 8.2). At the same time a number of projects were carried out in the more central localities as part of the urban renewal programme. In both city-states, however, land shortages have been forcing development progressively further from the metropolitan core.

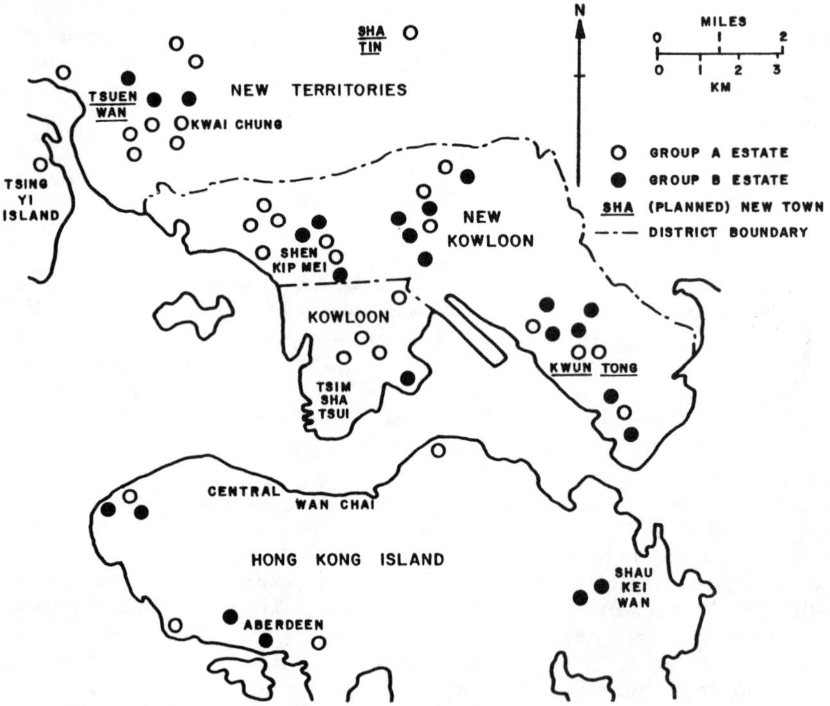

Fig. 8.1. Location of Public Housing Estates and New Towns in Hong Kong.

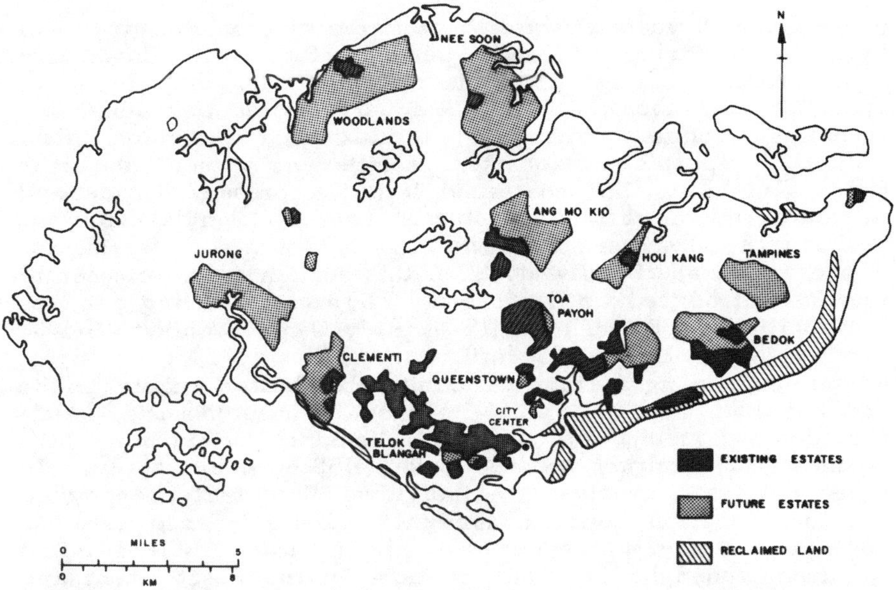

Fig. 8.2. Location of Public Housing Estates in Singapore.

Hong Kong

Hong Kong began its public housing programme in 1954 after an extensive fire in the Shek Kip Mei district had rendered 50,000 squatters homeless. Before this, the prevailing hope had been that the refugees might return to China once the political turmoil had settled. Certainly the government was reluctant to invest public funds in large-scale resettlement since the trading embargo of the Korean War had put the traditional economic function of the Colony in jeopardy. In the two decades that followed the Shek Kip Mei fire, the resettlement programme became an important justification for widespread squatter clearance. However, philanthropic motives were less important than the simple need for valuable building land to satisfy the demands of general urban development. Only much later was the scope of the resettlement programme expanded to incorporate rehousing on compassionate grounds.

The early resettlement blocks were built to very low standards. The six- to eight-storey buildings had only communal washing, cooking and toilet facilities, and no lifts. A bare concrete room averaging 11 square metres was the normal allocation for a five-person family. There was a genuine desire to keep rents as low as possible so that the monthly rental for the standard Mark I or II room was pegged at US$3 for many years. The low initial standards were justified in view of the prevailing circumstances, but the government adhered to these criteria for 10 years despite the remarkable economic growth of Hong Kong during the same period. Only after 1963 were improvements introduced to the new estates so that the space allocation was increased to 3.3 square metres per adult and amenities gradually incorporated into each individual flat.

The emphasis on squatter resettlement at minimum standards and rents has continued into the present decade and presents several difficult problems for the Colony's planners. Perhaps the most serious is the neglect of the slum tenements. A programme specifically aimed at this section of the community was not introduced until 1964 when Low-cost Housing projects were initiated for families with monthly incomes under US$100, but by 1970 such projects still comprised only 10 per cent of all public housing units. Concomitantly, better quality public housing had been provided by the semi-autonomous, semi-subsidised Housing Authority and Housing Society for which families with monthly incomes below US$260 could apply. In these estates not only were individual flats better appointed and more spacious but management and maintenance were far superior, avoiding, for example, the common problems posed by uncontrolled hawker congregations in the Resettlement and Low-cost Housing estates.

In developing the more recent peripheral estates, employment prospects and journeys to work have posed difficult planning problems. For instance, in 1968-1969 the Hong Kong government had to suspend work on the massive Kwai Chung development in north-west Kowloon because of its unpopularity. Since then several changes have resulted in faster growth rates in peripheral estates; these include cheap transport by minibus service, standardised fares on public buses, greater provision of educational and shopping facilities in the new estates, and increased employment opportunities in the wake of container port development.

Up to the early 1970s the most positive planning was found in the programmes to promote the new towns of Tsuen Wan and Kwun Tong. Industrial development was encouraged very early in these two centres, unfortunately preceding major house-building activities. This caused extensive squatting around the existing villages, much of which still persists, and also precipitated large-scale commuting from the main metropolitan area which is less than 10 miles away from either town. The close proximity of Kowloon to Tsuen Wan and Kwun Tung has in fact prevented the development of truly self-contained and independent new towns.

In the period 1953-1973 public housing construction in Hong Kong proceeded essentially on an ad hoc basis with the construction programme being geared more to the uncertain economic and political climates of the early 1950s than to the substantial economic progress made since. Until 1973 the public housing programme had been in the hands of several separate agencies. Although all have benefited from government subsidies in one way or another, principally through the provision of cheap Crown land, conflicting interests have prevented the adoption of an overall planning strategy with respect to housing provision for the urban poor. Minimal background research also meant that the policy recommendations proffered by the advisory Housing Board often bore little relation to reality.

In 1973 a 10-year housing programme was outlined by the Governor, Sir Murray MacLehose. The programme aimed at the provision of 2.1 million individual housing units in the period 1973-1983. Although the objective of extending social welfare to the masses is laudable in itself, a number of inherent weaknesses in the conceptualisation of the programme reduce the likelihood of attaining the stated goals. The programme was also inadequate and unrealistic in that it proposed a continued emphasis on squatter rehousing similar to that of the previous 20 years. However, since 1973, land has been regarded as a government contribution to public housing. Previously the Housing Authority had to borrow from the Development Loan Fund in order to pay land premia. Government's contributions to public housing as of 31 March 1977 were estimated to be at about US$1000 million, representing direct and indirect subsidy by the administration. The forecast expenditure on public housing over the 10-year period 1978-1988 was given at US$870 million.(2) The most significant change embodied in the programme was the basic structural reorganisation of the housing administrative system. All four housing bodies which existed before 1973 were amalgamated into a new, centrally coordinated Housing Authority which would be responsible for the planning, clearance, construction and management of all public housing. The implementation of this proposal since 1973 has eliminated the erstwhile rivalry and contradictory programmes among the housing bodies in question. All former resettlement housing has been redesignated as Group B, whereas all other units and those built by the new Housing Department are identified as Group A (see Fig. 8.1).

The present emphases in Hong Kong's housing programme are three-fold. Firstly, there is the continued building programme itself which is strongly oriented towards the existing and planned New Towns where accommodation for 900,000 people is being built. All units are now self-contained and a minimum space allocation of 4.6 square metres per adult is the target for future construction. In addition, new estates are provided with a full range of services and amenities, from supermarkets to kindergartens.

Within the existing estates there are two main developments at present. The first consists of an extensive improvement programme in most of the older areas, ranging from the provision of individual facilities to the complete conversion and renovation of some of the oldest blocks in Shek Kip Mei. In addition to this physical upgrading, there have also been extensive changes in the system of management, the most important of which was a rental review in 1974. As a result, rents have been increased in all types of accommodation although they have remained very low in the older resettlement estates. As a whole, Group B estates run at a loss which is partially covered by the surplus from the newer estates. However, with land, labour and material costs rising rapidly, more frequent rental adjustments seem unavoidable.

Singapore

In contrast to Hong Kong, attempts were made quite early in the century to tackle the problem of housing the urban poor in Singapore. The first efforts towards public housing began half-heartedly as early as 1927 under the Singapore Improvement Trust (SIT). Limited by meagre financial support and ineffective legal powers, the Trust provided at best stop-gap palliatives in the face of soaring housing needs. At the time of its dissolution in 1959, the Trust had built only 23,000 dwelling units, the bulk of which was completed in the post-war period.

When the People's Action Party (PAP) assumed power in 1959, the Housing and Development Board (HDB) was formed, with much enlarged financial and legal powers. In 1960 a 10-year building programme was charted. It was estimated that during this period 150,000 dwelling units would be required to meet the housing demands which stemmed from the need to relieve over-crowding in the central city area and from the pressures of urban renewal and population growth. Allowing for 40,000 units to be built by the private sector for the upper- and middle-income groups, there would still be a balance of 110,000 needed to be provided by the government for the lower-income groups. Accordingly, two 5-year building programmes were formulated for the periods 1961-1965 and 1966-1970, during which 54,000 and 64,000 units respectively were constructed. Thus, 1960 marked the beginning of the present phase of large-scale and integrated development. The Third Five-Year Building Programme (1971-1975) added another 113,819 units of flats and shops, and the Fourth Five-Year Building Programme (1976-1980) targets a further total of between 125,000 and 150,000 units. By March 1978, 68,479 units had been completed and work was ahead of schedule.(3)

Together with the quickening tempo of construction, an ever-increasing proportion of Singapore's population has been drawn into this emerging way of life. In 1978 an estimated 1.4 million people or 60 percent of the population lived in public flats, subsidised at an annual rate of US$30 million. In terms of general policy, three socio-economic guidelines in the HDB programmes merit note. First, it was decided that the rents for all categories of flats should not exceed 15 percent of the family income. Second, in keeping with the national objective of building a multiracial, multilingual society, flat allocation policies since 1960 have been premised upon a judicious admixture of different major ethnic groups. Third, within the limits set by certain prescribed standards, there has been a conscious attempt to search for minimum cost. The streamlining of the administrative machinery and the tendering system are examples. It should also be noted that, compared with public housing in Hong Kong, Singaporean standards are far more generous. SIT flats had an average space allocation of 7.2 square metres per person, and HDB flats average from 10.0 square metres, 10.7 square metres, 14.6 square metres, 16.6 square metres and 20.8 square metres per person in one-, two-, three-, four- and five-room units respectively.

To enhance the attractiveness of public housing and to adjust to changing conditions, three major policy revisions were made during the last decade. First, the HDB stopped building the one-room flats with communal toilets and cooking facilities in 1966. In response to the economic progress made by the Republic and to the rise in expectations of the population, the recent emphasis has been one in which the building programme favours four- and five-room flats with larger floor space and improved floor design. Second, the home ownership scheme, launched initially in 1964, was officially given a fillip in 1968 when flat buyers were allowed to draw upon the balance of their Central Provident Fund (social security contributions) for deposits and monthly payments. In an attempt to broaden home ownership, the monthly family income ceiling for eligibility to buy public flats was revised from US$450 to US$530 in 1970, and again to US$670 in 1971. The result of this policy change was anticipated: there was a flood of applications to purchase flats, the waiting list for which has, through accelerated construction over the past few years, been reduced in 1978 from about 3½ years to 2 years. For the first time, more residents lived in owned homes than in rented flats; 53 percent of all public flats was owner-occupied. Third, as the housing situation improved and, consistent with the national population policy of striving towards zero population growth, qualifications for renting and purchasing flats have been relaxed. Until 1967 the minimum household-size requirement was five persons; it has since been reduced to two persons for any type of public housing unit. In fact, small families enjoy certain advantages in subletting and allocation. For instance, the year 1978 saw the relaxation of the rule which forbade single persons over 55 years old from renting or buying public flats.

At the local level, careful planning is reflected in the detailed arrangements within public housing estates. The neighbourhood principle is relied upon as a guide for orderly and tractable development. This has been adapted from British and European town planning practices to suit local needs. The basic planning philosophy of the neighbourhood concept is maximum self-sufficiency in the satisfaction of basic needs by the community. Thus, shopping facilities, medical care, schools, recreation and the like have been planned on the basis of neighbourhood units, which in Singapore comprise from 2000 to 5000 households at an average of six members each. Studies have been made testing the viability of neighbourhood units and neighbourly relations, and in spite of the views of critics of neighbourhood planning, the opinions of the residents themselves have been quite favourable.(4)

After 18 years of intensive development, Singapore has reached a stage towards which Hong Kong still aspires. The public housing programme has changed from one meeting a housing crisis to another which is a stabilizing force in society. In place of expediency and speed, the current emphasis is on quality and amenity; as later sections will show, Singapore now faces rather different problems from Hong Kong.

HOUSING PROGRAMMES EVALUATED

In spite of the absence of public advocacy of redistribution with growth, actual policies and programmes have, in practice, had considerable effect in promoting redistribution of resources. The public housing programmes in particular have played an important, although indirect, role in this process. This is not to say, however, that total equality is a desired or attainable goal in either society and any evaluation of the respective housing programmes must take into account the prevailing political as well as socio-economic circumstances.

Hong Kong

Viewed in terms of numbers alone, the government housing programme in Hong Kong has been impressive. Some 5000 to 6000 new units are completed each year and standards have steadily improved over the years, notably since the administrative reorganisation of 1973 which placed virtually all government building under the control of a reconstituted Housing Authority. However, the 1.8 million persons living in public accommodation in 1975 is somewhat lower than the 2.1 million predicted at the beginning of the decade when annual construction rates were higher.

Despite the impressive totals of units built each year by the public sector, it is important to note that domestic construction by the private sector is usually double that of the government - an important difference from the Singapore situation. Although most of the new units in Hong Kong still comprise tenements and small flats, their average size has increased by approximately one-third over the last 5 years, while the corresponding rents have almost doubled. The average rent for a small tenement in 1975 was US$125 which effectively restricts such units to the middle-income groups. The trend of tenement redevelopment is therefore to meet the demand of families that have been forced into the slums because of lack of suitable alternative accommodation.

Notwithstanding the ratio between private and public construction activity, there is still an annual net movement of families into government accommodation. The reason for this apparent contradiction is that government emphasis is now on rehousing the displaced slum families rather than on resettling squatters from clearance schemes. This represents an important, but not widely recognised, shift in policy over recent years.

However, despite the new policy changes, the bulk of government housing in Hong Kong is still representative of the old emphasis on quick, cheap construction to rehouse squatters. Two-thirds of the present 1.8 million residents live in Group B units, formerly Resettlement Estates. Implicit, therefore, in the above overview of Hong Kong's public housing programme is that one of the major shortcomings is not quantity but quality.

In the past the government pitched its programme at a very low level. While this policy was understandable during the economic uncertainty of the early 1950s, its retention over the ensuing years was not. Over-crowding is still appalling in the oldest resettlement estates which house almost half a million people, and in 1975 there were some 400,000 living below the original 2.2 square metres per person allowance. The mobilisation of resources to build on such a massive scale was undoubtedly impressive, but the sacrifice of standards on the altar of expediency has produced severe problems and has virtually resulted in the creation of new slums. A major policy decision within the last few years, therefore, has been the refurbishing of these earlier resettlement blocks to more acceptable standards.

The present plan originally intended to renovate completely the oldest and worst resettlement estates by expanding allocation standards and installing individual amenities within each newly created unit. More open spaces for extra marketing and recreational facilities are also planned. However, experimental conversion carried out to date in the Shek Kip Mei estate has produced cost-benefit analyses which favour complete reconstruction of old estates in future. The conversion process is too expensive in relation to numbers rehoused, since some blocks have to be demolished to make way for new markets and play areas, while the newly converted blocks themselves house far fewer people than before.

Much more important in terms of their housing needs is the large population resident in substandard tenement accommodation. As outlined previously, these people have been severely neglected when compared with squatters, despite the fact that both were the product of the same population influx following the 1949 Civil War. In many of the small subdivided tenements, living conditions are worse than those prevailing in squatter settlements and it was estimated in 1975 that almost 750,000 lived in substandard private tenement slums. On the other hand, the number of urban squatters had decreased to 188,000 by 1971. In this light, the continued emphasis on squatter resettlement as propounded in the 10-year housing programme clearly indicates misplaced priorities.

Singapore

In Singapore the public housing programme seems to be more successful. By most criteria, there have been notable gains, not only in housing standards, but also in terms of economic production. For example, the construction sector has played an important role in maintaining rapid growth during a period when the British military withdrawal augured a recession. From 1960 the construction sector grew at an average annual rate of 23 percent and its contribution of GDP rose from 2.0 percent to 6.8 percent in 1973.(5) Over this period more than 60 percent of the total construction was attributable to the public sector.(6)

As more and more people move into public flats, overall housing conditions are progressively improved. In comparison with the tenement slums in Chinatown, the HDB flats are vastly superior in terms of internal and external densities on a per capita basis. Floor space and open space per person have increased manifold and overall density is a fraction of that prevailing in the traditional shophouse tenements. These marked improvements are the direct result of new planning practices which now allow for more favourable plot ratios and much reduced building coverage. In a similar fashion, Yeh and Pang have shown that the average number of households per dwelling was reduced from 2.8 in 1964 to 1.2 in 1970.(7) Comparing the household conditions in 1954 and 1970, the average number of rooms per household grew from 0.9 to 2.2 and the average number of persons per room decreased from 4.8 to 2.5. The appreciable progress in these national housing standards can be ascribed to the contribution by public housing.

Within the HDB building programmes themselves, there have been some important shifts in character and emphasis over the years. One such change is the accelerated rate of construction. The average annual production of 12,000 units in the last decade has been increased to more than 20,000 units per annum in the Third Five-Year Building Programme. This rate will be further increased to 30,000 units a year over the next 5 years. A second noteworthy feature is that the average size of flat has been increased over the years from 41.8 square metres to 65.0 square metres. This is a reflection of the sustained upgrading of the building programme and of the changing complexion of public demand. In the 1960s, up to 70 percent of the applicants for public housing preferred one- and two-room flats. In 1975, however, only 12 percent wanted one-room flats and 9 percent two-room flats; the bulk of the applicants favoured larger though more expensive units.(8)

A measure of the success of Singapore's public housing programme can be gauged by the results of a series of tenant and household surveys. In one early survey undertaken by the HDB in 1968, it was found that, in terms of the general housing environment and other aspects of the residents' daily lives, a very high level of satisfaction was expressed.(9) A similar HDB sample household survey in 1973 produced evidence that up to three-quarters of the residents were satisfied with the estate, the block, the floor, and the flat in which they lived. The increase in the satisfaction level with respect to the general housing environment was readily discernible.(10)

Singapore is also faced with a problem of ethnic and cultural diversity in its public housing programme. It is often alleged, for example, that inter-ethnic differences exist in the adaptation of new residents to highrise public housing; in particular, that Malays encounter great difficulty in adjusting from their previous kampung milieu. Contrary to this popular impression, Hassan (1976) has shown that Malays exhibit high levels of satisfaction with both flats and environment, although it must be noted that as resettlement is a voluntary process this survey does not cover those Malays who reject the offer of government housing. Other, more predictable, results from Hassan's surveys have indicated that satisfaction is positively related to economic status and inversely correlated with family size. However, there is a notable lack of independent studies on the social effects of living in the flats and tenements built by government in Singapore and Hong Kong and this makes it difficult to provide a rounded evaluation of their housing programmes.

It is the policy of HDB to set aside 10-15 percent of the land within each public housing estate for industrial use, usually of a labour-intensive and pollution-free kind. As the results of the HDB Employment Survey in 1972 indicate, the policy of generating within-estate employment has, to a large extent, been successful. In particular the pool of female labour has been effectively tapped and unemployed female labour dropped dramatically from 13 percent in 1968 to 4 percent in 1973. Employment within estates has been so successful that, coincident with the Singapore economic boom in the early 1970s, labour imbalance was noticeable in some of the estates. In the light of the shortage of female production workers, it has been suggested that the best policy to pursue is to redirect within-estate industries, along with the recent national development goal, towards a high skill intensity and high labour productivity rather than the prevailing emphasis on high labour intensity and low labour productivity.

Viewed from various national perspectives, the Singapore public housing programme is regarded as a notable success. One of the reasons for this is the existence of an able administrative leadership at the middle level, complementing the political leadership at the top. Integrated with national development policy, public housing is at once an economic contribution generating employment, a force for social equity, a social overhead, and a stabilizer in the cost of living through its rents. The results are mutually reinforcing: the government continues to devote greater commitments to public housing and the people reciprocate with more express legitimization of public policies. The overwhelming victory of the PAP in the 1976 national elections lends itself to such an interpretation.

However, while the government housing programme in Singapore has been relatively successful in terms of its political and economic goals, it is debatable whether those in greatest need have received commensurate benefits. For instance, Liu has noted that, despite the acceleration in housing construction between 1966 and 1970, squatter housing continued to increase from 30 percent to 34 percent of the total housing stock.(11) In the urgency to create a stable, middle-class society, there is therefore a possibility that the urban poor may have been bypassed and that the real economic gap between the under-privileged and the rest of Singaporean society has widened.

Comparative Evaluation

Finally, it would be instructive to compare the Hong Kong and Singapore housing programmes using some of the evaluative criteria as spelled out in Chapter 2. In terms of equity considerations, there is no question as to their overall redistributive effects in both city-states, although the Hong Kong programme appears to have fared better in this count. In Singapore, the present proportion of 60 percent of the population living in public flats is anticipated to increase to 75 percent by the mid-1980s, a reflection of the fact that housing conditions are improving for most families. The alleged economic distance between the minority urban poor and the overwhelming majority in public housing mentioned above may be an inevitable side effect of the Singapore programme. By and large, it is the housing demands of the lower-middle and middle-income groups which are sustained, determining the needs to which the HDB has seen fit to respond. By contrast, in setting its sights towards the lower-income groups, the Hong Kong programme has apparently reached the really needy. The stringent criteria of income and over-crowding qualifications have ensured that a relatively well defined target population is catered for. Even then, the waiting list is long and, since 1967, 340,000 families have applied. Under these conditions public housing is undoubtedly a factor of social and economic equity. Although the proportion of the population benefiting from the housing programme has been increasing over time in Hong Kong, one of the challenges to the policy-makers and planners is how to meet the seemingly insatiable demand.

From the standpoint of choice, both the Hong Kong and Singapore programmes offer a range of options at different levels of operation. Occupationally speaking, public housing estates in Singapore are planned with employment opportunities provided by light industries within them, particularly for the female labour force. This planning consideration, on the other hand, is not explicitly embodied in most of Hong Kong's developments. However, in both programmes qualified families do have a choice of the location of the housing estate and, to a lesser extent, the housing unit within it. The choice of the size and type of public flats is related to the income level, family size and other characteristics of the applicant. There is also the choice of purchasing or renting a flat. Once settled into life in the estates, residents in Hong Kong and Singapore are encouraged to take part in community activities and nation-wide campaigns. For example, a total of 525 mutual-aid committees have been established and accommodated in premises in Hong Kong housing estates; regular meetings are held with the management staff to discuss problems of mutual concern. Similarly, within Singapore's housing estates church groups and community organisations are also active as rallying points of social and cultural activities.

With regard to participation of the residents in the planning process, both the Hong Kong and Singapore programmes can be characterised as top-down in approach in which the three-actor scenario involving the planners, the planned-for, and the politicians, as outlined in Chapter 2, applies. Despite the lack of obvious input into decision-making by the users in both systems, the periodic tenant and household surveys and regular informal visits assure some feedback to the planning and policy apparatus. Monthly rent collection in Hong Kong, for example, provides one such occasion for informal contacts to be made. Although the system as prevailing in the two city-states may not be as democratic as found in some Western countries, lines of communication are clearly open between the planner-technocrat and the users. Far from viewing public housing as "free handouts", beneficiaries of the programmes in Hong Kong and Singapore take pride in their new housing and the record of rent payment is highly satisfactory.

PROBLEMS AND PROSPECTS

This case study has so far outlined and assessed the salient features of the public housing programmes in Hong Kong and Singapore; it remains to highlight the significant recent developments and issues.

Hong Kong

In Hong Kong, although the 10-year housing programme announced in 1973 suffered from certain inadequacies, remarkable changes and improvements have since occurred. There is now much more evidence of coordinated planning both on the spatial macro-scale and at the micro-level of the individual estates and blocks. The major changes in policy since 1973 are worthy of re-emphasis. First of all, future development in public housing is to be tied in with new towns in the New Territories, at increasing distances from the metropolitan area. Much of the current attention has centred on new town developments at Tuen Mun and Sha Tin, but plans for developing Castle Peak and Yuen Long have also been drawn up. Second, in order to remedy the previous neglect in planning for shopping facilities, more licensed hawker pitches and regular retail shops are being built into the new estates. The lessons from the past have been well learned: the inadequate provision of shopping facilities had led to a great loss of revenue, both from trying to clear hawkers and in being forced to permit private retailing activities to operate in the larger estates to satisfy demand. The new policy is to construct sizeable shopping complexes, including market centres, which will be leased at reasonably competitive rents.

A third major policy change has been in the allocation of public housing. Flat allocation is now facilitated by one master waiting list which is compiled according to a fairly uniform standard with simple size variation. To be eligible for the waiting list an applicant must be over 21 years of age with a minimum family size of three persons, living at a density of worse than 3.3 square metres per adult. The ceiling of total family income per month has been revised on a sliding scale which varies with family size. The range is from a maximum monthly family income of US$325 for a family of up to six persons to that of US$475 for a family of ten or more persons.

In addition, there has been a change in official attitudes towards the remaining squatters, most of whom occupy land on steep hillsides unlikely to be required for development in the immediate future. Toleration has now reached the stage where positive improvement of these settlements has been taking place through, for example, the provision of communal water and sewerage connections. In following this line of action, Hong Kong is in essence effecting the squatter upgrading common to countries without the resources to promote large-scale rehousing.

While improved squatter settlements and government housing are both available to the urban poor in Hong Kong, the pressure of the housing shortage on the middle-income groups has shown few signs of being alleviated. Medium-sized flats still account for only 10 percent of total private sector domestic construction and, although the tenement redevelopments appear to be geared towards the lower-middle income households, this is more in terms of a pricing response to an artificial demand. Many of the middle-income families resident in these new tenements would prefer to move out to larger flats if they were available at reasonable cost. Some form of government assistance is, therefore, overdue for such households either by direct government building, as in Singapore, or by providing cheaper credit to encourage house buying and stimulate a response from the private developers.

Very recently the Hong Kong government decided, for the first time, to build public housing for sale. However, this move was stimulated more by the demand from within the present government estates rather than by a desire to meet middle-income needs in general. In 1976 it was decided that a revolving fund of US$65 million would be set up to help finance the Housing Authority's flats-for-sale scheme. According to the proposal, new blocks of public housing will be constructed for sale to existing tenants of the Housing Authority's estates, so that their present flats can be reallocated to poorer families on the waiting list. In 1978 a total of 8400 flats in six localities were offered for sale. The public response was most encouraging, with the number of applicants outnumbering the available flats by more than four to one. About 22 percent of the applicants were from public housing tenants who were allocated by balloting half of the flats. In six phases over 8 years from 1978 to 1986, 42,000 flats will be built for sale for families with incomes up to US$750 a month.

It was emphasised that the primary focus of the building programme would still be on flats for rent. This policy change is significant and, depending on its success and other relevant factors, may steer Hong Kong closer to the Singapore model.

Singapore

In Singapore, ownership of public flats has been available since 1964. Because of the general success of the public housing programme and of sustained government encouragement, the demand to purchase and rent public flats has been increasing sharply since the late 1960s. Although a certain proportion of these demands was induced, accelerated construction of new flats to meet this backlog of applications has been a significant element of the Third and Fourth 5-Year Building Porgrammes. At the end of March 1976 there were 89,803 applicants on the waiting list to buy and rent flats. By March 1978 this figure declined to 61,696 applicants, of whom 12,042 wanted to rent and 49,654 to buy flats. In fact, after discounting 16,186 applicants who would vacate their smaller flats to move into larger ones, the actual demand was about 45,000 applicants.(12) It is further anticipated that, by the end of 1980, between 65 and 70 percent of the total population of 2.5 million will be housed by the HDB and that 1 million Singapore citizens will be living in their own purchased public flats.

Although the situation is far less acute than in Hong Kong, Singapore has taken positive steps to meet the housing demand of the middle-income groups. Towards this end the Housing and Urban Development Company (HUDC) was recently established to building housing for middle-income families whose incomes do not exceed US$860 per month. Nearly 1000 of these housing units were constructed by the HDB in the Lakeview, Farrer Road, and Amber Estates and were ready for occupation in late 1976. The public response to this component of the housing programme has been encouraging. All the housing units built under Phase I have been sold and more than 2000 applicants have been registered for about 1240 units under the Phase II programme.

Hand in hand with the continuing need to meet quantitative targets is the trend to improve the quality of public housing. In 1966 a design and research unit was established in the HDB with the objective of evolving and improving planning and physical designs to upgrade general living conditions in public housing estates. In addition, there are other problems which have resulted from the active urban renewal programme. Among other things, urban renewal projects have generated many construction activities in the private sector which has been competing with the HDB for the increasingly scarce construction labour force. Allied to this problem of labour shortage is the struggle to maintain rental rates at their present level. Only in mid-1973 were the rentals and selling prices of HDB flats increased after remaining stable for over a decade since 1960; the selling prices were again revised on 1 January 1974. These revisions were necessary as more of the cheaper and available land around the city has been exhausted. More important, inflationary trends emanating from abroad began to impinge more forcibly on Singapore after 1973.

While the steady upgrading of Singapore's housing programme is commendable, fears have been voiced that it is becoming increasingly geared to the needs of higher income groups. One of the principal criticisms is that there exists a group of very poor families who have been displaced by the urban renewal scheme into other slums because they have been unable to afford the rents of government housing. The magnitude of the affected population is difficult to ascertain, although a sample study in the central city area in 1968 showed that 37 percent of the households could not pay the rents in the HDB flats they were offered.(13) It is entirely possible that the urban poor have since been significantly reduced in number and proportion, given Singapore's remarkable economic growth over the last decade. However, without knowing the size of the population in question, any assessment of the housing programme from the viewpoint of equity and other evaluative criteria established earlier in the volume would be largely speculative. It was, nonetheless, concluded previously that the overall redistributive impact of Singapore's programme had been positive.

It is important to prevent the continued alienation of the very poor group from future building programmes and to bring them into the mainstream of life in Singapore. Perhaps this can be achieved by more intensive follow-up surveys on the poorest households affected by urban renewal and resettlement. An understanding of their post-relocation problems may point to new policy directions for the HDB. On the other hand, the difficulties of the urban poor in Singapore may involve a much more complex series of factors than simple housing provision.

CONCLUSION

The examples of Hong Kong and Singapore in their provision of public housing in the post-war period illustrate how, under certain conditions, success is attainable in one of the most intractable urban problems in the Third World. Public housing programmes evolved in rather different conditions in the two cities, with each following dissimilar planning and development practices. Yet the governments decided to embark on housing the urban poor for reasons which were politically compelling, economically justifiable, and socially desirable. Their experiences in dealing with the housing problem suggest several implications for policy and planning in cities in the developing world.

The first consideration is the need to establish housing priorities. Hong Kong's resettlement of squatters and Singapore's large-scale developments of the early 1960s both emphasise that immediate housing shortages should be met first. Relative standards can be sacrificed at this stage for the short-term goal of bridging the household-home hiatus, but long-term considerations need not be abandoned if flexibility is built into the initial estates. This flexibility was theoretically characteristic of the early resettlement blocks in Hong Kong where the original design provided for conversion to self-contained flats. However, the standards were so low and adhered to for so long that their convertibility has been devalued and is finally being abandoned.

Once the commitment to public housing programmes has been made, the next priority is that of creating an efficient administrative organisation. A single unit responsible for public housing is essential to coordinate efforts and finance while reducing unnecessary overlap. Despite its achievements, Hong Kong had, until 1973, four separate bodies competing for land and money. On the other hand, Singapore has long had a centralised administrative authority complete with a research and planning unit. In both cases, nonetheless, the main advances in planning and efficiency occurred after reorganisation into a single policy and executive housing body.

In view of the emphasis by both Hong Kong and Singapore on high-rise, high-density public housing, it is doubtful whether they offer models for metropolitan Asian cities to follow. It would be beyond the scope of this paper to analyse in detail the differences between the city-states' experience and that prevailing in other Third World countries. In brief, it may be pinpointed that success in the public housing programmes in Hong Kong and Singapore is attributed to clear urban priorities, high administrative capacity, intensive population planning measures, and the absence of a rural hinterland to divert scarce capital resources. These conditions are frequently not present in other Third World countries.

From the standpoint of cost, development on a scale and intensity as exemplified in Hong Kong and Singapore is quite beyond the means of most urban governments. In some of the cities in Southeast Asia where the high-rise approach has already been tried, the results have been very mixed. Notwithstanding their unique situation, Hong Kong and Singapore do offer a wealth of experience to other developing Asian cities in land assembly, planning, design, housing management, administration and finance, and other spheres of activity in large-scale housing development. It is hoped that this reservoir of experience will eventually be of greater use and value to other cities and nations as their ability to pursue mass housing programmes develops.

NOTES

(1) In 1977 the per capita GNP in Singapore was US$2,648; for Hong Kong US$2,080.

(2) Hong Kong Housing Authority (1977); p. 41.

(3) Singapore Housing Development Board (1978); p. 5.

(4) See Yeung (1970) and Yeung and Yeh (1975).

(5) Teh (1975); pp. 18-19.

(6) Yeh and Pang (1973).

(7) Yeh and Pang (1973); pp. 16-17.

(8) Yeh (1975), p. 351.

(9) Yeh and HDB (1972).

(10) Yeh and Tan (1975).

(11) Lin (1975); p. 126.

(12) Singapore Housing Development Board (1978); p. 5.

(13) Western et al. (1973); p. 593.

REFERENCES

Drakakis-Smith, D.W. (1975) "Perspectives on Urban Housing Problems in Developing Countries", Canberra: Department of Human Geography, Research School of Pacific Studies, Australian National University. Unpublished.

Hassan, R. (1976) "Public Housing", in R. Hassan (ed.), Singapore: Society in Transition. Kuala Lumpur: Oxford University Press, pp. 240-268.

Housing Authority (1977) Annual Report, 1976-1977. Hong Kong.

Housing Development Board (1978) Annual Report 1977-78, Singapore.

Liu, Thai Ker (1975) "Design for Better Living Conditions", in Yeh (1975: see below), pp. 117-84.

Teh, Cheang Wan (1975) "Public Housing in Singapore: An Overview", in Yeh (1975: see below), pp. 1-21.

Western, J.S., Weldon, P. D. and Tan, Tsu Haung (1973) "Poverty, Urban Renewal and Public Housing in Singapore", Environment and Planning, 5, pp. 589-600.

Wong, L.S.K. (1978) "An Overview of Housing Provision and Housing Needs in Hong Kong", in L.S.K.Wong (ed.), Housing in Hong Kong: A Multi-Disciplinary Study. Hong Kong: Heinemann.

Yeh, S.H.K. (1974) "Housing Conditions and Housing Needs in Singapore", Malayan Economic Review, 14(2), pp. 47-71.

Yeh, S.H.K. (ed.) (1975) Public Housing in Singapore: A Multi-Disciplinary Study. Singapore: Singapore University Press.

Yeh, S.H.K. and Statistics Research Department, HDB (1972) Homes for the People. Singapore: Government Printing Office.

Yeh, S.H.K. and Pang, Eng Fong (1973) "Housing, Employment and National Development: the Singapore Experience", Asia, 31, pp. 8-31.

Yeh, S.H.K. and Tan, Soo Lee (1975) "Satisfaction with Living Conditions", in Yeh (1975), pp. 214-239.

Yeung, Yue-man (1970) "Viability of the Neighbourhood Unit in Singapore's Public Housing Estates", Bandar, 2, pp. 11-19.

Yeung, Yue-man (1976) "Location of Housing in Urban Development Plans in Southeast Asia". Paper presented at the Low-cost Housing Workshop at the Habitat Forum, Vancouver, June 1976.

Yeung, Yue-man and Yeh, S.H.K. (1975) "A Review of Neighbourhoods and Neighbouring Practices", in Yeh (1975: see above), pp. 262-280.

9

Upgrading of Low-income Residential Areas in Jakarta and Manila

John L. Taylor
David G. Williams

DESCRIPTION OF THE JAKARTA KAMPUNG IMPROVEMENT PROGRAMME

Background and History

Jakarta is the capital and largest city of Indonesia. Situated along the north-western coast of Java, it functions as the commercial and administrative centre of the world's fifth largest nation. With a present population of about 6 million and an annual average per capita GDP of about US $160 (1971), the city is one of the largest and poorest in the world. Jakarta is growing at an estimated 4.5 percent annually, with over half of that growth due to net immigration from other parts of Indonesia. Physically, the jurisdiction of the Special Capital Region of Jakarta (DKI) extends over 560 km^2, but the city's urbanised area was a relatively compact 12,000 hectares in 1969 and is presently estimated to be over 18,000 hectares. Since 1964 Jakarta has been administered as a special district with the status of a province. This status gives it an advantage over other Indonesian municipalities in its taxing powers and in greater accessibility to the financial and technical resources of the Central Government.

Jakarta's recent history was dominated by government decisions in the 1950s and 1960s aimed at giving the city an image of modern prosperity. In the 1960s a high-income suburb, Kebayoran Baru, was developed south of Jakarta, and a series of limited access roads were constructed around the city. Although these highways were built through paddy fields beyond the fringes of what was then urbanised Jakarta, they have proven to be an extremely important force in channeling later physical and economic develpment. During the

1960s, major construction activities, including a sports complex for the Asian Games and several office buildings and hotels, created thousands of jobs for unskilled labourers, thereby stimulating migration into Jakarta. Thousands of rural families moved into crowded quarters with friends or relatives; thousands more hastily erected temporary shelters on land they did not own. A further wave of in-migration occurred during the repression of the abortive communist putsch in 1965/66. These population influxes increased densities and added to the number of existing "kampungs", of low-income neighborhoods, which had been settled in an unplanned manner throughout the city for more than a hundred years.

It is important to understand the definition of the term "kampung" in the context of Indonesia. The term refers to predominantly residential areas which were often rural villages that have been engulfed by rapid urban expansion and incorporated within the city. These "urban villages", which include middle-income as well as low-income families, are characterised by generally inadequate physical infrastructure and social services. However, many of them are viable communities, and the term kampung is neither synonymons with slums nor squatter settlements where residents have no rights of occupancy.(1) The latter hardly exist in Indonesia since occupancy confers considerable right of possession.

In Jakarta, these kampungs account for 60 percent of the city's area and about 75 percent of its population. A 1969 survey of Jakarta housing conditions demonstrated the inadequacy of urban facilities and services in these kampungs; 65 percent of the houses had no private toilet facilities, 80 percent no electricity, and 90 percent had no piped water connection. Approximately, 30 percent of the households depended solely on water vendors for their supply at prices 5 times greater than the charges for piped water. Jakarta has no water-borne sewer system. Even houses having piped water flush sanitary wastes into septic tanks or more frequently into open ditches along the roadside. Much of the population, however, has no alternative other than to use the drainage canals for bathing, laundering and defecation. Much of the city's uncollected garbage (over 30 percent of the daily production) is thrown into adjacent canals, clogging the drainage system of the city. Permanent houses with solid walls, cement floors, and tile roofs constituted 24 percent of the total housing stock; temporary houses of bamboo matting walls, earthen floors, and thatch roofs comprised 44 percent; and semi-permanent structures having some combination of temporary and permanent materials accounted for the balance (32 percent).

The DKI-initiated Kampung Improvement Programme (1969-1974)

Prior to the establishment of the Kampung Improvement Programme (KIP), little was done to improve the living conditions of the people in these areas because the programmes proposed were often designed to standards which were beyond the means of the population they intended to serve. However, the DKI recognized these kampungs as permanent settlements and became increasingly concerned about the deterioration of conditions within them.

During Indonesia's First Five-Year Development Plan (1969-1974) the DKI inaugurated a programme to improve the physical infrastructure in some of the worst kampungs in Jakarta. The KIP is an attempt to meet minimum infrastructure needs of large numbers of urban poor at low cost. The programme represents the lowest level of investment in this direction as it upgrades community infrastructure in low-income areas. The DKI realised that it would be unable to provide all the resources necessary to rebuild the kampungs and it decided instead to concentrate its available resources on improvement of those physical infrastructures which the people found most difficult or impossible to organise and construct by themselves. The KIP did not involve direct investment in housing per se. Rather, it would concentrate on providing paved roads and footpaths, drainage ditches, communal water taps, sanitary latrines, garbage bins, and social services such as schools and health clinics. By providing these basic community infrastructures, the DKI hoped that kampung residents themselves would be encouraged to improve their own dwellings as improvements were made in their environment. These elements were to be planned and installed in a careful and sensitive manner to minimise disruption and relocation of households.

It should be emphasised that the KIP was a locally initiated programme at the outset. Not only was there no foreign assistance prior to 1974, but it was the DKI rather than the Central Government that took the lead in launching the programme.(2) A publication of the DKI mentions some of KIP's specific objectives:

> "(i) To build the main requirements for the city population, such as roads, footpaths, drainage, sanitation, drinking water supplies and schools and health centres;
>
> (ii) to identify the poorer part of the population which has suffered from inadequate environmental conditions;
>
> (iii) to draw up a programme of investment which can be enjoyed by the widest section of the population; and

(iv) to encourage the population to realise its potential for self-sufficiency and cooperation within their own kampung."(3)

From 1969-1974 DKI managed to upgrade about 2,400 ha or 20 percent of its 1969 urbanised area (see Table 9.1). The programme directly benefited about 1.2 million residents, which was estimated to be approximately 40 percent of the kampung population as of 1974. On the average, the first 5 years of KIP cost US $6500 per ha and US $13 per capita. (Cost figures are given in current costs.) In return the city of Jakarta gained 399 km of paved roads and footpaths, 140 km of feeder drainage canals, 101 km of water supply pipes, 71 sanitary units, 394 rubbish bins and 26 health centres. In all, 89 kampungs were improved.

Table 9.1. Summary of Jakarta Kampung Improvement Programme

Urbanised area (1969) (ha)		12,000		
Area in kampungs (1969) (ha)		7200	(60%)	
	Results from three phases of KIP			
	1969-74	1974-76	1976-79	Total
Area improved (ha)	2400	1980	3000	7380
Percent of 1969 urbanised area	20.0%	16.5%	25.0%	61.5%
Population benefited ('000 persons)	1200	890	1200	3290
Average cost per ha (US $)	6500	18,000	24,000	17,000
Average cost per capita (US $)	13	40	60	37

Source: The World Bank.

A few comments should be made about some of the salient features of KIP during the initial years. First, the programme consisted entirely of providing physical facilities without any social or economic components. Secondly, roads and footpaths alone accounted for approximately two-thirds of total expenditures during the 5-year period. Thirdly, standards were kept very low; for instance, only one communal toilet facility consisting of twelve closets and areas for washing and bathing was provided per about 3500 people. And finally, the programme's inputs were provided on a relatively homogeneous basis; that is, there was little room for much variation in type and standard of improvements on the basis of community participation.

The World Bank Supports KIP (1974-1979)

In 1974 the World Bank joined to assist with finance for the next 2 years (1974-1976) of the Jakarta KIP programme, as part of the Bank's first urban loan to Indonesia.(4) The Bank had for some time been advocating upgrading of infrastructure within existing residential areas as one of the most desirable policy options for LDC cities, and it saw in the Jakarta KIP a prime opportunity to support just such an effort. The Bank's support for the KIP, coupled with 5 years of previous DKI experience, enabled a moderate increase in the programme's standards and components, and a dramatic increase in its pace or rate of activity. The construction of primary schools and provision of garbage trucks were added to the list of KIP components included in the programme during the first 5 years. Standards were raised for specific components, in particular with regard to water supply and sanitation. The most dramatic change at this time was the accelaration of the pace of the programme. Whilst less than 500 ha were improved per year during 1969-1974, 1890 ha were upgraded during the following 2-year period (1974-1976), or a doubling of pace to nearly 1000 ha per year. This 2-year period directly benefited approximately 890,000 people. Because of higher standards, and higher prices as well, KIP costs were about 3 times higher than during the earlier period: US$18,000 per ha and US$40 per capita.

In 1976 a second loan was made by the World Bank to continue the KIP programme in both Jakarta and Surabaya, Indonesia's next largest city. This 3-year (1976-79) period of support to the Jakarta KIP has again involved some increase in scope and standards, while the rate of improving 1000 ha per year established during the previous 2-year period was maintained. With regard to scope, 1976 marked the first year during which a concerted effort was made to introduce a social component into the programme, with the addition of training for community health workers to staff the physical facilities being built.

A more flexible approach was introduced regarding standards which gave the DKI increased latitude in designing the KIP for each kampung, in part through greater participation in the planning process on the part of local representatives, within a framework of established design objectives and allocation procedures. Several modifications were made in service levels of which the most important were (i) changing from large communal toilets to individual pit privies (because of land acquisition problems and lack of public acceptance of communal facilities); (ii) increasing the coverage of footpaths and reducing the amount of roads provided; and (iii) improving standards of water supply.

Information on the actual achievement of this most recent 3-year period indicates that about 3000 ha has been upgraded, directly benefiting another 1.2 million persons. Costs have increased to US$24,000 per ha and US$60 per capita ($40 per capita at post-devaluation prices).

During 1979 yet a third World Bank loan was negotiated for kampung improvement which is intended to extend the programme to the newer remaining kampungs and to improve the water supply and sanitation in the oldest kampungs in Jakarta. Assistance for KIP is also being extended to four other cities in the country. A fourth loan from the World Bank has just been realised which will extend KIP to a further six cities. The Asian Development Bank and bi-lateral donors are now assisting KIP in a range of additional cities and the Government plans to have KIPs underway in a total of 200 cities within the next 3 years.

Programme Planning and Management

The key to the phenomenal output of physical works in congested urban areas which the KIP units have been able to attain first in Jakarta, and now in other cities, lies in effective programme management, a simple design approach and a high degree of discipline with regard to timing and the budget cycle. Construction for a set of kampungs is scheduled for the dry months of the year, and the planning cycle begins one year before.

In May the KIP unit, in conjunction with the City Planning Office, and with assistance from air photos, other sectoral agencies and information from the Lurahs and Camats - the lower-level of local government officials in the city - defines the following year's list of kampungs to be improved based on their density, environmental conditions, service deficiencies and dispersion across the political subdivisions of the city. Rough outline budgets are then prepared and in June the KIP Steering Committee reviews and approves the programme, followed by approval of the City Council and the Governor. During July outline sketch plans are prepared based on an analysis of each kampung's deficiencies and the facilities required to bring the kampung up to a minimum standard level of service. These plans are discussed with the community in meetings organised by the Lurah. Often there is controversy over cases of unavoidable acquisition of land or buildings in order to insert a footpath or widen a road. The financial compensation is frequently inadequate unless the individual has a strong "right" on the land. Fortunately, less than 5 percent of the dwellings in KIP are cut or demolished due to the flexible standards adopted and the efforts made by the site planners to thread the infrastructure in along existing access-ways.

During August and September ground survey checks along access-ways are made and the airphoto bases turned into survey drawings, detailed site plans are drawn up and discussed again with the residents. Each household is required to sign the plan before the work on the kampung proceeds further. The popular demand for KIP is such that community pressure is sometimes brought to bear on dissenting households, and contributions in money or land to ease the relocation or resiting problems of adversely affected households are often made by other kampung residents.

From October through February detailed engineering designs are prepared. These use standard quantities and cross sections and are more simple and understandable to local contractors than the elaborate drawings common in developed countries. As soon as the year's budget has been approved in mid-March, bids are solicited and contracts let. Each contract usually covers one kampung or area of a large kampung, thus achieving an integration among the various facilities provided. There are frequent on-site changes due to unforseen circumstances and to the rough and ready nature of the engineering drawings. The Camat is designated the site project manager and his main role is as intermediary between the residents and the contractors. KIP engineers supervise the works and authorise payments which are passed to the DKI Directorate of Finance for disbursement. The physical works usually take about 9 to 12 months to complete. Management of the schools and health centres is taken over by the relevant authorities, and operation of the public water taps, washing places and toilets is let to concessionaries. Maintenance of footpaths and drains are left to the local kampung committee and vehicular roads are taken over by the DKI.

The Overall Effect of the Jakarta KIP

To conclude this description of Jakarta's upgrading programme, a few general comments are in order. With a volume of activity that currently provides improvements to 1000 ha per year benefiting about 450,000 persons annually, Jakarta is the first major LDC city which has been able to mount a sustained programme at a level sufficient to catch up with both the backlog and current growth within a reasonable period of time. By the end of 1979 the city had upgraded the physical infrastructure in kampungs covering 7,380 ha, thus benefiting nearly 3.5 million persons (see Table 9.1 and Figure 9.1, the latter being a map of Jakarta which shows the geographic extent of the programme). This represents at least 80 percent of total kampung area and population at the present time. Within precisely a decade, Jakarta has come close to eliminating the backlog of unserviced residential areas.

Although a more complete evaluation will be made in conjunction with Manila's upgrading programme at the conclusion of this chapter, the following points pertaining specifically to the Jakarta KIP can be made at this stage. First, the programme was locally initiated and demonstrates that an innovative effort can be implemented under dynamic leadership. Secondly, it has been quite well managed. Although KIP has not been marked by a high degree of community participation, it demonstrates that "command" planning may at times be appropriate. Finally, there have been problems with the programme, including the following: (i) Maintenance of improvements, especially in the kampungs where KIP was first undertaken, has not been what it should be. (ii) Inadequate reform of the city property tax system which carries the main burden of cost recovery for the programme. (iii) KIP has made no attempt to deal with the long-standing problem of clouded land ownership titles, so that the need for an organised urban land registration system has not been met.

DESCRIPTION OF MANILA'S SLUM UPGRADING PROGRAMMES

City History and Structure

With over 6.3 million population, and growing at 5 percent per year, greater Manila is over 4 times the size of the next largest city in the Philippines, a country of 40 million people. Although, at US$240, the average annual per capita income of Manila (1977 levels) is almost twice that of the country as a whole, 40 percent of the people earn less than US$170/capita, below the country's absolute poverty line as defined by the World Bank, and about 30 percent of the population live in unserviced slums and squatter settlements scattered throughout the 37,000 hectare urbanised area of the city.

The present structure of the city was developed following the devastation during World War II. Along with the rebuilt port, new industries were quickly established and attracted thousands of migrants from the countryside which was, and is largely still, in the hands of large agricultural landowners. With its friendly people and English as a lingua franca, the

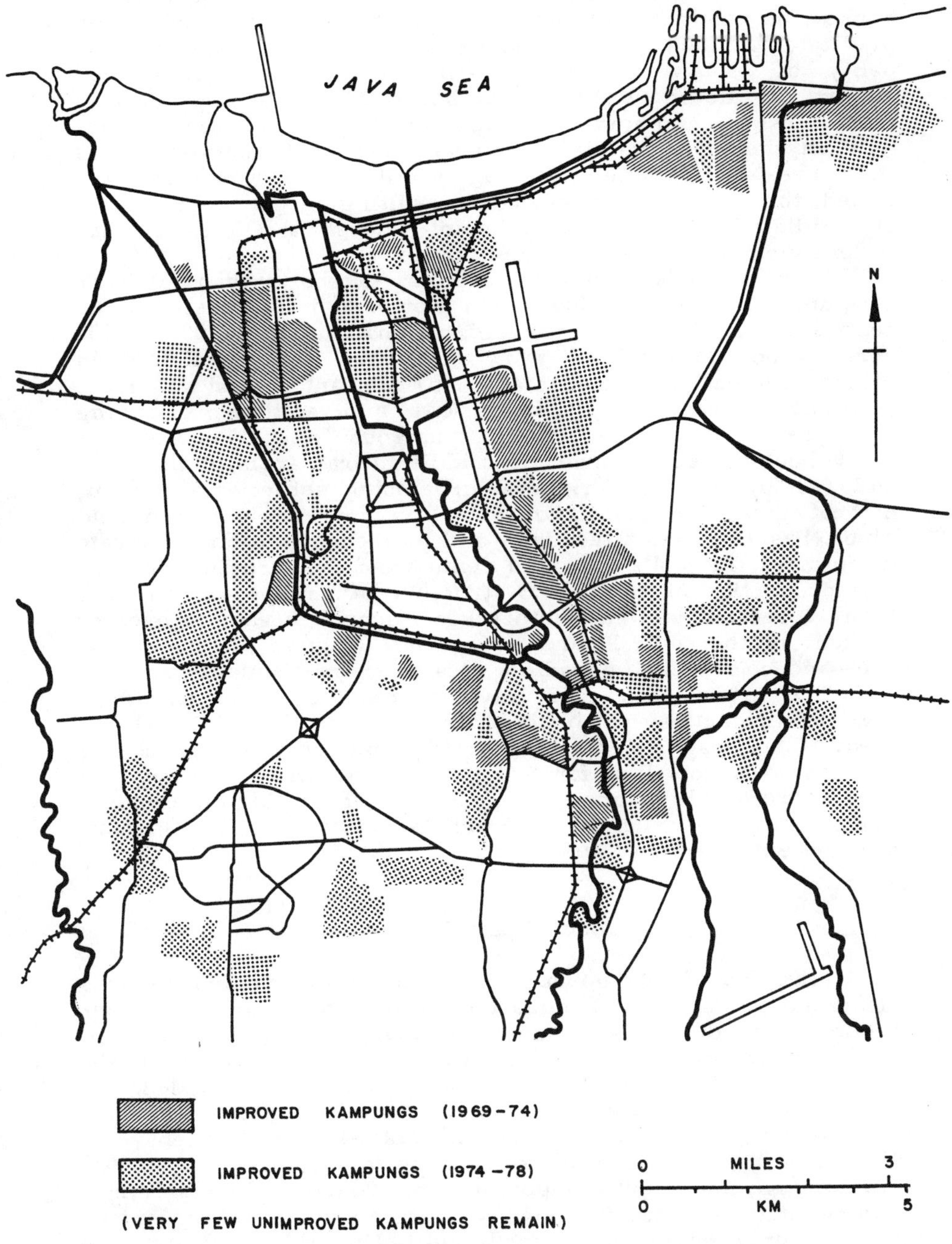

Fig. 9.1. Jakarta Kampung Improvement Programme

city then attracted the offices of international businesses, banks and insurance companies which built large buildings on privately planned and developed land in the central municipality of Makati. A little earlier the government-planned suburb of Quezon city was established to form a new administrative centre and new roads to link these developments were built in the 1950s and 1960s. A wide range of employment was thus created for the emerging middle class which in turn fueled the demand for services, resulting in the densification of middle class areas to the point where many are now deteriorating into densely crowded slums.

Metro Manila's slum areas are less extensive than Jakarta's kampungs and exhibit four main morphological types: (a) the central slums which are very high density areas (700 to 2000 persons per hectare) of two- and three-storey buildings in blocks divided by regular roads; (b) "linear" coastal and river settlements occupied by fishermen, and settlements strung along rail lines and canals; (c) numerous "pocket" slums of ¼ to 10 hectares dotted over the middle-income areas of the city; and (d) low-density peripheral urbanising settlements. About half of these unserviced areas are on government-owned land which has been squatted upon and half belong to large private landowners who collect ground rents from the structure owners. The proportion of renters to structure owners grows from less than 10 percent in the peripheral low-density areas, to over 60 percent in the central slums. Figure 9.2 shows the major land uses and community upgrading sites in metro-Manila.

The urbanised area is divided into four cities and thirteen municipalities which together comprise the Metro-Manila area. This fragmented administrative pattern is slowly moving towards a metropolitan form of government under the aegis of the Metro-Manila Commission (MMC) which is increasingly undertaking provision of city-wide services and the financial management of Metro-Manila.

The Tondo Upgrading Project

Until the late 1960s government policy was oriented towards clearance of slum and squatter areas and relocating their occupants to distant sites up to 40 km from Manila. With few work opportunities and high commuting costs, most of the relocatees moved back to the city proper. The residents of the largest slum, called Tondo, successfully resisted efforts to be resettled and demanded provision of services and tenure of the government land they had squatted on since the 1940s. Comprising about 180,000 persons the Tondo residents form a strong political force in the city since they are well organised with powerful community councils elected by the residents. By 1972 the government had realised that this slum-removal policy

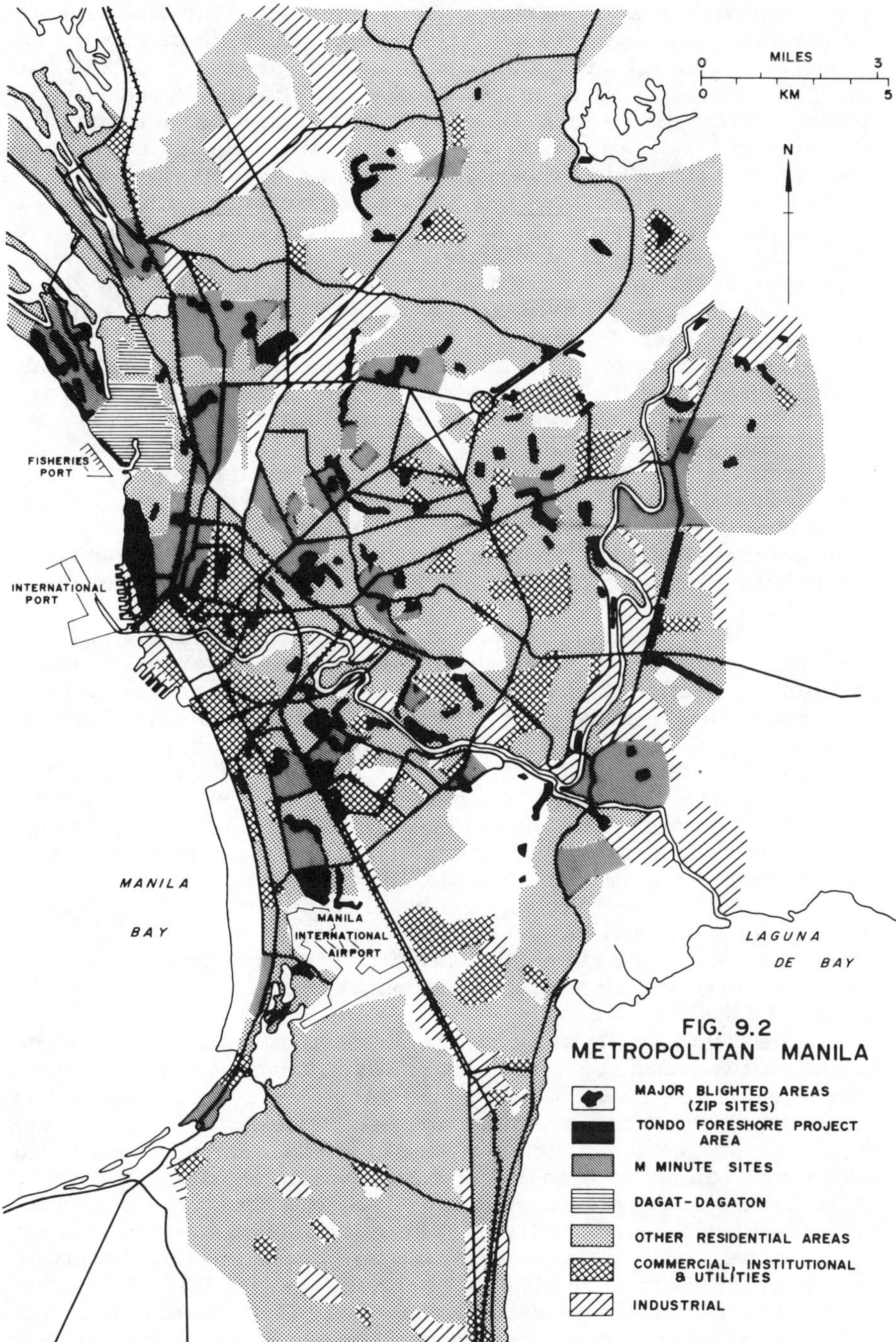

FIG. 9.2
METROPOLITAN MANILA

was unworkable and started discussions with the Tondo community for a scheme which would meet their demands. With assistance through a World Bank loan a project was initiated by the National Housing Authority to up-grade the whole Tondo area and which involved no relocation outside the community. The approach was an intensive one involving long discussions with Zoto, the main community council, and with the residents on a block by block basis, over alternative layouts and levels of service for the community. The components of the scheme included land tenure for the structure owners, provision of roads, footpaths, drainage, piped water supply to each house and individual sewerage connections, schools, clinics, playgrounds and loans for building materials for individuals to improve their houses, and assistance to small-scale businesses. The costs of services and land were to be recovered through mortgage payments and user charges for water and these terms were discussed and agreed by the community. The mortgage payment for the development and land costs amounts to US$13 per month, affordable by over 80 percent of Tondo's households. Occupants who are not structure owners, usually the poorest 20 percent, will also benefit by enjoying improved services, but would have to remain as tenants.

The NHA designers developed three site-planning options for each block which were discussed with each group of block residents. While no scheme involved relocating houses beyond the community, they ranged from minimum disturbance of existing structures to maximum movement of houses into a grid-iron pattern. This phase of the design is called "reblocking". Most resident groups chose the maximum relocation model and subsequently moved their wood-frame houses through community self-help to the new plot locations. Each house was lifted by twenty to fifty people into its new position. This approach, while being a remarkable demonstration of community cooperation, tended to slow the process of upgrading the community and thus delay the benefits of upgrading for others, and also involved families in an additional expenditure averaging about US$100 each.

The Tondo scheme is now half completed and the results are already amazing. The community has been transformed into a clean and attractive place and secure land tenure has encouraged most households to put enormous efforts into building up their structures in an individual and at times eccentric manner. Two- and sometimes three-storey Spanish style town houses have replaced many of the original shacks and the variety and quality of the building has created a much more human and liveable environment than the best institutional architecture could ever achieve. The NHA has monitored the physical and social changes carefully and indications are that all these improvements have been done by the original settlers who have not sold out to higher-income groups but have put all their savings, and often those of their relatives, into improving their houses. The loans for building materials have all been called on and the US$350 maximum allocated for each loan is probably inadequate in view of the average expenditure of US$600 per house, many families adding extra rooms for renting. The residents' ability to mobilise personal savings has been greatly under-estimated and indicates that income should not be the sole criterion for judging affordability. A weaker feature is the assistance to small-scale enterprises, which has not yet got established due to the inexperience in the component, and the requirements for collateral by the local banks.

The approach taken in Tondo has demonstrated in a dramatic way that low income people are willing and able to mobilise considerable assets to improve their environment and individual plots provided that their own priorities concerning land tenure and services are respected and they are brought in as serious partners to the planning process.

Plans for the Future

The activities at Tondo stimulated the interest of many other slum communities in Metro-Manila and encouraged the NHA to initiate a metro-wide programme of slum improvement called ZIP (the Zonal Improvement Programme), which is designed to provide tenure and services to over 1.8 million people in about 300 depressed areas of the city over a 12-year period. A programme of this magnitude and complexity on hundreds of sites and with a high degree of community participation could not be undertaken efficiently by one office, and will instead be implemented by the local governments with the assistance of four district offices under the overall guidance of the NHA and the Metro-Manila Commission. The popularity of ZIP was such that it became one of the main platforms for the government in the two recent elections. Planning for ZIP has been underway for almost 2 years and has included intensive discussions with each of the communities, and the first sites are now under construction.

While more streamlined physical design and implementation methods will enable the ZIP to up-grade the depressed areas faster than Tondo, it is nevertheless a slow process and stands in danger of being outpaced by the speed of slum formation. Furthermore, there are many areas in the city which are not slums but still lack essential services. Two complementary programmes of up-grading called "MMINUTE" (Metro Manila Infrastructure Utilities and Engineering) and "PROGRESS" (Program for Removing Sewage from Streets) were therefore devised by the Ministry of Public Works and take what could be called a "network" approach to up-grading as compared to the "area" approach of ZIP. MMINUTE will involve the secondary and tertiary networks of streets, drainage, public sanitation and water supply which can be improved and installed in existing rights of way, but will not deal with tenure, minor footpath access, individual plot services or reblocking of plots. PROGRESS is similar to MMINUTE but deals only with micro-drainage. These approaches are thus closer to KIP in Jakarta, but will also involve a measure of direct cost recovery through a betterment levy on street improvements in addition to the indirect charges through water consumption rates and sewage surcharges. They will be targeted at the poorest and worst areas first and will be able to move much more rapidly than ZIP by avoiding the issues of land acquisition and tenure. They are expected to improve conditions for about 3.5 million people in large areas of the city over a 10-year period. The most congested blocks bounded by these network improvements which need tenure and individual plot services will then be treated to a ZIP in the later phases of the Zonal Improvement Programme. MMINUTE, PROGRESS and ZIP will all use district level teams to implement the works and these teams will also include a maintenance section to strengthen this important but often-neglected area of municipal service. Another component of the effort to direct services to the urban poor in Manila is a programme of serviced sites on open land at the urbanising fringe of the city within easy commuting distance to existing employment and in locations where new industries are growing. About 2500 plots per year will be developed on which families can build their own dwellings which, together with the large sites and services development at Dagat-Dagatan (just north of Tondo), will provide for the expansion needs of additional families from the lowest 15th to 70th percentiles of Manila's income distribution. These new sites will also include schools, clinics, plots for small industries and land for sale to larger industrial and commercial enterprises. Half of the plots will be developed by the Government in the conventional manner and for the other half an experiment is being tried to interest private developers in building serviced sites for low and moderate income families. In the latter case the Government would restrict its involvement to assisting with part of the construction finance, providing off-site infrastructure and offering mortgage financing for plot beneficiaries, controlling land location, planning standards and plot sale prices. All these incentives and controls would be part of an agreement negotiated with each developer. A new effort has also been made to deal more effectively with the "livelihood" needs of low-income people, by taking a more comprehensive view of the needs for small and informal businesses and local production cooperatives and credit unions. A division of the Technology Resource Centre (TRC), a government corporation specialising in business operations is taking a leading role to evaluate the operations and opportunities for small-scale enterprises in Metro-Manila and to develop project packages to assist them, using the skills and abilities of other government and private agencies. As from 1980, a 3-year slice of the ZIP, MMINUTE, PROGRESS, sites and services and livelihood programmes are being financed with the assistance of World Bank loans.

Together with complementary efforts to focus investments in water, sewerage, solid wastes and transport on helping low income groups, the programmes described here represent a major effort to redirect investments in the capital city towards the urban poor. The combined impact of these programmes on reducing deficits in urban services is expected to be considerable, as illustrated in figure 9.3.

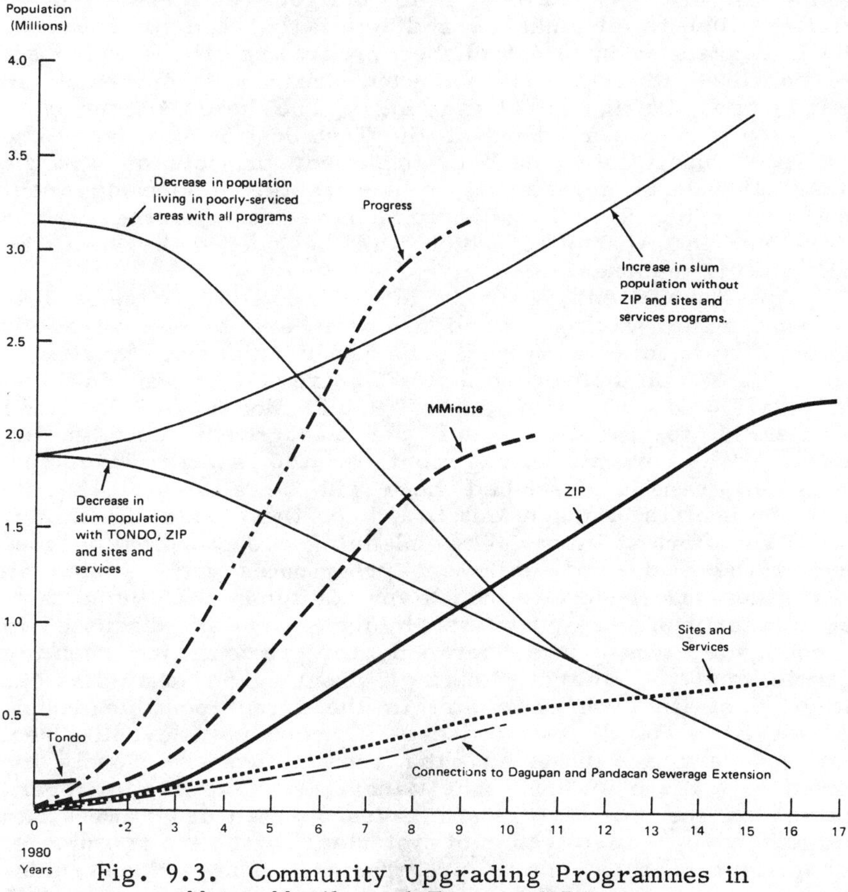

Fig. 9.3. Community Upgrading Programmes in Metro-Manila and Expected Impacts on the Unserviced Population.

Programme Management

Initiating five major municipal works programmes concurrently in one city through four different agencies could lead to great confusion, especially since they will affect all of the seventeen local governments which comprise Metro-Manila. The need for effective coordination is paramount. This is expected to be achieved through a Management Coordinating Board which has been established and on which each major implementing agency sits together with the key Ministries of Finance and Budget. The Board is chaired by the Assistant Governor of Metro-Manila, and is assisted by a Technical Secretariat. It has powers to review each agency's financial and physical programme and to consolidate the individual yearly budgets for submission to the Ministry of Budget, to review and reschedule agency programmes according to budget revisions, and to resolve problems of linkages and inputs between programmes. The lead agencies have established programme offices which set the policies and standards for each programme and establish their scope, timing and budgeting. The heads of the programme offices are members of the Technical Secretariat. The District Teams, noted earlier, implement projects on specific sites. It will be interesting to see whether this management structure (Fig. 9.4) is able to achieve the degree of collaboration and discipline which will be needed between the implementing agencies.

The Management Board is also expected to develop into the main policy making arm to prioritise and budget all public sector investments in Metro-Manila. This planning function - called the Capital Improvement Folio review - was initiated during 1979 by the Ministry of Public Works and is being transferred to the MMC and the Management Coordinating Board. The overall management of the specific municipal works programmes described here will be a test of the effectiveness of the Management Board for these wider functions.

This effort at inter-agency planning and coordination goes beyond the design of settlement programmes and initiates an interesting model for metropolitan planning and budgeting. Programme priorities and overall budget levels are discussed in a collegiate atmosphere between the various implementing agencies and the Budget Ministry. Each agency maintains the integrity of its programme and to the extent possible decentralises it to its district offices. Where land title and direct cost recovery are involved, the communities are closely involved with the planning. The Management Coordinating Board focuses on coordination, interlinkages between programmes and budget levels, but does not interfere with the nature of management of the sectoral programmes. The national Ministries of Human Settlements, Public Works and Budget maintain a watching role. In this way the function of each level of

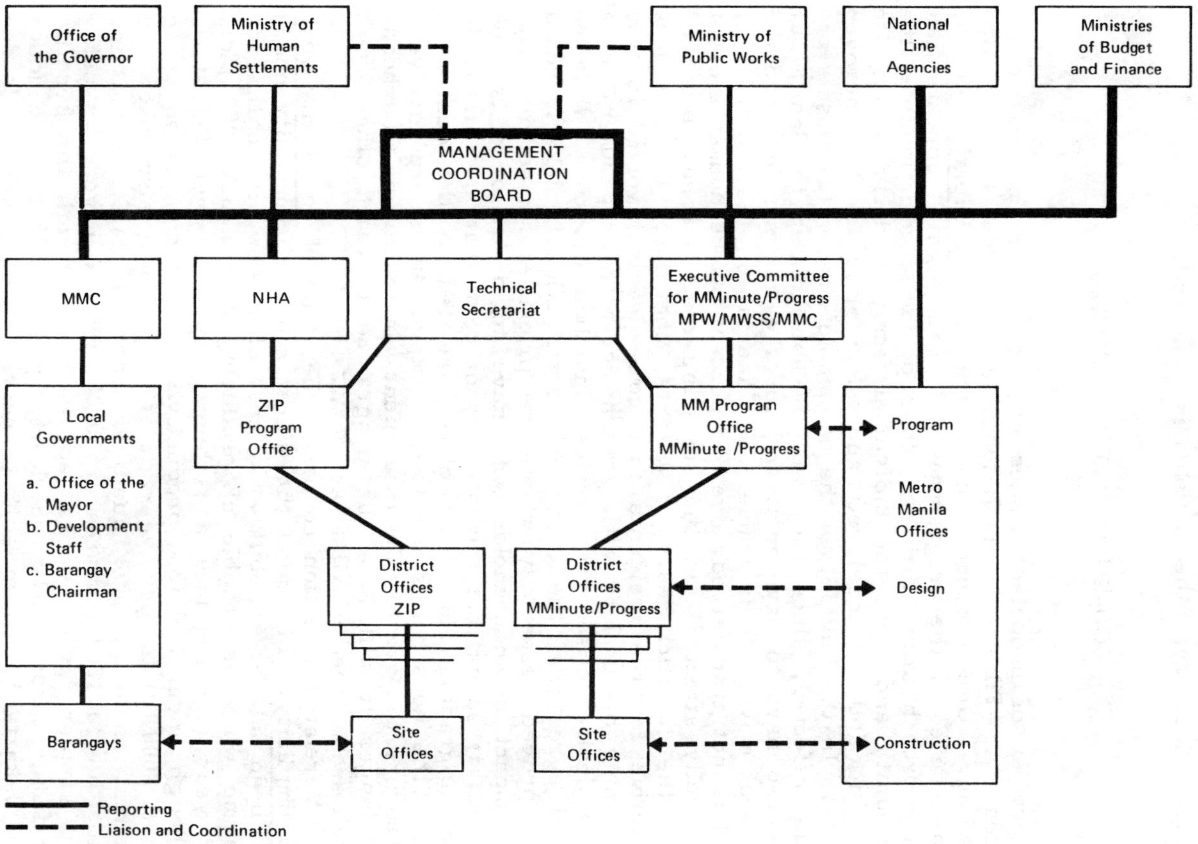

Fig. 9.4. Institutional Structure for Zip and MMinute Programmes.

government and community appears to be properly used, and trespass into each other's fields is minimized.

COMPARATIVE EVALUATION

A number of important issues emerge from a comparison between the Filipino and Indonesian approach to slum upgrading. One concerns the degree of participation of the beneficiaries of the programmes. At first sight it appears that the approach under ZIP is much superior since it involves the community and even the individual family in decisions on site planning and service levels and their priorities for improvements. In the Philippines the household's individual assets are being affected, since they will be able to own the land, but will also have to pay for it and for the new services and the costs of moving their house. In Jakarta, on the other hand, land is not transferred, over 95 percent of the houses are not physically affected and the servicing costs are not recovered from the beneficiaries. In Jakarta, therefore, there is less incentive for the residents to become deeply involved in time consuming discussions with government planners, but rather a great desire to see the services installed quickly. While we would agree that the degree of participation in Jakarta could be improved, especially where the priorities for services and the impact on households who have to be removed is concerned, it seems that the intensity of participation desirable in slum upgrading should be closely related to the degree in which the household's assets and expenditures are involved. Moreover, the greater the time spent with each neighbourhood, the longer it will take the programme to reach other areas which are in need of vital services.

A related question concerns the issue of complexity versus simplicity. In Tondo the widest range of community needs has been addressed, but at a cost of a slow, in-depth programme which is capable of producing only about 5000 plots per year and requires a technical input of over 200 staff. Although under ZIP this productivity is expected to go up to about 8000 plots per year, staff input will also rise. In Jakarta, about 200 less qualified technical staff can now upgrade up to 1200 hectares or 60,000 plots per year by using their simpler "public works" approach. Although the benefits per family through KIP are clearly much less than those under ZIP, Jakarta has been able to service most of the city's depressed areas within a fairly short time of 10 years. It will be interesting to see whether the dual approach which the Filipinos are now adopting by using both ZIP and MMINUTE/PROGRESS will offer the best of both worlds. Naturally, other factors have to be considered when choosing the type of up-grading programme, such as cultural attitudes to land tenure, and the skills and numbers of technical staff available in the country. There is a very strong urge in the Philippines among all income groups for freehold land ownership, originating in Spanish colonial attitudes, as compared to the ambiguous and indeterminate condition of the many levels of land rights in Indonesia where tenants traditionally have a strong right to continued occupancy.

In terms of other criteria noted in Part I, both ZIP and KIP score high in terms of equity by reaching the lowest income groups in the city. Growth and Distribution of assets for individual families is already a proven feature in Tondo, although the greater number of tenants in some ZIP sites will require that greater attention is paid to tenants' security of tenure and potential share of assets. It would not be possible to offer each tenant a new plot and the present practice in Tondo is that most tenants move with the structure owner during reblocking. Preliminary indications are that there has not been a high turnover of tenants and that rental costs have not escalated greatly beyond the average rate of increase in the city. In Jakarta, surveys have shown a similar trend in stable rentals but this may be largely explained by the extent and speed of the KIP, diluting the surge of values in any one area, and the low physical standards inhibiting the influx of higher income groups. Further attention is being given to this matter in the ZIP, especially in the central slums where high tenancy ratios are common, and different tenure options involving condominium and cooperative ownerships, and legal divisions of the existing building and plot, are being explored. Community participation may then focus more on these legal options than on numerous alternatives in physical design.

The experience in Tondo has also developed leverage to enable those in government concerned with the conditions of the poor, to develop and implement the ZIP, MMINUTE and PROGRESS programmes, and also to influence the distribution of investments in water and sewerage projects in Manila so that their service networks are directed more towards lower-income groups in the city than had first been planned. The leverage has been mainly exercised by residents of other slum communities who have seen the Tondo example and have pressed the politicians and administrators to continue the upgrading projects.

The efforts to grapple with the planning process is also instructive. Whereas Jakarta already had a fairly effective planning and budgeting process for major city investments and the KIP has been a process of continual improvement in the efficiency of managing a single programme, in the Manila the administrators are more ambitious in launching several new programmes which they hope will also serve as a catalyst to bring about a more effective urban management system. At the same time an overall review of government investments in Metro-Manila is underway to determine their priority with respect to social and economic objectives and their affordability to the city and national fisc.

In summary, experiences in slum up-grading both in Indonesia and the Philippines have been very positive and can be counted among the more effective urban programmes in the developing world.

NOTES

(1) For further definition, see PADCO (1976).

(2) However, Central Government grants do provide on important source for KIP.

(3) DKI KIP unit (1975).

(4) For details reviewing the impact of KIP from 1969 and a projected programme for expansion, see P.C.D. (1973).

REFERENCES

Government of the Special Province of Jakarta (DKI), KIP Unit (1975) "A Paper Describing the Development and Progress of a Scheme for Improving Physical and Social Conditions in Urban Kampungs in Jakarta."

PADCO (1976) "Towards a National Policy for a Kampung Improvement Program." Unpublished report for the Director-General of Housing, Planning and Urban Development (Cipta-Karya).

P.C.D. (1973) "Request for funding to the World Bank for the Kampung Improvement Program, Jakarta." Unpublished report to the Director-General, Cipta Karya.

10
The Malayasian Urban Development Authority: A Case Study

Peter W. Amato

BACKGROUND AND HISTORY OF MALAYSIA

Peninsular Malaysia has a relatively small population; 9 million persons distributed over 131,590 square km or 68 persons per square km; 20 percent is cultivated, 60 percent is forested and only 1 percent can be termed "urbanised". Exports have provided the main thrust of economic growth for the country since independence from England in 1957, particularly during the boom years of 1963-1974. However, to understand Malaysian development activities, planning priorities and goals, one must understand its racial composition and social goals and concerns. Moreover, in seeking directions and priorities for the planning of human settlements, various historical and ecological considerations and patterns of behaviour must be understood.

Early Malaysian communities were riverine settlements established at the confluence of major rivers. These settlement patterns underwent major changes with the influx of Chinese traders and tin miners in the nineteenth and early twentieth centuries. Migrants from India followed to work in the newly established rubber estates. Colonial policy encouraged Malays to remain in rural areas as farmers which tended to compartmentalise the various races into economic activity and spatial location. Thus, urban centres are largely populated by Chinese, while Malays dominate in the rural areas. Indians tend to be located on rubber estates with additional concentrations in professional and retail business activities in urban centres.

Another event which has had important impact on the settlement pattern in the country was the Emergency period 1948 to 1960. In order to hinder Communist infiltration and threats within rural Chinese communities, New Villages were established close to urban centres to facilitate military supervision and control. These New Villages have remained to this day as tight Chinese settlements with severe development problems, not being absorbed into surrounding traditional Malay villages and testifying to the difficulties of racial integration within the nation.

Malays, although predominantly employed in the primary sectors of the economy, form the majority of the electorate, with 57 percent of the population, and have controlled the government and the political life of the country since independence. The Chinese, who make up 31 percent of the population, are mainly employed in secondary and tertiary sectors and control the major interests in manufacturing, construction, wholesale and retail trade. Indians account for only 11 percent of the population in peninsular Malaysia and have much less influence in either the political or economic activities than Malays or Chinese. The mean monthly incomes in 1970 showed Chinese with the highest at US$154, followed by Indians at $124 and Malays with $71.(1)

Given the economic disparities between Malays and other races, particularly the Chinese, and on the heels of the 1969 racial riots which occurred in Kuala Lumpur, the government adopted its Second Five-Year Plan in 1971, calling for 30 percent of corporate wealth and control to be in the hands of Malays by 1990. Improvement is to occur, at least according to the Second Five-Year Plan, without expropriating the wealth of Chinese and others, which puts a burden on a continuous and accelerated expansion of the economy.(2)

The goals of the New Economic Policy (NEP) are directed at restructuring society in order to achieve a "national unity" by (1) eradicating poverty by raising income levels and employment opportunities for all Malaysians irrespective of race, and (2) accelerating the process of restructuring Malaysian society to correct economic imbalances so as to reduce and eventually eliminate the identification of race with economic function.(3)

To give the NEP direction and execution, the government created various entities to facilitate "bumiputra"(4) participation in commercial and economic activities - PERNAS and MIDFIC in the industrial development area, MARA in training, SEDCs in state infrastructure; and the Urban Development Authority, UDA, in real property ownership, development and management.

THE URBAN DEVELOPMENT AUTHORITY (UDA)

Introduction

The Urban Development Authority (UDA), set up in 1971 as a quasi-governmental statutory body, attempts to redress several of the problems outlined above through urban development projects directed at achieving a distribution of opportunities, particularly in the real property field and other related activities, among the various races.(5)

The UDA employs over 400 persons of which approximately 20 percent are professional or managerial. It is organised into six divisions under the general control of the Chairman and Deputy Chairman, who, together with five other part-time members, constitute the Members of the Board. The UDA is presently responsible and reportable to the Prime Minister's office. Each of the organisation's six divisions (Secretariat, Finance, Business and Entrepreneural Development, Properties, Land Development and Research, and Technical Services) fall under the charge of an executive officer appointed by the Chairman.

The UDA's cash sources come from government treasury loans and are repayable in fifteen annual instalments at 6 percent interest starting from the sixth year after loan receipt. Consequently, the UDA tries to meet its social responsibilities under the New Economic Policy by locating financially profitable projects to minimise losses and to fulfil its legal responsibility to return loan monies plus interest.

The UDA's major cash sources consist of government grants (for administration purposes), treasury loans and loans from other sources. Other cash sources include rents, interest, dividends, profits from land sales, profits on hire purchase sales and other minor sources. Under the Second, and now, Third Malaysia Plan, the UDA desires to develop a real increase in the "Bumiputra" (Malay) property ownership and effective participation in commerce and industry, particularly in those fields generated by, and related to, property development. The Third Malaysia Plan (1976-1980), launched in July 1976, continues the Second Malaysia Plan strategies but with a greater stress placed on eradicating poverty irrespective of racial origins.

Development Planning and UDA's Mission

In a narrow sense, developmental planning may be considered that set of strategies which attempts to direct the flow of capital investment into a particular sector of a developing country's economy--basically an economic input. In a broader sense, it deals with human well-being and the quality of life and may be considered as those strategies directed at improving human settlements, developing more viable communities, advancing housing and living conditions, and doing so within a process of devolving power and decision making to lower levels and encouraging self-reliance by individuals and community groups. The task of designing a developmental strategy in a multiracial country like Malaysia is complicated by the serious economic imbalances which exist between the races and the greatly different growth and development rates in the various states and regions of the country. Moreover, the country lacks a tradition and orientation for urban and regional development planning.

The UDA's activities which were initially confined to Kuala Lumpur have now been extended to other major urban areas as well. Four major programmes have been devised to carry out the UDA's mandate. These are:

<u>Programme A - The provision of ready premises</u>:

The objective of this programme is to facilitate the entry of bumiputra businessmen into strategic locations in urban areas. It includes such activities as the purchase and leasing of ready premises; and the provision of loans, equipment and the booking of premises under construction. The UDA has expended almost half of its budget on these activities, ranging from 40 to 45 percent during the years since 1975. Activities under Programme A mainly benefit existing businessmen, those better educated and knowledgeable with business acumen. Since the UDA must pay back its loans, projects directed at upper income Malay businessmen have been thought to be less of a risk than those attempting to purchase or lease business premises for individuals with little or no business background.

<u>Programme B - Developing new premises</u>:

The objective of this programme is to develop shop units and premises in towns and new urban centres by providing financial, technical and management assistance. The Authority also participates by buying into properties owned by non-Malays in selected urban areas, as well as by developing joint venture companies with various State Economic Development Corporations (SEDCs). Activities under Programme B have been the second most important programme, exceeded only by Programme A. Total budget expenditures for Programme B were 36 percent in 1978 and a projected to 39 pecent in 1979. Again, as in the case of Programme A, the majority of recipients who have benefited have been those Malays in the middle and upper income ranges.

Programme C - Participation in business:

The objective of this programme is to assist the promotion of Malays in the business sector by the provision of capital, management, control and supervision by the Authority. The strength of this programme lies in the ability to train a commercially-oriented group of Malays either as potential entrepreneurs or as employers in business enterprises. The programme is relatively small in terms of percentage of expenditures. In 1975, approximately 6 percent of UDA's total budget was committed in this effort, whilst in 1978 and 1979 it was only 2 percent. Similarly, as in Programmes A and B, attention has been given to the more enterprising Malays who are predominantly in the upper or middle-income groups.

Programme D - Comprehensive urban development:

The objectives of this programme are to undertake comprehensive urban development, including urban renewal and activities related to the development of new communities and towns.

Housing studies for several of the major cities in the peninsula indicate that inadequate housing is one of the most difficult and pressing urban problems. In many urban areas in the country, over 20 percent of the population occupy land but do not own the land nor legally rent it and can thus be considered "squatters".(6) Squatting, although technically in violation of the law, is the result of an inadequate supply of available and suitable land for purchase or rent, an inadequate supply of low-cost housing, and of poverty in general. Understandably, government cannot provide housing built and financed along traditional lines for such numbers. New and innovative approaches are needed.

The Federal Territory or capital city of Kuala Lumpur(7) in Malaysia is no exception to the housing problem. Within the Territory there are about eighty-seven squatter areas covering a total of over 1215 hectares, of which approximately 77 percent of the squatter occupied land is government owned (former mining land and other open lands) and only 23 percent is privately owned. There are an estimated 22,700 housing units or over 28,000 squatter families (approximately 153,000 people) living in the Territory.(8)

Chinese make up the predominant squatter group, 45 percent; Malays 41 percent; and Indians 4 percent. Studies indicate that Chinese squatters tend to have higher incomes than others and may often have small commercial or industrial establishments on or near their housing site. There is an urgent need to deal with the squatter problem in conjunction with the larger picture relating to restructuring society and to reduce the incidence of poverty among the urban poor irrespective of race. The government has continuously attempted to deal with the housing for squatters and other low income members of the city's population by providing new high-rise and low-cost flats, but the demand has continuously overrun the supply.

To provide completely affordable housing units for large numbers of the urban squatter population does not appear realistic. However, some form of minimum housing for low-income groups may be more attainable. An investment in such housing would return substantial benefits in real national income by directly increasing employment and indirectly increasing productivity.

The nation has reached a level of output productivity and national income where surplus from business and an efficient taxation system has mobilised substantial savings, including those for the housing mortgage market. While it may be argued that the government should play a role as a long-term guarantor of housing for low- and moderate-income groups and that a secondary mortgage market should be created for fund liquidity, the fact remains that the country has no adequate institutions in place to handle the risk.

The 1971 Act setting up the Urban Development Authority specifically entrusts to the UDA the functions and power to promote and carry out projects in urban development areas for "development, redevelopment, settlement, resettlement and public housing". Consequently, the undertaking of housing projects are clearly within the UDA's mandate. The Act goes on to state that the promotion and carrying out of projects in urban development are aimed at distributing opportunities among the various races.

Moreover, the Third Malaysia Plan (TMP) 1976-1980 seeks to ". . . reduce the incidence of poverty among the urban poor by . . . improving their real income through the provision of low-cost housing and other public services . . ." and ". . . enhance the quality of life of all Malaysians and in particular the poor through the expansion of education, health services, family planning facilities and housing".(9)

The UDA has been particularly active in the building of new communities and is presently associated with thirty-seven housing projects of varying types and sizes spread throughout the Federal Territory and ten of Malaysia's thirteen states. In total, the UDA is connected with the development of over 35,000 dwelling units of which approximately 20 percent were completed at the beginning of 1978.

The UDA's involvement in these housing efforts consists of 100 percent UDA financing in 20 percent of the total effort; joint ventures with non-bumiputras in 44 percent; joint ventures with bumiputras in 25 percent; and the remaining 11 percent spread out between UDA partnership with government agencies, 7 percent, and UDA assistance mainly to small bumiputra developers, 4 percent.

Consequently, through its heavy involvement with private developers, the great majority of the UDA's housing efforts have and continue to consist in the development of housing for upper and middle income classes. Those efforts which can be considered directed mainly at low- and low-middle income population are the UDA partnership activities with government agencies, including the 419 units presently completed in the Salak South area which is examined later in this study.

It should also be noted that, since more SEDCs are entering into new town development efforts, the UDA's activities earmarked in this area are being reduced as a percentage of their total expenditures from 14 percent in 1978 to an estimated 11 percent in 1979.

It could be reasoned that the UDA should engage in more socially oriented activities than are presently represented by Programmes A, B, C and D, as outlined above, thereby addressing a wider spectrum of Malaysian interests, particularly those of very low-income households which are specifically addressed in the TMP. Nevertheless, although the UDA Act clearly spells out that housing (including public housing) is one of its legitimate activities, the Authority has proceeded very cautiously in the housing field, catering to households in the middle and upper ranges. It appears that the UDA's economic constraint of having to pay back its loans has led it to concentrate on projects directed at upper-income Malays where higher profit margins may be achieved. Notwithstanding these arguments, a strong case may be made for a more diversified portfolio in which those projects of more direct social benefit and somewhat lesser profitability may be traded against those of higher profitability.

DEVELOPMENT INSTITUTIONS IN THE CONTEXT OF MODERN MALAYSIAN SOCIETY

Difficulties in Achieving Adaptive Planning

Environments in most developing countries generally consist of rapidly changing, unstable conditions. Within such environments, we cannot often predict the outcome of secular trends or actions of government. Under these conditions, planning needs to be <u>innovative</u> and <u>adaptive</u>, able to cope with conditions of uncertainty, insecurity and crisis--many of the types of conditions Malaysia has faced since the Emergency Period of the late 1940s. Thus, we may define adaptive planning as that which is aimed at improving human well-being, the quality of life and the flow of capital investment in a particular sector under conditions of rapid change. In addition, adaptive planning requires the ability to respond rapidly to feedback information in a positive fashion.

Organisations have been classified by sociologists into "open" and "closed" systems. Whereas open systems emphasise decentralisation in operations and diffusion in decision-making, closed systems rely on centralisation of command and hierarchy of authority. As in most countries, bureaucracies in Malaysia operate more as "closed" than as "open" systems. UDA's organisational structure may be considered to be a hierarchical closed system in which all policy decisions come from the top at the level of the Chairman and Deputy Chairman. They, in turn, attempt to pursue the goals for the organisation in line with the functions as enumerated earlier. This approach can be fairly efficient in delivering a standard product over a long period of time (public highway authorities are often good examples). However, when the nature of the problem changes from place to place and over time, and involves several agencies - conditions which are common in urban and community development - flexibility, openness and willingness to collaborate are essential requirements, but ones which do not come easily to government bureaucracies. Nevertheless, UDA has sensed the need for innovative responses and an example of such an effort is described below. But first we should examine more closely the national context which influences and constrains UDA's operations.

Malaysian Society in Transition: Opportunities and Constraints

Society in Malaysia is in transition. And, although the New Economic Policy goals of totally eradicating poverty for all Malaysians and correcting gross economic imbalances among the various races appear unlikely to be achieved in the immediate future, progress has been made. More and more Malays are entering urban communities, taking up a new way of life, and moving from primary to secondary and tertiary sector occupations. Some are enticed by government sponsored programmes formed under the New Economic Policy of the Second and Third Malaysia Plans (SMP and TMP). Others migrate to urban areas simply in search of work and new opportunities.

Programmes under the SMP and TMP have witnessed the emergence of a small group of technically competent Malays, as well as those with entrepreneurial skills. In these efforts, governmental institutions including PERNAS, MIDFIC, MARA and the UDA can rightfully take a large share of the credit. Nevertheless, mistakes in the management of large projects and enterprises, ranging from new community land development schemes of DARA to oil exploration and joint venture activities of Petronas, point out some of the difficulties between good ideas and intentions on the one hand and the ability to execute them on the other hand. Experience has shown that there is no substitute for good management skills in government.

The government through the offices of the Prime Minister has dramatically moved against corruption in public office. Promising careers have been ruined and others made, based upon the ability to maintain the public trust. A greater attention to efficiency in government has also emerged in the form of a technocratic orientation to process and method in the delivery of the public goods and services. Moreover, some Malays have exhibited a greater confidence in their technical and organisational abilities and have to a certain extent imparted this confidence among the non-Malay community.

Notwithstanding many of the gains as outlined above, the transition period has witnessed many difficulties. The pre-existing feudal class structure of Malay society has tended to ensure that those Malays of aristocratic origin in association with wealthy Chinese entrepreneurs have received most of the economic benefits under the NEP with few exceptions (most notably the agricultural development schemes of FELDA). In addition, the conservative, capitalist economy has inhibited the distribution of benefits to all Malaysians irrespective of race and has suppressed or co-opted the development of viable labor unions. Criticisms of these policies even by moderate minority parties, such as the Malay Partai Rakyat, have tended to be suppressed in the name of national unity. Moreover, a series of laws were passed which disallowed discussion of many of the fundamental political issues of the country, including the position of the sultans and the status of the bumiputras, the stated pre-eminence of Islam as the national religion and the organisation of the communist party. On the heels of these laws followed others severely limiting legal defence of persons accused of assisting communist or terrorist elements. These laws and measures not only induced fear in the opposition, but also caused great anxiety and apprehension even among many Malays. The effect on the government was to encourage a rigid bureaucracy whose heads often fear the discussion of alternative policies or the development of new ideas for fear of being labelled divisionist.

Consequently, under such conditions of closed institutional settings where new and innovative approaches may be discouraged, achieving sufficiently adaptive planning is difficult. However, recent political events do offer some hope for an improvement in bureaucratic attitudes and responses. Malay interest groups show signs of fragmentation on some of the heretofore "sensitive" national issues. This may eventually lead to more open dialogue both with other Malays and other racial groups. Moreover, Malays with high technical and administrative expertise are beginning to head a number of important bureaucracies. Their own confidence and the growing recognition of their abilities by others is allowing them to take more open attitudes towards contentious issues including race and class. Furthermore, the top leadership in the country has become committed towards the development of genuine ability and self-reliance among Malays. This attitude, as contrasted with earlier emphasis on patronage and rhetoric, should propel the country much further towards its quest of creating a better and more socially just society for all Malaysians.

Nevertheless, many pockets of resistance remain in changing old ways and habits. Explosive issues between the races remain unresolved beneath a surface calm, but are ready to burst out again as in a recent dispute concerning a university primarily for Chinese students. In this context of tension, uncertainty and social change, mistrust among all sections of the community is rampant and tends to undermine efforts at concensus among moderate politicians. Openness, fairness and trust are essential to re-establish a basis for a sense of national unity. Efforts to establish a planning process which is both open and responsive to the needs of the poor of all races in the community, and which opens itself to influences among the agencies of government, could play an important role in generating a foundation of trust. In 1974 some tentative steps were taken in this direction by UDA in its involvement in a resettlement project for low-income families in Kuala Lumpur. An examination of this case study follows.

A UDA HOUSING RESETTLEMENT PROJECT

Summary and Objectives of Project

We noted earlier that on the ground of equity UDA might well diversify its portfolio of projects and give more attention to low-income Malaysians, particularly in the area of housing. In 1974 UDA agreed to take this step by becoming the executing agency on behalf of the Kuala Lumpur Government for a low-cost housing project financed in part by World Bank funds, a step which would provide a pilot experiment and also be very compatible with the constraints of UDA's financing.

This pilot housing resettlement effort was jointly developed by UDA staff working with a United Nations technical assistance team. The project was intended to meet a crisis need: to resettle squatters displaced by the construction of Federal Highway I which links Singapore in the south to Kuala Lumpur and to the east-west highway presently under construction in the far north of Malaysia. Studies conducted in the areas in which the road first enters and traverses the Federal Territory indicated that well over 300 squatter structures were affected and about the same number would be indirectly affected. The affected structures included not only residential units but businesses and small-scale industry as well. The great majority of the occupants are Malaysians of Chinese origin. Their incomes fall within the 20 to 50 percentile of the income distribution for Kuala Lumpur.

An immediate question posed was whether UDA, ostensibly set up to promote "bumiputra" interests, would venture into a resettlement project for low income Chinese. After some discussion within the agency, a redevelopment effort was begun which would assist not only the Chinese settlers and business owners immediately affected, but would develop in phases a larger scheme to integrate low-income Malays who may wish to join the project either in its first or in later stages of development. The redevelopment site is in Salak South, close to the area affected by the road.

Initial resistance to offering land ownership in the resettlement site was changed after a terrorist attack on a military airport close to the project site. This precipitated a crisis situation where the government concluded that it was important to offer low income urban residents a personal stake in the city whatever their racial origin. The overall objectives of the pilot effort were:

(a) to relocate squatters living within or immediately adjacent to the freeze order zones of Federal Highway I and the Southern Middle Ring Road, within a short period of time with a minimum dislocation to employment, existing community ties and business operations;

(b) to demonstrate that a sites and services programme including residential and business activities is a practical approach to meet the needs of low income and/or squatter households;

(c) to test affordability and cost recovery and hence replicability for future low cost settlement programmes in the country;

(d) to demonstrate that low-income people can build their own houses through self-contracting and self-construction cheaper and more responsively than government-built low-cost housing;

(e) to assist the restructuring(10) of society by reservation of a portion of the lots within the pilot project for low-income Malays who wish to join the scheme;

(f) to generate employment through labour-intensive construction methods and through the allocation of small-scale industrial and commercial lots for sale within the project; and

(g) to upgrade existing communities affected by the road schemes but not requiring relocation. In this instance the objective seeks to evaluate the upgrading approach in transforming squatter areas into stable communities with adequate infrastructure at low cost within the financial abilities of the recipients.

Project Benefits

The planners anticipated that several benefits would result from the project, including improved living conditions and urban services for the recipient households, direct employment on project construction, and indirect employment through self-help activities. One of the most important project benefits involved an examination of the feasibility of providing minimally serviced sites for self-contracted housing which could become a model for squatter and low-income settlements in the country as a whole. Another benefit was that the possibilities of providing racial integration in the overall scheme could be explored.

It was also anticipated that the project would offer an attractive alternative to further squatting by permitting households to gain title to land and a certain residential stability through security of tenure. As such, the project should improve the government's ability to plan and implement urban settlement programmes. It would emphasise "restructuring", the concept of bringing more Malays and other low income households into the mainstream of the economic life of the country. In addition it would provide important linkages to urban services and employment opportunities under the New Economic Policy. A comprehensive housing programme for low income households tied to employment and restructuring goals can be timed and programmed to provide necessary staging for public works activities, which will displace squatters and other households from affected areas. This programme can also be tied to the upgrading and/or removal of squatters located near sensitive and strategic government and public facilities within the Federal Territory and other areas in Malaysia.

As outlined above, there are many potential project benefits and objectives for the pilot effort in Salak South. Most importantly, the plan tests the desire and adequacy of existing institutions to undertake sites and service activities along a broad front. This includes such questions as: Are existing institutions adequate? Will land be made available for such activities? How do civil servants respond to the concepts advanced under a sites and service approach? Do present building codes and subdivision regulations need revisions to accommodate broader based sites and services activities? Can the administration adequately handle the present system?

Evaluation by the UDA will seek to determine whether the objectives mentioned elsewhere are being met on time and whether both physical and institutional project components yield the desired social and economic impacts on project participants and/or institutions related to the project. Evaluation will be carried out in three phases--before the project is initiated, during execution, and after the project's closing date.

LESSONS TO BE LEARNED

What Happened in the Pilot Project

The first major effort on the part of the UDA to develop low cost core houses in Salak South shows a number of weaknesses, inconsistencies and conflicts. The first phase of the project took approximately 2½ additional years beyond the originally scheduled completion date. At the time of writing, resettlement into the project area has not yet taken place. This means that the project's original function to act as a resettlement area for squatters displaced by the construction of Federal Highway I is not likely to happen, since the squatters have by now been dispersed, relocated to other temporary sites or put into public housing. Moreover, the original survey on which the project was designed and which carefully enumerated the needs and capacities of all households and businesses may have been wasted. This raises the question as to whether the project, as designed, will relate to the needs of its eventual occupants, whoever they may be. Further complications between UDA, City Hall, the land office and the Public Works Department arose from poor project coordination. Affected businesses were not moved concurrently with residences. Consequently, the project site designated for business relocation was used by the Public Works Department for relocation of squatter households from another part of the road.

Also, the original concept of providing minimally serviced sites which included no more than water, sewers and electrical lines to the property lines of each plot, with approximately half of the plots provided with latrines, posts and roof, has evolved into the provision of more complete housing shells, together with higher planning and overall site construction standards. Many of these changes took place at the insistence of City Hall which believed that squatters would not be able to build within the existing city codes and ordinances and thus would erect other "slums" similar to the ones which they left.

Moreover, the original upgrading component has been changed from sites directly affected by the new roadworks and adjacent to the new relocation project area, to areas basically unrelated to the resettlement component. These new upgrading areas in which new roads would be laid and electricity, water and sewerage would be provided are primarily inhabited by Malays.

Clearly, a number of the problems enumerated above could be expected with a programme as complex and new as squatter relocation and sites and services development in which several agencies are involved. Issues were complicated by the division of responsibility in implementation between City Hall, the UDA and the Department of Public Works. The UDA showed reluctance to become directly involved in the negotiations in receiving and giving title to predominantly Chinese squatters on government-owned land, and asked City Hall to perform this task.

On the other hand, the Department of Public Works, pressed by the timing of World Bank financing in the road construction, moved hastily in resettling squatters during the initial phasing of the work without adequate consultation with the UDA and City Hall to integrate the resettling efforts into the overall development scheme. As pointed out earlier, this resulted in settlers being moved to sites earmarked for business relocations. Moreover, the Bank, in negotiating the original road construction programme with the Malaysian government, sidestepped relocation needs of affected settlers along various portions of Federal Route 1.(11)

The resettlement scheme as proposed was not part of the original contract but became part of a second Urban Transport project after the original alignment had already been negotiated and begun under the first project. This raises the question as to whether another route would have been chosen away from Chinese squatter areas if such relocation was to be part of the overall project's requirements.

Evaluation of the Pilot Project

There are several important lessons to be learned from an evaluation of the Salak South experiment. The agencies involved, particularly the UDA and City Hall, attempted in the planning stages to implement a new kind of approach to settlement of low-income families and used the project to assist all low income racial groups. Nevertheless, the failures during implementation indicated a certain loss of faith in the approach and a slackening of the will to implement it. This indicates that, although a crisis situation is often needed to precipitate new ideas and policies, there has to be an underlying opening for change in the political sphere. Various approaches, including pilot projects and more frequent discussions between agency staffs, would have been beneficial to expand ideas and help the planning system become open and adaptive. Moreover, there must be strong support for the pilot project by top management to retain its impetus and to ensure that effective agency coordination takes place.

Moreover, the responsibility for the major elements of project implementation, including land acquisition and removal of occupants, should be firmly in the hands of the executing agency. And each major aspect of the project which involves a change in policy or administrative procedure should be fully discussed with various agencies before implementation commences.

The planning effort in Salak South attempted to be responsive to user needs by providing security, identity and equity, but these qualities were lost sight of during the implementation phase as the good intentions of the UDA and United Nations staff planners were eroded by a breakdown in coordination between agencies and a lack of will on the part of decision makers to execute the project as planned. In addition, participation by the users in the planning process was generally lacking.

With regard to the criteria mentioned by the editors in Chapter 2 which fall under the rubric of "matching actions with resources", the Salak South project as implemented has not been successful in terms of factor endowment. Although a least cost solution to the problem of low-income settlement was planned, those responsible for project implementation failed to show the openess and flexibility necessary for realisation of project objectives. For example, the institutions dealing with building and housing codes were very reluctant to lower standards as required by both sites-and-services and upgrading components of the project. In general, civil servants have shown a reluctance to change existing practices and procedures, particularly as regards housing for low income groups. Consequently, whilst one of the pilot project's objectives was to test the affordability and cost recovery and hence replicability of the low cost sites and services approach to squatter relocation and settlement, such a test could not be properly undertaken because both infrastructures and dwellings have actually been built to higher standards. This is consistent with our earlier observation on the prevailing closed system existing in many of the institutions in the country.

Most importantly, it remains to be demonstrated whether a project such as the resettlement effort in Salak South, to a great extent developed and conceived by "outsiders" working within an authority such as the UDA, will maintain sufficient focus and attention to have a lasting impact. While there are several important advantages of using an urban development authority such as the UDA for changing social and economic imbalances in the country, there are also many weaknesses.

This points out another lesson to be learned. Planners and financing agencies should make efforts to discuss the policy implications of new approaches more fully with local agency personnel, including those at executive, operational and technical levels. Seminars and discussions among operational staff and policy-makers should be encouraged. This would enable outsiders to gain a better understanding of the political and cultural roots of institutional behaviour before advocating particular types of projects and policies.

UDA is primarily a physically oriented real estate development agency operating within a set of often conflicting objectives. On the one hand, the UDA is to be responsive to national interests, which includes all Malaysians of low-income status according to the TMP. Yet, on the other hand, it is also charged politically with direct assistance to "bumiputra" or Malay interests. This latter charge is put constantly before the UDA by the heavily pro-Malay government spurred by the party's youth organisation, UMNO youth.

In addition, while the NEP stresses assistance to poor Malaysians of all races, poor in the rural areas of the country are generally synonymous with Malays, but poor in the urban areas of the country where UDA mainly operates are primarily Chinese. This raises the question as to the extent to which the government will assist non-Malays in business, employment and settlement. Projects such as major infrastructure improvements which do not transfer assets to non-Malays will probably proceed in urban areas. On the other hand, it is possible that projects which involve strengthening assets and rights of multi-racial and non-Malay groups, such as slum upgrading, serviced sites and low-cost housing for sale, will be resisted.

It should be remembered that the heightened interest to develop a resettlement project by the UDA, particularly for low-income Chinese, was due in large part to a crisis situation in Kuala Lumpur: the need to resettle squatters displaced by the right-of-way of a new highway and the need for appeasement following a terrorist attack. Nevertheless, an alternative approach for UDA projects which could yield greater social benefit yet maintain economic solvency is inherent in the Salak South type effort. At this time the crisis has passed and it remains to be seen as to whether the interests in the larger questions of national unity and racial harmony as espoused by the Third Malaysia Plan are to be achieved.

As the TMP so eloquently states:

> . . . racial conflicts and emnity which exist even in the rich industrial nations show that economic prosperity alone does not necessarily ensure the achievement of such unity and harmony. It requires a high degree of mutual tolerance among the various races, respect for each other's culture and religion, the integration of basic norms and values in regard to the nation and its identity and the establishment of a

> commitment to a common set of goals and aspirations that transcend communal interests. These form the conditions that the Malysian society will attempt to satisfy in order to achieve racial harmony.(12)

Whether Malaysian society is up to the task, and whether a project response to low income housing needs as undertaken by the UDA may prove to be a starting point for additional national efforts and one which would promote better social relations, remain for future appraisal.

NOTES

(1) 1970 Population and Housing Census of Malaysia (1972), and Third Malaysia Plan, 1976-1980 (1976), p. 142.

(2) Second Malaysia Plan, 1971-1976 (1971).

(3) Op. cit.

(4) In the Malay language *bumiputra* means son of the soil. It is a term which is presently used in Malaysia to signify the racial groups which are Malay and at the same time Islamic, and toward which much of the New Economic Policy is directed.

(5) Perbadanan Pembangunan Bandar Act, 46 of 1971, as amended by Statutory Bodies Act, A348, 1976.

(6) Amato, Peter W., Siear Hooi Koon, and Emiel Wegelin (1975).

(7) Kuala Lumpur, the country's capital, has grown from a town of 20 square km with a population of slightly over 32,000 persons in 1901, to a municipality of 94 square km with a population of over 316,000 in 1957, to a Federal Territory of 244 square km with a population of over 730,000 in 1974.

(8) Wehbring, Kurt J. (1976).

(9) Third Malaysia Plan, 1976-1980 (1976).

(10) The term *restructuring* is used in the Second and Third Malaysia Plans to indicate that process under the New Economic Policy by which lower income groups, particularly bumiputras, are brought into the mainstream of the economic life of the country. This often means changing employment from the primary to secondary or the tertiary sectors, and mixing the residential locations of racial groups.

(11) Amato, Peter W. (1978).

(12) Third Malaysia Plan, 1976-1980 (1976), p. 104.

REFERENCES

Amato, Peter W. (1978) "Development Standards and Conflict Management in Southeast Asia", Ekistics, Vol. 45, No. 270.

Amato, Peter W., Siear Hooi Koon and Emiel Wegelin (1975) "Urban Housing in West Malaysia: 1975-2000 Needs and Programs". Kuala Lumpur: UNDP Project Technical Report, Mal 72/015 (unpublished).

Perbadanan Pembangunan Bandar Act, No. 46 of 1971. Kuala Lumpur: Government Press.

1970 Population and Housing Census of Malaysia (1972) Kuala Lumpur: Department of Statistics.

Second Malaysia Plan, 1971-1976 (1971) Kuala Lumpur: Government Press.

Third Malaysia Plan, 1976-1980 (1976) Kuala Lumpur: Government Press.

Wehbring, Kurt J. (1976) "Squatters in the Federal Territory: Analysis and Program Recommendations". Kuala Lumpur: UNDP Project Technical Report, Mal 72/015 (unpublished).

Planning and Implementation of Selected Sectoral Programmes

The last two case studies presented in this volume form a kind of residual group. These are sectoral programmes which do not deal with housing and residential development, but which address two other aspects of urban development: (1) a solution to the urban traffic problem is illustrated by Singapore's area licence scheme; and (2) health and nutrition needs and programmes are discussed with particular reference to Jakarta and Manila. These sectoral programmes are indicative of the many schemes which do not attempt to attack urban problems comprehensively, but which narrow the focus and formulate implementable projects for only one basic problem at a time.

Edwin Holland and Peter Watson, in their contribution entitled "Singapore's Area Licence Scheme: Results and Lessons", present the book's single case study on urban transport. The selection of this particular case is not arbitrary. Rather than programme costly new systems, the Singapore project represents an effort at maximum utilisation of the capacity of existing systems. It also illustrates several characteristics of what can be considered a well managed programme.

In the final case study, S. S. Basta discusses public health and nutrition programmes, highlighting specific projects in Jakarta and Manila. Although it would have been ideal to have included a number of examples of social development programmes, space limitations meant that only one such case could be presented. This case must suffice as at least a partial attempt to balance out the above-mentioned programmes dealing with the physical environment with an effort in the social field. Interestingly, several of the points which Basta makes regarding the characteristics of a good programme in health and nutrition are very similar to those required for programmes dealing with the physical environment.

11

Singapore's Area Licence Scheme: Results and Lessons

Edwin Holland
Peter Watson

INTRODUCTION

With or without planning, cities in developing countries are growing at an unprecedented rate. The effect of rapid growth on transport is twofold: a more than proportionate increase in the demand for transportation modes--trucks, buses and motorised vehicles of all types; and the need for roads on which to travel. Accommodating the demand for access to road space is an especially difficult problem in older cities where narrow streets were never intended for use by motor vehicles. This problem also exists in the more recently planned cities where the expanding population and concentration of industry and commerce lead to more movement into and through the city centre, and an increasing number of the population can afford to buy automobiles and attempt to use them instead of walking or using public transport. The potential for these problems to intensify as incomes grow is illustrated by the fact that in some cities, already notorious for traffic congestion, car ownership levels are quite low.

The traditional approach to urban traffic congestion has been to expand capacity, that is, to build more roads. In recent years it has become increasingly obvious that the economic, social and environmental costs of highway construction programmes can be unacceptably high. The costs of urban highways have escalated rapidly, in large part as a result of dramatic increases in the price of urban land. The costs in terms of disruption during protracted periods of construction are extremely high, prompting some observers to speculate that, in terms of their present values, the benefits forecast for a given project may be exceeded by losses during construction. Disruption can also occur after a project is completed, with urban freeway projects having the effect of splitting neighbourhoods or isolating communities. After construction, the operation of highway and automobile based systems have important implications for levels of air and noise pollution, not to mention the problems caused by over-dependence on petroleum fuels. Most of these problems are particularly severe for countries in the developing world, which have limited resources to devote to transport projects and even more limited capacity to absorb the foreign exchange demands of increasing petroleum imports.

It might be possible to accept all these problems if it were clear that urban transport problems were being solved, but the opposite is true. It seems that the creation of capacity is a continuing stimulus creating travel demand. How often do we read of highways, bridges, etc., designed to accommodate traffic predicted for 10, 15 or 20 years in the future, that are operating at capacity and under increasingly congested conditions 18 months after they have been opened?

WHAT ALTERNATIVES?

The key to a search for alternatives is that the problem being addressed in urban transport is one of dealing with the excess of demand for road space over its supply. The traditional solution is to increase the supply--a solution, it is argued, that is costly and not completely successful. The problem might also be addressed through attempts to reduce the demand. This can frequently be achieved by raising the price of a good or service--in this case--travel. The solution is not so simple. Not all travel is the same, nor are all roads or vehicles the same. There may be no necessity to take action in areas where congestion is not severe. On the other hand, in congested areas, it may be appropriate to take action to treat different road users, such as automobiles and buses, differently. Within this basic framework a system of modern urban transport planning is evolving that emphasises selective increases in capacity together with measures aimed at increasing the price of travel in congested areas.

Increasing the Capacity of Existing Networks

What is meant by selective increases in road capacity? Basically, it means avoiding undesirable road construction. Traffic engineering solutions have often produced significant increases in the effective capacity of a road system by eliminating bottlenecks. The measures can be simple: eliminating bottlenecks at intersections by prohibiting certain turning movements or channelling traffic into storage lanes. Frequently, traffic flow can be improved dramatically by improving the geometry of an intersection, especially if turning radii for buses can be improved. In the road itself, maintaining a consistent cross-section can be highly beneficial. At a different technological level, modifications can be made to traffic light systems to speed the flow of traffic, ranging from simple changes in timing and offsets to sophisticated systems of bus priorities and area traffic control systems.

The principle advantage is that the tool kit is extensive and the possibilities of measures such as those described above should be exhausted before new construction is considered. New construction should be approached cautiously, with an open mind, and on the basis of active consideration of a range of solutions. While new four-lane, divided highways may often have high benefit-cost ratios, it has frequently been found that widening the existing road can yield as much as 80 percent of the benefits at as little as 50 percent of the cost. In some cases, upgrading, resurfacing, adjusting alignments, eliminating bottlenecks, repairing gutters and drainage, can be as effective and much cheaper than widening. This is especially true in the developing countries where available road space is more often subject to obstruction and bad maintenance than in developed countries.

Under what circumstances might new road construction be justified? In some cases it is quite clear that a road network is incomplete and that a certain link is required to permit adequate operation of the network. In others, new roads are required to open up or give structure to rapidly developing parts of a city. In yet other cases, it is necessary to undertake new construction to allow the provision of special facilities such as exclusive bus lanes. Overall, the application of economic tests will reveal whether the less expensive solution is acceptable, through examination of the respective marginal net present values. Only after a proposed solution has been compared with cheaper and more expensive alternatives, and the implications of reducing the scale of investment examined, can a new road construction project be considered to have been evaluated. None should be accepted without such an evaluation.

Reducing the Demand for Road Space

Reducing the demand for road space generally means reducing the number of automobiles in use. A given number of individuals can obviously travel in fewer cars by car pooling or otherwise increasing occupancy. Further savings in demand for road space are achieved if riders shift from cars to buses and other high occupancy vehicles such as minibuses and jitneys. Such shifts may be encouraged, to some extent, by giving priorities such as exclusive lanes to buses and perhaps other high occupancy vehicles to enable them to offer better service. To provide exclusive bus lanes from existing road space would reduce the space available to cars resulting in increased congestion and lower speeds (i.e. increase the cost in terms of trip time) unless there is a corresponding drop in the number of cars in use. In most less developed countries the impact of this effect will fall mainly on a relatively small and affluent segment of the travelling public, while the benefits of improved bus service will accrue to the more numerous middle and low-income groups.

Campaigns to attract motorists on to the bus and park-and-ride schemes have met with limited success, even when special express, air conditioned services have been offered. Such schemes appear to be highly sensitive to the locations of the fringe parking lots, to the bus fares and parking charges levied, and to the speed of the shuttle buses relative to the level of automobile congestion in the central area. Campaigns to encourage the formation of car pools have enjoyed a certain degree of success, especially when car pools can enter exclusive lanes on freeways or through toll plazas, thereby bypassing the remaining automobile traffic. On the other hand, setting up such schemes coupled with the inconvenience associated with adapting varied travel and work habits make car pools unacceptable to a large number of motorists.

If persuasion and the limited incentives accorded to the users of park-and-ride systems or car pools do not succeed in attracting motorists out of their automobiles, have disincentive schemes met with any greater success? Most schemes aimed at creating disincentives for automobile users have attempted to create delays in one form or another. This may be done simply by holding up cars to give buses priority at a bottleneck intersection. It may be more extensive: in Nottingham, England, a sophisticated "ring-and-collar" scheme was introduced as an experiment. It used a technique similar to metering on freeway ramps to hold motorists at the edge of the congested area, thus creating delays to motorists while allowing buses to flow freely. In practice, the length of delay was unpredictable and the scheme caused much confusion and frustration. It was eventually abandoned. Overall, it seems fair to conclude that, except on a very small scale, the deliberate creation of delays to motorists is unacceptable to planners and public alike.

Increasing the Monetary Cost of Driving

If persuasion and time disincentives have not proved to be very successful in discouraging motorists from using their automobiles in congested areas, a logical alternative is to increase the cost of driving. Several possible methods can be used. At a general level, a high import duty on automobiles may work well. Another general measure is to have high annual registration fees. Increasing the price of petroleum through taxes can be used to limit the amount of driving undertaken. However, these measures operate on all travel and fail to discriminate against trips in specific areas that contribute to congestion. Specific charges can be levied to raise the price of trips on specific routes or to specific destinations. The former effect is frequently achieved through the use of tolls; the latter can be achieved through surcharges on parking in specific areas. One thing these methods have in common is that they are all known and accepted by the motoring public. There is, however, an additional method that is relatively unknown: road pricing.

Road pricing is better known by the terms associated with some of its specific operational forms, such as "supplementary licensing" or "area licensing". Whatever form it takes operationally, road pricing is an attempt to overcome the fact that motorists generally do not pay the full social costs associated with their journeys. The price perceived by the car driver generally includes the costs of fuel, oil, tires and parking; it does not include the other costs that the trip imposes on society, e.g. environmental pollution, noise, congestion, etc. The result is that, for many car trips, the benefits to the traveller may exceed the costs perceived by the traveller, but may not exceed the costs to society. When this is the case, trips take place that, from a social viewpoint, should not be made. The basic concept underlying road pricing is that the motorist should be made to pay a price which more closely resembles the total social costs of the journey.

Although this basic concept has been promoted by economists for many years, it has until recently been perceived as politically infeasible. Recently, however, planners and politicians in several cities have considered the possibility of making it operational, and in 1975, the government of Singapore introduced road pricing in the form of its Area Licence Scheme. The remainder of this paper is devoted to a description of the scheme, an assessment of its effects, and a discussion of the potential for developing similar schemes for other cities. (For fuller details of the scheme, its development and its impact, see (1).)

SINGAPORE'S AREA LICENCE SCHEME

The Singapore government set itself the specific goal of designating a scheme to reduce peak-hour traffic by 25 to 30 percent. It was estimated that this reduction would restore reasonably good traffic conditions equivalent to those found during off-peak hours. In the Singapore context, the key concept underlying the Area Licence Scheme is that a special supplementary licence must be obtained and displayed if a motorist wishes to enter a designated restricted area within which congestion is to be reduced.

The restricted zone (see Fig. 11.1) includes the areas with congestion problems, leaves diversion routes for motorists who do not have destinations in the zone, minimizes the number of entry points that have to be monitored, and takes advantage of existing facilities for use as fringe parking lots. The zone covers about 500 hectares and has twenty-two entry points.

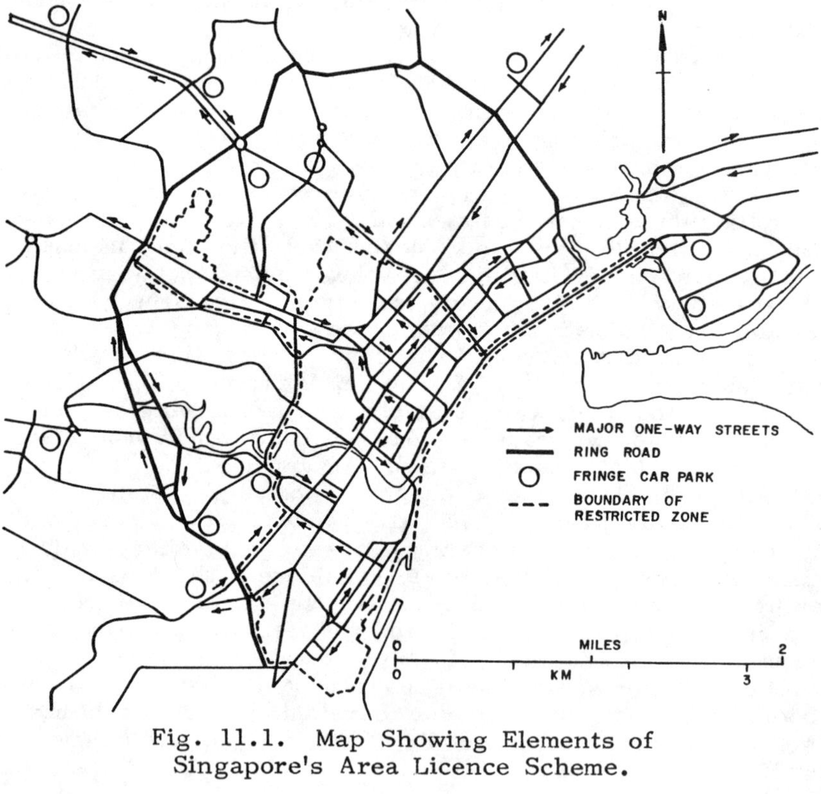

Fig. 11.1. Map Showing Elements of Singapore's Area Licence Scheme.

The licence. The government had no previous experience to guide it in setting the licence fee. Thus, it was necessary to set the fee by judgement. Licences were initally sold for S$60 (US$26) a month, or S$3 (US$1.30) a day. They have since been raised to S$80 a month or S$4 a day.

Categories of vehicle. The requirement to display an area licence does not apply to buses or commercial vehicles, car pools (defined as cars carrying at least four persons), and motor-cycles. Taxis pay half the fee applicable to private cars.

Restricted times. The aim of the Singapore government was to reduce the congestion arising during the morning peak period, so the scheme was designed to operate from 7:30 a.m. to 9:30 a.m. After implementation, congestion developed after 9:30 and the time period was extended to 10:15 a.m.

The park and ride scheme was designed to complement the Area Licence Scheme. Ten thousand spaces in parking lots around the periphery of the restricted zone were opened to commuters, and special shuttle buses were introduced to carry commuters from the fringe parking lots to the central area. This service attracted very few patrons.

Parking policy. The third element of the scheme was an increase in parking charges within the Restricted Zone. Previously, there had generally been a flat rate of US$0.40 (US$0.18) an hour. The new rates are designed to reflect the geographical distribution of congestion and to favour short-term as opposed to all-day parking. In the most congested part of the Restricted Zone, the new rates are S$0.50 (US $0.22) for the first hour, S$1.00 (US$0.44) for the second hour, and S$1.00 (US$0.44) for each subsequent half-hour. The monthly rate for all-day parking in the central area was increased from S$40-60 to S$50-80.

THE IMPACTS OF THE SCHEME

With more than a year's advance notice of the introduction of the scheme, the World Bank's Transport Research Division, in cooperation with the government of Singapore and with support from the United Nations Environment Programme and the United States Department of Transportation, was able to design and carry out an extensive programme of data collection before the Scheme went into effect and a follow up programme afterwards.

Changes in Traffic Flows and Composition

Measurements showed that the number of cars entering the Restricted Zone between 7:30 and 10:15 a.m. fell by 73 percent from 42,790 in March to an average of 11,363 in September and October 1975. The volume of cars entering during the half-hour before 7:30 a.m. rose by 23 percent as people started their trips earlier to avoid paying the Area Licence Fee. The exemption from the licence requirement for car pools (cars with four or more occupants) induced a large increase in occupancy during the restricted hours. The proportion of car pools entering the Restricted Zone during the restricted hours jumped from less than 7 percent to 37 percent. Flows of vehicle types other than cars changed by smaller proportions and the net result was a 44 percent reduction in total traffic during the 7:30 a.m. to 10:15 a.m. restricted period.

A surprising finding was that traffic flows in the evening peak (4:00 p.m. to 7:00 p.m.) changed very little. It had been expected that reductions in the morning peak flows would be reflected by a sizeable reduction in the evening. When the flow data showed only a 6 percent decline in the evening peak, it could not be explained until a detailed analysis of the home interview data gave enough clues to piece together the explanation. The main factors were "trans-Restricted Zone trips", trip scheduling, and taxi trips. Many car drivers making work trips with an origin on the one side of the zone and destination on the other used the ring road to bypass the zone in the morning but returned home through the zone in the evening. Another group of commuters, with work places in the Restricted Zone, took to driving in before 7:30 a.m. but still drove home during the evening peak. Taxis entered the zone in greatly reduced numbers in the morning restricted period, but the number of taxis operating during the evening peak seems to have markedly increased.

Change in Vehicle Speeds

A method of licence plate matching was employed with observers at each end of a link recording licence numbers and time signals from which vehicle speeds were calculated. Unfortunately, this procedure was not perfected until after the Area Licence Scheme went into effect. Thus, before-and-after comparisons were not possible. However, in the later period reliable data were obtained at different times of day, so that comparisons could be made between restrained and unrestrained conditions and inferences drawn on changes because of the Area Licence Scheme. There was a 22 percent improvement within the zone during the restricted hours (33 k.p.h. vs. 27 k.p.h.). On parts of the ring road, speeds were 20 percent lower in the morning restricted period.

Impacts on Travel Behaviour

Impacts on people making work trips:

For people who travelled to work in the Restricted Zone, the monthly cost of commuting by car rose from S$153 (US$65) to

S$228 (US$97). In response, the proportion of trips that members of vehicle-owning households made by car fell from 56 to 46 percent while the bus share rose from 33 percent to 46 percent. Within the declining car mode, the car pool share rose by a factor of 3, from 14 to 41 percent of all car trips. In addition to the modal changes, the proportion of work trips that were started before 7:30 a.m. rose from 27 to 40 percent for car drivers and from 17 to 28 percent for car passengers. The data indicate that about the same numbers of people from vehicle-owning households chose the options of changing to the bus, joining or forming car pools, and making the trip at a different time. People from non-vehicle-owning households did not change their behaviour--90 percent travelled by bus before and after the introduction of the Area Licence Scheme.

The changes in travel time for travellers who did not change mode were very small. Car drivers, on average, took about 1 minute longer; bus riders from vehicle-owning households reported taking, on average, half a minute longer. However, bus riders from non-vehicle owning households, who constitute the vast majority of bus riders in Singapore, reported taking, on average, about 1 minute less. Car drivers who changed to the bus took an average of 9 minutes longer, and bus riders who changed to the car took an average of 9 minutes less.

For travellers who travelled to work through the Restricted Zone to destinations on the other side of the city, the proportion of trips made by car fell from 53.5 to 50 percent, but the proportion of trips made by car pools rose from 9 to 28 percent. The proportion of trips started before 7:30 a.m. rose from 50 to 60 percent. Of course, these travellers had the additional option of detouring around the Restricted Zone. Before the introduction of the scheme, 88 percent of trips passed through the zone. Afterward, only about 66 percent drove through the zone, and of these, only 13 percent drove through during the restricted hours. The remainder changed time to avoid the fee.

Impacts on people travelling outside the Restricted Zone:

It is useful at this point to note that over 70 percent of all trips and over 60 percent of work trips are made outside the Restricted Zone. The majority of trips to work outside the Restricted Zone are made by bus, and the majority of shopping trips are made on foot. The people making these trips have been unaffected by the Area Licence Scheme. Those motorists who use the ring road have been slightly adversely affected by the increased congestion and reduced speeds.

Other Impacts

Impacts on business:

In-depth interviews were conducted with selected leaders in the business community. They generally agreed that the Area Licence Scheme had an important impact on the business climate. It was believed that the increased parking charges had further depressed central area retail sales that were already suffering from recession and decentralisation. It was also believed that the restrictions on car travel to the city centre were accelerating the existing trend toward decentralisation. In both cases, the Area Licence Scheme and the increase in parking charges were viewed as adding to existing problems and not creating new ones.

Effects on pedestrians:

Observations of pedestrian movements at various times of day were made by time-lapse photography at a number of different locations within the Restricted Zone. The films indicated that, with less traffic, people were crossing in more leisurely fashion, so that longer crossing times were observed in some cases. Analysis of the frequency with which pedestrians had to change pace or back up in response to challenges by motor vehicles showed that the ease of crossing streets had clearly improved.

Changes in air pollution levels:

The Singapore government's Anti-pollution Unit measured air pollutants at several downtown locations. The most clearcut result was that the carbon monoxide level during the restricted hours, which had formerly been at peak, was reduced below that in the middle of the day. All-day average levels were also lower.

Public opinion:

A public opinion survey revealed that Singaporeans believed that the Area License Scheme had relieved congestion and improved conditions in central Singapore. Pedestrians, bus riders, taxi riders and motor-cyclists believed that they personally were better off as a result of the scheme. Central area residents reported that it was easier and safer to cross roads, that general conditions in the Restricted Zone had improved, and that the level of fumes had been reduced. Motorists reported that they were worse off but not greatly so. All, including the motorists, believed that the effect on Singapore as a city was favourable.

Problems Encountered

Although the Area Licence Scheme was implemented without difficulty and appears to have had largely beneficial results, not all of its effects turned out as expected. Some problems arose and had to be dealt with.

Level of the licence fee:

Without precedent to guide them, the officials had to set the fee on the basis of an "educated guess". That they set it within the right order of magnitude showed very good judgement. Nevertheless, in terms of the target specified they set it somewhat too high. That was probably better than setting it too low, but it did pose the question of whether to reduce it or leave it alone. Choice of the latter alternative was justified in terms of conditioning motorist's attitudes so as to postpone future congestion problems. (Subsequent increases were not based on technical considerations; overall fiscal considerations led the government to increase what was already too high a fee.)

The evening peak:

Singapore officials, the World Bank research team and consultants all believed that if morning peak traffic were reduced by the targeted amount, evening peak traffic would also drop considerably. All were surprised when that did not occur. There were discussions of the possibility of imposing restraints of some kind in the evening, either on inbound or on outbound traffic. However, there seemed to be no way to do that without unfavourably affecting business--for example, in the restaurant and entertainment sectors as well as the retail trade. No good solution to this problem was found and no restraints have yet been imposed in the evening.

Park-and-ride:

The designers of the scheme believed that car drivers would be attracted by the possibility of driving to the outskirts of the central business district, parking and taking a shuttle bus downtown. In the event, only 6 percent of the parking space was used, and the shuttle buses were so under-utilized that the operators were in immediate financial difficulties. The government acted quickly to revise the shuttle bus operations, making them essentially a supplement to the regular bus service on profitable routes where more capacity was needed. Over a longer period, they found new uses for much of the parking lot space.

Ring road traffic:

Although improvements had been made to some segments of the ring road prior to implementation of the Area Licence Scheme, other parts proved inadequate for the unexpectedly heavy flows that developed as drivers to destinations beyond the Restricted Zone sought to bypass it. The initial problem was somewhat alleviated by retiming the traffic lights or directing traffic manually at critical intersections between radial roads and the ring road. Further relief will be provided by long-run projects to improve conditions at critical intersections.

Taxis:

Whether taxis should be exempt from the licence fee as public transport vehicles or subjected to it as equivalent to private cars in their road space has been a matter of debate. In Singapore, taxis were initially exempt, but they entered the Restricted Zone in such numbers that the government felt they were defeating attempts to reduce congestion. Accordingly, taxis were made subject to the licence requirement. After that, it was almost impossible to find a taxi driver willing to travel into the central area during the morning peak unless the passenger first agreed to pay at least a substantial part of the cost of an area licence. After nearly 2 years of this inconvenience, the situation was much improved by establishing a distinctive licence for taxis at one-half the private car price.

Financial Aspects

The total capital cost of establishing the Area Licence Scheme was about US$2.75 million. Over 90 percent of these costs were associated with the construction of the fringe parking lots. Thus, it is clear that road pricing schemes can be implemented very cheaply. The scheme currently yields a revenue (net of operating expenses) of US$216,000 per month. In Singapore these funds are treated as general tax revenue. In other cities it may be appropriate to earmark them for specific purposes, such as road improvements, traffic management and public transport improvements.

Conclusions

Motivation for the planners of the Area Licence Scheme was the general objective of changing the public's attitude toward the use of cars for commuting. The aim was to prevent the existing moderate congestion from growing progressively worse. To solve the problem, the planners perceived that they had to explain the rationale behind the need for more widespread use of public transport and other high-occupancy vehicles, and induce motorists to review and fundamentally change their attitudes toward ownership and use of cars. This revision of motorists' attitudes--and hence behaviour--was expected to reduce the problems caused by congestion and at the same time create an environment in which public transport services could be improved. A target of 25 to 30 percent reduction in traffic entering the central area in the morning peak was set to translate this objective into practical and measurable terms. This target was more than achieved. It is clear that the Area Licence Scheme has forced motorists to modify their behaviour, at least in the short run. The Area Licence Scheme has reduced congestion in the central area, largely by inducing a shift toward public transport and car pools. Whether these are short-term behaviour modifications or whether they represent fundamental changes in the attitudes of motorists cannot be determined at this point. It seems likely, nevertheless, that in the long run continued use of such measures will result in a more widespread acceptance (rather than tolerance) of public transport and car pooling.

IS THE CONCEPT APPLICABLE ELSEWHERE?

It is likely that in different cities the objective will vary from those of the Singapore government. One city might wish to limit or reduce the number of people going downtown, rather than to influence their choice of mode without inhibiting their trip making. Another city might want to exert less impact on trips to downtown destinations but discourage motorists from driving through town to destinations beyond the central area. Another city may also wish to tax commercial traffic. Since different objectives require different measures, it is important to have the objectives defined and agreed at the outset in working out the design and operating details. It is worth noting that a variety of physical, legal and fiscal measures may be combined with different approaches in a policy package. For example, Singapore, in addition to the Area Licence Scheme, also made use of parking charges, reserved bus lanes and prohibition of trucks with more than two axles from the area inside the ring road.

If the selected approach to reducing traffic congestion is pricing, i.e. charging fees for some aspect of the use of the city streets, the selection of the most suitable form of pricing in any city warrants careful study of the effects of the different approaches in the context of local conditions. Some are discussed below:

Method of Implementation

One method demonstrated in Singapore was the practicality of administering and enforcing a system of charging for entry to a zone by using dated windshield stickers. Another proposed method that would solve the one-day licence problem uses a windshield sticker or ticket from which portions are cut off by the user in such a way as to show the date on which it is to be used and rendering it invalid for any other date. The user can purchase these singly or in quantity without committing himself to using them on a specific day. More sophisticated methods would use chemical "self-cancelling" stickers, on-vehicle meters, or automatic vehicle identification equipment. These methods have not progressed beyond the prototype stage, although tests have shown the reliability of AVI equipment in toll collection situations.

Impact of Different Bases of Charging

Zone entry or exit:

Singapore's zone entry charge affects traffic from outside, whether it is bound for within-the-zone destinations or crossing the zone to go out again. Traffic originating within the zone is unaffected so long as it either stays inside or goes outside without returning during the hours of restriction. The fact that enforcement is by visual observation makes it possible to grant exemption to high-occupancy cars, which would be difficult to do with an electronic system.

Presence in the zone:

Except for some differences in dealing with particular hours of restraint, a charge for presence within the zone would affect entering and transiting traffic in the same way as the entry charge, but would also apply to residents within the zone. A plan proposed for London would have charged for presence rather than entry because that was believed more feasible to enforce under the prevailing local conditions.

Other pricing methods:

Electronic devices, once they become operational, would open up possibilities that would otherwise be infeasible. There might be dozens of "pricing points" with different prices, all varying by time of day, to fit the price in each place more closely to the degree of potential congestion or the social marginal cost. Charges could reflect not only entry into a congested area but also the length of time spent, or distance traveled, in it. There is, nonetheless, a danger that the motorist would not have sufficiently clear and accurate understanding of the prices confronting him to be able to respond as he is expected to. Thus, care should be taken to keep the scheme relatively simple, with prices known in advance.

Delineation of a Pricing Zone

If charging for entry to a zone is chosen as the principal approach to be used, delineation of the zone is a basic step in designing the system. This step will depend heavily on the size and shape of the city, its traffic-flow patterns, the local geography and the pattern of roads. An important consideration in defining the zone is that there should be a reasonably convenient route for those who wish to bypass it. That may, in practice, be one of the most important determinants of the zone size and its boundaries.

Hours of Restriction

Given that the purpose of a pricing scheme is to prevent excessive congestion, it is obviously not necessary to keep the scheme in effect 24 hours a day. The question is whether it should be in effect only for the morning commuting hours, or for one period in the morning and another in the afternoon, or during the whole working day. This depends on the intended impact of the scheme and on local conditions such as normal business hours, whether it is customary to drive home for lunch and so on.

Setting the Price

When the Singaporeans set the price for the area licence, there was no previous experience to guide them. Now there is one case. The Singapore experience could be used as a rough basis for choosing a price by relating it to the other costs of making trips, the mean income level and the desired reduction in traffic. However, whatever price is set must be regarded as an experiment, and the authorities must be prepared either to change it after they observe its effect or to accept the resulting reduction in traffic congestion even if it is different from what they had intended.

If the effect is greater than intended, it may be that the price, while too high for the immediate conditions, is right for a future situation when there will be higher incomes and more cars. In that case it may be best to leave it alone rather than reduce it and have to raise it again in a couple of years. If the effect is much too little, the price should be raised before users get used to it. It is probably unwise to start with a very low price and increase it gradually to seek the right level. When the pricing scheme is first introduced, it is important that it have some shock effect to make users re-evaluate their travel habits rather than merely adjust their budgets to absorb a small change in costs.

Exemptions and Different Prices

Discrimination among types of vehicle is feasible, in terms of exempting certain types from the licence requirements and charging different prices. This has been demonstrated in Singapore, where buses, commercial vehicles, emergency vehicles, motor-cycles and scooters are exempt and where three different prices apply to business-owned passenger cars privately owned passenger cars and taxis. The three different prices are signified by six easily distinguishable shapes of windshield sticker, three for monthly licences and three for daily use. There are hazards and difficulties in making such distinctions, and there should be compelling reasons for any departure from charging the same price to all without exception.

Another exemption, in Singapore, is for cars and taxis with four or more occupants. Essentially, this was aimed at giving another option to car drivers who found it hard to afford the licence fee and difficult to use other modes. Since having four riders in a car automatically reduces the cost per person, it has been argued that exemptions for car pools are not necessary. In Singapore they were introduced to reinforce the concept of encouraging high-occupancy vehicle use and to counteract arguments that the Area Licence Scheme only allowed the rich to drive into the central business district.

Granting special prices or exemptions to particular categories of car owners (starting, probably, with government officials) is a temptation to be firmly resisted. Once that door has been opened, there is no end of groups that will voice their need for special treatment, and in any exempt category there will be many individuals to whom the rationale for the exemption does not validly apply. Exemptions of this sort are also an invitation for corruption, as someone has to decide on the qualifications of individuals. It is far better to have no exemptions--especially for government officials, who should set a proper example for others.

Complementary Measures

Reducing the inefficient use of cars is not a policy to be considered in isolation. It should be viewed in the context of an overall transport policy for the city. If it is to be adopted, it will probably need to be complemented by other measures in the realms of traffic management and public transport.

Provision for charges in traffic patterns:

A convenient route should be available for drivers wishing to bypass the restricted zone. Unless a ring road with excess capacity already exists, it may be necessary to upgrade or widen some roads along a circumferential route, modify intersections to handle increased traffic, and perhaps convert some parallel two-way roads into one-way pairs. If the public is to be induced to give up driving into the city, there must be other means of getting there. Car pooling will accommodate some travellers. Some may switch to motor-cycles, bicycles or walking. In most cities the main alternative is public transport, usually buses or jitneys. If there is not sufficient public transport capacity to absorb the increased load, public reaction could force the pricing scheme to be abandoned.

Essential Factors in Implementing the Scheme

Successful implementation of the Area Licence Scheme in Singapore has led some people to proclaim that it could now be done anywhere, while others say that Singapore is a unique case and proves nothing. In a sense, both are partly right, and totally wrong. It has been demonstrated that an area licence scheme can be successfully implemented under some conditions. The following factors, all of which were present in Singapore, are judged to be essential to the successful implementation of any pricing scheme.

(a) Competent management, with an organisational structure that fosters comprehensive policy-making and planning for all aspects of transport in the metropolitan area, including traffic management, traffic policy, bus services and motor vehicle registration.

(b) Carefully worked out, detailed provisions for issuance of licences, erecting signs on the approaches to the restricted zone, enforcing the rules and handling administrative details.

(c) Good design of the scheme, including upgrading the circumferential route, expanding public transport facilities, and laying out the boundary.

(d) Advance education of the public as to the reasons for the scheme, its expected benefits, both short and long run, exactly how it will work and what choices can be made.

(e) Pragmatism, as exemplified in Singapore by an effective programme of monitoring results and quickly making traffic management changes, or modifying the rules of the scheme to overcome observed problems.

Other Contributing Factors

Some other factors undoubtedly make successful implementation of the scheme in Singapore easier but are not deemed absolutely necessary for success elsewhere: (i) the fact that automobiles were used by only a minority of downtown commuters, even before the Area Licence Scheme was instituted; (ii) cultural-social attitudes favourable to compliance with regulations, Singaporeans are disposed to believe government acts in the general social interest, and to accept rules and costs imposed on them; (iii) the relative ease of planning and decision-making in a city-state, with one level of government dealing with one geographical area; (iv) laws that made enforcement simple; and (v) the relative isolation of the region from outside traffic.

Considering both the essential factors and those that were helpful but not absolutely necessary, the possibility of successfully implementing area pricing schemes in other cities has to be judged on a case-by-case basis. Given a conviction that such a scheme would be worthwhile, appropriate organisational and administrative arrangements, and competent personnel in charge, it should be possible to design and implement a workable scheme within the constraints of local conditions of a wide variety of cities.

RELATIONSHIP WITH EVALUATION CRITERIA

One group of criteria outlined by the Editors in Chapter 2 are primarily concerned with the provision of basic needs of the urban population (especially its poorer members), including the method by which those needs are ascertained and the efficiency of resource use in meeting them, as well as the long-run viability of the supply system.

The Singapore Area Licence Scheme was not a development project but a policy measure designed to avert what was seen as an undesirable side effect of development. Thus, many of the criteria are simply inappropriate for evaluating the scheme. For example, the whole set of questions on whether the scheme facilitates provision of basic needs for the poor evokes the answer: "No, but that is not what it was meant to do." Similarly, the first group of questions having to do with growth, employment and affordability are not relevant because we are not evaluating a process of production.

On the other hand, it is pertinent to consider the mode of implementation, the equity of distribution of costs and benefits, the economic suitability of the technique chosen in terms of factor inputs, and the questions on simplicity, adaptability, flexibility, risk and monitoring. These we proceed to discuss.

The editors, in the chapter on criteria, described a "responsive" process whereby all those affected by a plan take part in formulating its objectives, and in choosing among alternative plans devised by the technical representatives to meet the objectives. This ideal process is contrasted with "repressive", "paternalistic" and "manipulative" processes of deciding and implementing plans. It is admitted, however, that the "responsive" process may depend on a higher level of education and understanding than may exist in most poor countries, that it is contrary to prevalent attitudes in many cultures, and that it may use up more time, technical expertise and scarce resources than are justified.

In Singapore it would have been unrealistic, for the reasons just alluded to, to try to implement a traffic regulation policy by the "responsive" approach. In our judgement the government did well to spend a year in a public dialogue to prepare participants for the scheme and then to carry it out "paternalistically", trying to see that no one was badly hurt by it and that relatively low-income groups gained the main benefits.

In terms of equity, there is no doubt that poorer commuters--those who were already using buses--were the main beneficiaries. The immediate savings in bus riders' travel time were admittedly small, but the true measure of benefit has to be the future time savings, considering the traffic growth that would have taken place without the scheme and the consequent creeping paralysis of both private and public transport such as has occurred in many other cities. Some former bus riders benefited by filling the demand by car drivers for passengers so that they could qualify for the "car pool" exemption. Presumably some rich people also benefited--those to whom the cost of the area licence is low relative to the convenience of driving on congestion-free streets. The losers were those in the middle who were accustomed to driving cars downtown in the morning and to whom the licence fee was either an additional burden on a tight budget or an expense that had to be avoided by the inconvenience of car-pooling, changing route or shifting to the use of buses.

In the context of the evaluation criteria concerning efficiency, the attempt to make better use of existing road space instead of building new roads and to promote the use of public transport at the expense of private cars clearly indicates the desire of the scheme's planners to make more efficient use of existing and appropriate resources. The use of basic warning gantries, simple widescreen stickers and visual-control measures represents the selection of a least-cost solution. The choice of a simple approach to the implementation of a road pricing scheme over more sophisticated alternatives and novel technologies is indicative of the planners' desire to use the simplest method to reach their objectives.

The objective of the scheme's planners was not specifically to influence patterns of urban growth. Nevertheless, the constraints on private car accessibility to the central area constitute an increase in the cost of central locations. In the context of a city with a land shortage, this leads to a degree of selectivity among potential city centre users so that only those with the highest need to locate in the central city do so, thus forcing less essential land uses to peripheral areas. To the extent that this has taken place in Singapore, the Area Licence Scheme may be interpreted as promoting a more efficient land use pattern.

The Singapore government undertook a significant monitoring programme and recieved additional inputs from the World Bank study. The willingness with which they introduced changes in traffic light timings, the hours of operation, the shuttle bus system, and the way in which taxis were treated demonstrate rapid feed-back and a significant degree of pragmatism in identifying and dealing with problems. The fact that Singapore was the first country in the world to introduce road pricing shows the open-mindedness of the planners. The scheme is easy to modify either by changing the hours of operation, the vehicles exempted, the price, or the zone boundaries. In fact, three of these have already been modified.

The approach adopted to risk was to provide extensive advance publicity to highlight potential problems, monitoring to identify specificational problems, and pragmatism in dealing with them. The responsibility for component parts was clearly defined, understood and accepted. Of course, achieving this is relatively easy in a single jurisdiction state.

The project was implemented in accordance with time and budget plans and achieved more than its planned impact. No strong adverse reaction from users resulted. No negative social side effects occurred and the environmental side effects were positive. The only major disbenefit proved to be under-utilisation of the perimeter parking lots and park and ride system.

Conclusions

A number of conflicts are inherent in urban transport planning: between automobiles and buses, between construction and upgrading, between creating supply and restricting demand. Attempting to find a compromise that balances these conflicting needs has resulted in the articulation of a set of principles that have been found useful in guiding the preparation of urban transport projects:

(a) priority should be given to traffic engineering and management measures that increase the functional capacity of the existing street system, together with institutional and organisational measures to improve the efficiency in bus fleet operations;

(b) only when the above measures are insufficient, when specific links in the road network are missing, or when special facilities, such as bus lanes, are required, should new road construction be considered; and

(c) priority should be given to projects that will improve public transport services, with a specific emphasis on services in, or used by people from, low-income areas.

A crucial point to note, however, is that the effectiveness of the type of traffic engineering measures advocated in this chapter are likely to be eroded as affluence, and hence car ownership, grow. In the long term, it will be necessary to introduce measures that will directly reduce the demand for travel by automobile in congested areas. The results from Singapore presented above demonstrate that such measures can be implemented successfully. The discussion of alternatives paves the way for consideration of these measures in other cities. What is most important, given the time required for planning such schemes and ensuring political acceptance, is that preparatory studies begin as soon as possible. Only if the planning phase is initiated now will "road pricing" schemes be ready for implementation at the appropriate time.

The overall conclusion is that the Singapore Area Licence Scheme was successfully implemented and achieved its objectives. In addition, the planning and implementation process received positive evaluations when compared with the editors' evaluation criteria.

NOTES

(1) Holland and Watson (1978) Relieving Traffic Congestion.

REFERENCES

Holland, E.P., and Watson, P.L. (1978): "Traffic Pricing Schemes: Some Design Factors", Transportation Engineering, Vol. 48, No. 2, February. (Also published in Traffic Engineering and Control, Vol. 19, No. 1, January 1978.)

Holland, E.P. and Watson, P.L. (1978) "Traffic Restraint in Singapore", Traffic Engineering and Control, Vol. 19, No. 1, January 1978.

Holland, E.P. and Watson, P.L. (1978) "Relieving Traffic Congestion: The Singapore Area License Scheme." World Bank Staff Working Paper No. 281, World Bank, Washington, D.C.

12

Health Programmes Directed to Urban Squatter Populations

Samir Sanad Basta

HOW SEVERE ARE HEALTH AND NUTRITION PROBLEMS IN URBAN AREAS?

This question deserves answering before we plunge into reviewing details of case studies. There is, of course, no question that levels of mortality, morbidity and malnutrition are much higher in LDCs than in developed countries, and that greater efforts and resources are needed to improve these conditions. But the question arises: given limited resources, where should the efforts be made to improve health conditions? Health indices for urban areas generally appear better than the averages for the country as a whole. Certainly the number of health facilities, especially hospitals, is proportionately higher for the urban population than for those in rural areas, and spatially closer to most of their potential users. Urban areas almost invariably receive higher *per capita* investments in infrastructure than rural areas. Consequently there has to be some compelling reasons why more resources should be placed in urban areas where *per capita* incomes and health levels appear higher than in the rural areas where the majority of LDC populations still live.

One obvious feature of urban areas which demands closer examination is the discrepancy in sanitation and environmental conditions between the low income and squatter areas and the rest of the city - differences which, at least visually, appear much greater than in rural areas. Are these apparent differences confirmed by health statistics?

The Extent of Malnutrition and Disease in Slum and Squatter Areas

For over 3 years I have attempted to collect data about health and nutrition in the slums and squatter areas of most of the developing world, but even the initial step in identifying and locating medical or nutritional information dealing with these populations becomes extremely difficult. Nearly all the data is on the city as a whole, and is not disaggregated into geographical sub-areas or on the basis of income groups. And since most cities do not even report statistics on squatters, or else include only a marginal number of them (many, for instance, are outside "city" limits), the data is often skewed towards middle- or relatively high-income patterns of disease and mortality. Even these data look bad in most LDC cities. Nevertheless, by referring to data on squatters obtained from the five or six cities in which these are reported, and comparing this to the overall "city" picture, one begins to have an idea of the extent of the problem.

For example, Tables 1 and 2 indicate that, for Asian cities such as Manila, infant mortality in squatter settlements near the port area is around 3 times what it is for the city as a whole. Birth rates are also more than 5 times as high in the Tondo and Navotas areas than they are for Manila City's official statistics. Third degree (severe) malnutrition cases are over 3 times higher in Tondo than for Manila City. Gastroenteritis is twice as high and tuberculosis is around 10 times higher for Tondo than the city as a whole.

For Calcutta, energy intakes for squatter/slum areas are one-third less than what the overall statistics show, even for this predominantly poor city. In Madras, deaths from dysentry are 3 times as high in squatter areas as in the metropolitan area as a whole; and in Karachi, whereas only 50 percent of the city's school children as a whole do not attend primary school, the corresponding figures for slum areas is 80 percent. In Bangkok, Khanjanasthiti and Wray(1) showed that in district I of the city, around 24 percent of infants suffered from protein calorie malnutrition, but for the slum and squatter areas of districts II, III and IV, the corresponding figures were 70 percent, 82 percent and 76 percent. This health/nutrition gap between squatter areas and the city as a whole is in many cases larger than urban to rural differences, and yet these differences rarely appear in the official municipal statistics.(2)

Why Are These Differences So Large?

The epidemiology of disease and malnutrition in squatter areas is known. What to do about it is quite another matter. But first, let us summarise briefly the reasons for such shockingly high morbidity and mortality rates.

In the first place, we have the absence of potable water in the homes, and inadequate sewage disposal. Even if a standpipe with reasonably clear water is situated at some distance from the house, families will store water in unhygienic containers for long periods of time. As such, the water is then contaminated from the air and more seriously from the hands of various members of the family who "dip" everything from cups to dirty hands into the container. Such contaminated water is then fed to everyone, but its effects will be most noticeable in the young infant or child. In slums and squatter areas, the common reduction or even cessation of breast feeding allows for such contaminated water to be used more and more in the dilution of cows' milk or other preparations, which are then given to the child. The hand or the air are the agents, the water is the carrier, and the child the biggest victim. In some cases, families boil large quantities of water, but because there are large quantities, they are then stored for long periods and the same thing happens.

In addition, because of inadequate hygienic practices, young children defecate on the floor, droppings are rarely swept away completely on a dirt floor, and even the presence of a pit in a corner of the house or yard ensures that everyone who uses it will, to some degree, become contaminated with faecal organisms. Over-crowding and constant dampness also ensures the spread of many diseases; from measles, a deadly killer for the malnourished child, to tuberculosis and various respiratory diseases that lead to pneumonia. Flooding of homes, a constant occurrence in the rainy season, ensures that a certain amount of everybody's waste is also thrown into living, sleeping and eating quarters, and the residual mud ensures that many organisms, especially intestinal parasites, will have an easy and long means of survival. Pools of stagnant water and canals will lead to ideal breeding grounds for malarial mosquitos and other insects, and the lack of proper windows, netting and doors ensures their constant presence, even if sprays, smoke, etc., are used.

From a nutritional point of view, lack of purchasing power and unsteady incomes mean that only foods with relatively high bulk and few nutrients will be bought, leading to very low intakes of most vitamins, minerals and essential protein to combat infections. Children will be looked after by older siblings who feed them dirty water to keep them quiet, and malnutrition in the adults will increase apathy, infections and lack of stamina. Dysentery and diarrhoea will lead to withdrawal of all foods, leading, for infants especially, to high mortality rates; and sporadic unemployment will ensure that, in crisis periods, food intake will be reduced even further. All foods must be purchased for cash, unlike the rural farming

Table 1. Characteristics of Squatter and Non-squatter Urban Settlements in Manila, Philippines

Parameter	City (non-squatter)	Squatter Settlement	Notes Squatter Settlement
Percent school dropouts before high school	20% (a)	35% (a)	
Hospital bed to population ratio	1:300 (b)	1:4000 (c)	Squatter settlements surveyed are Tondo, Malabon and Navotas (pop. 714,924)
Infant mortality rate	76 (b)	210 (b)	Tondo and Navotas Port Area (pop. 2,100)
Birth rate (per 1000 pop.)	33 (b)	177 (b)	Tondo and Navotas Port Area (pop. 2,100)
Neonatal mortality rate (per 1000 live births)	40 (b)	105 (b)	Tondo and Navotas Port Area (pop. 2100)
Tuberculosis: rate per 100,000 population	800 (b)	7000 (b)	Greater Tondo Area (pop. 0.4 million)
Gastroenteritis: rate per 100,000 pop.	780 (b)	1352 (b)	Tondo Area (pop. 0.4 million)
Third-degree malnutrition	3% (d)	9.61 (e)	Tondo area nutrition survey on 6000 households (Operation Timbang)
Second degree malnutrition	21% (d)	37.5% (e)	"

(continued)

Table 1. (Continued)

Parameter	City (non-squatter)	Squatter Settlement	Notes Squatter Settlement
Anaemia	10% (d)	20%(e) -	"
Per capita calorie intake	1700 (d)	1550(e)	"
Typhoid (rate per 100,000)	33 (b)	135(b)	Tondo Area
Diphtheria (rate per 100,000)	48 (b)	77(b)	Tondo Area
Measles (rate per 100,000)	130 (b)	160 (b)	Tondo Area
% Clinical signs Vit. A deficiency	50% (f) (Cebu barrios)	72% (f)	Cebu City

Sources:

(a) M. Lopez and M. Hollinsteiner, The Face of Poverty - Implications for Urban Development (a survey of squatters and non-squatters in and near Barrio Maligamgan). Ateneo de Manila Univ., Institute of Philippine Culture, Quezon City, 1975; pp, 7-15.

(b) Republic of the Philippines, City of Manila Health Department Statistics, Division of Preventable Diseases, Manila, 1973.

(c) Tondo Foreshore Development Authority, Interim Report: Socio-Economic Characteristics, Manila, 1974.

(d) Food and Nutrition Research Centre Survey on Four Regions and Greater Manila, 1973 - as quoted by B. Popkin, in Nutrition Problems, Consequences and Long Run Strategy Considerations in the Philippines, School of Economics, University of Philippines, August, 1975.

(e) Nutrition Foundation of the Philippines and Tondo Foreshore Development Authority, unpublished survey on 6000 households, May 1975, as quoted in (d).

Table 2. Food-intake Characteristics for Squatter and Non-squatter Urban Areas in India and Pakistan

City	Parameter	City or High-Income Average	Squatter/ Slum Areas	Notes on Squatter Settlement
Calcutta	Mean cost of daily diet (in paisa's) of children 3 to 5 years of age	108.8 paises	49.4 paisa[a]	
Calcutta	Mean caloric intake daily diet children 3 to 5 years	960 ± 321 calories	789 ± 237 calories[a]	Group with monthly income less than or equal Rs.20 *per capita*
Calcutta	Mean vitamin A intake daily diet children 3 to 5 years	709 ± 843 i.u.	410 ± 678 i.u.[a]	Group with monthly inincome less than or equal RS.20 *per capita*.
Calcutta	Average *per capita* intake of calories	1422 calories	1061 calories[a]	Group with monthly income less than or equal to Rs.20 *per capita*
Calcutta	Average intake of protein	45 g/day	34g/day[a]	
Calcutta	Vitamin A	2139 i.u.	1400 i.u.[a]	

(continued)

Table 2. (Continued)

City	Parameter	City or High-Income Average	Squatter/ Slum Areas	Notes on Squatter Settlement
Madras	Death rate per 100,000 pop.:			
	Dysentery	7.6	21.8[b]	
	Tuberculosis	16.4	37.5[b]	Marina city section
Karachi	Population: dispensary rate	12,800:1	62,100:1	Mahmoodbad, Karangi[c] Baldia; total pop. = 0.2 million
Karachi	Beds per 1000 female population (15-49 years)	2.07	0.49	Average of 5 slums[c]
Karachi	Primary schools: minimum not enrolled aged 5-9	57% (old city and Federal area)	80% (North Karachi[c] and Mahmoodbad)	

Source:

(a) A Study of Food Habits in Calcutta, United States Agency for International Development, New Delhi, Lalchard, Roy Co. and Hindustan Thompson Associates, 1972.

(b) Shanker, T.C. Annual Report of Health Department, Corporation of Madras, 1972, pp.238-250.

(c) UNDP/Gov. of Pakistan, National Pilot project No. 3, Master Plan for Karachi Development Area, Part II. Report No. MP/RR/84-11. Karachi Information Centre Master Plan Dept., July 1973.

family, which typically grows some 80 percent of its food needs.

Soft drinks, tea, coffee, drugs, alcohol and cigarettes will become habitual palliatives and, for the infant, additional competitors for his already meagre food supply. Occasional visits to fee-paying physicians, the purchase of expensive and usually useless drugs and herbs, and constant over-crowding, filth and callousness of neighbourhood clinics and hospitals will do little to help. In many cases, these can also be agents of disease. A recent study in Recife, for instance, revealed that child mortality rates were declining in city slums, but increasing among hospitalised children, so that overall there was little change in the city mortality rate. The author of the study hypothesises that poor sanitary conditions and overcrowding in hospitals is leading to many unnecessary deaths(3).

Even assuming that we know the extent of the problem, the strategies to follow are not necessarily clear. There is a chasm between public health needs and the organisational and political realities, and little in the form of a bridge to show us the way. In some cities political support and prestige is associated with large and visible infrastructure works and public health is not accorded a high priority. Often the will exists, but the present structure of health services may not address itself to providing either sufficient funds, manpower or resources to squatter areas. In most if not all cases, a municipal health office, if it exists at all, is under two main obligations. The first is probably to ensure that existing services under its tutelage, services already established in _bona fide_ sections of the city such as garbage disposal, street cleaning, municipal clinics and hospitals, and out-patient services for the most communicable diseases, are prevented from collapse. In other words, maintenance of existing services, already very difficult because of fiscal and manpower constraints, becomes almost the _sine qua non_ of its existence. Secondly, in most cases, a municipal health office is under the strong patronage of the Ministry of Health, which controls most of its budget, policies and senior appointments. If, as is usually the case, this Ministry is "traditional", most of its philosophy and hence that of the municipal health office will be oriented towards curative services. That is, a heavy dependence on expensive infrastructure such as city hospitals and referral systems which shunt the patient from physician to physician. Long waiting times, over-crowding and little attempt to attack the root cause of the conditions which lead to the disease are characteristics of the system. This in turn leads to very high costs, both in terms of operating the system as regards infrastructure and because it needs a large number of physicians to operate it. Moreover, only a small proportion of the target populations can be covered because of high _per capita_ cost. This inclination to see people only when they are ill also ensures that there is little interaction or feedback from the vast but needy majority who are not directly in contact with the physicians and hospitals. Conditions and diseases, therefore, persist and, among the poor, only the most patient or the very ill are contacted.

TWO CASE STUDIES OF NEW APPROACHES

"New" approaches, oriented towards improving the whole health environment rather than on purely curative treatment, and using community health workers, traditional healers and other types of para-medics are now being tried in several countries. These new approaches all seek to employ the simplest and most direct means, namely the residents in the area, to obtain their objectives. They usually attempt to attack health problems through simultaneous improvements in neighbourhood water supply, drainage and sanitation facilities, vector control, nutrition, immunizations, family planning and health education. The software components are cheap (around US$3 to US$10 per capita per year) and sometimes include various options whereby the community can pay recurrent costs (about US$0.20 to 0.50 per family per month). Let us examine what has happened in two recent projects in which these new approaches have been attempted.

Integrated Community Health Care in Tondo

In Manila an urban project designed to improve housing, environmental sanitation, small-scale business and social programmes for about 180,000 Tondo Foreshore people was begun in 1975. The health/nutrition component, in addition to sanitation improvements through the physical infrastructure, consisted of the following:

(a) Barangay Volunteer Medics (BVMs):

Three hundred volunteers from the Tondo community were to be trained over a 12-18 month period by the National Housing Authority (NHA), the lead agency implementing the integrated upgrading scheme, in coordination with the Department of Health and other government agencies involved in the training of volunteer workers. The training of each BVM would take about 2 months and include education in family planning methods; follow-up referrals; first-aid treatment for malnourished children; weighing procedures and recognition of malnutrition; recognition and referrals of communicable disease; vaccinations; administration of deworming drugs; vermin control and waste disposal; and the preparation of records and statistical information. The BVMs were also to be trained to dispense certain medicines and injections.

(b) Identification, location and feeding of malnourished children:

Weighing scales were to be provided to an ongoing programme, involving the weighing of all children less than 6 years old, to discover suspected cases of malnutrition. Follow-up treatment and family counselling for children in primary, secondary and tertiary stages of malnutrition was included. The project was based on issuing yellow cards to families of secondary malnutrition cases and red cards to tertiary malnutrition cases. These admit the children to clinics on a priority basis; and, after counselling and treatment, the BVMs instruct the mothers how to weigh their children and to keep a record of their status, using a simple weight chart. Mothers can also attend nutrition classes at regular intervals in the community centres. However, all mothers of critically malnourished children are required to attend these classes at least once a week. NHA and the Nutrition Foundation of the Philippines were to administer this programme. The weight of children from selected families would be monitored from time to time, to evaluate the programme. A religious foundation would provide a corn-soy mixture for children to be prepared at home, and for 4-6 year-old children at day-care centres.

(c) Food preparation:

As part of the infant nutrition programme, mothers were to be taught the use and preparation of a simple, nutritious food mixture using local ingredients. The mixture would include mango nut powder, rice, red palm or coconut oil, and unsalted anchovy or shrimp powder in a proportion of 2:6:1:1. For a 1-year-old infant, about 50 g/day are needed, in addition to breast feeding and to the usual mixtures of strained fruits and vegetables. The mixture would cost about $0.12 per 100 grammes, or $0.06/day, at current shop prices in Tondo. It could be prepared in the home by grinding the ingredients in a dish or a grinder. The Nutrition Council of the Philippines was to be in charge of this programme, as well as Project Tulungan, Office of the President.

(d) Vitamin and iron supplement programme:

It was estimated, from records obtained from clinics in the area, that about 5 percent of the children in Tondo suffer from some degree of visual impairment due to vitamin A deficiency. The survey carried out by the Nutrition Foundation, in the spring of 1975, revealed that 36 percent of the children over 4 years of age are deficient in vitamin A, and nearly 50 percent of the adults were consuming diets that were not meeting the basic physiological requirement for the vitamin. Accordingly, since a deficiency of this vitamin leads to a much greater susceptibility to infections, as well as eventual blindness, it was proposed to include a mass-dose vitamin A programme which would entail twice-yearly oral administration of 100,000 i.u. of vitamin A palmitate to around 40,000 children between the ages of 2-6 years of age, by a combined force of BVMs, Nutrition Foundation personnel and clinical staff. The programme would be under the administration of the National Nutrition Council. In terms of iron deficiency anaemia, surveys indicated that over a third of lactating mothers and young children suffered from the disease. In view of the established connection between this disease and apathy, predisposition to infections and reduced productivity, all clinics, Tulungan centres and social workers were to be responsible for supplying all eligible females in the study area with cheap, but effective, take-home iron supplements. Haemoglobin (blood iron) levels were to be monitored on a yearly basis in a sub-sample to evaluate the success of the programme.

(e) Nutrition education for adults:

A programme of nutrition and health education conducted in the barangay centres and in schools by personnel from the Nutrition Foundation of the Philippines. Particular emphasis was to be given to breast feeding and to cooking nutritious food mixtures. The preparation and erection of posters and advertising was to be conducted through the National Media Centre. Follow-up surveys would be carried out to evaluate the inputs the mothers receive.

(f) Immunization:

Based on the data gathered from the health centres and clinics there were, in 1974, 210 deaths and 2662 confirmed cases of communicable diseases (diphtheria, measles, typhoid, cholera, poliomyelitis) in Tondo Foreshore alone. In order to arrest the spread of infection, the project was designed to include the provision of DPT (diptheria, pertusis, tetanus), measles and poliomyelitis vaccines to about 30 percent of the children in Tondo (about 14,678 vaccinations a year), and cholera-typhoid to about 98 percent of the inhabitants of Tondo. The Department of Health was to be responsible for the programme. Given the high prevalence of tuberculosis, an ancillary programme to detect, treat and prevent tuberculosis in adults was also included, that would cover all adults in Tondo District.

The capital expenditure was mainly for an X-ray laboratory, located at Rawis Tulungan Centre in Tondo.

(g) Deworming Programme:

Because of the presence of worms (mainly Ascaris lumbricoides) in nearly 90 percent of all the children surveyed at random and 80 percent of the adults, and the concomitant decline in productivity, health and longevity, a deworming component was included in the project. While some 10 percent of the children in the Foreshore had already been dewormed, the major activities under this component would take place after sewerage and water connections to individuals' households had been installed for maximum effectiveness. The target was about 46,000 children, between ages 4 and 12 (100 percent coverage); and as many adults as possible would also be included, using a two-dose approach. The programme would run for 3 years and would be financed and administered by the Department of Health. Stool samples would be collected at regular intervals.

(h) Family planning:

The delivery of family planning information, services, etc. was to be via the Health and Tulungan centres, in addition to the Barangay Volunteer Medics who were being trained to also function as family planning motivators and advisors. The target for the family planning programme for a 10-year period, 1974-1984, was the reduction of the birth rate from 3.3 to 2.5 percent. Operational targets for each year have been set up. Personalised follow-up letters, campaigns geared to adult males, adult education classes in schools, referral systems, roving mobile units, monitoring and evaluation systems, etc., were features of the programme and, at the local level, were to be under the responsibility of one person in each barangay (physician, barangay chairman and/or volunteer medical worker). The Population Commission of the Philippines (POPCOM) was to supervise, fund and design the programme.

(i) Vermin and rodent control programme:

The large number of rats and vermin, such as lice, present in Tondo were to be eliminated or reduced considerably, in order to reduce many of the communicable diseases in the area. Accordingly, the City Health Department agreed to finance a sub-project to reduce vermin and rodents in the area with a capital expenditure of US$6000 (sprays and fogging equipment) and the recurrent expenditure of US$4000 per year.

(j) Clinics:

Nearly all the government clinics needed some degree of physical upgrading, such as improvement in sewerage and water connections, repairs to walls, roofs and, in one case, reconstruction. Some minor equipment also needs to be replaced and updated, and at least fifty beds need to be provided in the area in order to meet acceptable standards. The project, therefore, involves upgrading of one centre, renovation of a second together with two small clinics, reconstruction of a third centre and construction of a further two new health centres with twenty-five beds each. The clinics were to be improved by NHA, then operated and maintained by the Manila City Health Department.

Although it may be too soon to predict the final outcome, let us examine 5 years later what has occurred. We must keep in mind that the whole complex project, including the physical infrastructure, was about 1 year late in starting due largely to management, staffing and political difficulties.

1. From 1976 when the programme began 120 BVMs have been trained out of the 300 expected. Interest on the part of the BVMs was high during training and while they were receiving an honoraria of US$7 per month which commenced in November 1977. However, the honoraria was eliminated in March 1979 and the number of volunteers has dwindled to about forty-five. These persons and some of the others continue to offer services since they have become identified with the barangays and many of their neighbours continue to seek their services. During the 9 months from January to September 1979, while their numbers were falling, they made 7000 referrals to health clinics and hospitals, treated 2700 emergency cases and contacted 3000 mothers (about 25 percent of those estimated to require contact). For the numbers of BVMs working during that time, which averaged about eighty-five persons, this seems to be a reasonable performance, and a service which has come to be appreciated and used by the residents. For what would be a relatively minor expenditure of US$25,000 per year (or US$1 per household), 300 BVMs could be paid the stipend and continue to provide a needed service. All concerned agencies agree that the BVM's service is valuable, but they continue to wrangle over who should pay the honoraria.

2. The BVMs together with the Volunteer Nutrition Aides of Operation Timbang have been weighing 8200 children quarterly, generally a successful level of operation. Monthly distribution of food to households covering 2300 malnourished children and direct feeding daily of 1700 children at twelve day-care centres is underway by the religious foundation. The programme is said to be reaching about 20 to 30 percent of those children in need, and appears to be operated well, although further expansion is needed for which there will be an opportunity as more day-care centres are built.
3. The food preparation (cooking demonstration) programme is tied in with the food assistance programme noted above and, over the first 9 months of 1979, 195 sessions were held attended by about 2000 mothers, about 15-20 percent of those which required contacting. This component is running well and expanding.
4. The vitamin and iron supplement programme has been a failure with only one allotment received from the Ministry of Health. The supervisory staff are too occupied with rural health programmes to run the component effectively.
5. The nutrition education programme has been successful in reaching 6300 mothers in weekly classes. Participation of the National Media Centre has been dropped because they do not provide free materials, and instead NHA now works with the Communications Foundation for Asia and the Dieticians and Nutritionists Association of the Philippines.
6. Up to 1978 the immunisation programme was conducted for all adults and children for cholera and typhoid because of the threat of epidemics. Since then, selective immunisations on a semi-annual basis for children has been carried out, with 2500 children immunised for DPT and 2200 for BCG during 1979.
7. Deworming commenced too early, before water and sanitation was installed and footpaths paved. However, it is now being synchronised with the physical upgrading. Funds have been limited and efforts are now focused on the 1860 food assistance recipients up to 6 years old, of which 1340 have been reached. It is not clear why funds are not available to treat a wider age range, as originally envisaged.

8. The reduced number of BVMs has meant that less families have been contacted for family planning advice than originally intended. Nevertheless, there were 2430 acceptors over the period from January to September 1979, and community response has been favourable.
9. The City Health Department has supplied chemicals and machinery for vermin control and NHA trained 100 residents who worked voluntarily on weekends. In 1978 the MHD stopped supplying chemicals but continued to supply machinery. The individual barangays now buy their own chemicals, but have limited the programme to rodent control, since they have found that the spraying is not very effective. Across the sixty-three targeted barangays, a "clean-up" operation has been mounted 900 times, 49 barangays have been fogged 167 times and 45 barangays sprayed 145 times. This component has thus been quite successful.
10. By the end of 1979 little had been done to the upgrading and construction of the clinics in the programme. Only one clinic has been built but is not yet occupied due to structural weaknesses. A preoccupation with completing infrastructure services in Tondo, and phasing problems of clinic location related to road alignment and landfill together with weak coordination between responsible agencies have delayed this component.

Performance on this project thus presents a mixed picture. Community acceptance for those elements of the project which were implemented has been positive, and the services well used. Unfortunately no systematic monitoring of the health impact has been undertaken and the effectiveness of the programmes has not been properly evaluated. The major problems have related to weak coordination between agencies, the absence of a full-time coordinator of the health/nutrition components and the chronic shortage of trained individuals to implement surveys for evaluation (base-line data does, however, exist). As from the end of 1979 a full-time coordinator was appointed, which may help to improve the situation. The other major issue concerns payment for the BVMs. The need for even a small additional income is very important to residents in very low-income urban communities, and much so-called spare time is used in looking for work. Volunteer time is relatively more onerous for low income individuals than for communities receiving more stable and regular incomes. It seems that some monetary payment is required to maintain momentum and interest on the part of the BVMs.

The Community Health Component of Indonesia's Kampung Improvement Programme

A second project, this time in Indonesia, was initiated late in 1976. It covered parts of both Jakarta and Surabaya and contained almost the same mixture of upgrading packages as the Manila project. Once again, the community health workers (CHWs) were to be the "core" of the health component, but here they were to be paid a sum of around US$15 per month for their services, and were to operate from one-room health "posts" built by the government or rented from the community. The total cost of the combined health/nutrition components, including salaries for the first year, were roughly of the order of US$500,000, or 1 percent of the total project cost, as in Manila.

One health post (Pos Keshatan) in each community (Rukun Warga or RW) of about 3000 people was planned. These were to serve as satellites for the health subcentres and as a base for health and nutrition activities in the community. A simple two-room facility would be provided, one room for the health activities in general and the other for a Young Child Centre (Karang Bahta), which would focus on nutrition, disease prevention and education of pre-schoool children. Twelve CHWs were to be assigned to each of the thirty-three health posts, thus providing one CHW to every 500 persons in the six communities where the programme was to be implemented. After the first year it was hoped that the community would fund their operating costs via a health "insurance" contribution of US$0.12 to US$0.24 per month per family. The CHWs would be selected from the community and would undergo basic training for 2 months, with a refresher course starting 4 to 6 months after they have been in the field. The curriculum and training was to be undertaken by the respective City Health Departments who would also manage the programme. Eight full-time supervisors were to be assigned to the project.

The programme got off to a slow start, due in part to differences of opinion on training curricula and the difficulty of hiring responsible administrative staff. Difficulties in acquiring land for building the health clinics which are the next level of facility above the health posts also delayed implementation. As of late 1979, 70 percent of the health posts had been built, close to the targeted number, and in Jakarta, where the programme is further ahead than Surabaya, nine of the fifteen health posts built are being well used. The others were either poorly sited for community access or the use and control of them are contested by local leaders. In Jakarta 116 out of the 180 CHWs trained are now working. The drop out of sixty occurred after the City Health Department discontinued the honoraria. In Surabaya, funding from the City was reduced and late in arriving, and so far only forty-six out of the projected 100 CHWs have been trained. Again, funds for the honoraria are in doubt. In neither city has a monitoring and evaluation system been set up to assess the impact of the work. In Jakarta, the City Health Department has tried to organise the family insurance scheme so that families would pay the US$0.15 a month instead of the present charge of US$0.30 for every visit to the clinic. Thus far the system has not been well received by the community which feels that the monthly payments are too high. In Jakarta the Health Department is increasing the number of nurses in the kampungs to provide better supervision and direction for the CHWs.

In both cities it is too early to make any definitive assessments. The authorities are trying to modify the programme in response to difficulties, which is a good sign. However, elimination of payments to the CHWs is symptomatic of chronic under-funding for staff and for equipment and supplies in the health programmes generally. It is not clear whether it also indicates a lack of support for the concept by the medical administrators.

One thing, however, is becoming increasingly clear. The relatively long gestation period for some of these projects, arising mainly from the lack of trained administrative manpower, increases the likelihood that administrators will change which in turn causes delays or changes in operational concepts or criteria.

WHAT ARE THE LESSONS?

First, to use an old cliche, money isn't everything. That is, "software" programmes such as the development of health care services are much more dependent upon the upgrading of human resources which cannot be done simply by pouring in financial resources. Second, even if programmes are designed by local authorities themselves with the best of intentions, the planner is well advised to make a thorough inventory of existing manpower and administrative capabilities. This is more important than the fine technical points of any health/nutrition programme. Third, even if the community in question seems well geared to accept a preventive or educational programme, out-reach services such as "barefoot doctors", medical volunteers or health/nutrition/family planning workers cannot be effective unless the medical hierarchy is ready to accept them and to allow them to practice their assigned role. Fourthly, a multiplicity of agencies, such as those involved in the Manila components, are to be avoided even if in the existing situation one agency is unwilling to take most of the burden. If this is the case, drop the programme or simplify it to the point where one or two main agencies can handle it. Fifth, a realistic perspective regarding local difficulties by the foreign planner or funding agency is important from the beginning. One must plan a framework that is simple and robust enough to accept local management capabilities. Supervision, monitoring and proper evaluation to see that benefits are accruing to the target population, or to help local agencies plan corrective action, are of course also an essential ingredient to the framework.

In addition, the eagerness and impatience of the original planners and funders made them wary about trying to enlist the support of the powerful central Ministry of Health. Had they done so, more logistical, financial and political support or pressure could probably have been brought to bear on the municipal health offices. Secondly, the rapidity through which funds were disbursed by the funding agencies became a problem in itself, since many of the local institutions could not adapt quickly enough to the administrative and logistical demands that come with the money. It is also probably true that, if the health component had been funded directly via a health or nutrition project rather than as a small component of a much larger multidisciplinary project, many of these delays and problems would not have occurred.

This may illustrate an underlying problem with the "small area" approach to health service delivery as implemented in the Jakarta and Manila projects. Whereas a small area defined by physical and community boundaries may be appropriate for the programming of physical infrastructure, it is often difficult for the agencies responsible for social services to operate in the same areas in isolation from the larger urban community. The hierarchy of catchment areas required for delivery of social services frequently demands at least a city-wide perspective which would allow for the necessary changes in administrative relationships.

From the limited examples given, it is not therefore sufficient to try to correct existing shortcomings by improving infrastructure (health posts, clinics), or by trying to reduce the dependence on curative services by measures such as increasing supply and training of community health workers, or by appealing directly to the people (nutrition education, recruitment of locals, home visiting, etc.). All this in the "new" theory should work, but the reason so much has been delayed is because the planners simply did not appreciate the complexity of providing the correct supervisory input by high level local administrators. The planners thought too much of the barefoot medic and too little of the physician or administrator who makes or breaks the decisions.

Thus, the key lessons to the planner who is attempting to implant new style "people-oriented" health/nutrition projects is to study well the existing referral systems and hierarchical chains of command. Then convince the administrators and obtain their full support. At all stages monitor everything carefully, from the production of training manuals to the methodology involved in home visiting and communications, to the manner and level each administrator or barefoot worker in the project is to be paid or "rewarded". And everyone has to be "rewarded". The gleam in the eye of the planner is not necessarily the same gleam in the eye of the local administrator. The latter is beset with problems, decisions and priorities which are in many cases quite different from the urban or health planner who is frantically trying to get his "project" off the drawing board. My evaluation of the two experiences in Indonesia and the Philippines has concentrated on their implementation which, as we have seen, was disappointingly slow and uneven. However, if these deficiencies can be overcome, the fundamental approach of the programme can yield immense benefits compared to the "curative" and traditional high technology approach to health care. With regard to the Editors' criteria, the grass-roots approach redresses equity in the system by reaching the poor and disadvantaged. It is a low cost approach able to be replicated on a large scale providing that the key ingredients of commitment and strong management are there. It addresses the most basic elemental needs of the population and elicits their cooperation and participation as an essential element. Improved health offers economic benefits which are difficult to quantify, but nonetheless real. Healthy people can work more energetically and productively and have more initiative to try new activities and expand their educational and social horizons. In this sense, the allocation of resources to expand this type of health care can yield immense economic and social, if not immediate financial, benefits to the government.

Finally, slowly, many of these things are occurring the Philippine and Indonesian projects just described. And one of the most important of these is that the target population has been CONTACTED. Contact is the <u>sine qua non</u> of everything. It is especially so for urban squatters who live in relative isolation (or dread) from local authorities. Secondly, local agencies themselves, realising their shortcomings and the urban explosion, and realising that money will not necessarily remedy them, are coming up with much more realistic formulas. A fundamental review of rural and urban health service delivery aimed at reaching the poor is underway by the Ministry of Health in the Philippines. In the Philippines and Indonesia the community health worker programmes described above are finally gaining momentum and the health authorities are taking an increasing interest in evaluating their effects. At the national level, the fertility rate in Indonesia has been lowered by 21 percent, compared to a planned 15 percent over the Second Five Year Plan, due in part to the extensive and effective family planning programmes. Success can be attributed here, at least partially, to the extensive use of field-workers and traditional midwives. Last, but not least, everyone, the local population, the agencies themselves, and the planners and funders, has learned something.

NOTES AND REFERENCES

(1) S. S. Basta (1977) "Nutrition and Health in Low Income Urban Areas of the Third World", Journal of Ecology of Food and Nutrition, Vol. 6, pp. 113-124.

(2) P. Khanjanasthiti and J. D. (Wray July 1974) "Early Protein Calorie Malnutrition in Slum Areas of Bangkok Municipality 1970-71", Journal of the Medical Association of Thailand, Vol. 57, No. 7, pp. 357-366.

(3) R. Nunes (1977) Preliminary material presented at "INAN" workshop on Recife Health/Nutrition Programmes at Brasilia. To be published.

III

PRINCIPAL CONCLUSIONS

III

PRINCIPAL CONCLUSIONS

INTRODUCTION

The purpose of this concluding chapter is to assemble the major conclusions which can be derived from the cases presented in Part Two. What can we learn from the actual plans, programmes and projects described in this volume? Rather than build our conclusions on theoretical arguments, the reasoning process applied here is inductive. All general propositions and statements have been formed on the basis of studying the specific cases.

In the search for meaningful patterns, and for a constructive framework, the following five questions emerged as useful headings for presenting our principal conclusions with regard to urban planning practice in the LDCs: (1) Who controls and benefits from urban development? (2) Where should urban development occur? (3) Who plans - and who decides? (4) How to plan and build? (5) What are the impacts of development?

It should be emphasised that these conclusions do not pretend to deal comprehensively with all aspects of urban development - for instance, neither with all problems and issues outlined in Chapter 1 nor all criteria covered in Chapter 2. This is because the case studies themselves represent a limited series of experiences which do not encompass all aspects of development. However, we have made every effort to cross-reference the points advanced in Part One, particularly the criteria of Chapter 2.

WHO CONTROLS AND BENEFITS FROM URBAN DEVELOPMENT?

Overall Socio-political Orientation

In enumerating the principal conclusions stemming from the case studies of this volume, one distinction should be made at the outset.(1) This relates to the relatively high degree of political control which socialist or communist societies are able to exert over every facet of social life. Among other uses, such political control or power can be applied by governments to limit urbanisation, regulate rural-urban migration, and otherwise effect national spatial strategies and patterns of population distribution. It should be borne in mind that a different set of tools are used in socialist/communist societies than in democratic/capitalist ones, tools which exercise a greater degree of control and limitations on individual freedom.

Of the case studies in this volume, the Peoples Republic of China is distinguished as the only socialist/communist state. Because of its greater political control, China has attempted to regulate rural-urban migration and prevent large-scale urbanisation to a degree which would have been impossible in democratic/capitalist nations. Cadres of urban workers and students have been "sent down" to join work brigades in the rural areas. Despite these efforts, however, China's actual success in limiting overall urban growth has been marginal, as will be discussed below.

Perhaps the crucial variable with respect to general socio-political orientation, at least from the perspective of this book, is the basic philosophy and stance which each nation's decision-makers adopt toward urbanisation. The Chinese rulers have perceived urban development as a destructive and inhibiting influence on the new order and on the primacy of the worker-peasant. Consequently, they have taken an anti-urban stance, recognising existing urban centres only as a necessary evil to support the industrial development which in turn would service agriculture.(2)

This philosophical position stands in contrast to that of the other nations represented here: in virtually all other cases, urbanisation is seen as an important vehicle for economic growth and modernisation, that is, in an essentially positive light. However, as will be amplified in the next section of this chapter ("Where Should Urban Development Occur?"), significant variations in specific attitudes toward urbanisation can be perceived. In both India and Turkey, for instance, the goal was to establish major secondary urban centres which would act as countermagnets to the established, neo-colonial metropoli. These new centres would function as major power bases for the emerging technocrats and bourgeoisie who were becoming increasingly important in the governments. In Malaysia, the approach was different: here the goal was to "urbanise the Malays" by taking the city to the country through a series of small centres serving agricultural hinterlands. The expectation here was that exposure to urban conditions would enable Malays to compete better in trade and industry with other ethnic groups. In the cases, the decision-makers realised that urban development has socio-political dimensions as well as economic and technical ones, which they attempted to utilise for their purposes.

Who Benefits from Urbanisation?

Although there is a tendency on the part of some urban planners to bury the basic issues of urban development under such technical concerns as "optimal densities", "appropriate land uses" and "unauthorised development", several case studies point up the fact that the needs and aspirations of various social classes within urban areas are in fundamental conflict. They tend to demonstrate that technical or physical solutions to urban problems either will not succeed or will only be partially successful until the larger social conflicts within the society are somehow resolved - or brought into an acceptable equilibrium. Basically, it comes down to the issue: who benefits from urban development, and how are the needs of various social groups taken into account? In this context, several of the criteria mentioned in Chapter 2 under the headings of "Distribution of Assets and Services", "Equity" and "Respect", which are concerned with supporting poorer groups in society, should be borne in mind. Under the criterion of "Distributing Assets and Services", for instance, it is stated that programmes should expand the supply of services needed by the urban poor in sufficient volume and at prices they can afford.

Tekeli and Okyay address this issue most directly. As the history of Ankara's growth is traced, they emphasise that the Turkish capital was planned and built primarily for the benefit of the "emerging national bourgeoisie". If this group's interests were in conflict with those of the lower income masses - for example, over the issues of urban land tenure or housing policy - it was clear what the outcome would be. At least as far as official planning and implementation activities were concerned, there was no question as to who was supposed to most benefit from the city's development. But in Ankara as elsewhere, the needs of those not accommodated officially do not simply disappear, as is demonstrated by the vast gecekondu areas in which the poor have taken the matter of living environments for themselves into their own hands.

This fundamental class conflict is also illustrated very effectively by the case of Malaysia's Urban Development Authority. Although the prime goal of this agency is to promote economic equity between the country's racial groups, there is some doubt as to whether the basic tool selected to achieve this goal - real estate development - will be successful. Amato seems to be saying that upper income Malay businessmen and bureaucrats, along with their Chinese "joint venturers", are better placed to benefit from real estate than the low-income Malays for whom the agency was presumably established.

In Karachi the different interests of the traditional land-owning elite, the newer industrial elite, the bureaucracy and the military, led to extended conflicts over the priorities for development and where investments in urban infrastructure and land development would go. As Herbert points out, there was not a single major agency that combined a sound social orientation with efficient management, political power and financial independence to launch and sustain programmes to benefit the massive low-income populations. The low-income groups were not well organised and he admits that insufficient effort was madé to contact and inform them, which could have allowed them to mobilise support for their concerns. This raises an important issue. The groups for which many plans are ostensibly made are either absent or poorly represented among the pressure and interest groups which influence the planning process. Is it possible, or desirable, for planners employed by the government to encourage the formation of groups representing the interests of low-income communities? Prior to any technical work, should more effort be spent on obtaining a more representative decision-making group, as a first phase of any new planning effort?

Inextricably bound up with the question of who benefits from urban development is the issue of general priorities in public investment: should LDC governments support activities in the modern or in the traditional sectors within urban areas? For example, should an improved primary highway network be built to speed the flow of private autos of the urban elites or improved public transportation to benefit lower income groups? As another example, should large-scale, capital-intensive industries providing high-wage jobs for the modern sector be fostered or small-scale, labour-intensive industries benefiting lower income groups? Regarding housing, should government programmes emphasise public housing and co-ops for middle income groups or upgrading and sites and services projects for the poor? The Chapter 1 theme of "Dualism between Modern and Informal Sectors" and the Chapter 2 criteria under the headings of "Employment and Productivity" as well as "Distribution of Assets and Services" and "Resource Allocation" are all strongly linked to this general issue.

Our case studies provide examples of governments having taken positions on such issues. In the case of Singapore's area licensing scheme, for instance, policy-makers were tough on high consumers and high-income groups to the benefit of lower-income commuters. There also appears to be a perception that the productivity of the whole urban area, and thus the long-term interests of rich and poor alike, would suffer unless something was done to improve efficiency in using road space. In the case of both Singapore's and Hong Kong's public housing, whilst most families are benefiting from these programmes, there remains a very poor group who have not been able to participate in the new government housing programmes. In these relatively wealthy city states, this group is a small minority and it may be that their problems cannot be solved through public housing programmes which benefit the majority of families.

In fact, the question of optimum solutions to residential development for lower-income groups is an excellent illustration of the general issue of who benefits from urban development. As we saw in the case of the Urban Development Authority, LDC governments, and especially their professional staff, are often reluctant to provide serviced sites or to engage in upgrading for fear that these developments will rapidly deteriorate into "tomorrow's slums". The Malaysian authorities never really agreed with the approach being advocated in the Salak South project. Yet what the lower-income groups require most urgently is land, basic infrastructure services and employment opportunities, not houses. But in Malaysia and elsewhere, housing agencies are often dominated by architects whose success is measured by the number of "housing units" erected.

An even more serious constraint, however, is that it may not be perceived to be in the best interests of the ruling elites to provide the poor with the kinds of living environments they want. Perhaps token provision of public housing a la Singapore, and allowing the remaining urban dwellers to fend for themselves, is felt to be closer to their political and economic interests. In the case of the Karachi Development Programme, for instance, the major upgrading project proposed for Lyari fell into limbo chiefly because it was in conflict with the entrenched interests of local property owners, and the first Metroville project was compromised and built to higher standards largely because of political and administrative (in this instance not technical) unwillingness to support the concept of new open plot and utility wall development. However, in two further cases concerning housing, both the Jakarta and Philippine governments recognised that something had to be done for the poor in depressed areas if only for reasons of political stability. In the case of Tondo, the critical factor which got the scheme going was the well-organised resistance of the community to government efforts to relocate them. By accepting the approach of leaving the people where they had settled and upgrading them in situ, they subsequently found this to be both a low cost and politically popular solution. Perhaps this is one of the reasons why these upgrading schemes seem to be so successful - that once tried on a large scale they appeal to the interests of both the majority of the people and to the political rulers.

A final, classic example of the issue of who benefits from development - in this case rural as well as urban development - is the case of the Pahang Tenggara regional scheme. In utilising large private and public corporations to develop, own and manage the means of agricultural production in this frontier region - rather than alternative mechanisms involving poor Malay settlers more directly - Kuala Lumpur created a climate in the name of presumed efficiency which would enable wealthier entrepreneurs and government bureaucrats, rather than the kampung Malays, to be the scheme's chief beneficiaries. Once again, the chance for a more thorough distribution of resources and opportunities seems to have slipped by.

WHERE SHOULD URBAN DEVELOPMENT OCCUR?

The first two themes raised in Chapter 1, the "Optimum Pattern of Urbanisation" and "Integrated Spatial Development", and the Chapter 2 criteria of "Factor Endowment", "Thresholds and Economies of Scale" and "Multipliers and Leverage", all address the broad issues related to national strategies of urban and regional development. What can be inferred from the case studies as to both the nature of alternative national strategies of spatial development and the effectiveness of various countries in implementing their strategies through different kinds of settlement planning and development?

Alternative National Strategies of Spatial Development

Four of the case studies deal with countries which have an explicit national strategy of spatial development. Although they vary widely in their resource endowment and political systems, all wish to spread the economic and social benefits of development to their less developed regions.

China and Malaysia have dispersed public investments in order to stimulate agriculture and improve the incomes of the rural masses who depend on it. Malaysia has used regional and urban development to expand agricultural production in previously uncultivated areas, using public infrastructure to offer a stimulus for both private estates and public enterprises

(FELDA) to open up land, and using new small towns as service centres and dormitories for the agricultural work force. China, on the other hand, has taken the work brigade and the existing agricultural village as the motor for stimulating productivity, with the development of public works in a secondary and supportive role.

Both Turkey and China have looked upon regional investments as a means to remove the political and economic power from the old colonial and trading centres, to redistribute it to different social groups and to use it to change the economic base of the country. However, the purposes to which rural and urban development were put and the social classes who directed it were very different. While the Chinese advocated rural development, the Turks, on the other hand, used the establishment of a new capital city as a means to unify the country under the new nationalist bourgeois order. To them industrialisation would transform a weak and vulnerable country into a strong power and this would be achieved by, and to the benefit of, the rising middle classes with the peasants supplying the manpower for the new industries.

As the case study of Durgapur points out, most of India's regional development concerns since independence, until quite recently, were focused on the development of heavy industry as a vehicle for economic self-sufficiency. This type of industry (mainly coal and steel) needed to be located close to the resource sites, and it was expected that they could act as poles for new industrial growth and thereby as a counter balance to pull new employment opportunities away from the large cities. The motivation for this type of regional development was thus mainly economic and was planned by technocrats.

Effectiveness in Achieving Objectives of National Spatial Strategies

What do the case studies tell us concerning the effectiveness of these countries in achieving the objectives of their urbanisation strategy? Here we must be cautious since, apart from Malaysia, the cases only discuss one illustrative settlement in each country and are focused primarily on the history of and future prospects for the internal development of that settlement. Nevertheless, five principal issues emerge, which revolve around migration and growth rates, economic base, the incubation and maturation period, management and costs.

In all cases, the new settlement strategy does not appear to have dramatically changed the growth of the existing cities, at least over the medium term. Despite the efforts of "sending down" in China, the large cities have maintained their growth, although the growth appears to have taken place during periods of unrest and change in policies when insecurity and loosening of social controls allowed waves of migration to take place. On the other hand, while China's policy does not appear to have substantially slowed migration, it has stimulated agricultural productivity and brought about great improvements in well-being of the agricultural work force through dispersal of investments and encouragement of responsibility and decisions at the village level.

In India the development of major resource industries, while contributing effectively to the government's import substitution policy, appears to have had little effect in slowing migration to the large cities or inducing spread effects to the hinterlands of the new industrial towns. Similarly in Malaysia, the expansion of estate agriculture in Pahang Tenggara is rapidly adding to the country's exports of palm oil, timber and rubber, but the numbers of new settlers are relatively small compared to the rural population as a whole and the programme has had little effect on migration rates to the large cities on the west coast of Peninsular Malaysia. In Turkey, the establishment of Ankara, together with the strategy under Ataturk of improving major transport links to the eastern part of the country and locating major industries at the intersections of these transport routes, has stimulated industrial and urban development in the central and southern cities of the country. Ankara thereby strengthened other urban areas but has had little effect on expanding agricultural employment or diffusing innovation to rural areas.(3) The rural populations have continued to migrate mainly to Istanbul where the enormous numbers of small and medium size businesses offer greater employment opportunities.

It appears from our case studies that new urban development, per se, does not necessarily improve the well-being and incomes for the majority of the population of the region in which the new town or industry is located. It would seem that, in order to help the rural population, development efforts have to be focused directly on them, with urban development providing a service role to support agricultural productivity and employment. Where small towns already exist, it appears that their economy cannot be easily linked into new large resource industries. In Durgapur the steel industry could not quickly develop these linkages mainly because most downstream industries are more market than resource-oriented and consequently have to locate close to the existing large markets, in the major cities. Nevertheless, more recently there do appear to be indications of limited spread effects to smaller towns on the north of the Damodar river. When considering new or expanded urban development there appears to be a myopia which focuses only on the city itself, often arising from the limited mandate of the development authority. In Durgapur the I.I.T. proposals for regional integration were not pursued and in Karachi the proposals to improve the agricultural productivity and water-resource base of the surrounding region were neglected. However, Ankara has been very successful in generating self-sustained internal growth. It appears that a government-based city can do this much more easily than a settlement based on primary industry, perhaps because government is essentially a labour intensive and services-oriented activity and a central government bureaucracy is not dependent on markets and other external factors. Indeed, it attracts business since there are many advantages for industries, professional organizations and service businesses in locating close to the centre of power and influence. We conclude from this brief review that both industry and government-based cities usually develop links with other urban areas of the country, but often at the cost of largely bypassing their own hinterlands and rural areas.

Another feature of new towns which are planned to modify the national spatial pattern is the long gestation and maturation period they need to undergo before becoming viable integrated communities. Durgapur is still in many ways a "company town". The small agricultural settlements of Pahang Tenggara have taken longer to develop than expected. Even Ankara, which is now such a rapidly growing city, took about 25 years from its inception before rapid growth occurred. This implies that a very careful look needs to be taken before a programme of new towns is initiated, particularly with respect to their costs and their promotion and management. A conservative view is needed of the lead time required before a new town can be self-supporting and of the costs to the national economy which are involved. The amount of new infrastructure which is required to establish the town and the costs of creating a job in that location against expanding facilities in existing settlements needs to be weighed against the probable political and long-term benefits of establishing a new settlement. A clear understanding of the function of a new settlement and how it will relate to the existing urban and rural employment structure is needed. And finally, when a decision is made to go ahead, the management of the new settlement and national policies regarding industrial and employment incentives and assistance need to be designed to give it the best chance of success.

WHO PLANS? WHO DECIDES?

Who Plans the City?

One issue that came up in several of the case studies was that of the role of foreign technical assistance *vis-à-vis* local initiatives in urban development. Foreign assistance can often play a catalytic and supportive role in planning for appropriate development, but there must be strong local interest, advocacy and commitment if a programme is to succeed. All of the more successful programmes described in this volume had the common feature of strong local support: China's rural development programming, Singapore's area licensing scheme and Jakarta's kampung improvement programme being three prominent examples. All were initiated without foreign technical or financial assistance.

The latter of these programmes provides a good illustration of the principles involved regarding this issue. Under the strong leadership of Jakarta's former Governor, Ali Sadikin, KIP originated as a locally initiated programme in 1969. To be sure, the basic upgrading approach had been strongly supported by international agencies whose representives had advocated this approach in Jakarta. But for 5 years the programme proceeded without foreign assistance, and it was not until 1974 that the World Bank became involved and helped to accelerate the programme. The Bank, perhaps wisely, did not suggest any major changes in the management and organisation of the programme but used its input to expand the scale and improve some of the design and distribution of services.

UDA's Salak South project provides a contrasting case. The basic initiative for what for Malaysia was to be an innovative sites and services cum upgrading project came from World Bank and UNDP planners. Key Malaysian policy-makers were not really convinced of the soundness of low-cost, "marginal" approaches to residential development for the poor, fearing that they would create slums in the future and expand assets to non-Malays. In the absence of underlying political support for this project, it was very doubtful that it could succeed.

In his discussion of public health and nutrition programmes, Samir Basta also brings up the role of the foreign planner and international funding agency. He stresses that the in-country political will must exist to give public health a high priority amongst other, more visible programmes. But even if the will is present at national and local levels, international assistance agencies may be too eager to provide money too quickly when the most urgent need is a gradual build-up of local manpower and acceptance of new ideas by the decision-makers. If foreign funders become too impatient, their support may be damaging rather than constructive.

Herbert offers, in his Karachi case, perhaps the most fascinating example of the relationships between numerous actors in the planning process, who in this case comprised international aid agencies, central and local government authorities, the military, three foreign consulting firms and local staff. Here again, the initiative for rational integrated planning came largely from the outside, and in any case did not include the real power structure. Given this veritable Tower of Babel, all participants having conflicting interests and viewpoints, it was surprising that the modest successes described were achieved at all.

There seem to be several lessons here. One is that an earlier and closer link with funds for specific purposes might have shortened the extent of argument and conflict. The second is that the most important outcome may be the mutual education of all parties which emerged from the discussion and effort which went in to the study. This can be especially useful for bureaucracies which may rarely discuss priorities or inter-sectoral relationships. Finally, it takes much longer than we imagine at the outset for even a partial concensus to emerge on concepts and policies. It seems that persistence and compromise are called for, with an early effort made to get something built, which will then help the momentum of future planning. In the absence of clear priorities and objectives enforced on all agencies, the answer to "who plans the city" must be "those holding land, money and political influence".

The second issue that needs to be addressed in connection with "who plans the city?" relates to that of the degree of participation of the local community which is appropriate under varying conditions. The Chapter 2 criterion of "participation, power and responsibility" dealt with this issue and stressed that the planning process should encourage a high degree of participation by local beneficiaries. But the key question would appear to be: participation for what purpose and at what scale? What is required is a crude model of participation in the planning process, which would attempt to deal with some of the most relevant variables. The caveat should be added at the outset that the manner in which such variables, and hence the model, are interpreted will not be the same in all societies. The meaning of community participation is very different in a democratic, industrialized, highly literate nation than it is in a nation whose people are generally illiterate and are emerging from a traditional society which is strongly hierarchical.

As discussed in Chapter 2, there are at least three main actors in the development process: the politicians (or decision-makers), the official planners (or technocrats), and the planned for (or users). Our particular concern at this point is the role played by the third group vis-à-vis the other two in making planning decisions about future urban development in a given situation. One important variable is the scale at which a planning decision is made, be it national, regional, urban or very local. If the decision is large scale (national), then the role of the people is different than if it is to be taken at the local level. In the latter case the need for local community participation is more compelling, whilst in the former the people's will may be more effectively transmitted through a hierarchy of representatives. This principle is well exemplified by China's rural development programme. Although the voice of ordinary people is rather faint at the national level, it is very strong at the level of the commune or village. Closely related to the issue of scale are the contrasting characteristics of rural versus urban settings with regard to the meaning and relevance of local participation. In rural areas, a high degree of co-operation and participation is built-in through the barter economy, greater personal control over time and frequent absence of external governmental support. Urban participation, on the other hand, must be structured, being less likely to occur naturally through voluntary efforts.

Especially in urban areas, therefore, we must ask the question "participation for what end?" That is, for what specific programmes and projects is local participation most relevant? In fact this question addresses the second major variable of our simple model, which is the nature of the decision involved. It seems to us that the crucial factor is the extent to which the decision affects people's lives. Is the decision affecting people's assets, such as their pocket book, ownership of property or some other key factor? If such assets are directly affected, then local people should be involved, whereas, if government is simply providing normal services, the level of community participation need not be so intensive.

The Jakarta and Manila upgrading programmes provide excellent samples of this point. Although the Jakarta KIP has been criticised for its lack of local participation, there is some question as to the degree of such participation necessary for a programme which merely provides basic infrastructure services with minimum taking of property and no payments by individual families. Part of KIP's success has been that it provides a relatively homogeneous, straightforward set of inputs that do not require a great deal of local participation. Consequently, the programme could be implemented efficiently with a minimum of manpower. As an upgrading programme expands its scope to deal with such matters as transfer of land ownership, direct recovery of costs from beneficiaries or generation of local employment opportunities, as in the case of Manila, greater participation in planning decisions by the local community would be indicated, despite the concomitant loss in efficiency and increase in manpower required for implementation.

In terms of planning the large-scale structure and spatial form of the city, two different pictures emerge. In the early stages of planning completely new towns, the physical planning authority and its consultants appear to play a primary role, but as we saw in Ankara, when more industries, population and other interest groups move into the city, the wide powers of the technocrats diminish. Their role will then inevitably change into that of initiators and stimulators in order to guide investments made by other parties. In Ankara they failed to take on this role and thus became largely irrelevant to the development of the city. In the case of expanding existing cities, financial planning and budgeting is more critical from the beginning, since existing line agencies such as the highway and port authorities, as in the case of Manila, have more influence and financial power than the city planners on the course of city growth. As we have seen in Karachi, the traditional land-owning elite may put pressures on infrastructure agencies to service the land they own, and consequently raise its value. Where government itself owns urban land, similar pressures may be applied to sell valuable land at a low price to influential groups. This often leads to development patterns which are both spatially inefficient and socially regressive, since the purchasing power of upper income groups and modern-sector industry and commerce is such that the small supply of developed land is instantly acquired for "high value" uses. The power of the owners of urban land also accounts for the reluctance of governments in many Asian countries to impose adequate development regulations or property taxes and explains why city governments are frequently kept weak in order to justify obtaining large subsidies from central government funds to pay for infrastructure development. In a rural context, Pahang Tenggara illustrates a similar case of the interests and control over land affecting both planning, financing and implementation of a regional development scheme.

Returning to the key issue at hand, however, what lessons can be learned from the case studies as to the degree and nature of local community participation which is appropriate in planning the overall development of large cities? In discussing the Karachi planning effort whose lack of community participation was acknowledged as a major weakness, Herbert offers two reasons for "a genuine involvement of the ultimate user in the planning and development process". Firstly, programme and project design will be more sensitive to their real needs and realistic in terms of their resources if users are consulted at the planning stage. And secondly, the chances of sustained implementation despite possible changes in agencies, funding or even governments will be greater if user groups - especially the low-income majority who are least able to form interest groups and bring effective pressure to bear on decision-makers - participate in both programme formulation and implementation. We would offer yet a third reason which is relevant both to large-scale development (as in Metro Karachi) as well as to local projects (as in the Jakarta KIP).

This is that maintenance of physical and social infrastructures will be much greater if users are involved in planning and building them - and hence think of them as their own. However, none of the case studies, including Karachi, offer much insight as to precisely how this process of user participation should be organised and carried out.

Who Builds the City?

In addition to the question of who plans the city, the case studies in this volume have made us aware of the fact that there can be a wide range of initiators or prime implementors of development. The institutions who build the city are widely scattered over the surfaces described by a three-dimensional matrix. One dimension involves public versus private sector institutions; the second describes the scale and allegiance of the institution - whether it is a municipal, metropolitan, provincial or central government authority; and the third dimension is whether the institution's functions are single or multi-activity. These institutional dimensions were discussed in Part One of this volume: the general roles of government, private sector and self-help activities were raised under the theme, the "Role of Government", in Chapter 1; whilst the specific roles of planning institutions were mentioned under the final theme in Chapter 1 and under the heading "Managing the Planning Process" in Chapter 2.

A review of the case studies indicates three general categories with regard to the first dimension. First, there are situations which involved implementation essentially by the public sector. In China, for example, the government-initiated production brigades play a key development role. Although Singapore stands as a major centre of capitalism in Southeast Asia, the city state was primarily built by large scale government agencies. Second, at the other extreme are situations in which implementation was carried out largely by the private sector. Despite its importance as a government centre, for instance, most of Ankara's development - commercial, industrial and especially residential - has been carried out by many small and medium-sized private companies and the major public service agencies are either private sector or public corporations.

The third general category involves mixed public and private implementors. For example, Durgapur was largely built by a series of separate, mostly public sector, industries, each of which developed both factories and residential quarters for many of the workers. Although ostensibly public sector, these institutions tend to behave much the same as would private sector firms. Malaysian developments also involve a characteristic mixture of public and private sector institutions. Although UDA is public, it enters the private sector (real estate) arena and there functions very much like a private firm. But its aim is to achieve certain public policy goals. However, most development in Kuala Lumpur is in the private sector. Pahang Tenggara also represents a mixed situation in which the means of agricultural production are largely in private hands, but the settlements are built by government.

Do the case studies furnish us with any insight as to the relative effectiveness of public versus private sector institutions? In view of the categories just enumerated, it would appear that public agency initiative is frequently important in dealing with many of the difficult urban problems of Asian LDCs. Despite very different political systems, both China and Singapore have implemented comparatively successful development programmes with public agencies. As both the Ankara and Karachi cases point out, on the other hand, the political will must exist before a society recognizes that government must take strong initiative in solving an intractable problem such as that of shelter for low-income families. But the case studies also show that government must function as a catalyst whose actions stimulate further actions on the part of the private sector or individuals. We see this multiplier effect operating quite successfully with the Jakarta and Manila upgrading programmes where public infrastructure investments have stimulated spontaneous self-help investments in housing and other facilities. Malaysia's UDA should have played a similar catalytic role in the Salak South and other projects, but the tensions between conflicting institutional objectives has reduced that agency's role. In the final analysis, however, it would seem that the quality of management of a given agency or city is more important than whether it is public or private sector. For instance, although Durgapur was built largely by public institutions, the multiplicity of agencies, poor relationship of planning and implementation agencies, and diffused management of urban development activities led to a number of problems.

Many of the public agencies discussed in the case studies are central government bodies with the exceptions of the KDA in Karachi, and the KIP operations in Indonesia which are almost entirely local government, and the Hong Kong and Singapore agencies which, of course, are both national and local. They tend to owe their allegiance to the central government which makes planning and inter-sectoral programming at the city scale very difficult. There may also be antagonisms between the central agency and the local government, all of which makes effective implementation difficult, as was the case between UDA and the City government and between DARA and the State of Pahang.

With regard to the single or multi-activity functions, the case studies point up at least three different categories.

First, there are situations in which planning and implementation functions are combined within a single agency, such as with Singapore's area licensing scheme, and both Hong Kong's and Singapore's housing programmmes.(4) At the other extreme are cases in which the planning and implementation functions are basically carried out by separate agencies, be they public or private. This situation was essentially the case in Ankara, Karachi and Durgapur. The third category falls in between, where planning and part of the implementation is conducted by one agency, but other agencies are also responsible for pieces of implementation of a given programme. This was the case with Malaysia's UDA, with DARA in Pahang Tenggara, with KIP in Jakarta and with the ZIP and MMINUTE programmes in Manila. Based on the experiences in the case studies it would seem that, where a highly integrated operation is involved, such as a housing or upgrading development involving movement of people and multiple works on one site and simultaneous linkages to off-site services, there are clear advantages in having a single agency to do the work. An exception to this is the KIP in Jakarta. Here, however, all of the implementing agencies are controlled by the city, and the city government has an extremely effective planning and coordinating mechanism. Where many activities disparate in space and character are involved, such as the numerous sectoral developments in large urban areas, a single agency is usually impractical and inadequate. Here the need for a powerful planning and budgeting function becomes relatively more important, and it would seem from the present experience in Manila that the implementing agencies themselves should be part of the coordinating and budgeting body. But the case studies demonstrate that there are a range of institutional options which should be based on the cultural and administrative traditions of the country.

HOW TO PLAN AND BUILD?

Ineffectiveness of Planning Divorced from Implementation

Daniel Burnham, architect of the Plan of Chicago (1907), was once quoted as saying "Make no little plans . . ." but, on the basis of the case studies of planning practice presented in this volume, the adage might be changed to "Beware of Big Plans, for they are more likely to be divorced from what can realistically be implemented". Although urban planners are tempted to create comprehensive, long-range planning documents, it would appear that the connection between such products and the possibilities of implementation is frequently inadequate. This was true in Pahang Tenggara where an ambitious regional plan failed to chart a realistic framework for implementation. It also appears to be a danger in Karachi, where the planning in being comprehensive may have failed to focus early enough on specific projects which would justify and reinforce the planning activity. It was also true in Ankara where three "master" plans failed to produce usable guidelines for actually channelling the city's growth and solving its increasingly critial and pressing problems. The case of Ankara also serves to point up the irrelevancy and inadequacy of using competitions as the basis for planning, in part because they place too much emphasis on the product rather than the process.

More than anything else, however, Ankara demonstrated that the traditional master planning approach, as described in Chapter 1, is irrelevant to accommodating growth and solving problems of urban areas. This approach is too inflexible, cumbersome and static to cope with the dynamic growth and change taking place in the typical LDC city. It fails to address the strategic nature of development in space and time, presenting only a static map of the city at some future point in time. That point in time is 20 years away, and the plan is vague as to the exact short-term programming necessary to achieve the long-term goal. A related problem is that large numbers of professional personnel are required to prepare detailed physical plans prior to development, but these personnel simply are not available - at least not in the immediate future in most LDCs. Frequently, the master-planning approach also fails to address the most critical needs of an urban area, such as provision of low-income residential settlements, creation of employment opportunities, or development of public transport systems. It would not be necessary to level such an elaborate criticism at physical master planning were it not for the fact that the approach is still being used in many LDC countries today, and hence a concerted effort needs to be made to document its failures. In the case of Ankara, the goal was to produce a "planned garden city" by means of technocratic physical planning but, despite the city's growth success, today's reality falls far short of the goal. In addition to all of the above problems, investments in roads, public transport and cheap land for settlement of low-income migrants failed to keep pace with demand. As an example of "economic master planning" at the regional scale,(5) the slow pace in implementing the Pahang Tenggara Master Plan also points up the limitations of that approach.

Generally speaking, the more successful programmes involved what were characterized in Chapter 1 as either the "current predominant paradigm" or the "tentative model" of planning practice. The emphasis in either instance was on achieving a close connection between planning, programming, budgeting, implementation, evaluation and feedback; that is, on a dynamic model in which "planning" and "implementation" are viewed as inseparable parts of the same process. With the exception of Karachi, these successful programmes were not comprehensive in scope, but concentrated on more narrowly focused proposals within specific sectors. Although their objectives tended to be more limited, programming was carried out to maximize coordination with related activities and implementation was vigorous. Examples of such narrowly focused programmes are found in Singapore's ALS, the Jakarta and Tondo upgrading efforts, and Hong Kong/Singapore public housing. Actually, these cases come closer to what Chapter 1 described as the current predominant paradigm, but in several respects they also fit the ideal model, especially in terms of these dynamic and flexible qualities.

Determining the Nature of Solutions Appropriate to the Problem

The case studies' descriptions of successes and failures in implementing urban development throw some light on the match of solutions with the problems and on whether these problems were correctly diagnosed in the first place. One important question is, given limited resources, whether one should expand the supply of services, or limit the demand for them. There is no doubt that, with the expansion of population in LDC cities, service networks need considerable expansion. Rather, the issue is whether these services should be expanded for all sectors and for all demands made upon them. The case of transport is a notable example where expansion of car ownership among upper- and middle-income groups may increase demand for major new road networks which are extremely expensive and can pre-empt resources from other services which may be required to satisfy more basic needs. The Singapore ALS scheme is a remarkable example where, instead of automatically expanding road networks, the planners have focused on restricting the excessive demands of higher income groups for an increasing share of the city's road space and its financial resources. Interest in this approach has been growing and now road pricing schemes are being implemented in Kuala Lumpur and Bangkok, although they are meeting more resistance from car-owning interest groups.

Examples of the opposite attitude can be cited in the housing sector where many countries have responded to influential groups, including government and military employees, to supply expensive, completed housing units and subsidised credit to buy them, thus reducing resources for expanding a more basic need in the same sector, namely the supply of serviced land for lower income groups. Pressures in this direction can be observed in both the Karachi and Kuala Lumpur (UDA) cases. On a broader scale, China has attempted to reduce urban migration partly through denying the expansion of jobs and services in large urban areas, although other socialist countries such as Cuba and Tanzania may have been more successful in this respect.

This leads to another issue - that of priorities. Samir Basta points out that, although the average level of health in urban areas may be higher than that in rural areas, the urban slums often show much worse health indices than rural villages. Yet the response of the health system is often to continue to provide hospitals which can be used by relatively few people instead of more broadly based health care at the community level. The priorities of low-income groups are usually for more basic services than those demanded by higher-income groups who have already satisfied their basic needs. It would seem that one of the most important functions for planners is to help determine the investment priorities both among service sectors and within each sector.

In order to supply these basic services to many people at a price which they and the city can afford, the design standards and costs of the service must be low, yet able to be improved over time if incomes increase. Both the KIP in Jakarta and the Tondo project in Manila demonstrate that this is possible and at the same time extremely popular with the people, despite the initial reservations expressed by architects and engineers before the programmes got underway. In the rural towns of Pahang Tenggara standards are now being reduced in order to keep within budgets and to prepare basic "reception areas" for the new migrants as fast as possible.

Once the priorities are clear and affordable standards determined, how comprehensive should the solutions be? It is usually agreed that an important goal is to eliminate the problem of the backlog in service. The question then arises as to whether the solution should be a multi-faceted, extensive approach or whether to concentrate on one or two sectors. This again may rest on the extent of the problem, the availability of trained staff and the ability of the planning process to coordinate many activities. One of the reasons for the success of KIP in Jakarta in providing basic services to almost the entire city in 10 years seems to be that it concentrated on only a few services in a systematic, city-wide programme which avoided difficult issues such as land acquisition, tenure and direct cost recovery. In Manila it has been realised that the extensive approach of ZIP will have to be supplemented by the simpler MMINUTE programme in order to deal with the backlog in services within a reasonable time period. Basta also makes a plea for a simpler approach, starting with a few elements and adding more later as experience grows. If some of the components are both innovative and small relative to the primary activities of the implementing agency, they may assume a low priority. On the other hand, use of several agencies for similar tasks can increase output providing the tasks are clearly defined and well coordinated. In a multi-sectoral programme, much will depend on the ability and interest of the lead agency to promote, coordinate and supervise all the components of the programme and on its leverage over other implementing agencies.

Tools and Techniques for Implementation

The case studies stress that one critical technique for ensuring implementation is to establish a strong linkage between spatial planning, programming and budgeting, as described in Chapter 1's tentative model of planning practice. This linkage has a clear temporal dimension, in which long-term planning is positioned at one end of a continuum and annual programming/budgeting at the other. A second dimension is sectoral, in that economic, social and spatial/physical aspects need to be tied together. Even if the inputs from a particular programme are not "comprehensive" in sectoral terms, it is important that a mechanism is developed in the government to maximize coordination between sectors and over time. In this regard, there appear to be three points at which coordination is often lacking and frequent "splits" occur: (1) There is the split between sectoral plans and spatial integration, in which priorities within given sectors come into conflict with the optimum intersectoral approach. (2) There is the split between vertical levels of governement (i.e. generally between national and local levels), especially over who controls and allocates public investments. (3) Finally, there is the split between various functions in the implementation process - such as land acquisition, infrastructure and superstructure development - especially if different agencies are responsible for different functions.

The case studies point up some of these coordination problems. In the planning of Durgapur, for instance, the sectoral needs of specific industries tended to take precedence over the need to develop a spatially integrated citywide plan. In the case of the Urban Development Authority in Kuala Lumpur, implementation was hampered both by rivalries between national versus local agencies, and also because authority was split between the land acquisition, squatter relocation and project implementation functions. In Karachi the greatest challenge of planning involved improving the efficiency and clarifying the social objectives of existing agencies, none of which were guided by a common development philosophy. The difficulty of forging a coherent indigenous vision of the city's future, plus insufficient attention by the planning team to early project execution, seems to have contributed to the mixed results of this experience. Perhaps, if the institutional mechanisms for controlling and allocating funds had been addressed earlier and at a national as well as a local level, a greater measure of agreement on project composition, standards and timing could have been obtained.

Another lesson-for-implementation that can be learned from some of the case studies is the need to carefully examine alternative policies and tools for solving a problem. Rather than rely on conventional solutions which may have been developed elsewhere, it is preferable to seek out cheaper approaches which may satisfy basic needs and remain in balance with available resources more effectively. Such an approach implies maximum utilisation of existing facilities, assets and institutions, instead of creation of new ones. The criteria discussed in Chapter 2 under the heading, "Matching Actions with Resources", deal with various aspects of this least-cost approach.

The Singapore area licensing scheme provides a positive example of this rule. The planners' strategy was to maximise utilisation of the capacity of the central area's existing street system before building costly new highways. In formulating their scheme, the local planners exercised considerable imagination - and no Western city has yet been able to implement such a solution. Upgrading programmes of the kind being carried out in Jakarta or Manila demonstrate a similar effort to utilise existing facilities, the housing stock in these cases, and thus to conserve on resources and costs. By improving existing neighbourhoods, rather than tearing them down and rebuilding, these programmes stretch limited resources much further to satisfy the basic needs of their cities' households more effectively. This principle can pertain to institutions as well as facilities, as we can see in the case of the Karachi development programme. One of the most important administrative recommendations of the planning team was that specific actions and programmes must be within the capacities of existing public and/or private institutions, at least in the relatively short run.

The studies in Part Two also furnish some negative cases of where existing facilities and institutions have not been utilised. For example, new towns as represented by both Ankara and Durgapur have generally been shown to be more costly with regard to public infrastructures than it would be to expand selected existing urban areas. But even if we accept that each of the two cities in question had ample justification for being built, it is difficult to defend Durgapur's very high capital costs and extravagent use of land. There is also a need to make use of existing institutions before creating elaborate new ones. In this context Malaysia's Urban Development Authority may not be fully justified as an institution, given the existence of state development corporations and several other federal agencies which could have shared a similar mandate.

Some Key Factors for Successful Planning and Implementation

Although a number of factors have already been mentioned, such as the need to link planning closely with implementation via the programming/budgeting mechanism, it would be useful to provide a check-list of some of the other factors required for good programmes which stem from the case studies.

Good public relations:

First, as exemplified by the Singapore area licensing scheme, it is critical to the success of any such programme to provide adequate publicity well beforehand and to inform the users of the alternatives they will have under the programme. Although the A.L.S. may appear on the face of it to be restrictive, it encompassed a package of alternatives which included improved bus services, park-and-ride facilities, etc.

Competent management:

Secondly, it is essential that the programme have competent management. This factor actually encompasses all the others. But, perhaps most importantly, the programme should be implemented with fairness and firmness. Having set a particular course of action, no exceptions are granted and all persons are treated in the same say within the framework of the policy. It is also important that the institutional basis for carrying out particular programmes be streamlined so that responsibility is clearly allocated. This was the case, for example, with the housing programmes in both Hong Kong and Singapore.

Consistency and clarity:

Programmes have a much better chance of success if there is consistency in policy and clarity in defining responsibilities between different levels of government and different agencies. Cases differing as widely as the Huaxi village building effort and the Indonesian Kampung Improvement Programme provide positive examples.

Sound personnel policies:

A fourth factor is a series of sound personnel policies within the implementing agency. These include a clear definition of job responsibilities and also decentralisation of responsibilities to the maximum extent possible. Another aspect here, of which Basta reminds us in his discussion of problems with voluntary community health workers, is that, if a programme wants good personnel, it must pay them a salary commensurate with their contribution.

Fiscal responsibility:

Several factors revolve around the aspect of fiscal responsibility. In particular, there is a need to generate local revenues by various means, a criterion which was mentioned in Chapter 2 as "Replicability, Affordability and Cost Recovery". First, a programme can be used as a lever to improve the tax base, as in the case of the Jakarta KIP. Secondly, consumer charges can be levied, as occurred with the Singapore A.L.S. It is important to look for opportunities for direct cost recovery from a programme's beneficiaries as with the Tondo and ZIP upgrading programmes. But perhaps the most essential element for fiscal responsibility is that each urban area formulate an overall financial programme which balances costs with revenues. As an example, the housing programmes of Singapore and Hong Kong have involved subsidies, but were possible because the city states have efficient tax-collection systems.

Flexibility:

The criterion of flexibility in planning and implementation was mentioned in Chapter 2 under the heading "Adaptability, Uncertainty and Risk". At the outset, flexibility should be a guiding principle of any initial planning strategy. This is illustrated by a number of recommendations in the Karachi development programme which stressed low-risk coupled with considerable flexibility in the choice of development locations and types of technologies. Many current planning products, however, tend to ensure the major proposals in laws and regulations which discourage the necessary subsequent modifications. Finally, as implementation proceeds, any successful urban development programme should be frequently evaluated and the lessons learned fed back into improving the programme. Again, as demonstrated by the Singapore/Hong Kong housing experience, standards have been raised when appropriate and, in the case of Hong Kong, remaining squatter areas have finally been accepted. Any good programme must build in an effective and practical monitoring and evaluation mechanism so that changes can be made before problems become insoluble.

WHAT IMPACTS OF DEVELOPMENT?

Short-term Versus Long-Term Returns

By synthesising experiences, what are some of the lessons that can be drawn from the cases with regard to one of the key variables mentioned in Chapter 1, the balance between short-term and long-range planning? From the case studies, it would seem a good argument can be made in favour of a short-term view of planning and development. There are several reasons for this. The backlog of services in existing cities in most LDCs is enormous and, as we have seen in Jakarta and Manila, addressing these immediate needs can yield dramatic improvements within a short period. Although it is difficult to determine, the resulting improvements in health and well-being will probably lead to higher productivity and incomes especially if, as in Tondo, there are increased opportunities for rental income and expansion of small business and female employment. The adage would seem to be to start where the people's needs and opportunities are and work from there. A short-term view may thus lead to higher short and long-term returns. Moreover, programmes to assist immediate needs are frequently more easily managed and have more political support than those focused on the long term, and they are thus more likely to be successful. Another advantage of the short-term view is that, in the volatile and fast-changing conditions of the present day world, especially in LDCs, what may seem to be a desirable long-term plan now may not appear that way within a few years when both external conditions and the perception of the problems have changed. The comparative success of most of those cases which have stressed short-term programming and implementation - which includes not only Jakarta-Manila upgrading, but Hong Kong-Singapore public housing, China's rural development and Singapore ALS - give testimony to these advantages.

However, there are dangers in a short-term view. As the studies of UDA and Pahang Tenggara show, attempts to bring low-income Malays quickly into the sophisticated world of urban real estate and plantation management may be too quick a jump and result in expanding the gap between the existing commercial entrepreneurs and those coming from low-income, rural origins. In this sense, starting from where people are and developing a network of manageable alternatives may yield more solid long-term returns.

There are sometimes other concerns which argue against a short-term view and which may offer important structural changes over time. Chief among these are political and regional considerations which could justify higher costs than a more narrow economic view would indicate. This was the case with Ankara which provided a base for the entrepreneurial class emerging from the dissolution of the Ottoman empire and which stimulated the economic expansion of towns in Anatolia and eastern Turkey. The development of Pahang Tenggara is also likely to lead to strengthening the economic power of the east coast states of Malaysia, although it will probably perpetuate the existing economic base of the country. To be successful, long-term planning should clearly be based on a realistic estimate of the potentials, resources and constraints of the country, and of the specific regions and settlements it wishes to help.

Turning to issues of planning within the city, some trade-off may be necessary between satisfying the immediate needs of the present generation and planning an efficient and liveable city for the future ones. Often one of the problems of dense central areas in LDC cities is a severe lack of open space for recreation and relaxation. It may not be desirable or possible to remove existing built-up areas in favour of large amounts of recreation space, but the opportunities should be taken in planning city expansion and regulating development at the urbanising perimeters to provide enough space for public needs. While avoiding excessive use of land, spatial planning should aim for a "loose fit". Techniques such as land re-adjustment used in Japan, Taiwan and Korea can help to obtain public space without heavy costs to the government. In this context, even the more successful short-term action programmes reveal some limitations. The Jakarta and Manila upgrading efforts, for instance, while concentrating on local improvements within existing built-up areas, cause policy-makers to lose sight of the needs for city-wide systems and for programmes of expansion on the urban periphery. And the earlier resettlement estates in Hong Kong, while praised in the short term for their use of realistically low standards, were criticised in the longer run for their inability to adapt to changing circumstances.

The planning initiative in Karachi is probably the best example among the case studies of an effort to define clear policy and programme alternatives, then combine the long-, medium-and short-term perspectives into a rational development programme, which, had the operating environment been more positive, could have led to a greater number of the proposals being implemented. As Herbert stresses, limited technical skills should not "be wasted on elaborate long-range planning of the kind traditionally associated with 'master plans' - work that will be out of date long before the proposals associated with it can be implemented. Instead, the skills which are available should be focused on implementable projects designed to deal with urgent and major issues, with the effort spent on long-range programming being just sufficient to provide a sensible framework for project identification."

Social Impacts of Physical Development

Among developed countries, interest in physical development of urban areas has recently tended to take a back seat and direct social programmes have become more important for achieving social welfare goals. Perhaps this is mainly because the most essential physical services have already been provided. In LDCs, on the other hand, most urban dwellers still live in unhealthy and insecure conditions, and in this context provision of physical services can yield very positive social impacts. As part of the upgrading programmes in Jakarta and Manila, social surveys were made of the residents' priorities. The highest priorities almost invariably turned out to be employment, security of tenure, physical services, education, health and recreation facilities. In Singapore, new housing developments are planned with adequate space for recreational activities, and in the Manila ZIP small parks and playspaces are being fitted into the existing physical structure of the settlements. But the need for new infrastructure should not obscure the importance of maintenance, often the Cinderella of municipal services. Especially where low standards are used, maintenance becomes very important to prevent rapid deterioration as the experience of the first years of the Jakarta KIP has shown. Where maintenance is poor and intensity of use is heavy, it is important to look at the life-cycle costs of an investment rather than only the initial capital costs. Related maintenance activities such as solid waste collection are extremely important and without these considerations the positive impacts of capital works may only have a short-term effect.

Negative social impacts from physical development are a recurring theme in the history of many housing and public works agencies in LDCs, although our case studies have not been selected to emphasise these periods. Two influences continually threaten the living environments of LDC cities. One is the impact of large, space-consuming projects such as roads, cultural centres and, in the case of the private sector, commercial and hotel developments. They tend to displace more poor people than similar projects in Western countries, due to the very high densities in low-income central areas of LDC cities. There is not only a clear need to plan facilities to avoid disrupting existing communities wherever possible, but also to look to alternative solutions, as exemplified in Singapore's ALS, which would avoid the need for extensive disruption. Another pressure with similar impacts often originates from planners, architects and politicians who sometimes feel embarrassed that the city does not look "modern" enough and wish to clear away unsightly slum and squatter areas. These motives often coincide with the interests of real estate developers who wish to redevelop central area land into higher value and more profitable uses. In many LDC cities efforts have been made from time to time to clear slum areas but, apart from the exceptional cases of Singapore and Hong Kong, the economic, social and political costs have been found to be too high for comprehensive redevelopment, since this may often entail tearing down 20 to 60 percent of the city. The economic and social costs of disruption are often magnified by inadequate compensation or lack of suitable alternative sites for those affected. Fortunately, in recent years the futility and social costs of this approach are becoming more widely recognised. A conceptual weakness of this "city-beautiful" attitude to urban development is that it fails to recognise that highly integrated, mixed land uses and activities are needed for the economic and social advancement of the poor who do not have sufficient income or stable jobs to bear higher transport costs, and that more segregated land uses will increase the number of trips in the city and consequently the need for more road space. It is fortunate that an increasing number of young architects and planners from LDCs feel that the vitality and variety of their cities offer a distinct advantage in human terms over the lifeless character of much of the monumental building of the last three decades. This appreciation of the value of the social and economic complexity of existing settlements comes over strongly in the Tondo and ZIP upgrading activities in Manila.

Environmental Impacts

In Chapter 2 we observed that land-extensive development in rural areas often created more severe impact on the natural environment than does urban development, which is more limited in area. The ecological problems created by Pahang Tenggara's development are a case in point. But within their land areas the settlement of Asian cities has created severe negative impacts on water resources, air quality and soil, mainly due to their high residential densities, lack of sanitation and treatment systems, and poor collection and disposal of solid wastes. As Basta notes, this has in turn severely affected the health and well-being of their poorer residents. Curative measures, especially for the collection and treatment of sewage and major improvements in macro-drainage, are usually prohibitively expensive.

As we noted earlier when discussing the needs for open space and recreation, preventive measures may hold more chance of success than curative ones. Guiding new developments away from environmentally sensitive areas such as water sources, aquifer recharge areas, swamps and steep slopes, through improved legal regulation and control, is one line of action. Even more effective would be complementary efforts, as have been made in Singapore, to direct new roads, services and employment centres along suitable corridors of development in order to make settlement attractive in these directions, and relieve the pressure to settle in more ecologically sensitive locations. But once all this has been done, settlement is still likely to occur unless these sensitive areas are used and protected. If the land is to be kept open, then appropriate uses such as recreation, forestry, agriculture or aquaculture should be encouraged. In Jakarta, for example, the canal banks which have not been squatted on are generally those which have been leased to local people for vegetable and flower gardens. If clear responsibility for protecting and using certain areas is given to specific individuals or communities, there is much less chance of violation.

Another problem in cities with steep land, such as Kuala Lumpur, Ankara or Seoul, is the way in which these slopes are developed. The worst offenders are the developers of high- and middle-income housing estates and industrial sites, who strip and heavily terrace the land, thus causing severe erosion, river siltation and consequent flooding. It may not be possible to prevent all development on such land, but regulations could be made for appropriate site planning and development practices and penalties exacted on developers who failed to conform.

In summary, the lack of knowledge and skills concerning good environmental land-use practice is causing many problems which could be avoided. There is a need to develop an environmental information system for each large city which can form the basis for environmental policies and regulations, and which can be used both by those who are formulating spatial and sectoral plans, and by private developers, to check the suitability of their proposals.

NOTES

(1) This distinction relates to the theme discussed in Chapter 1, "The Nature of Power and Decision-making", in which major issues include the degree of political control vis-à-vis individual freedom and the extent to which power should be decentralized within a nation.

(2) It will be interesting to see whether this anti-urban stance continues under Teng Hsiao-ping's current modernisation programme.

(3) An exception is recent development in the agricultural areas around Adana. However, this is probably due more to major investments in irrigation and mechanisation of agriculture in this area than to any impact from Ankara.

(4) A related factor is whether there should be a single or several public agencies functioning within a given sector such as housing. Both the Singapore and Hong Kong housing experiences suggest advantages of the former option, but present work in Manila, where the Ministry of Public Works is implementing one type of upgrading programme (MMINUTE) and the National Housing Authority another (ZIP), indicates that the strengths of several agencies can be used, providing there is a strong mechanism for coordination and programming.

(5) See the discussion of economic master planning as a regional variant of the traditional paradigm of planning practice in Chapter 1.

Biographical Notes

AMATO, PETER W.

A U.S. national, he is Professor of Urban and Regional Planning, University of Wisconsin, Madison, and has been a member of the faculty since 1967. He holds a B. Architecture and M.S. (Urban Planning) from Columbia University, and a Ph.D (Urban and Regional Planning) from Cornell University. He was formerly Consultant and Project Chief, Puerto Rico Housing and Urban Development Administration, Consultant to U.S. AID mission in El Salvador; and United Nations Project Manager with the Malaysian Urban Development Authority, Kuala Lumpur, Malaysia. Recently Professor Amato acted as consultant on national urbanisation issues in Egypt and is presently on leave serving as Behaviorial Science Advisor-Urban Analyst, USAID, Cairo. Professor Amato has published widely in the area of housing, land use and urbanisation issues in developing economies.

BASTA, SAMIT SANAD

Was born in Cario in 1943. He holds a Doctor of Science Degree in Nutrition from Massachusetts Institute of Technology, USA, and Bachelor of Science Degree (Honors) from Surrey University, England. In 1968 he was appointed as research fellow at the National Institute of Nutrition, Ministry of Health, Mexico, where he worked on milk production of low-income lactating women and on growth of malnourished children; in 1970 he was accepted as research assistant and doctoral student at M.I.T., Cambridge, Massachusetts. His initial work was on protein synthesis and molecular biology, and subsequent work on public health problems in developing nations, with particular emphasis on anaemia, parasite diseases and productivity. In 1972 Dr. Basta was appointed Editor of the International Nutrition Congress. In 1974 he was employed at the World Bank as nutrition consultant and helped to initiate the work of the Nutrition Unit. After being accepted to the Young Professional Program of the World Bank, Dr. Basta was appointed Nutrition Expert first with the Urban Projects Department, where he specialised in Health/Nutrition programmes directed at slum and squatter populations, and later as Nutrition Expert and Project Officer in the World Bank's Nutrition Division. Currently, he is Nutrition Expert to the new Population, Health and Nutrition Department of the World Bank where he is heavily involved in evaluation and preparation of nutrition projects in a number of countries.

DRAKAKIS-SMITH, D.W.

A British national, he received his initial degrees from the University of Wales, and his doctorate was awarded from the University of Hong Kong whilst he was a lecturer in the Department of Geography. During this period he undertook research on urban housing problems in Southeast Asia. Dr. Drakakis-Smith then moved to the University of Durham in the United Kingdom, and during this period undertook fieldwork in Turkey, again on urban housing problems. He is currently a Research Fellow in the Research School of Pacific Studies at the Australian National University. In recent years he has undertaken research in Southeast Asia, the Pacific and more recently on problems of Aboriginal under-development in Australia. He is the author of many papers on urban development, has written three monographs, and is about to publish a book, Housing and The Development Process, with Croom-Helm.

HERBERT, JOHN D.

Born in New Zealand, he is an urban and regional planner and economist. He obtained his degree in architecture from the University of New Zealand, and his Masters in City Planning from Berkeley in 1958. He received his doctorate in city and regional planning from Pennsylvania in 1964. He is presently Senior Vice-President of PADCO, Inc. and has worked as principal in charge of regional development planning projects in the Cameroons (1979), Sumatra, Indonesia (1978-1980) and

San Salvador (1976-1978). He was Head Planner on metropolitan planning projects in Karachi, Pakistan (1971-76), Port-au-Prince, Haiti (1973-1976), Santiago, Chile (1970), Brazil (1969-1970) and Ecuador (1969). He was the Senior Planner in the Ford Foundation's Advisory Group in Calcutta (1966-1968), and has consulted on several occasions with the World Bank and U.S. AID. Earlier he worked in the United States and Canada and taught planning in the Universities of California and Pennsylvania. He is the author of several publications on urban planning practice and policy.

HOLLAND, EDWARD P.

A U.S. national, he became an economist after a career in aeronautical research and development during and after World War II. He received his Ph.D. in Economics in 1958 from the Massachusetts Institute of Technology, where he remained as a research associate in the Center for International Studies until 1961. There, and later in Venezuela, he carried out some of the first computer simulations of the dynamics of developing national economies. After 2 years in the U.S. Agency for International Development in Washington, he joined the World Bank staff in 1969, working at first on macroeconomic analysis and later in the field of transportation. He took part in the supervision of urban transportation studies in several cities of less-developed countries and was proposing a study of possible schemes for restraining traffic in Singapore when officials there told him they had already decided on a scheme and were getting ready to implement it. He requested and was given permission to monitor the effects of their action, and thus the study reported here was initiated. Dr. Holland retired from the World Bank at the end of 1977 and now does occasional consulting work.

KIRKBY, RICHARD

Was born in Britain and received his degree in Geography from Bristol University and Diploma in Architecture from the Architectural Association, London. After a brief spell in Local Authority Planning in London he spent some time in Poland studying the planning system. He first visited China in 1973, then lived in Nanking from 1975 to 1977 where he was employed as an English Language Advisor to the University. From 1977 to 1978 he was a research member in the Universities Service Centre, Hong Kong. He returned to the People's Republic from 1978 to February 1980 where he was employed by Shandong University. His chief purpose in China and Hong Kong was to learn more about Chinese urban problems. Mr. Kirkby has contributed a number of articles on urban development to professional journals and is presently preparing a manuscript entitled "Perspectives on Chinese Urbanism" to be published by Pergamon Press in 1981.

OKYAY, TARIK

A Turkish national, he holds a B.Sc. in Civil Engineering, Robert College, Istanbul, a Masters Degree in City Planning, Middle East Technical University, Ankara, and a Masters Degree in Transportation and Environmental Planning, Birmingham University, England. He later took his Ph.D. Degree, Department of Geography, Bristol University, England. He has worked as a regional planner in the State Planning Organisation, Ankara, Turkey. He is presently lecturing in the City and Regional Planning Department, METU, Ankara.

SIVARAMAKRISHNAN, K.C.

An Indian national, he was educated at Loyola College, Madras University, where he received a B.A. with honours in Economics and Politics in 1955 and a B.L. at the Law College in 1958. Later that year he joined the Indian Administrative Service. In 1963, after a spell of magisterial and administrative work in the districts of West Bengal province, he shifted to the urban field. He was Director of the Asansol Planning Organisation, engaged in preparing a regional development plan for a mining and industrial conurbation. Later he was Chief Executive Office of the Durgapur Development Authority. In 1970 he became Secretary of the Calcutta Metropolitan Development Authority where he was responsible for implementing a multi-sectoral development programme in metropolitan Calcutta. During 1976/77, a Homi Bhabha Fellow and visiting Professor at the Indian Institute of Management, Calcutta, he was engaged in writing a book on new towns in India and directing a comparative study on the organisational framework for metropolitan development in Calcutta, Bombay, Madras and New Delhi. Mr. Sivaramakrishnan was a Parvin Fellow at the Woodrow Wilson School of Public and International Affairs, Princeton University, during 1964/65 where he participated in an urban affairs programme. He has contributed frequently to journals and has lectured at several universities in India, the U.S.A. and Canada. He has also been a consultant with the Economic Development Institute (World Bank), the UN, the Asian Development Institute, etc. Mr. Sivaramakrishnan has been with the Economic Development Institute of the World Bank since July 1977.

TAYLOR, JOHN L.

A U.S. citizen, he received his BA from Oberlin College in 1957 and his Masters in urban planning at Pratt Institute, New York, and is a Ph.D. candidate in the same field from the University of California at Los Angeles. He is presently the UNICEF consultant on urban planning in Indonesia. From 1978 to 1980, he worked on developing a national training strategy for provincial, regency and urban planning officials in Indonesia under a USAID Contract. Earlier, he worked in Calcutta on urban/regional planning and training with the Ford Foundation (1965-1968) and on community development and comprehensive planning in the United States (1959-1964). From 1968 to 1970, Mr. Taylor directed the Brooklyn office of the New York City Department of City Planning. He has taught planning theory and practice at the Asian Institute of Technology in Bangkok and, from 1973 to 1976, was Associate Professor and Head of the Graduate Planning Programme in the School of Housing, Building and Planning at the Universiti Sains Malaysia. He is the author of a number of studies and reports related to planning and settlement activities.

TEKELI, ILHAN

A Turkish national, he obtained his M.Sc. in Civil Engineering, Istanbul Technical University, his Masters Degree in City and Regional Planning, Middle East Technical University, Ankara, and a further Masters Degree from the Regional Science Department of the University of Pennsylvania, U.S.A., followed by a Doctorate Degree at Istanbul. His Ph.D. dissertation was on "Social Systems, Social Change and Settlement Systems", and his master's thesis on "A Macro Approach to Settlement Systems for Turkey". He has worked as a planner in the Ministry of Housing and Reconstruction and as a consultant for the Municipality of Ankara. He lectured for a year in UCLA and for many years in METU, Ankara. He is presently the Head of City and Regional Planning Department, METU.

WATSON, PETER L.

A British national, was educated in Sheffield and at the University of Edinburgh, Scotland. His Ph.D. thesis was on the subject of the value of time and behavioural models of mode choice. From 1970 to 1974 he was an Assistant Professor of Economics and a Research Associate in the Transportation Center at Northwestern University, where he taught courses in economic theory and the economic aspects of travel analysis and behaviour. His research interests were in the area of travel demand analysis, including econometric models of travel demand, the value of time, and urban goods movements. Dr. Watson has written a book and numerous articles on these subjects. In 1974 he joined the World Bank as a transport economist working on traffic restraint in Singapore and practical applications of urban strategic planning models. In April 1977 he joined the Latin American and Caribbean Urban Projects Division, where he has worked on urban transport projects in Brazil and Costa Rica and housing and integrated urban development projects in Brazil.

WILLIAMS, DAVID G.

A British national, he received his degree in architecture from Birmingham, England, Masters in City Planning from M.I.T. and Masters in Landscape Architecture from Harvard University. He was involved in community development work in India (1962-1963), and practised architecture in Pakistan (1964), Britain (1961-1962, 1967-1969), Japan (1965) and Canada (1966). Most of his work since 1971 has been in regional and urban planning and project development, first working on the Kampung Improvement Programme in Jakarta (1972-1973) and later as chief urban planner for the Pahang Tenggara Development Authority, Malaysia (1974-1976). Since 1976 Mr. Williams has been a staff member of the Urban Projects Department of the World Bank, with major responsibilities in the Philippines and Indonesia. He is the author of a number of articles in the fields of architecture, sociology and planning.

YEUNG, YUE-MAN

Dr. Yeung is currently on the staff of the International Development Research Centre in Ottawa, Canada, and was previously Senior Programme Officer of the Social Sciences Division of the IDRC, Asia Regional Office, Singapore. Prior to this appointment, he was lecturer in geography at the University of Singapore. He has a B.A. and Dip.Ed. from the University of Hong Kong, an M.A. from the University of Western Ontario, and a Ph.D. in Geography from the University of Chicago. His recent publications include National Development Policy and Urban Transformation in Singapore (1973), Changing Southeast Asian Cities (Co-editor) (1976) and Hawkers and Vendors in Southeast Asian Cities (Co-author) (1977).

B2